The Rule of Saint Benedict

THE NEWMAN PRESS
SIGNIFICANT SCHOLARLY STUDIES

The Newman Press imprint offers scholarly studies in historical theology. It provides a forum for professional academics to address significant issues in the areas of biblical interpretation, patristics, and medieval and modern theology. This imprint also includes commentaries on major classical works in these fields, such as the acclaimed Ancient Christian Writers series, in order to contribute to a better understanding of critical questions raised in writings of enduring importance.

The Rule of Saint Benedict

A Commentary in Light of World Ascetic Traditions

Mayeul de Dreuille, O.S.B.

translated from French with the collaboration of
Mark Hargreaves, O.S.B.

THE NEWMAN PRESS
NEW YORK/MAHWAH, N.J.

The Newman Press is a trademark of Paulist Press, Inc.

First published in 2000 by
Gracewing
2 Southern Avenue
Leominster
Herefordshire HR6 0QF

Library of Congress Cataloging-in-Publication Data

    Dreuille, Mayeul de.
    The Rule of Saint Benedict : a commentary in light of world ascetic traditions / by Mayeul de Dreuille.
       p. cm.
    Includes bibliographical references and index.
    ISBN 0-8091-0538-1
    1. Benedict, Saint, Abbot of Monte Cassino. Regula. I. Benedict, Saint, Abbot of Monte Cassino, Regula. English. II. Title.

BX3004.Z5 D74 2002
255'.106—dc21

                           2001058367

Jacket design by Cheryl Finbow.

Published in the United States of America in 2002 by
THE NEWMAN PRESS
An imprint of Paulist Press
997 Macarthur Boulevard
Mahwah, New Jersey 07430

www.paulistpress.com

Printed and bound in the
United States of America

CONTENTS

PREFACE

Commentaries on the Rule of Saint Benedict are not lacking. Even without counting the numerous collections of spiritual reflections, our time has been rich with scientific studies on this text and on its place in Western monasticism since the sixth century. Studies in the textual and literary analysis of the Rule published during the last half-century were often of great quality and they shed much light on Benedict and the monasticism of his time. Barring some highly improbable discovery of new manuscripts, it is difficult to see how new studies along the same lines could produce more understanding of the Patriarch of Western monasticism and his Rule.

The great mixing of cultures in our time, which provoked the meeting in many parts of the world of cultures that had existed side by side for centuries while ignoring each other, and also the progress of interreligious dialogue since Vatican II, have made us more aware than before of the fact that various forms of monasticism exist outside Christianity, and even existed many centuries before the coming of the Messiah. Not only were there various Christian monastic traditions at the time of Benedict, as well as before and after him, but many great spiritual traditions of the past developed forms of monasticism each time they reached a sufficient degree of spirituality. It is nowadays accepted that monastic life is a universal human archetype. A careful comparison of the Benedictine monastic tradition with all those forms of ascetical life could be very revealing.

A comparative study of all forms of monastic life, Christian and non-Christian, could be done. This is not Father Mayeul de Dreuille's aim. What he proposes to us in this book is to get a deeper understanding of our Benedictine tradition in the light of other traditions, and to discern the basic values that are embodied, although in various ways, in all those forms of monastic life. Nobody is better prepared to meet this challenge. Benedictine monk for the last sixty years, founder of a monastic community in Madagascar half a century ago, formator of monks from various cultures in several continents, it was after acquiring a familiarity with his Christian Benedictine tradition over a period of several years that he encountered other traditions, those of Buddhism and Hinduism in particular. He studied them with respect and critical sense.

This commentary is neither an exhaustive analysis of the various monastic traditions, nor a comparative study of Western and Eastern monasticism. It is a commentary on the Rule of Saint Benedict, enriched with lights drawn from other traditions. As such it is directed first of all to Christian nuns and monks who will find in it an instrument to deepen their own experience and to develop respect for that of other spiritual traditions. Members of other religious families could similarly find in the description of the diverse ascetic traditions insights into their founders' charism. The comparison shows, by similarities and differences, what is proper to each Institute. Buddhists and Hindus desiring to get to know Christianity better – many of whom have learned to appreciate Father Mayeul – will also draw profit from it. Lastly, although this book is not primarily addressed to the specialists in comparative studies of religions, it can be helpful to them also, revealing to them a lived experience of the Christian monastic tradition characterised with a great respect for the other religions.

Armand Veilleux
Abbot of Scourmont

INTRODUCTION

As long ago as the third century AD, Clement of Alexandria indicated the presence of Hindu and Buddhist ascetics in his city. But it was only during the present century that monks of the various world religions finally met together, when Christian monasticism sought its counterparts in India, while Eastern religions spread to the West. Recent years have also seen a renewed interest in the Founders of Christian monasticism, due to the publication of their writings.

During my years of monastic formation, such figures were not my main interest. However, in 1954 I was sent to Madagascar, to take part in the foundation of a new monastery. There I discovered that the young monks were much more at ease with the style and imagery of the Fathers of the fourth century than with the abstract literature of the modern West. So it was with these Malagasy novices that I rediscovered the Fathers of the Desert, Cassian, Pachomius and their contemporaries. At the same period also my confrère, Père Adalbert de Vogüé, started to publish his researches on the *Rule of Saint Benedict* (*RB*). Since I also had to teach it, I took great interest in his research from that time onwards, work which he readily shared with me.

From 1965 to 1977 I lived in India, taking part in the formation of young Benedictine monks from several monasteries. This long stay allowed me to discover a very rich culture, with forms of monastic life that were thousands of years old. Little by little, I got to know them, by reading their essential texts, but above all, by contact, whether in villages or universities, with Hindu and Buddhist monks and lay people, and also with Muslims. I subsequently made extended visits to mosques, ashrams, Hindu and Buddhist temples, both in India and Sri Lanka, and also to Tibetan monasteries, asking questions and building up friendly relations.

During this period in India, I collaborated with the Secretariat of *Aide Inter-Monastères* (AIM), being given the task of visiting the monasteries of Asia and Africa. I subsequently visited nearly all those of Western Europe and North America, with the purpose of creating mutually beneficial links between monasteries of the old and young churches. This work gave me the opportunity of comparing my experiences with those of the monks and nuns of three different continents.

My time in India over, I went to help an African monastery for a period of five years and, in 1988, left it with regret, to come and work in Rome. The Eternal City, however, with visitors from every kind of background, has enabled me to develop my previous contacts.

In each part of the world, I found the same questions being asked. Monks and nuns of all races and religions feel a deep kinship between them. What do they have in common? What is the special contribution or requirement of Christianity and, among all the religious orders, what are the specific contributions of Saint Benedict? These points were the general guidelines of my researches.

The result was conceived as a trilogy, whose first two parts, intended initially for the monasteries of India, were written in English. They concern, respectively, the history of monasticism in Asia and the West, and the founders of Christian monasticism.[1] A third part, this present book, makes a comparison of the Rule of Saint Benedict with its western predecessors and the ascetic traditions of Asia.

My sojourns outside Europe show both the extent and the limitations of my research. I have met only a few of the branches of Hinduism, Buddhism and Islam, and make no pretence to describe them for themselves. Each one merits a study in its own context. Any generalisations I have made express merely the overall impression that my contacts gave me.

Further, despite numerous footnotes on each page, this book is not a work of erudition, with the resources of a well-stocked library. Rather, it was written in monasteries far from towns, with some basic texts and the books that were available on site, making use of moments of time snatched from the daily work schedule of the small houses I was living in, where one had to do most things for oneself. This book, then, is above all the fruit of experiences matured by reflection in the silence of the jungle, and by contact with the young people I had to educate.

It is divided into two parts. The first is a study in detail of the Prologue of *RB* and the first seven chapters, which form the doctrinal part of the Rule. The second discusses the way life is lived in the monastery, as described in the remaining chapters. These are grouped together by themes, trying to follow the order in which Saint Benedict placed them as much as possible.

It remains for me to thank all those who have helped me. I have already spoken of Père Adalbert de Vogüé. I also thank the Abbots of La Pierre-qui-Vire and the Abbots President of the Subiaco

---

[1]   De Dreuille, Mayeul, *History of Monasticism from East to West*, and *Seeking the Absolute Love: the Founders of Christian Monasticism*, published by Gracewing, 1998–1999.

Congregation, who have constantly encouraged me during this long work. Then there are my Benedictine confrères of India and Sri Lanka, who made possible my contacts with Hindus and Buddhists. I thank the professors of the Major Seminaries of Bangalore, Delhi and Kandy, whose competence was a great help to me. Finally, thanks go to my Hindu, Buddhist and Muslim friends of Bangalore and Kandy, who allowed me to share their religious experience in their family. I must not forget my confrères and friends in Rome, through whom the text of this book was put on the computer. My gratitude goes also to my friend, Abbot Armand Veilleux OCSO, whom I have met in every part of the world and who, despite a very heavy schedule, has kindly written the preface to this book.

Finally, because this work is due to the collaboration of so many male and female religious belonging to different continents, cultures and religions, I hope that it will stimulate all 'seekers of God' to imitate their zeal and charity. For all of them, I wish the Divine Peace, so much loved by Saint Benedict, found in the Buddhist compassion, in the Hindu meditative presence of the *Aum Shanti*, and in the Arab *Salam*, used by the Malagasy people as a greeting.

Mayeul de Dreuille, O.S.B.

SIGNS AND ABBREVIATIONS

ABR	*The American Benedictine Review*
ACW	ANCIENT CHRISTIAN WRITERS, New York
AG	*Ad Gentes* (Vatican II)
Av *RB*	A. DE VOGÜÉ, *La Règle de St Benoît*, vol. I/ss. S C 181–187
AV *Communauté*	A. DE VOGÜÉ, *La Communauté et l'abbé*
AV *Mon. Egl.*	A. DE VOGÜÉ, *Le monastère, Eglise du Christ*
AV	A. DE VOGÜÉ
BASIL, LR	*Rules of St Basil, Longer Rules*
BASIL, SR	*Rules of St Basil, Shorter Rules*
BG	Bhagavad Gita
CC	CORPUS CHRISTIANORUM
CESARIUS, *RV*	CESARIUS OF ARLES, *Regula Virginum*
CIC	*Codex Iuris Canonici* (Canon Law)
CIST STUD	*Cistercian Studies*
COLL CIST	COLLECTANEA CISTERCIENSIS
CSCO	CORPUS SCRIPTORUM CHRISTIANORUM ORIENTALIUM, Louvain-Washington
CWS	CLASSICS OF WESTERN SPIRITUALITY, New York
DOROTHEUS *OS*	DOROTHÉUS OF GAZA *Oeuvres Spirituelles*
Hist Mon	*Historia Monachorum in Aegypto*, Latin transl. by RUFINUS
LG	*Lumen Gentium* (Vatican II)
LW	L. WIEGER, *Vinaya, Monachisme et discipline hinayana*
MANU	*Laws of Manu*
NF	NICENE AND POST-NICENE FATHERS, Grand Rapids
PACHOMIUS, *VC BO*	*Coptic Life of St Pachomius*, Codex Bohairic
PACHOMIUS, *VC S*	*Coptic Life of St Pachomius*, Codex Sahidic
PACHOMIUS, *VG*	*Première Vie Grecque* FESTUGIÈRE Codex Sahidic
PACHOMIUS, *Cat*	*Catéchèses*, CSCO 160
PACHOMIUS, *Praec*	*Praecepta*, CSCO 160
PC	*Perfectae Caritatis* (Vatican II)
PG	MIGNE, J.P., *Patrologia Series Graeca*, Paris

PL	Migne, J.P., *Patrologia Series Latina*, Paris
Qumran	Qumran (Textes)
Qumran *DD*	Qumran *Document de Damas*
RAM	*Revue D'Ascétique et de Mystique*
RB	*The Rule of Saint Benedict*[1]
RHE	*Revue d'Histoire Ecclésiastique,* Louvain
RM	*The Rule of the Master*, French transl. by A. de Vogüé (sc 105–106)
sc	collection sources chretiennes, ed. Le Cerf, Paris
UR	A. Degraces-Fahd, *Les Upanishad du Renoncement*
VA	Athanasius, *Vita S. Antonii*, cf. ACW and NF PG 26
VP	*Vitae Patrum*, pl 73

---

[1]Quotations from the Rule of St Benedict in almost all cases follow the translation of Abbot Parry osb (Gracewing, 1990), with occasional revision by the author.

PART I

PRINCIPLES OF MONASTIC LIFE

CHAPTER I

THE PROLOGUE

An invitation to an inner listening to God

1. PRESENTATION OF THE TEXT

Saint Benedict inherited a tradition and, in the Roman manner, knew how to use the work of his predecessors to make his own construction solid. A good part of the Prologue of his Rule is taken from a work, written some years before by an unknown abbot, entitled, 'The Rule of the Master'.[1] This Rule begins with a long introduction in which several scriptural commentaries are juxtaposed: the Our Father, Psalms 33 and 14 – all of which very probably come from a baptismal catechesis.[2] It ends with an invitation to enter into the service of the Lord.

From this collection, *RB* uses only the commentary of the Psalms. Some lines of introduction replace the preceding text. This opening is very important for the whole Rule,[3] since Saint Benedict usually put general principles at the beginning of the parts that he composed.[4] In these first lines he describes the fundamental attitude of every 'seeker of God'; so we can expect to find some parallels with the monastic systems of other religions.

[1] We use the following signs: *RB* for the Rule of Saint Benedict and *RM* for the Rule of the Master. In this chapter, only the references to *RB* are in italics. The passages of the Prologue which are proper to Saint Benedict are printed in bold italics.
[2] The Master is perhaps the author of this catechesis; this kind of literary genre was quite common in his time. Cf. A. DE VOGÜÉ, *La Règle de saint Benoît*, vol. IV, pp. 48–49, henceforth cited as AV *RB*, followed by the indication of the volume in Roman numerals.
[3] When we speak of the *Rule*, without other qualification, we always mean *RB*.
[4] The importance of the first lines of *RB* is not diminished by the fact that Saint Benedict borrows certain ideas and expressions from the Prologue and the *Thema* of *RM*. He chose them with a deliberate purpose and moulded them to fit his concise style.

2. SAINT BENEDICT'S OWN INTRODUCTION TO THE PROLOGUE:
The fundamental attitude of Inner Listening and the Spiritual Combat (*Prol.* 1–4)

Prov. 1: 8; 4: 1	*Listen, my son, to the precepts of your master and incline the ear of your heart.*
Prov. 6: 20	*Willingly accept and effectively carry out the advice*
(Deut. 6: 4)	*of your loving father*
Matt. 22: 9–10	*so that, through the toil of obedience you may return to him from whom you have separated by the sloth of disobedience.*
Luke 15: 11–32	*To you, then, whoever you may be, my words are addressed who renouncing your own will to do*
(Matt. 27: 37)	*battle under the Lord Christ, the true King take up the strong and bright weapons of obedience.*
(2 Tim. 2: 3–4)	*First of all when you begin any good work, beg of him with most urgent prayer to bring it to completion.*[5]

Note the impressive list of quotations or allusions to Scripture contained in these few lines. They show how the thought of the author is entirely impregnated with the Bible, an impression confirmed by the entire text of the Rule.

This short passage divides into three clear parts: an invitation to listen, a description of the spiritual combat and a prayer.

THE INVITATION

Listen, my son

Following several ancient Rules, these first words repeat God's invitation to his people to make a covenant with him.

> Listen, Israel: the Lord our God is the one God. You shall serve the Lord your God with all you heart, with all your soul and with all your strength (Deut. 6: 4–5).[6]

---

[5] The scriptural references are in the left-hand column; those in brackets being passages which are alluded to, without being directly quoted.

[6] *Dt.* 6: 4. The text of *Prov.* 1: 8; 4: 10, 20 is nearer to that of *RB* but the *precepts* remind us rather of the giving of the Law on Mt Sinai. The biblical context is made explicit in several ancient monastic documents: ORSISIUS opens his *Testament* with the words: *Listen, Israel*; A. DE VOGÜÉ also quotes Pseudo-Basil, Pachomius and Pelagius (AV *RB* I, pp. 412–413).

Christ has extended this call to the whole of humanity, giving to each one a special vocation, inviting certain people to leave everything and follow him.[7] But all are to be united with him intimately, in the depths of their heart.

In other religions, only rarely do we find people dedicated to the search for the Absolute who also think of their spiritual efforts as a response to a divine call.[8] Among the greater part of Hindus and Buddhists, desire for monastic life is usually considered as the result of good actions carried out in a previous existence. The monk's state is the highest that can be reached in human life, and is the preparative stage for union with the Absolute.

The monastic systems of the various religions do, however, agree that it is this search for union with the Absolute that stands at the centre of their entire life. This common goal defines them and creates a fundamental unity, although their ideas about the Absolute and the means of attaining to it are different.

In most monastic systems, the Absolute is considered as present in the deepest part of the human being. Their insistence on this point can help to bring to light an important value of the Christian tradition: the Fathers considered the divine presence in the human heart to be the source from which the soul arose, in its primitive beauty, created in the image of Christ. Saint Augustine speaks of God as 'more intimate to me than I am to myself'.[9]

Saint Benedict also had this experience; he alludes to it several times in the course of his Rule, in particular with regard to prayer and silence,[10] passages that suppose an inner kind of listening, here described for the first time:

---

[7] This choice made by Christ is well illustrated by the examples of being called in the Gospels: the Apostles (*Mk*. 1: 16, 20 and parallels), the disciples who accept the call (*Mk*. 3: 13; *Lk*. 10: 1) others refuse it (*Mk*. 10: 17–22; *Lk*. 9: 51–62). These examples are in some way lived out again by the Fathers of monasticism; thus, Saint Antony (ATHANASIUS, *VA* ch. 2, 3 and 4) and PACHOMIUS *VC Bo* 6; 10 and *passim*.

[8] Outside of Christianity, the case of a special vocation seems to be reserved for exceptional people, found from time to time in the course of history, beginning with the Indian *rishis* and leading up to the founders of religions or sects in the modern period.

[9] *Tu autem eras intimior intimo meo*, AUGUSTINE, *Confessions*, 3. 6, 11. The Alexandrian Fathers spoke in the same way of the restoration of the image of God which had been tarnished by sin; Saint Antony and Isaac of Skete invited the monks to struggle to recover *the natural state* of man as friend of God before the fall. ATHANASIUS, *VA*, 20; ISAAC OF SKETE, *Logos* 2.

[10] *RB* ch. 7, 1st step; we could, perhaps, find another similar allusion in Saint Bernard's *Commentary on the Song of Songs*, 2: 14, where the rock is the heart of Christ, and the soul is the dove which goes to rest in it. He thus manages to invoke, in some way, the Hindu symbolism of the cave of the heart where one can rest with the Presence.

incline the ear of your heart, accept willingly ... 'libenter accipe'

This listening is conditioned by an inner attitude of faith, good will, openness and generosity, in response to the love which is offered by God, an attitude that is characteristic of the monk, which Saint Benedict tries to develop or to re-establish in every area of life.

The Father of western monasticism, Saint Benedict, here echoes all the Christian monastic tradition, which incessantly calls for docility towards the God who calls us. Pachomius, Theodore and Orsisius make this the subject of their exhortations to the monks.[11] Basil, in the Prologue to his Greater Rules, gives three reasons for serving God: the fear of a slave, the hope of a reward (like a salary) and the love of a son. This son:

> must remember the words of the Apostle: do not make sad the Spirit of God, that Spirit whose seal is upon you.[12]

Gregory Nazianzen, Gregory of Nyssa and Augustine also insist on sincerity of heart, in the love of the Lord.[13] These inner dispositions are so fundamental, that one also finds them in other religions. For instance, the Buddhist novice is asked:

> not only to be eager to work, but to be receptive, docile, open and devoted to his master.[14]

This availability also corresponds with an attitude of *letting go*, cultivated by Zen practitioners, so as to become aware of the presence of the Infinite everywhere. But Saint Benedict immediately introduces a Christian note here, in saying that the disciple should remain attentive to the Father who loves him and speaks to him.

Carry out effectively ... 'efficaciter comple'

RB here recalls two other words – '*accept willingly*' – and complements them with '*carry out effectively*'. Good will is indispensable but it needs to continue into action.[15] Saint Benedict wants there to be as

---

[11] PACHOMIUS, *VC Bo.* 17; 93; THEODORE, *Catéchèse à propos d'un moine rancunier*, CSCO 160, p. 50; ORSISIUS, *Testament*, ch. 33.

[12] BASIL, *LR*, Prologue.

[13] GREG. NA, *Orat.* 3; GREG. NY. *Hom. I in Cant.*; AUGUSTINE, *Lettres* 83, 3; 33, 292; DOROTHEUS OF GAZA, *Instruction* III, De la conscience.

[14] THARTANG TULKU, *Gesture of Balance*, p. 158, a Tibetan text which summarises the numerous and detailed Rules of the *Vinaya* on this subject.

[15] See further on the sections that deal with obedience and the spiritual master.

near perfect a correspondence as possible between idea and action.[16] This concern for efficacy is one of the characteristics of his Rule.[17] The word of God, received in the heart, runs the risk of developing only an empty kind of compliance, if personal conduct is not constantly confronted with that word, and remodelled on it. Saint Benedict's concern for efficacy is not, therefore, simply the reaction of a pragmatist, but a desire for fidelity to the Gospel, in all domains of monastic life. He thus puts his natural gifts of organisation at the service of God.[18]

This discourse is not addressed to monks in general (unlike the title of the Rule itself a few lines above) but rather to each individual monk in particular, using the phrase, *my son*. The requirement of perfection is tempered with a fatherly affection that is even more marked in the words that follow:

Listen, my son, to the precepts of your master and incline the ear of your heart. Willingly accept ...

Master, Father: these two words describe the attitude of respect and of love which Saint Benedict likes to show towards God and, for his sake, towards everyone. The accent is on love, the basis of the precepts and of his concern for efficacy – the responsibility of the master – while faith and good will are asked of the disciple. We will see, further on, that obedience and love are always put in close relation with one another during the course of the Rule.[19]

This love comes from God. It is the love of God that is transmitted to the disciple by the Abbot. Our text seems to give a double meaning to the words 'master' and 'father', so that they imply both God and the superior of the monastery. The same act of fidelity and love takes in all the aspects of obedience of a monk. The Abbot, for his part, must show to each monk the same love of Christ.

The affection and mutual respect between master and disciple, emphasised by Saint Benedict, are considered, in other forms of

---

[16] We find the same concern for spiritual efficacy in Saint Antony, see for example Antony, 16; 19.1.

[17] See in particular the duty he lays on the abbot to correct the brethren so that they may amend: *RB* ch. 2.

[18] This concern for fidelity implies a certain suppleness in the structure, which must be able to adapt, so that it can incarnate the same gospel values in changing circumstances. Saint Benedict also modifies quite a number of the details of organisation of prayer, work, clothing, food, etc.

[19] The relation between obedience and love is particularly emphasised in *RB* at the beginning of ch. 5 and in ch. 7, 3rd step. In this last, Saint Benedict adds 'for the love of God' to the text of the *RM*.

monasticism, as an important element that helps the disciple to learn. The *Laws of Manu*,[20] the Buddhist Rules and the Sufi writings often describe the gestures of respect on the part of the disciple for his master and the qualities of gentleness, welcome and understanding which the master must show towards those he has to guide.[21] This ideal remains very much alive in Asia. Many of those who have followed the gurus in the East testify to the disinterested kind of love which they received from them. For some of them, this was a unique experience in their lives.

Through the toil of obedience you may return to him from whom you have separated by the sloth of disobedience.

This phrase leads us to consider the various ways towards the Absolute source of unending happiness. The monastic systems of the world religions describe several of them,[22] but all recognise as a preliminary the need for *toil*, that is, an ascetic effort that stops the human passions from being dominant and brings an interior peace.

The Bible also shares these ideas, but considers the return to God more as a loving submission of the human will to the divine. This is one of the principal themes of Scripture.[23] God wishes to save humanity, and sent his Son to redeem it from its faults and to give it a share

---

[20] MANU, 2, 119–162; 190–246; 6, 47–48.

[21] *Vinaya*, LW 6, 'Instruction sur les règles des novices masculins', p. 161, ff.; J.S. TRIMINGHAM, *The Sufi Orders in Islam*, ch. 6 and 7.

[22] Here are the principal ways of journeying towards the Absolute in the Eastern religions. First, we have the suppression of transitory desires. If they are no longer present, the disciple can become aware of the presence of a Reality which is not transient. Then comes the way of union, which sometimes means the identification of the human essence (*atman*) with The Being, source of all that exists (*Brahman*). Lastly, we have loving abandonment (*bhakti*) to a mediator who gives salvation. Almost all of these different approaches are found in each religion, in different combinations, following the tendencies proper to each branch. Buddhism, in general, insists on the suppression of desire as a preparation for illumination. The *bhakti* movement, with its devotion to a mediator is one of the most usual forms of Hinduism, but is also found in the cult of the *Bodhisattvas* (cf. note 69) of *Mahayana* Buddhism. If the Hindu *Vedanta* uses almost exclusively the identification of the *atman* with the *Brahman*, in practice it is often combined with a kind of *bhakti*.

[23] See, for example: God, father and spouse of Israel, awaiting its return, in spite of its infidelities: *Deut.* 32; *Ezek.* 16; *Isa.* 63–64; *Jer.* 2; 11; *Hos.* 2; 11; *Amos* 2; *Mic.* 6; *Ps.* 106–107. The Messiah will invite Israel to a new beginning, in fidelity and happiness: *Isa.* 35; 40–52; 56; 62–64; repentance and return to God as preached by John the Baptist: *Mt.* 3; by Jesus: *Mt.* 4: 17; *Lk.* 15: 11–32; by the Apostles: *Acts* 15–22 *passim*; 5: 31; 7: 35 ff.; 1 *Cor.* 5: 7; 10: 1–6; *Gal.* 4: 18; 1 *Pet.* 1; 2; *Jn.* 1; 3; 6; 8: 12; 13; 14; 17; 19; 1 *Jn.* 3.

in his divine life. In response to this love the Christian monk must try to conform himself to Christ who brings him into the joy of the Father. The first Christian monks are unanimous in their development of this theme.[24]

Saint Benedict borrows the expression *toil of obedience*[25] from the Fathers of the Desert, in whose writings it is taken to mean asceticism and their zeal to be conformed to Christ. Among the biblical references, the Rule seems to give a privileged place to the Prodigal Son (*Luke* 15: 11–32) which forms a background for the Prologue. The monk is invited to *rise from sleep* and *run* so that he can *return* to his Father who is waiting for him.[26]

Obedience, as described by Saint Benedict, goes a long way beyond the narrow framework of an order given by the superior. It assumes all the effort which a monk makes to put his intimate feelings in harmony with God.

While *RM* speaks several times of preferring the will of God to one's own, it always associates this idea with the fear of death and with a reminder of the last things. Saint Benedict eliminates the notion of fear in this context, and considers the encounter with God as a happy one. The monk is thus placed between the errors of his past life and a future of reintegration into the divine friendship, with the aid of grace.

The same enthusiasm is shown with regard to the combat in which he must engage, to attain that friendship.

THE COMBAT (*Prol.* 3)

Whoever you may be . . .

These words allude to the parable of the wedding feast,[27] in which God invites the whole of humanity to share his friendship. We are a long way from the perspective of the Hindus and Buddhists, which sees the monastic state as the final part of a progression by stages through various lives. For them, the monastic system would be reserved for a kind of elite, predisposed to accomplish the tasks.[28]

---

[24] BASIL, *LR* 35; *SR* 1; 98; 114; 303; EVAGRIUS, *Praktikos*, No. 78–79; CASSIAN *Conf.* 18: 7–8; ATHANASIUS, *VA* ch. 2; 3; 4; *VP* I, 1, 11; DOROTHEUS OF GAZA, *Instr.* 3. These ideas will be developed in ch. 7 of *RB*.

[25] '*Obedientiae labor*' *VP*5 14, 15.

[26] We could add that these words of Saint Benedict seem to have been inspired by Saint Augustine's *De Civ. Dei* 11. 28, which quotes the parable of the Prodigal Son.

[27] *Lk.* 14: 15–24; *Mt.* 22: 9–10.

[28] Many Hindu monastic orders only admit men who have been 'reborn' into the highest castes.

The Gospel sees things differently. Saint Benedict finds it normal that the monastery should include not only men from different social backgrounds, but also people who are weak in the sight of God.[29] It is a consoling fact that the necessity of conversion does not admit any exception. Who, in fact, does not feel weak sometimes, during his life? The important thing is not to be strong, but to turn towards God with perseverance and sincerity. This idea returns at the conclusion of the Rule in ch. 73, where Saint Benedict uses the same words as a definition of the monk: *you, whoever you are, who are hurrying forward to your heavenly fatherland*:

> **who renouncing your own will to do battle under the Lord Christ, the true King take up the the strong and bright weapons of obedience.**

The return to God by obedience, as described in *RB*, is a combat for Christ and against self-will. This was one of the favourite themes of the Desert Fathers, found frequently in their vocabulary.[30] The term *self-will* here means all the things in us that are in opposition to God. It is the false and superficial self, the *old man* (Col. 3:9–10) that we must get rid of, in order to follow Christ totally and receive from him the perfection of our being with the divine life.

Fuller details will be given about this struggle in chapter 7 and in several other passages of the Rule.[31] But all monastic systems are once again united over what the Hindus call *detachment from the impermanent* and the Buddhists, under another aspect, *renunciation of desires*. It is faithfulness to the *dharma*, the eternal law that is inscribed in the depths of the heart, which makes this abandonment possible. The Gospel parable of the seed (Matt. 13: 3–23) reminds us that a plant cannot grow freely unless it has been disentangled from weeds and stones. All religions thus recognise that a man's true personality develops by mastering the passions that disturb it.

From these diverse experiences, it is evident that the renunciation required by all religions has the very positive goal of promoting in man all that is of the best. But the special characteristic of Christianity is that it finds the perfect law in Christ, coming from God and leading to his light. We certainly could not accuse the Father of Desert monks – Saint

---

[29] *RB* several times alludes to monks coming from different social milieus: *RB* 2; 18; 59: 73. It is also opposed to the custom in *RM* of dividing monks into two categories, the fervent and the rest, especially on the subject of silence and obedience.

[30] *Renunciat propriis voluntatibus*: *VP* 5.1; 19; *Hist Mon* 31. This theme of spiritual combat is one of the most richly represented ideas in the Fathers; we also find it several times in *RB*, notably with regard to Lent (*RB* 59) and obedience.

[31] *RB* ch. 1; 4–7; 68; 71–72 and *passim*.

Antony – of laxity, yet his teaching puts less emphasis on mortification than on the positive aspect of following in the steps of Christ, and the attraction that radiates from him through his love and beauty.

> 'Let us, then, be full of confidence, and rejoice always, because we must be saved and because the Lord is with us ... and, since he is with us, the demons will not be able to do us any harm' (ch. 13) ... Antony's words filled those who were there with joy, increasing the love of virtue in some and chasing negligence away from the spirit of others (ch. 14) ... 'Do not be afraid of the demons but believe in Jesus Christ and look for no other thing but to serve him ... work with all your strength to unite yourself first of all to him and then to the saints, so that, after your death, they will receive you as friends into the eternal tabernacles' (ch. 22).[32]

Saint Benedict also proposes that we make a step towards the light, towards Christ, source of life. This is why the weapons of obedience are *strong* and *glorious*, and the toil will be a battle carried out with enthusiasm. Christ is present, the true king, the only one who can give right instructions and true rewards. Under his guidance, and following his example, we participate in the mystery of the redemption of the world.

These lines, we should remember, replace and, in part, repeat the baptismal catechesis of the Rule of the Master. The monastic ideal, considered in such a positive way by Saint Benedict, is also a development of the incorporation into Christ by Baptism.

PRAYER (*Prol.* 4)

Whenever you begin any good work, you must ask Christ with the most urgent prayer to bring it to completion.

Christ gives not only the desire for combat but also the strength with which to succeed. Spiritual progress demands effort – but this cannot be acquired merely by will power; it is a gift of God which needs to be asked for insistently. Saint Benedict returns several times to the idea of grace and the presence of the Holy Spirit in the soul.[33] This was already a traditional practice. Further on in the Prologue, he recalls the teaching of Saint Paul, who attributes none of his success to himself. Saint Antony also said in one of his discourses to his monks:

---

[32] ATHANASIUS, *VA*, ch. 13; 14; 22.
[33] Cf. *RB*, Prol. (end); ch. 4; 5; 7; 20; 49; 72; 73.

We are much in need of prayer and asceticism in this life that we have professed, so that we can receive the gift of discernment from the Holy Spirit.[34]

Most of the mystics of the theistic religions recognised the love that God has for humanity and the help that be brings to it by his grace. In the *Bhagavad Gita*, for example, the Lord Krishna says that, with this help, the faithful follower will:

> overcome all dangers, ... and will reach the highest love of abandonment to me ... Because of this love, says Krishna, he will come to know me as I am ... when he knows me, he enters into me immediately.[35]

The experience of this action of God in the heart of man leads Saint Benedict to establish the priority of prayer over action; that is to say, a priority of time but also of importance. Along with all the monastic tradition, he wants the monk to have a permanent contact with God, so that he can *pray without ceasing* as the Gospel prescribes.[36]

Prayer, then, ought to precede and surround every action, asking for strength and directing the intention, so that the work that is accomplished will bring man nearer to God. It also thanks the Lord who permits human actions to bear fruit.

In this beginning of the Prologue we see that the originality of Saint Benedict is to present the effort of harmonising the human heart with God's as the great way, the method which leads to perfection. It shows us the monastic vocation as a return to the Lord who calls us; as an intimate union with him, thanks to his grace and to a constant effort to conform our being to the plan which Christ, in his love, has devised for us.

Here we have one of the major ideas – if not the key idea – in the whole Rule. Saint Benedict calls it *obedience*, but he gives a very rich meaning to the word, and wants it to mean, above all, obedience to God. The associations it evokes of spiritual combat, of sharing in the universal redemption, of prayer, and of love, are developed in the commentary on Psalms 33 and 14, passages which he took from *RM*, as an end for the Prologue to his Rule.

---

[34] ATHANASIUS, *VA*, ch. 9.

[35] Cf. R. V. DE SMET, *The Status of the Scriptures in the holy history of India*, p. 7, which cites the *Bhagavad Gita*, 18: 54; 57; 58. Here we could quote innumerable texts from the Egyptians, the Hindu *Bhatas* both old and modern, the *Mahayana* Buddhists and the Sufis.

[36] *Lk*. 18: 1; cf. *Rom*. 12: 12; 1 *Thess*. 5: 17. This idea is frequently expressed in the Fathers, in particular in their comparison of the monastic ideal with the life of the angels who stand constantly before God and intercede for humanity.

3. COMMENTARY ON PSALMS 33 AND 14

This long piece is composed of an introduction, and then come several verses of Psalms 33 and 14, each followed by its commentary. A conclusion introduces the last part of the Prologue: The School of the Lord's Service. Within this framework the author presents the call of God, and the desired response from the monk, in a very free way. These themes follow one after another, shedding light on one another, almost as in a conversation.

THE INTRODUCTION: *a call from God: 'Who desires life?'* (*Prol.* 5–15)

In Saint Benedict, as in the Master, the lines which introduce Psalm 33 are a prayer to Christ, followed by an exhortation, in which he is presented to us as Father and Judge (*RB Prol* 5–7). This text comes after the part that is proper to Saint Benedict:

> *so that he, who has now deigned to reckon us in the number of his sons, may not later on be made sad by our wicked actions. For we must at all times serve him with the good gifts he has placed in us, so that he will not later on, as an angry father, disinherit his sons; nor like a feared lord, who has been roused to anger by our sins, hand over to eternal punishment us wicked servants who refuse to follow him to glory* (*Matt. 18: 32–34*).

Let us notice, first of all, how Saint Benedict emphasises once more the reciprocal action of the gift of God and the free will of man; this is not merely an occasional event, but a state of life: one obeys by means of '*the good gifts he has placed in us*'.

The image of God as feared Lord, which occurs frequently in *RM*, but is avoided by Saint Benedict at the beginning of the Prologue, is here used to add colour to his description of the respectful love which one vows to God. The allusion to the parable of the merciless debtor shows that the same respect should also be offered to everyone.

If, in the rest of the Prologue, Saint Benedict keeps the texts of the Master about the last things, these are not seen as punishment, but as an encouragement to apply oneself to the task in hand. In the same way, the exhortation concludes with words of the Prodigal Son, when he decides to return to his Father:

> *Luke* 15: 18   *Let us then at last arouse ourselves, even as Scripture incites us in the words,*

Rom. 13: 11	*'Now is the hour for us to rise from sleep.' Let us, then, open our eyes to the divine light, and hear with our attentive ears the warning that the divine voice cries out to us daily.*
Ps. 94: 8	**'Today if you hear his voice, do not harden your hearts,'** *and again,*
Matt. 11: 15	*'He who has ears to hear, let him hear what the Spirit*
Rev. 2: 7	*says to the Churches.' And what does the Spirit say? 'Come, my sons, listen to me; I shall teach you the fear of the Lord.'*
John 2: 35	*'Run while you have the light of life lest the darkness of death overwhelm you.' And as the Lord seeks his workman in the mass of people, he again cries out to him in the words,*
Ps. 24: 12	*'Who is the man who desires life and is eager to see Good Days?' If you hear this and reply, 'I do', God says to you, 'If you want to have true and everlasting life,*
Ps. 33: 13	*keep your tongue from speaking evil, and your lips from uttering deceit. Turn aside from evil and do good; seek peace and follow after it.'*

There are a number of themes in this introduction that will be discussed several times in the course of the Rule. First of all, the idea of listening, which we have already seen at the beginning of the Prologue; it is here repeated twice and underlined by the verse of Psalm 94 added by Saint Benedict: *'Today, if you hear his voice, do not harden your hearts ...'*. This alternates with an invitation to action, *'Listen ... run ...'*, with the Gospel theme, *'divine light'*, and with the idea of a calling, presented as God's initiative, since he is the one who sends out the call. A person freely responds to it in accepting the conditions that are set out in the quotations from the Psalms.

These themes have interesting parallels in other religions, where the mystics often speak of the purification of the soul as if it were a light that burns up the veil of ignorance. The Koran states that God is light, and the Sufis see the approach of man towards God as the removal of successive veils that obstruct man's vision.[37]

Zen calls the discovery of profound reality 'illumination', referring to the name of the Buddha himself, which means 'the illuminated one'. For the Buddhists and Hindus, this new perception is, at base, the distinction between the transitory and the permanent. It is the gift

---

[37] *Koran*, 24, 25. Some Sufi mystics, using this as a base, developed 'emanentist' theories with Mazdean origins; according to them the 'Mohammedan light', the essence of the Prophet, which emanates from God before all time, is the source of all faith. Cf. L. GARDET, *Mystique musulmane*.

of the third eye, the one that sees beyond the senses, symbolised by the red point, which men in India often carry between their eyebrows. It is also worth noting that, for many Hindus, this light dawns in their heart when listening to sacred texts that speak of God:

> It is a holy thing to sing and hear the praise of the Lord. He is the friend of all religious men. Present in the heart of those who listen to his story, he destroys their sins.[38]

However, we are also in touch here with one of the specific points of Christianity. Several times in both the Prologue and in the whole Rule, Saint Benedict attributes the divinisation of the soul to a transformation effected by grace or, more precisely, by the Holy Spirit. These other religions speak rather of the discovery of the Infinite reality which is always present in man, the source of full human existence, than of transformation.[39] To become aware of this Presence, we must purify the soul, take away the veil of corruption and ignorance which impedes our vision,[40] and realise that the *true self* is the

[38] *Bhagavad Purana*, 1, 2, 17–18.

[39] For the Buddhists, obviously, there is no question of God. They insist on the ephemeral state of the human being, in sensory perceptions, in the passions and in ideas or conceptions. The only thing that remains is *wisdom*, the intuition of the *Unlimited*, or of the *Ocean of Peace*, which all the different ways of meditation are seeking. A Tibetan poem explains this:

> (22)
> Whatever appears to be truly existent
> Is merely what mind in delusion creates;
> This mind of ours also is, from the beginning,
> Devoid of an essence inherently real.
> Then, realising Truth is beyond the conceptions
> We have of the known, and the knower as well,
> Dispel the belief in inherent existence –
> The Sons of the Buddha all practise this way.

> (30)
> Perfection of charity, patience and morals,
> Absorption and effort alone won't suffice;
> Without the Perfection of Wisdom these five are
> Unable to bring us to full Buddha-hood.
> With the methods of pure Bodhicitta develop
> The wisdom to see that the actor, the act,
> And the acted upon lack inherent existence –
> The Sons of the Buddha all practise this way.

The Thirty-Seven Practices of all Buddha's Sons 22; 30, pp. 11–12.

[40] The mystics' intuition serves to discover these 'veils': the Hindus compare them to the layers of an onion and the Sufis say there are seventy thousand of them. Cf. J. S. TRIMINGHAM, *Sufi*, pp. 154–155.

Infinite, or, in Hindu terms, that the Atman, the human being which has its source in the Being, is identical with the Brahman, Being in itself. Even love, expressed so vibrantly in the Hindu *Bhaktas*,[41] is usually conceived as a means of attaining this inner reality:

> When devotion to the Lord Krishna is strengthened, detachment and intuitive understanding soon grow ... When, through devotion to the Lord, the spirit of man is purified and freed from all attachment and obtains understanding of the divine reality, then he has 'realised' God in his heart.[42]

In the same way, the idea of grace as a free gift coming from on high[43] is not unknown, but is, in general, considered as a light which reveals man's inner Reality and helps him to purify his conduct so as to attain this reality.

Another difference is brought to our attention by the last lines of this paragraph of the Rule that, once again, describe the Christian conception of vocation. Such a vocation is not a privileged state, but a free response to a free call from God, inviting us to the happiness of being with him as his children: '*Who desires life?*' This appeal from God brings grace, and we respond by opening our heart to the light that comes from Scripture. Psalms 33 and 14 shows us how to enter into the joy of God.

QUOTATIONS FROM PSALMS 33 AND 14: *A Christian perspective*

The Master and Saint Benedict emphasise the importance of these themes by placing them on the lips of Christ.[44] Psalm 33 is introduced by the words:

As the Lord seeks his workman, ... he cries ...

---

[41] *Bhaktas*, those who practise the way of *Bhakti*, or devotion towards a deity.

[42] *Bhagavata Purana*, 1. 2. 7, 20–22, following the English transl. of SUBHASH ANAND. Cf. *The Narada Bhakti Sutra*, English translation of A. GISPERT–SAUCH.

[43] In Hindu literature, the notion of grace appears for the first time in the *Katha Upanishad*, 1, 20, 23; it was subsequently developed in the *Bhagavad Gita*. It seems to be absent from *Hinayana* Buddhism (Buddhism of the Small Vehicle), but is found in the *Mahayana* (the Great Vehicle), using the aid given by the *bodhisattvas*.

[44] Further on in the text, Saint Benedict replaces the *Dominus* of *RM* by *Deus*; this is not a contradiction, but rather a reaction against the improper use of the second person of the Trinity by the Master, at the expense of the first person. Christ calls and shows us the road to follow, but judgement is reserved to the Father. Cf. AV *RB* I, p. 64, n. 129.

and Psalm 14 by:

> *Let us listen to the Lord's answer ... saying ...*

Thus these texts should be seen from a Christian point of view; it is not just a question of creating a peaceful atmosphere in the community. It is *for the love of Christ*, and in imitation of him, that the monk is invited. The commentary also shows how to attain union with God by humility and by the *'struggle to obey his commandments'*.

Our authors are here inspired by Saint Augustine's commentaries on the Psalms. To these they added some references to the messianic prophecies and the New Testament, thus christianising the text and adding the consideration of Christ's goodness to this programme of moral effort.

COMMENTARY ON PSALM 33: *The Lords calls us to intimacy with him* (*Prol.* 15–22)

The psalm: First, good will towards others.

> *Ps.* 33: 13–16
>
> *'Who is the man who desires life and is eager to see Good Days?' If you hear this and reply, 'I do', God says to you, 'If you want to have true and everlasting life, keep your tongue from speaking evil, and your lips from uttering deceit. Turn aside from evil and do good; seek peace and follow after it.' 'When you do this my eyes will be upon you, and my ears will be open to your prayers.'*

These quotations have not been chosen haphazardly. Psalm 33, beginning and ending with praise of the God who keeps watch over his servant, fits perfectly in the context:

> Magnify the Lord with me ...
> I sought the Lord and he answered me,
> From all my fears he delivered me ...
> The Lord hears those who call to him,
> he delivers them from all their troubles.

Between these two passages of praise the psalmist gives the conditions for remaining in the divine friendship:

> *Who is the man who desires life and is eager to see good days?*

We might wonder why Saint Benedict, following the Master, looks to the Old Testament to find these fairly standard moral precepts as a way of indicating intimacy with God. But we should note that the monastic texts of the other religions also repeat the same things.

To do good, to avoid evil, to seek peace, justice, truth, not to speak evil about others – all this is the essence of the great way of non-violence, made famous by Gandhi, but common to all the monastic systems of Asia.[45] A Buddhist monk comments on it as follows:

> A monk should acquire above all else, truth and sincerity. No cunning schemes! Do not injure another, do not speak flippantly, do not use flowery words. Do not speak flattery to their face, only to injure them afterwards, behind their back. Be slow to accuse – and never do it without proof. Do not speak about the faults of others. When you preach, explain the doctrine faithfully, without either repeating it over again or exaggerating. When you come across people who quarrel, try to make them agree.[46]

Similar recommendations are found among the Qumran texts:

> Do not speak angrily to your neighbour with complaints or with obstinacy; do not speak with the malice that comes from an evil spirit. We should not hate someone who persists in error, but should rather give him advice.[47]

The fact that these ideas are found everywhere indicates that we have here a fundamental value of monastic life. Mastery of the self is always considered as the first step in the search for union with the Absolute. In this ascetic effort, the control of the tongue, right conduct, and charity towards one's neighbour are practices to be observed, especially by cenobites.

The commentary

The Lord loves us

The first words combine Psalm 33 with quotations from Isaiah, which prophesy the happiness of messianic times and place it in the presence of the infinite goodness of God:

---

[45] See, for example: MANU, 2, 161; 167; 6, 8; 48; 60–69; 92; in the *Lingayat* tradition, SUNYASUMPADAYE, vol. 1, p. 3.

[46] *Vinaya, LW*, p. 157, No. 4

[47] QUMRAN *Règle*, col. 5, 23; 6, 1.

Ps. 33: 16   **When you do this my eyes will be upon you, and**
                 my ears will be open to your prayers, and
Isa. 65: 24; 58: 9 **before you call upon me**
                 I shall say to you: 'Here I am'.

The desire of the soul wanting to share the divine happiness, responds to this experience of love:

> *What can be sweeter to us than this voice of the Lord as he invites us,* **dearest brothers?** *See how, in his loving mercy, the Lord points out to us the Way of Life.*

In this text, which speaks for itself, there are several significant expressions. First, the qualificative phrase *'dearest brothers'*, added by Saint Benedict, to designate the members of the community. For him, they are not just 'monks', but persons dear to him in the love of Christ. This love, announced by the prophets, surrounds and envelops us and, even now, its presence is our reward.

The Lord, in fact, is calling us to the intimacy of family life. The idea is suggested in the last phrase, by the words 'fatherly kindness' (*pietate*),[48] which colours the images presented further on by Psalm 14. First, we have the image of the 'tent' (*dwelling-place*), which reminds us of the 'everlasting tabernacles' or tents. In a more radical sense, however, this is the place where the nomadic tribal family, dispersed throughout the day, would come together for the evening meal, and continue chatting into the night. The evocation of the tent seems important, because it returns several times in the space of a few lines.[49] It gives an affective warmth to the more impressive, but perhaps more distant, images of the holy mountain and the temple, the privileged places of encounter with God. These last images, in their turn, help one to go beyond human sensibility and show the transcendent and sacred character of the divine intimacy. Through these allusions, Saint Benedict inserts in the Rule the very rich theme of God's dwelling with his people, under its twofold aspect of intimacy where God speaks to the heart, and of a place where the people assemble to listen to him and to pray. For the Rule, this place is the monastery, *school of the Lord's service* and *house of God*. The vow of stability will again bring together these various aspects.

---

[48] In Latin, *pietas* means the mutual love of parents and children. This word introduces the feeling of affection with which Saint Benedict interpreted the parables of the kingdom, to which he subsequently makes allusion.

[49] The image of the tent seems privileged in *RB*. It is cited three times (*Prol.* 22, 23, 24) and in verse 39 it summarises all the other images. On the kingdom, cf. *Mt* 5; 13; 13–21 and parallels in the Synoptics.

Having thus evoked the experience of the love of God, the Rule translates it into the practice of the monastic life.

Walking in faith, under the guidance of the Gospel

Eph. **6: 14–15** *Let us therefore make for ourselves a girdle out of faith and good works*

1 *Thess.* **2: 12** *let us walk in his ways, under the guidance of the Gospel, so that we may deserve to see him who has called us to his Kingdom.*

Here we return to the theme of the light of the Gospel, which we met above, but we are also reminded of the early monastic systems, which attempted to be the Gospel put into action, in as radical a way as possible. The fact that such Rules, Lives, and other writings of the great forefathers (like Antony, Pachomius, Basil and their imitators or successors) had great authority, is due to the fact that such writings were recognised as a means of living the Scripture, in day-to-day monastic life. It was a way of living made possible by the charism of wisdom and discernment, which these saints possessed.[50] The Master presents himself as a spokesman for God. Saint Benedict was more aware of the limitations of the Abbot, yet did not consider his Rule

---

[50] Antony became aware of his vocation while meditating on the Gospel; his response was to imitate the Apostles in their following of Christ (ATHANASIUS, *VA* 1). Later, at each stage of his life, we see him meditating on Scripture so as to 'put Christ in his heart' (ibid. 3). PACHOMIUS does the same: all the instructions which we see him giving to his brothers are based on Scripture and, at his death, Saint Antony praised 'the marvellous way in which he walked according to Scripture' (FESTUGIÈRE, *La première vie Grecque*, No. 120). The first reaction of the young BASIL, faced with the problems posed by his contemporaries about the monastic life was to study Scripture. He published his conclusions in his *Moral Rules* in which he quoted more than 1,500 verses of the Bible. Later, in his *Long Rules* and in his *Short Rules*, he also makes frequent references to Scripture.

All these Rules, and the numerous others which follow them, up to that of Saint Benedict, are inspired by Scripture in different ways: first, because they cite it explicitly and apply it to the subject in question; then – and this is the most frequent case – because they are inspired by its spirit and even its vocabulary, without making direct quotations; long meditation on these texts made it natural for the writers to use their language. The allusion to the parable of the Prodigal Son in the Prologue of *RB* is a typical case; taking this tendency to the extreme, it came about that the Rules used the words of Scripture in an accommodated sense, giving them a meaning which they did not have in the sacred text. (cf. AV, *Sub Regula vel Abbate*, pp. 209–241, and *Per Ducatum Evangelii*, pp. 186–198. The continuous reading of and meditation upon Scripture is a practice traditionally recommended to monks as a means of approaching God and dispersing temptations.

any less an application of the Gospel for the monks of his time. Beyond the regulations, then, it is the example of Jesus that he invites them to follow. In doing so, they will discover an intimacy with God the Father.[51]

The mention of '*faith and good works*' demonstrates the idea of walking in the light of the Gospel, a way that is at once supernatural and pragmatic. To achieve this goal, the monk must discipline his life. Such discipline is also an act of faith, by which he clings to Christ and imitates him. Faith recognises the call of God, and makes the heart alert to follow the Lord, like Abraham and Saint Paul.[52] Clement, Origen and many others consider faith as the first step towards God. It becomes thus an act of love which makes a monk '*run ... and make haste*', as *RB* repeats several times. Here again is that theme of concern for efficacy and the zeal of love that we noted at the beginning of the Rule.

These traditional ideas of Christianity are also found in all monastic systems, although they are envisaged rather differently. It is remarkable that the attitude of faith is often much emphasised. In the Hindu *Bhakti* disciples ask their guru, Suta, to instruct them, in a text taken from the beginning of the *Bhagavata Purana*:

> O you, the holy one, give us, by means of your discernment, the essence of all knowledge and teach us, who are full of faith, so that our spirit may find repose. Speak to us of grace. We are listening avidly ... Tell us, who are full of faith, the high deeds ... of Krishna the Long-Haired, who is truly the Lord, hidden under the appearances of a man.[53]

It is difficult to assess this faith which, in Hinduism, can vary from simple confidence in an experienced master to a true faith in the God of love. Among the Buddhists it ranks alongside the liberating power attributed to the way of the Buddha. The first duty of the monk is to 'take refuge in the Buddha, his Law and his Order' (*Dharma* and *Sangha*). To doubt these things is to commit a capital offence.

In several religions, faith also refers to the sacred texts that transmit the religious experience of their sages. The Hindu commentators of the first verses of the *Narada Bhakti Sutra*[54] list the qualities required for entry into the way of devotion (*Bhakti*): these are neither caste, nor knowledge, nor sex, but faith in God, in the Scriptures and

---

51 The details of the regulations which Saint Benedict occasionally gives are only the practical application of the Gospel principles taken from his predecessors and applied to concrete situations.

52 Cf. *Heb.* 11.

53 *Bhagavata Purana.* 1, 1; 13; 11; 17.

54 Cf. GISPERT-SAUCH, *Narada Bhakti Sutras*, p. 4.

in the guru who explains them. But even several centuries earlier, the great Hindu theologian Shankara had shown the way, finding his inspiration and the criteria for his judgements in the oldest Holy Books of his country.[55] The whole of the Koran also seems like the word of God regulating human lives. This evocation of faith is so universal that one could see in it, along with L. Gardet, a statement of 'the incapacity of any created intellect to know God by its own powers'.[56]

Faith and the testimony of the sacred writings are not, however, sufficient for opening the heart to contact with the Infinite. Another Hindu theologian, Ramanuja, mentions the control of desire, diligence, the spirit of service to others, holiness in words and actions, serenity and peaceful joy.

Faith, devotion, the practice of good works, the search for inner peace – these are the common traits of all religions. The proper note of Christianity, underlined by *RB* in its commentary on Psalm 33, is to make us enter *'under the guidance of the Gospel'* into intimacy with the Holy Trinity. The lines that follow emphasise the role of Christ in the life of his disciple, the monk, and invite him humbly to hand himself over to him.

COMMENTARY ON PSALM 14: *Who shall dwell in your "tent"?* (*Prol.* 23–24)

The one who is charitable (*Prol.* 23–27):

Ps. 14: 1	*But let us question the Lord with the prophet, saying to him, 'Lord, who shall dwell in your "tent"? who shall rest on your holy mountain?' And*
Matt. 17: 4	*then let us listen to the Lord's answer to our questions, as he shows us the way to this "tent", saying, 'He*
Ps. 14: 2–3	*who walks without fault and does what is right; he who tells the truth in his heart; he who works no deceit with his tongue; he who does no wrong to his neighbour; he who does not slander his neighbour.'*

We find here again the themes of Psalm 33, on the virtues necessary for community life. The commentary is linked with a paraphrase of Psalm 136, which indicates the necessary qualities for one who wishes to live with the Lord:

---

[55] The *Narada Bhakti Sutras* date from the eleventh century. Shankara lived in the ninth and saw in the *Vedas* a truth which came from on high.

[56] L. GARDET, *Mystique musulmane*, p. 144.

The one who dashes temptations against Christ (*Prol.* 28–32)

Ps. 14: 4 *He who casts the wicked devil, even as he beguiles him, out of the sight of his heart, along with the temptation itself, and so reduces him to impotence, and takes the*
Ps. 136: 9 *incipient thoughts that he suggests and dashes them*
(1 Cor. 10: 4) *against (the rock of) Christ.*

This spiritual interpretation of Psalm 136, based on 1 *Cor.* 10: 4, 'That rock was Christ,' is a commonplace in monastic literature.[57] But the number of times it is used underlines the importance that such a recourse had among the Fathers for a faithful monk who found himself in difficulties.

Among the temptations, pride is given special consideration by Saint Benedict:

Ps. 14: 4 *Those who fear the Lord and do not become conceited about keeping the law well, but*
Phil. 2: 13 *realise that the good in themselves cannot be their own work but is done by the Lord, and who praise the Lord working within them, as they say with the prophet,*
Ps. 113: 1, 9 *'Not unto us, Lord, not unto us, but unto your name, give the glory.'*
1 *Cor.* 15: 10 *For neither did the Apostle Paul give himself any credit for his preaching, but said,*
2 *Cor.* 10: 17 *'By the grace of God I am what I am.'* **And the same Apostle also said, 'He who boasts must boast in the Lord.'**

It is this humble confidence in Christ, in his grace and his doctrine which is the source of all assurance for the faithful one. *RB* accentuates this idea by replacing the text of *RM*, containing the psalm, with a quotation from 2 *Cor.* 10: 17. Saint Benedict thus generalises the perspective, and applies the rest of the paragraph to every situation where the trust of the disciple might be tested. The text, in fact, extends the image of Christ the Rock, using the related image of the house founded on rock.

---

[57] BUTLER gives references to Hilary, Ambrose, Jerome, Augustine and Cassian. The commentaries of Dom DELATTE and that of A. DE VOGÜÉ add some others. Parallels can also be found in BASIL, *SR 75;* PALLADIUS, liv, II. ch. 42 and in the Fathers of the Desert: MARTIN OF DUMES 1–4. This text is found also in *RB* 4: 50.

CONCLUSION OF THE COMMENTARY ON THE PSALMS: *The rock of humble trust in Christ (Prol.* 33–34)

Matt. 7: 25   *And so the Lord also says in the Gospel, 'Everyone who listens to these words of mine and acts on them, will be like a sensible man who built his house on rock; floods rose, gales blew and hurled themselves against that house, and it did not fall; it was founded on rock.'*

The image of a rock, unmoved by the river's flood, takes on a particular interest since it is also found in the Buddhist *Dhammapada*:

By effort, resolve, discipline and mastery of self, the wise man makes himself like an island that no flood can submerge.[58]

The comparison of these two texts shows clearly the doctrinal difference that exists, in spite of the similar external attitudes. In Buddhism, trust is founded on firmness of resolve and strength of will; the monk goes ahead alone in pursuit of his ideal, and must attain it by his own efforts. This attitude is well described in the poem of the rhinoceros:

> Play, pleasures, mirth and worldly joys,
> Be done with these and heed them not;
> Aloof from pomp and speaking truth,
> Fare lonely as rhinoceros.
>
> And turn thy back on joys and pains,
> Delights and sorrows known of old;
> And gaining poise and calm, and cleansed,
> Fare lonely as rhinoceros.
>
> Astir to win the furthest goal,
> Not lax in thought, no sloth in ways,
> Strong in the onset, steadfast, firm,
> Fare lonely as rhinoceros.[59]

The Christian monk must also make a renunciation, and the Fathers

---

[58] *Dhammapada* 25. Cf. WALPOLA RAHULA, *L'enseignement du Bouddha; Dhammapada* II.

[59] *Sutta Nipata*, towards the beginning, from CONZE, *Buddhist Scriptures*, pp. 81–82.

insist on the necessity of an immovable resolve[60] to attain the goal. But the disciple of Christ does not depend on the firmness of his own decision, but rather finds his strength in a humble trust in the Lord. The central place of Christ is one of the principal points of divergence with the other monastic systems. It is he who gives life, strength and happiness, he whom one seeks as the perfect model, and he to whom the monk will be united for an eternity of love and peace.

4. THE SCHOOL OF THE LORD'S SERVICE

INTRODUCTION: *Necessity of formation* (*Prol.* 35–44)

The following paragraph of *RB* (*Prol.* 35–39) is also borrowed from *RM*. The idea of a school is introduced, acting as a summary of what went before. The Father, full of goodness, offers the intimacy of his tent, and *'daily'* waits for our conversion. The invitation becomes more and more pressing: we must *'make ready our hearts and bodies'* for the *'warfare of holy obedience to his command'* and pray for the help of his grace. Then, the vivid reminder of the last things shows how necessary it is to enter into the School of the Lord's Service:

Thus the Lord concludes his reply, and daily expects us to respond through our dutiful actions to his holy precepts. Therefore in order that amends may be made for sins, the days of our life are prolonged to give us a time in which to amend our evil ways, as the Apostle says,

Rom. 2: 4   *'Do you realise that the patience of God is meant to lead you to repentance?' For this loving Lord says,*

Ezek. (18–23); 33: 11ff   *'I do not wish the death of the sinner, but that he should change his ways and live.'*

We have asked the Lord, my brothers, about the kind of man who dwells in his tent, and we have heard what is required in order to do so. So let us fulfil the task of such a dweller. That means that we must make ready our hearts and bodies to engage in the warfare of holy obedience to his commands, and

---

[60] The *Apophthegmata* have a whole book on perseverance (liv. 7); see also, MARTIN OF DUMES, 26; DOROTHEUS OF GAZA, 7: 86, who quotes Antony; BASIL, *LR*, Prologue 29; 34; EVAGRIUS, *Praktikos*, Prol.; ch. 28–29; CASSIAN, *Conf.* 4: 12; 14: 3; 5–7. These last two authors envisage perseverance above all as a psychological disposition necessary for conquering the passions. The Master shares with Benedict the concern to christianise the theories of Evagrius which were repeated by Cassian. We will see other examples in the chapter on humility.

> *because our nature has not power to do this, we must*
> *ask God to send forth the help of his grace to our aid.*
> *And, if we wish to escape the punishment of hell and*
> *reach eternal life,*
>
> *John* 12: 35   *then while there is still time, while we are still living*
> *in this body and this life gives us the light to do all*
> *these things, we must hurry to do now what will*
> *profit us for ever. We propose, therefore to establish*
> *a school of the Lord's service.*

After these words, Saint Benedict again interrupts the text of *RM* to introduce a paragraph on the means of formation which were in use in his institute.

THE SCHOOL OF THE LORD'S SERVICE

Before citing the text proper to *RB*, we should look at the particular meaning given to the word 'school'. At the time of the Master and of Saint Benedict, the *schola* or school meant both the place where teaching was given, and the scope *for which* it was given, such as public service, e.g. in the army, or in the various spheres of public life.

In *RM*, the monastery appears like a technical college, preparing people for the service of the Lord. Already reborn in baptism, a person joined this school as a response to a second appeal from Christ: 'Come, learn from me ...'.[62] The monastery thus became the intermediary between baptism and the kingdom.

These ideas of teaching and service, in the context of *RB*, are like an echo of the first lines of the Prologue, asking that we should listen to Christ the teacher, and of the preceding sentences, which recall that we must '*make ready our hearts and bodies*' for the '*warfare of holy obedience.*' Such a life cannot fail to have its problems – and so the paragraph proper to *RB* begins with an allusion to the difficulties encountered by the monk in his life of service.

SAINT BENEDICT'S ADDITION

> *Matt.* 11: 30   *In setting up [this school] we hope we shall lay down*
> *nothing that is harsh or hard to bear. But if for*
> *adequate reason, for the correction of faults or the*
> *preservation of charity, some degree of restraint is laid*

---

[61] Note once more how obedience is directed first towards God with the goal of conformity to his will.

[62] *Mt.* 11: 28–30, cited by *RM* at the beginning of the *Thema*.

	down, do not then and there be overcome with terror,
Matt. 7: 14	*and run away from the way of salvation, for its*
	entrance must needs be narrow. On the contrary, as we
	progress in monastic observance and in faith, our
Ps. 118: 32	*hearts are opened wide, and the way of God's*
	commandments is run in a sweetness of love that is
	beyond words.

Even in the first words, we move away from the menacing threat of punishment for sin, which *RM* had envisaged in the preceding lines. Saint Benedict wanted his Rule to be, like the Gospel, an 'easy and light' yoke (*Matt.* 11: 30). There is no question of heroic physical performances, but rather of conversion of heart. This brings relief to the weaker members of the community, while encouraging them to progress towards the common ideal.

It is, nonetheless, recognised that there will have to be:

some degree of restraint, for the correction of faults [and] the preservation of charity.

These words summarise the method the Fathers used to attain to union with God. Following Saint Paul (1 *Cor.* 9: 27), they considered the struggle against the passions as the narrow way which leads to contemplation.[63] But this personal effort should always be balanced by the social dimension of charity. Pachomius had already spoken of this, calling it *Koinonia*, an essential means of union with Christ, while Cassian sees it as the final stage of purification of the heart, and the summary of all the virtues.[64]

In using these traditional ideas, Saint Benedict once more refers to Psalms 33 and 14. He also completes the indications he gave at the beginning of the Prologue and lays down, as a principle, the necessity of both ascetic effort and fraternal charity when searching for intimacy with the Lord.

The monastic systems of the other world religions have also recognised the dual necessity of asceticism on the one hand and, on the other, an attitude of good will towards one's neighbour. Non-violence is one of the cardinal virtues of the Hindu monk, while compassion is used in the meditation methods of the Buddhists to avoid the danger

---

[63] The mastery of the passions is the object of the *Praktikos* of EVAGRIUS: see also CASSIAN, *Institutes* 54: 5–12: *Conferences* 11: 6–8; BASIL, *LR*, 5; 8; 13; 16–25. The Fathers of the Desert were specialists in this kind of search and the Systematic Collection of the *Apophthegmata* is classed according to the vices to be combated against, and the virtues to be encouraged.

[64] Cf. PACHOMIUS, *Catechesis*, p. 2; 15; 21; 38; ORSISIUS, *Testament*, 50; CASSIAN, *Conf.* 1: 7; 3: 7–8; 24: 6.

of revulsion against created things (something which might occur with continuous reflection on the transitory nature of things). Here, for example, is the prayer of a Tibetan monk:

(18)
Understanding the meaning of renunciation,
(Having thought about suffering as well as its cause),
May I always uphold, till becoming Buddha,
The banner of freedom, for which I'd not break
The least Rule of pure moral behaviour,
That I vowed I would keep, though my life be at stake.

(27)
May I fully develop the love of a mother
Towards all sentient beings, especially towards those
Who verbally thrash me and always have harmful
Intentions against my life, body and wealth.[65]

The fact of devoting oneself to helping others in their spiritual progress is also considered as a meritorious work of which the Buddhist *Bodhisattvas*[66] give us an example; but it is a practice equally recommended by the Hindu gurus and the Muslim sheikhs. These altruistic efforts have the goal of purifying the monk from selfishness, as well as promoting an inner calm, and a peaceful atmosphere in community – all of which help to facilitate union with God. Although several schools, above all in Hinduism, recognise the presence of the Infinite in each human being,[67] it seems that the *Koinonia*, fraternal love seen as a direct means of union with God, is proper to Christianity.

Having shown the obstacles to be foreseen in the journey towards God, Saint Benedict turns to the brother in difficulty:

> **do not then and there be overcome with terror, and run away from the way of salvation, for its entrance must needs be narrow.**

Comparing this phrase of *RB* with the Tibetan practice, it is interesting to note that, in the great Tibetan monastery–universities, one of the roles of the spiritual master is to make sure that the young monk is provided with all necessary help, so that he will not be discouraged by excessive severity, and be tempted to return home.

The concern for weaker members of the community is one of the characteristics of *RB*, and the words, *'do not run away'* will be

---

[65] Tibetan poem given in *The Thirty-Seven Practices*, pp. 23, 25.

[66] *Bodhisattva*: people who, in *Mahayana* Buddhism, delay their immersion into the Infinite Peace of Nirvana, so that they may help others to attain it.

[67] The *Lingayat* Hindus, in particular, affirm the equality of all human beings and the duty of respecting them on account of the divine presence which lives in them.

repeated in connection with manual labour in the instructions given to the Abbot (*RB* 48 and 64). The discouragement of the weak and their abandonment of duty should be avoided, on the part of the authorities, both by a concern for moderation and by the loving support of the brethren, and, on the part of the religious in difficulty, by an effort to hold fast.[68] Saint Benedict also reminds him of the attractiveness of the divine gentleness, something that will help him to enter into the narrow way which leads to salvation.

As we progress in monastic observance and in faith, our hearts are opened wide, and the way of God's commandments is run in a sweetness of love that is beyond words.

If the beginning is narrow, that does not mean to say that it will become wider later, but rather, according to Psalm 118 (traditionally quoted in this context,[69]) that the *heart* will grow, giving the monk the strength to run in '*the way of God's commandments*', because his heart is now in harmony with them.

Saint Benedict, influenced by Saint Augustine's commentary on Psalm 118,[70] adds love to degrees of spiritual progress, religious life and faith, which were already mentioned when dealing with Psalms 33 and 14. This passage of the great Doctor mentions the work of the Holy Spirit. Saint Benedict will speak of it in chapter 7 but, in this final part of the Prologue, the shortness of the phrase is no doubt responsible for its omission. On the other hand the qualificative, '*beyond words*', testifies to a true mystical experience.[71]

The passage, as a whole, gives us a synthesis of the various stages of the spiritual life. We start with a phase of struggle and personal effort, the soul advances in faith and leaves the initiative to God. This schema was already the classic one in the Fathers,[72] and is found

[68] Here we find again the theme of firmness in one's vocation, already seen in connection with the image of Christ the Rock – a theme which, as we said, is abundantly treated in the monastic tradition.

[69] The link between Psalm 118 and the two ways of the Gospel is a theme treated by Hilary, Ambrose and Augustine in their commentaries on this psalm. Cf. AV *RB IV*, pp. 90–91 and notes 177–178.

[70] AUGUSTINE, *Enarr. in Ps.* 118; cf. *Serm.* 10; 11; 20; 70, 3; *Hom. in Mt.* 11.

[71] No doubt Saint Benedict practised the *krupté ergasia*, that is, he was careful to hide his spiritual experiences, something that was considered essential by the Father. Cf. *Apophthegmata*, 'Euloge prêtre' 1; Poemen, 144. There are other examples in the life of Pachomius.

[72] Cf. AV *RB IV*, p. 92 which quotes *Apophthegmata* 2 of Synclectica: 'After many struggles an unspeakable joy will arrive' (cf. 1 *Pet* 1: 8); MACARIUS, *Hom.* 18 and 21 (*PG* 34, 633; 635); GREGORY OF NYSSA, *De Inst. Christ.* 77; 85; 86; DIADOCHUS OF PHOTIKE, Cap. 93; CALESARIUS OF ARLES, *Serm.* 236. 5; JEROME, *Epist.* 22, 40; AUGUSTINE, *Tract. in Joan.* 48: 1; CASSIAN, *Inst.* 4: 39, 3.

again in *RB* 7 and 63. It shows how, like them, Saint Benedict conceived the monastic life as a means of entering into profound union with God. Guided by the Rule, and under the guidance of the Spirit, the monk follows Christ who leads him to intimacy with the Father.

The mystics of all religions would be able to endorse the expression *'experience beyond words'* which designates the goal of their meditation, since contact with the Infinite is beyond all expression. Some consider it to be also an experience of love. But the characteristic Christian note is to see that this is brought about by the Holy Spirit, who unites the monk to Christ, and introduces him into the mystery of the Trinitarian God of love.

After this brief glimpse of the marvellous horizon of intimate union with the Lord, Saint Benedict resumes his quotation from the Master, which asks for perseverance.

CONCLUSION OF PROLOGUE *RB/RM*: *Perseverance, Union with Christ the Redeemer*

Acts 2: 42	*Let us then never withdraw from*
2 John 9	*discipleship to him, but persevering in his teachings in the monastery till death,*
Phil. 2: 8;	*let us share the sufferings of Christ through patience,*
1 Pet. 4: 13;	*and so deserve also to share in his kingdom.*
Rom. 8: 1–17;	
(Luke 10: 30–42; 14: 27)	

We return here to the idea of the School of the Lord's Service but, in *RB*, this phrase becomes a final word of personal advice to the monk in difficulties. While reminding him of the necessity of a firm decision to persevere, his attention is centred on the Saviour. He is the Master to whom he should attach himself, and it is to expose himself to his teaching and to share in his life, in the mystery of the redemption by the cross, that he remains in the monastery until death.[73]

In underlining the role of Christ in the spiritual journey, Saint Benedict joins the experience of the first monastic Fathers, like Antony, Basil and Pachomius, who attached a great importance to the

---

[73] The richness of the scriptural allusions in these few lines show the importance for the Christian life of perseverance and union with the passion of Christ.

[74] The life of Antony gives many examples of his intimacy with Jesus: ATHANASIUS, *VA*, 3–5, 13–14; 22. PACHOMIUS addresses his prayer to Christ at the moment of his conversion, saying that he wanted to follow his example in 'serving the human race', like the Good Shepherd who takes care of his monks (*VC* p. 119); BASIL always preached the example of Christ both to monks and superiors: *Reg. Mor.*, *PG* 31; *PR* 1; 98.

relationship of the monks with their Lord.[74] This almost instinctive reference to Christ in *RB* is found each time there is a question of difficulties or sufferings to be endured.[75]

Perseverance in the monastery until death will be the object of the vow of stability. Let us be aware of its positive motivation: the monk likes to live in the monastery so that he can be with the Lord and listen to his teaching without ceasing, like Mary at Bethany. Together with her he is invited to 'choose the better part' (*Luke* 10: 38–42).

In taking a general view of the Prologue of *RB*, we note that Saint Benedict's presentation of monastic life touches the major part of the ideas which are essential to all the religions. His approach is a Christian one and he brings his own special contribution to the debate.

In the first lines, he presented the fundamental attitude of one who seeks union with the Absolute: an inner listening to the Infinite, present in the heart, and the struggle against selfishness which, for the Christian, is done by following Christ. In *RB* this '*toil*' is called '*obedience*', which gives the word a wider sense than usual.

Saint Benedict chose to develop his theme by using passages from *RM* which comment on Psalms 33 and 14. They express the desire for Union with the Infinite that lives in the human heart. Faith shows the call of God within this attraction, the God who loves each person and makes him share the intimacy of his '*tent*' which is also the '*holy mountain*' and which the mystics of several religions call the 'cave of the heart'. They are all in agreement, also, about the conditions necessary for attaining this dwelling-place and for remaining there: the flight from selfishness, good will towards other people and a strong resolution which, in Christian terms, is a humble confidence in Christ. In conclusion we see the necessity for a specialised formation in order to acquire mastery over the passions and to develop a universal charity.

Speaking as a Christian, Saint Benedict makes clear that the Infinite is a God who loves us, and speaks by means of the Bible, which '*leads*' each person onwards through Christ, the model and support of the faithful one. The particular note given by the Father of Western monasticism, is his constant concern for the weaker members of the community. He wants teach the disciple to listen to God present within him, so that he can constantly model his conduct on Christ, while trusting in his help.

---

[75] *RB* chs. 2; 4; 5; 7; 23; 27; 36; 63; 72; 73.

CHAPTER II

THE DIFFERENT KINDS OF MONK
(*RB* 1)

It is clear that there are four kinds of monk

The monastic reality, of which Benedict spoke in his own day, is also found in the monastic life of today's great world religions.

1. PRE-CHRISTIAN FORMS OF MONASTIC LIFE

One of the principal forms of Hindu monasticism – and, no doubt, the oldest – is the *ashram*, in which a spiritual master instructs a group of disciples who share his life.[1] When the time passed in formation is sufficient, the monk becomes a *samnyasi* (renunciant), and embarks on an itinerant lifestyle[2] that will help him to achieve inner purification by means of the external renunciation already begun under his master. The most fervent monk–pilgrims, who do not found an ashram themselves, often go to a hermitage. Feeling the approach of death, they set out for the north-east, the region of the high mountains where the gods live, so as to die on the road which heads in that direction.

Taken as a whole, the Hindu monastic life could be considered as an ever more radical way of purification, lived in view of union with the Absolute. Nevertheless, inner progress can also be pursued in each of these stages, which then become themselves a way of life. The itinerant monk goes from village to village, handing out his wisdom, in

[1] On the development of asceticism in India, cf. *The origin of asceticism and of the Ashram Dharma* in BHARATI BULLETIN OF INDOLOGY, Benares Hindu University 8, 1964–1965; F. ACHARYA, *Le monachisme en Inde*, COLL CIST, 1967, No. 3.

[2] *Samnyasi*: a description is given by ABHISHIKTANANDA in *Sagesse hindoue et mystique chrétienne*, p. 46, note 2; and J. GHUYRE, *Indian Sadhus*, Popular Prakasham, Bombay.

exchange for a little food. The continual succession of leave-takings is a way of detachment, peace, and union with the Infinite, as far as he is concerned. Here is how the *Laws of Manu* describe him:

> *He should no longer have either hearth or home. Let him keep absolute silence; his food, roots, and fruits. Let him be exempt from all inclination toward sensory pleasures, chaste like a novice, his bed the earth; not seeking a dwelling according to his taste, but rather living at the foot of the trees. He should receive in alms what is necessary for his subsistence ... he should study the different parts of the Scriptures, so as to unite himself to the Supreme Being ... and if he finds that he has some incurable malady, let him direct his steps towards the invincible region of the North East, and walk that way with decisive step, aspiring after union with the Divine, living solely on air and water, until the moment of his bodily dissolution.*[3]

The itinerant life can be pursued either alone or in a group, as is the case with the ascetics who follow the way of *Bhakti*, or devotion. They journey in companies, to be able to chant together the poems that celebrate the love of the god to whom they have consecrated themselves. For the Jain monks and nuns, this pilgrimage lasts the whole of their life.[4] Others retire to hermitages, and often take a vow of silence, whose duration can be as much as several years.

Hindu and Tibetan hermits are still numerous now in the Himalayas and in other sacred places of India. One can also find Buddhist hermits in Sri Lanka[5] and in the other countries where this religion is freely practised. In Islamic countries, the Sufis had many hermits, who often passed a part of their lives as pilgrims or itinerant missionaries.[6]

In general, the hermit does not immerse himself in solitude until formed by a master. He should have learned perfect self-control, which permits him to concentrate on the Absolute, with whom he wishes to be united. Here is the portrait of the hermit given by the *Bhagavad Gita*:

---

[3] MANU, 6: 24–26; 31.

[4] N. SHANTA, *La voie Jain, histoire, spiritualité, vie des ascètes*. The first Buddhist monks were also itinerants who came together only at the rainy season. The life of a Zen monk is sometimes itinerant.

[5] The existence of hermits and cenobites in Sri Lanka goes back to the beginnings of Buddhism in the country, cf. WALPOLA RAHULA, *History of Buddhism in Ceylon*, p. 196. Among the cenobites, a distinction is still made between two types: the meditative and the intellectual, this last being often also a teacher (ibid. p. 158). The Buddhist hermit, however, remains always attached to a monastic community. Cf. MOHAN WIJEYARATNA, *Les débuts du monachisme bouddhique comparés à ceux du monachisme chrétien*, COLL CIST 1983, 1, T. 45.

[6] J. SPENCER TRIMINGHAM, *The Sufi Orders in Islam*, p. 5 and *passim*.

Equal in his treatment of friend and foe, the neutral, the indifferent, the sinner and the saint ... he practises continual union with the Self, sits apart, alone, all desire and every idea of possession banished from his mental horizon; controlling his entire being with his all-pervading conscience.[7]

Shri Aurobindo gives the following commentary on this passage:

When all desires and passions have ceased, when the mind is no longer allowed to project itself outside in the form of thoughts, when the practice of this silent and solitary yoga has become the rule, what further action or relation is possible with the world of exterior contacts? ... The cave, the forest, the summit of the mountain seem henceforth to be the most suitable locations, the only possible place for his continuing life and the constant ecstasy of the samadhi, his only joy and his sole occupation. But, at the beginning, in the course of solitary yoga, the Gita does not recommend that one should give up every activity.[8]

Formation for the eremitic life is therefore a gradual process. However, as we have seen, not all the solitaries are closed to other people. Some of them return to their fellow men, to instruct them, to challenge their routine way of life and attract them towards the great adventure of the search for the Infinite. This is the story of many founders of monastic Orders and religious reformers in the course of the centuries among the Hindu and Buddhist monks. Several Sufi Orders also began with saintly hermits. It was thus quite natural for the eremitic life to give rise to cenobitic groups.

The qualities of the cenobitic life are evidenced in the history of Buddhism and the experience of the Hindu master, Shankara.

The first Buddhist monks lived in little itinerant groups, as did most of the ascetics of their time. They came together in community during the rainy season, and made use of the occasion to recite together the doctrine of Buddha. As they became established, this study was developed, to the point where some of their houses became celebrated centres of philosophical research,[9] giving rise to schools of thought, which would in turn create the various branches of Buddhism during the following centuries. In these seats of learning also, the missionaries and spiritual masters, who would later spread the doctrine of Buddha throughout Asia, received their education.

At the time of Shankara's birth (eighth century AD), the flourish-

---

[7] *Bhagavad Gita*, 6: 9–10.
[8] Shri Aurobindo, *Bhagavad Gita*, French transl. C. Rao and J. Herbert, p. 171.
[9] Such as the universities of Takchaçila and Nalanda, or the great monasteries of Tibet.

ing of contradictory teaching had thrown Hinduism into confusion, provoking either scepticism or a reluctant conformity. It is a mark of his genius that he was able to synthesise these diverse elements, thus bringing new meaning to religious practice, while establishing a due limit for the ritualist tendency. He began as a peripatetic teacher, forming disciples and entering dialogue with those who held different doctrines. Following the example of the Buddhists, however, he created a religious order, whose members were organised in large monasteries, which would later become the intellectual fortresses of his followers.[10] His imitators did the same in the following centuries[11] and, even in our own time, these establishments remain centres of orthodoxy for different religious groups.

The principal monasteries act as houses of formation for their order, and their influence is reinforced by the presence of other monks living in small communities, taking care of temples or ashrams. The members of these main Orders are recruited exclusively among certain castes of Brahmins; they devote themselves to study of the sacred texts, meditation, and the spiritual service of the members of their group. However, during the troubled period of the Muslim invasions, each order felt constrained to set up a branch of monk–soldiers, recruited from all classes of society. At the coming of peace, these warriors became itinerant monks, or were attached to the service of certain temples.

The Lingayat Hindus created an original form of monastic life, combining cenobitism with the wandering life. In this system, some monks lived together in *maths* and others, called *Charamurthys*, would journey around for a large part of the year, preaching to the faithful and giving advice on their spiritual practices.[12]

Modern Hindu religious orders, like the Ramakrishna Mission, have rather important *maths*, where their aspirants make their noviatiate, and other houses which have only a few monks. In general, they all have schools or other social works. Several great contemporary gurus have themselves founded ashrams, some of which have developed into centres of social work and retreats for lay people.[13]

---

[10] Cf. O. LACOMBE, *L'Absolu selon le Védanta*, pp. 21–24. The first and most important of these monasteries was Sringeri, near Mysore; after that came Puri on the east coast, Dwarka in the north-east of India and, finally, Badari at the foot of the Himalayas.

[11] In particular Ramanuja and Madhva, whose doctrine differs in several areas from that of Shankara. Cf. O. LACOMBE, *L'Absolu*, pp. 29–30.

[12] The Indian *maths* are a type of monastery. At present, among the *Lingayats*, many of the *Charamurthys* are themselves assigned to secondary *maths*, which are dependent on another more important one where the superior has his residence.

[13] We can cite, for example, Aurobindo at Pondicherry and Chivananda at Rishikesh.

A century before the coming of Christ, we also find communities among the Jews. At Qumran in Palestine, for instance, the monks prayed and studied the Law, as a preparation for becoming soldiers of the Messiah. At the same period, Philo tells us of the existence in Egypt of men and women contemplatives, who lived as solitaries during the week and came together on the Sabbath for prayers and a common meal.[14]

An overall view of these institutions leads us to conclude that, among the greater part of those religions which adopted monastic life, the cenobitic and eremitic forms were practised together, sometimes staying in the one place, at other times itinerant.

The cenobitic life offers certain advantages for the spiritual and doctrinal formation of monks[15] while the itinerant life develops detachment. The eremitic life, which is, in principle, reserved for monks matured by experience, allows a person to concentrate on the search for union with the Absolute, in solitary meditation.

Each of these forms produces holy monks. However, one also finds individuals who, for less praiseworthy causes, take advantage of the respect given to the monastic habit. Among these are debauched or 'parasite' itinerants, eccentric hermits and sectarian cenobites, or those who are attached to the goods of this world.[16] All these faults, however, are due to human weakness. We know that they can also be found in the history of Christian monasticism.

Each type of monastic life has thus its own virtues and dangers. The history of religion condemns none of these types. On the contrary, it considers it normal that they should coexist, and that monks should follow the form of life they find most satisfactory for their spiritual advancement.

2. DIFFERENT KINDS OF MONK BEFORE SAINT BENEDICT

Moving to Christian monasticism, one notices that the eremitic, itinerant, and cenobitic lives have existed simultaneously since its

---

[14] Cf. QUMRAN, *Règle;* PHILO, *De Vita contemplativa.*

[15] Again we see that the novitiate at Qumran was made in a fairly large community. From the point of view of spiritual formation, it is interesting to note that at the Congress of Asian Christian Monasticism in Bangalore, 1973, it was a Tibetan monk who emphasised the role of the community in orientating the monk towards spiritual experience.

[16] It is a fact, for example, that riches have often been the cause of spiritual ruin and of the disappearance of Hindu and Buddhist monasteries. Currently the most ancient and famous centres are not always the most welcoming. Some masters show only scant openness to the problems posed by modern life.

origins. Saint Antony lived as a hermit in the desert of Egypt, but at the end of his life travelled a great deal, visiting his disciples in one hermitage after another, perhaps in response to an appeal from other people who valued his counsel.[17] Saint Pachomius, inventor of the Christian cenobitic life, was his contemporary, as was Saint Amoun, the founder of Nitria, where the monks lived as a hermits in groups of various sizes, from two or three to several hundred.[18]

This variety of forms in monastic life is attested throughout the entire Christian world, East and West. From the fourth century, itinerant Syrian monks founded Christian communities in India and later went as far as central Asia and China, following the caravan routes. In the Middle East, the monastic institutions usually combined the cenobitic and eremitic lives.[19]

In the West, Saint Augustine and Cassian knew both hermits and cenobites. A little after their time, the Celts made a monastic virtue out of 'pilgrimage for God',[20] leaving their home country to preach the Gospel to the peoples of northern Europe.

A certain liberty in the form of life was the usual practice, right up to the end of the Middle Ages, and monks could pass individually from one form to another with ease. From the beginning of the thirteenth century, however, the hermits were required to belong to a religious Order. This same period saw them creating several new congregations or reforms of old Orders. The eremitic life disappeared in Latin Europe during the upheaval provoked by the French Revolution,[21] but it is flourishing again at the present time, and has always existed in the Eastern Church.[22]

Evaluation and judgement of the varied forms of monastic life is as

---

[17] Cf. ATHANASIUS, *VA*, 47; 91; etc.

[18] Antony, born about 250; died 356: Pachomius, younger than he, died however in 346. Amoun lived at Nitria around the year 330.

[19] Cf. D. J. CHITTY, *The Desert a City*.

[20] On the subject of Celtic monks, see J. RYAN, *Irish monasticism and Irish monks in the Golden Age*; L. GOUGAUD, *Gaelic pioneers of Christianity*; RIBB, *Les Saints irlandais hors d'Irlande*, RHE Louvain 1934.

[21] The Benedictine reformers of the thirteenth and fourteenth centuries, like Saint Sylvester and Saint Bernard Tolomeo, were originally hermits, as was the English mystic Richard Rolle. For England, see: SIDNEY HEATH, *In the steps of the pilgrims*, 2; in the thirteenth century, it was pressure from Councils and Popes (especially Innocent IV and Alexander IV) that made the hermits belong to a religious Order. This was the origin of the hermits of Saint Augustine; there were hermits and recluses in England right up to the Reformation and in France until the Revolution of 1789, cf. Dom L. GOUGAUD, *Ermites et reclus*.

[22] P. DESEILLE, in *L'Evangile au Désert*, gives details on the eremitical life in the ninth-century East; he cites Youssef Bournaya (*PG* 34, 468 ff.). Saint Charbel Maklouf, of the last century, is part of that tradition.

old as the life itself, as far as Christianity is concerned. The advantages and difficulties of each type of life have been assessed, right from the beginning, leading to the general conclusion that the monk ought to choose the vocation that seems best able to lead him to perfection:

> *When you see something that brings most profit and advantage to your mind, do it.*

Thus says one of the *Apophthegmata*.[23] Therefore, for the people of the time, the different categories of monks were equally meritorious.[24] Furthermore, Saint Antony, hearing of the death of Saint Pachomius, praised the institution which he had founded.[25]

Often, however, the eremitic life was considered a higher form of life in principle, because it was more austere. As it was more difficult to practise, it was also more easily subject to errors. It was this that led Saint Basil to write against the eremitic life,[26] in reaction to the abuses of the Messalian and Eustathian heretics.

Tradition also shows us the conditions that the elders judged indispensable for the hermit. One of the principal qualities required was a reliable power of judgement: to be able to walk with God, without the need of frequent advice. According to one Father of the Desert, the hermit should:

> *be capable of teaching, and not in need of it.*[27]

Cassian returns to this subject several times.[28] Maturity of spirit is acquired by formation. In the Fathers, such formation was acquired either by becoming a disciple of a solitary, or in a community. However, all were unanimous on the need for it. In the great centres of eremitic life, such as Nitria, Egypt, or the *Lavras* of Palestine, the monks could not take up the solitary life of the desert until after quite a long period of probation in the common life.[29]

---

[23] *Apophthegmata*, Joseph, 8; in the same vein, see Poemen, 29.

[24] Cf. WALLIS BUDGE, *The Paradise of the Holy Fathers*, vol. 1, p. 108; vol. 2, p. 8, No. 21.

[25] PACHOMIUS, *VG*, 120.

[26] BASIL, *LR*, 3 and 7.

[27] *Apophthegmata*, Anonymous 89; we should note, however, that the Fathers of the Desert frequently sought the advice of the elders. The whole corpus of the *Apophthegmata* is made up of such consultation.

[28] CASSIAN, *Inst.* 5: 36;*Conf.* 19: 14.

[29] Cf. CHITTY, *The Desert a City, passim*; CASSIAN, *Inst.* 5: 36; *Conf.* 3: 1–2; 19: 10–11; JEROME, *Ep.* 22, 36; 125, 9; DESEILLE, *Evangile*, pp. 221–222. In ninth century Syria, the eremitic life was permitted only after three years of formation.

Besides giving him maturity of judgement, formation also helped the monk to conquer his vices. Solitude, and absence of friction with other people, can actually allow faults to develop in a hidden way, until occasion arises for them to manifest themselves in all their force.[30] Preparation for the eremitic life should also give particular attention to the struggle against pride and attachment to created things:

> *Since they have learnt the virtue of humility together with that of nudity [total detachment] and have been completely purged of their vices, they are able to penetrate the profound secrets of the desert, to confront the demon, in terrible combat.*[31]

Cassian reminds us that the true motivation of the hermit is the search for intimacy with God, and not an escape from his personal problems:

> *Only monks who are perfectly purified should seek the desert ... those who are purified from all their faults, through living in the midst of other brethren, those who do not seek the desert as a refuge from their weakness, but rather wish to find this divine and superior contemplation, which only the perfect can attain, in solitude.*[32]

In most cases, the hermits lived in the neighbourhood of the monastery. The spirituality of the community was enriched by the presence of the solitaries, and the hermits could be sure of solitude and liberty of spirit, since the community relieved their material needs and removed indiscreet visitors.[33] The arrangements were adapted to the needs of each hermit, to remove the temptation (well known among the Fathers of the Desert) to search for another and better location.[34]

The itinerant life was also recognised as valuable, under certain conditions: detachment (which meant that one had to accept the perpetual insecurity of travel without resources, in lands that were sometimes hostile) and missionary zeal. These were the hallmarks of

---

[30] CASSIAN, *Inst.* 8: 18–19; BASIL, *LR*, 7.

[31] CASSIAN, *Conf.* 19: 12; cf. *Inst.* 5: 36, 1.

[32] CASSIAN, *Inst.* 8: 18, 1; cf. *Conf.* 18: 6; 19: 10.

[33] We have already spoken of Nitria and the *lavras* of Palestine. In these institutions, the hermits came to the monastery for the Sunday Eucharist; they brought their work with them and received, in exchange, their weekly food ration and the materials necessary for their work. In the sixth century, two famous hermits, Barsanuphius and John, lived near the monastery which was under the direction of Dorothéus of Gaza. Cf. BARZANUPHE and JEAN, *Correspondence*, Solesmes.

[34] '*Drink, eat and sleep, but do not leave your cell*' says one of the *Apophthegmata* (Heraclius, 1): a monk in difficulties might need to relax his observance for a time, or modify it, but it is important that he persevere in the place where he is.

authenticity for such men, 'intoxicated with God'. The situation was less uncertain for the pilgrims who went from hermitage to monastery, taking advantage of the already legendary hospitality of the monks. Cassian himself practised this way of life for a long period, and sometimes lets us see the way the Fathers distinguished true monks from lazy ones, who only wanted to live off other people.

The first test was to see if the visitors applied themselves to the usage of the place, such as the horarium, the manner of prayer, food, dress, etc.,[35] or whether they took advantage of their status as guests to do what they liked instead. Next, they discerned whether a desire for perfection and imitation of virtue were the true motives of their stay. Cassian's accounts, like those in the *Apophthegmata*, list a number of searching questions and some humorous remarks, designed to test the visitors and invite them to act sincerely.[36] Those who have sat at the feet of Hindu gurus or Zen masters have noted that they use similar techniques, to remove the masks which, more or less consciously, their visitors tend to wear.[37]

Cassian wrote the major part of his *Institutes* and *Conferences* for cenobites. Despite his esteem for the hermit way, he sees it as a growing out of the community life,[38] which he seems to have preferred.[39] In *Conference* 18,[40] for example, he appears to be describing the various types of monks – but, in reality, envisages only

[35] CASSIAN, *Conf.* 18: 2–3.
[36] CASSIAN, *Conf.* 18: 11; *Apophthegmata*, Sisoes, I; WALLIS BUDGE, *Paradise*, 2, p. 44, No. 198; p. 52, No. 237.
[37] It can happen that one is not permitted to engage in serious dialogue with the master until one has put up, without flinching, with brusque or facetious remarks which, in normal circumstances, would appear very impolite.
[38] CASSIAN, in the *Institutes* (2, 5) and in *Conference* 18, thinks that the cenobitic life was handed down as a tradition by the Apostles and is continued by people who live in common, according to the ideal described in chapter 4 of *Acts*. The most fervent of these would go out into the desert to live a more detached life. Although the existence of groups of virgins and celibate men is attested in the first centuries (cf. V. DESPREZ, *L'ascéticisme chrétien entre le NT et la début du monachisme*, in *Lettre de Ligugé*, 224 ff.), this theory has little historical foundation (cf. AV, *Communauté*, pp. 54–55). It remains true, however, that the example of the primitive Church has always been a source of inspiration for hermits and cenobites alike. Antony, for example, found his vocation by meditating on the lives of the Apostles and first Christians, as given in *Acts*. Pachomius speaks of it several times (cf. PACHOMIUS, *VC Bo*, 120). After him, the tradition gave the name 'apostolic life' to monasticism, because it tended to imitate that of the Apostles and first Christians reunited around Christ and in his name.
[39] It is characteristic that CASSIAN puts the comparison of the eremitic and cenobitic lives into the mouth of a certain Abbot John, an old hermit who had returned to the common life in the monastery (*Conf.* 19).
[40] CASSIAN, *Conf.* 18: 4–8.

the cenobitic life. The hermits he speaks of are solely those who might serve as examples for his cenobitic community in Gaul, chosen because of their formation under a master, and their thirst for spiritual progress.[41] For him, the 'first' kind of monk was the cenobite, and it is from cenobite ranks that the anchorites or hermits (the second kind) are to be recruited. There is also a third and degenerate type: the sarabaites, that is, those who have no formation, and are not under the guidance of a superior. Cassian does not give a name to the fourth type,[42] whose way of life contrasts with the hermits', just as the sarabaites' does with the cenobites'. Later tradition, however, unfavourably impressed by their wandering style of life, called them the 'gyrovagues'.

The author of *RM* found the same deficiencies among monks and, taking his inspiration from Cassian, spoke of four kinds of monks, while bitterly criticising the last two.

This, then, is the context of Saint Benedict's first chapter. We should remember also that he had himself experienced the eremitic life.

3. CHAPTER I OF *RB*: THE DIFFERENT KINDS OF MONK

The text of *RB* copies *RM*, as regards the first two types,[43] and gives a summary for the others. *RB* 1 is thus composed of four short paragraphs, followed by a conclusion. The whole text is homogeneous and well balanced. Each different type of monk is treated with approximately the same length of text. However, in fact this arrangement gives the hermits a special emphasis, since *RM* allowed them only a few lines, squeezed in between long pages devoted to the sarabaites and gyrovagues.

It is clear that there are four kinds of monk (RB, 1: 1)

Saint Benedict, like the Master, here alludes to a text of Cassian that had inspired them both.[44] They were also aware that monastic life can be lived in several forms, of which two, at least, are to be highly

---

[41] Cf. AV, *Communauté*, pp. 54–55.

[42] CASSIAN describes the gyrovagues in *Conf.* 18 and in *Inst.* 10: 6 The way of life of these monks is also criticised by PACHOMIUS (*VC Bo.* 88), BASIL (*LR* 36) and AUGUSTINE (*De opere monachorum*, 28).

[43] *RM*, 1, is inspired directly by CASSIAN, *Conf.* 18.

[44] CASSIAN, *Conf.* 18 and, no doubt, also JEROME, *Ep.* 22, 34–36 and AUGUSTINE, *De Moribus Ecclesiae* 1, 31, 66–68, as shown in AV, *Communauté*, p. 52.

valued. At a time such as our own, when the eremitic life is developing and when more attention is being given to the diversity of vocations within the monastery, these facts take on a new importance. Some monks feel drawn towards the liturgy, others to study or silent prayer, others find the Lord more easily in material or spiritual services rendered to their brethren or to visitors. By recognising these varied gifts, we can create an atmosphere of mutual comprehension and fraternal collaboration that helps the community to grow in unity. The different proportions of individual charisms help to make up the special physiognomy of each monastery.

THE CENOBITES

The first kind [of monks] are the cenobites (RB 1: 21)

In speaking of the 'first' kind of monk, the Master and Saint Benedict are following Cassian who gave the cenobites priority at the time. But, also like Cassian, despite a theoretical esteem for the hermit life, they are really interested in the cenobitic way, giving it a priority that led western monasticism to narrow its horizons during recent centuries, up to the point where cenobitic life was almost the only way. Today, thankfully, a broader view tends to prevail.[45]

> *The first kind are the Cenobites, that is those who live in monasteries and do battle under a Rule and an Abbot (RB 1: 2b).*

The monastery

RB copies the phrase of *RM*, in which the monastery is considered principally as the location of the two essential and defining points: the Rule and the Abbot. But *RB* also introduces the idea of stability, in opposition to the gyrovagues. This was the theme which ended the Prologue, and, in chapter 4 (on the Tools of Good Works), Saint Benedict continues in the same vein:

> *Now the workshop in which we diligently execute all these tasks is the enclosure of the monastery combined with stability in the community (RB 4: 7–8).*

Benedict also created a special vow of stability, which binds the monk so that

---

[45] The new Code of Canon Law officially recognises the existence of hermits, men and women: CIC 603–604.

he may not leave the monastery, nor cast off from his neck the yoke of the Rule.[46]

One can feel his opposition to the gyrovagues here, but another motivation is seen in the fact that these two authors do not use the phrase 'in the monastery' (*RB* 1: 2) but rather, an adjective derived from the word 'monastery': *monasteriale*. The corresponding word, in English, might be, perhaps, 'conventually'.[47] What is intended here is stability: the quality that makes the community life, and fraternal communion, into a road that leads to God. The monk fights in the name of all against the demon of division between persons. The fraternal charity of the community life thus becomes a witness to the Gospel.

Doing battle (*militans*)

Here again is the word used in the Prologue to define the monastic life as combat in the following of Christ. The idea is traditional in the Fathers, and Saint Benedict will make use of the same words again in chapters 2, 58 and 61.[48] The monastic vocation is thus presented to courageous spirits, those who have made the decision to struggle right to the end on the way of perfection, loving their neighbour, controlling themselves and practising the kind of detachment that leads to God. This point will be emphasised once more when speaking of the hermits.

Under a Rule

The word *Rule* obviously designates the written text of the Master or of Benedict. However, they borrowed it from Cassian, with whom it has a special traditional and monastic meaning, due to the way the first monastic legislation was composed. We saw in the Prologue that the goal of the monastic authors was to apply the Gospel to their way of life, based on the charisms granted to the founders. Their writings were thus charged with the force of Scripture and the experience of the Fathers. The questions posed by events led their successors to clarify certain points. Thus, little by little, a treasure of monastic tradition was built up, which had acquired the name 'Rules' by the time of Saint Benedict.[49]

---

[46] *RB* 58: 15–16.
[47] Cf. This fact is noted in the *Commentaire de la Règle* of Fr BERTRAND ROLLIN, En Calcat.
[48] *RB* 58: 15–16.
[49] It was usual for founders and abbots of the West, in the fifth and sixth centuries, to write a *Rule* for their monasteries. The most famous among these were made into a collection by BENEDICT OF ANIANE in his two works: *Codex Regularum* and *Concordia Regularum*.

As the fruit of the experience of previous generations, the Rule invites the monk to enter in their experience, making a personal check of its validity and adapting it to the conditions of the time. Far from being a fixed 'dead letter', the Rule supports the personal and community life, inviting each one to move beyond his personal point of view towards an ideal that unites the monastic family.

And an Abbot

The Abbot is considered by tradition as the representative of Christ and the heir of the Fathers, who handed on their doctrine, charism and wisdom. The role of the Abbot is to communicate this spirit to the community and to apply it to the problems that it must face. Thus, he needs to make a link between the received tradition and daily life, guiding the community members towards the Gospel ideal. He can only achieve this by radical commitment.

Community, Rule and Abbot

These three form the pillars of the monastic institution. Historically speaking, the Abbot was the main protagonist; the Rules developed, little by little, but the Master and Saint Benedict are the first to include the Rule of the monastery in the definition of the cenobite. The community life, currently highlighted by our society, should not eclipse the importance of the other two components of monastic life, but rather harmonise and evolve with them.

The brother who lives under a Rule and an Abbot is in the best environment possible for the following of Christ, where he can make use of the spiritual experience of his predecessors. However, this primitive definition of the cenobite was sketchy. Following the Master and Cassian, it was up to Saint Benedict to clarify it, by making a comparison between the cenobite and the other forms of monk.

THE HERMITS

In making the treatment of each kind of monk about equal in length, *RB* highlights for the cenobites the points which Cassian and the Master had emphasised for the hermits. These were the necessity of formation, and unceasing spiritual combat. According to the Fathers, they could purify the heart and open it up to contemplation.[50] Saint

---

[50] Cf. *Apophthegmata*, Macarius the Egyptian, 22; Matoes, 13; Anonymous, 1; Dialogue of the Elders, 23. This is also the theme of the *Praktikos* of EVAGRIUS PONTICUS and that of 'purity of heart' in CASSIAN.

Benedict alludes to this when he speaks of hermits who,

> **well-equipped to leave the fraternal battle-line for the solitary combat of the desert, are strong enough to do battle against the vices of the body and the mind on their own.**[51]

The hermit life is not presented here as a *choice*. No comparison is made between the different types of life. It appears, instead, as a *further progression*, something that crowns the cenobitic way, which should not be closed in on itself, but always open towards solitude, the condition of intimacy with God. The hermit life also challenges the institutions, to make them ever more faithful to the ideal that they must incarnate.

SARABAITES AND GYROVAGUES (WANDERERS)

The same desire to seek the good of those who consecrate themselves to the search for God led Cassian and the Master to disapprove of the way of life of the sarabaites and gyrovagues. If *RB* reduces the criticisms to two short paragraphs,[52] it nevertheless uses them by way of contrast, to show the stumbling-blocks which cenobites must avoid.

These remarks show that Saint Benedict is here attacking a spiritual disorder, and not the institutions themselves. The types of monks that he describes are more like ways of being, determined by the goal that is being sought, rather than external forms of life. These forms are, more or less exactly, incarnated in the monks whose conduct he condemns or praises accordingly.

Sarabaites live alone, or in little groups, just like the hermits. Their distinguishing feature, however, is that they are unable to judge whether their desires really come from God. They lack formation, have no Rule, no shepherd:

> **Whatever they like or choose, they call holy (RB 1: 9)**

The gyrovagues'[53] manner of life was similar to that of the monk–pilgrim, whom Benedict esteems in his Rule.[54] However, in addition

---

[51] *RB* 1: 5.

[52] *RB* 1: 6–12.

[53] In Saint Benedict's time, as in the period of the Fathers of the Desert, hospitality in a monastery was given free for a period of a few days; later on, if the guest wished to stay on, he had to work. A similar kind of rule seems to exist today in some Hindu ashrams. The gyrovagues disappeared quickly in order to avoid work.

to the faults of the sarabaites, the gyrovagues added instability and gluttony:

> *Always roving and never settling, they follow their own wills, enslaved by the attractions of gluttony (RB 1: 11).*

All these tendencies are, of course, very human and Saint Benedict mentions them to put the cenobites on guard against them.

> *Let us pass them [the sarabaites and gyrovagues] by, and with God's help set about organising the strongest kind of monks – the Cenobites (RB 1: 13).*

The strength of the cenobites, as the conclusion of the chapter shows, is that, far from following the way of the sarabaites and gyrovagues, they develop instead the monastic qualities praised by the Fathers.[55] Their approach fosters the fraternal life and offers support in the struggle against vices and something to imitate in the search for virtue; it also allows self-will to be controlled, and checks whether or not one *'truly seeks God'*.

ON THE MARGINS OF MONASTIC LIFE

Before finishing this study of the different types of monks, we should notice another category of people closely affiliated to the monastic order, who live, as it were, on its margins and, in the midst of their family life, wish to make progress in seeking God by prayer and asceticism.

The Rule does not speak about them as such. Nevertheless, even during Saint Benedict's own lifetime, there were lay people who felt drawn towards the monasteries. The same could be said of Saint Antony, and of the first monks whose friendly lay supporters benefited from their advice. Later, in the West, we see the arrival of the *conversi* (lay brothers) and of the oblates and Third Orders. From time to time, during the course of history, this 'lay' form of life became an institution; and it is interesting to note parallel forms in other religions.

Sufism, for example, gives perhaps the most remarkable instance: the dervishes are usually married people, but they sometimes lead their followers into a kind of cloistered life for a period of time,

[54] *RB* 53: 2 and 15; 56: 1; 61: 1.
[55] CASSIAN, *Conf.* 19; BASIL, *LR* 7.

in which ascetic practices and prayer are used.[56]

Among the Buddhists, the zealous faithful go regularly, for a short time, to take part in the life of the monks in their temples. Buddhist monasticism, which normally lives off alms, has only ever been able to exist in areas where the local populace gave sufficient support. In a similar way, a certain number of very pious families gravitate towards Hindu ashrams, supporting them with their goods and assuring the spread of their spiritual influence.

In order to survive and develop, the monastic life seems to require, or, at least, must try to set up, an entourage of co-religionists who share its ideals.[57]

OVERVIEW

Throughout the centuries, the monastic life has taken on only a limited number of forms in the various world religions. These are the hermit life (either stable or itinerant) and the cenobitic life (lived in small or large communities). When, due to unfavourable external circumstances, one of these forms disappears, it tends to spring up again, of itself, after a certain passage of time.[58]

The different types of monks seem to complement one another, and their coexistence down the centuries is so continuous that it constitutes one of the essential parts of monasticism. These ways of life delineate the habitual paths for people who wish to consecrate their life to the search for the Eternal. Equally, they share certain traits that, no doubt, come from their common goal: the search for union with the Absolute.

Among these traits there is, first, an ever-increasing desire for perfection and purification, flowing from the confrontation of human limits with the Infinite. Then the need becomes apparent for a type of formation that ensures the mastery of the passions, restrains selfishness and illusions, and teaches the disciple how to discern lasting

---

[56] Sufism has sometimes led to the creation of celibate communities, but only in the Middle East and in India, that is, in places where there was already a well-developed form of monastic life, Christian in the first and Hindu in the latter case. Cf. J. S. TRIMINGHAM, *Sufi*, pp. 83; 98; 170, note 2: 'The celibate Sufi was exceptional ... but, in general, Sufis at this stage [the Sufis of Cairo in the fourteenth century] though few were celibate in the strict sense, found that a normal family life was incompatible with the dedicated pursuit of the Path.'

[57] In Christianity, it is not only lay people that are involved, but also religious or priests who understand and value the ideal of the monastic life.

[58] The phenomenon of resurgence has occurred several times in the history of Buddhism and we can see it for ourselves today, in the revival of the hermit life and of small communities, in Christianity.

values amid all that passes away. The presence of a spiritual master allows for progress in the ways of perfection, and helps the disciple to recognise the obstacles that are met along the road.

The eremitic and cenobitic lives coexist, though each has its own characteristics and utility: they are different vocations. In general, monastic formation is better acquired in a community, which guarantees support and spiritual direction. For the persevering, it also curbs self-will and reduces self-centredness by means of service of others, while the solitude of the eremitic life (generally reserved for those who have already mastered their passions) allows the disciple to make contact with the Absolute, in silence.

In order to develop, monastic life has to have an environment that understands and supports its spiritual goals. Monasticism always appears as a challenge to remind humanity of its eternal destiny, in the midst of a society almost entirely orientated towards the satisfaction of earthly desires.

This particular point is common to all religions. Christian monasticism adds, however, that spiritual progress is made by *following Christ*, in a tradition drawn from the Gospel and filtered through the wisdom of the Fathers. The Gospel also indicates that God is found not only in one's heart, but also in one's neighbour, who is another bearer of the presence of Christ – thus adding a new dimension to community life.

Saint Benedict assigns to Rule, Abbot, and community the duty to pass on the Gospel and the wisdom of the Fathers, while adapting them to varied circumstances. Despite a real regard for hermits, he sees the cenobitic way as a better school of formation to bring the disciple to the summits of the spiritual life. In his search for God, Saint Benedict, like all Christian monks, feels in solidarity with all humanity and, in particular, with guests *'who are never lacking in a monastery'*.[59] He wants to help them to direct their steps towards the Infinite Love that alone can satisfy them.[60]

---

[59] *RB* 53: 16.
[60] SAINT JOHN CHRYSOSTOM had already remarked upon this role of the monasteries, *Hom.* 14 in *1 Tim., PG,* 62, 574; *Hom.* 72, 3 in *Matt., PG,* 58, 670.

CHAPTER III

WHAT KIND OF PERSON THE ABBOT SHOULD BE (*RB* 2 and 64)

Saint Benedict, Father of western monasticism, was not the first to deal with the subject of the superior: there was already a long tradition going back before the time of Jesus Christ. The experience of all these sages helps us understand more clearly the role of the Abbot in Christian monasticism and, especially, in the mind of Saint Benedict.

1. TWO TYPES OF SUPERIORS IN NON-CHRISTIAN MONASTICISM

The history of non-Christian monasticism shows two types of superior, both of which continue to exist in our own time. In the first case, the spiritual master, or guru, attracts a group of disciples and organises them little by little into a structured body. In the second, a community of ascetics, united by a common ideal, learns by experience the need of a superior who would be its focus of unity and ensures that the group makes spiritual progress.

The guru type is found most frequently in Hinduism, Islam, the Tibetans, and Zen; also occasionally in certain reformed branches of other Buddhist orders, especially in the *Mahayana*.

The members of the group (depending on their philosophical and religious tendencies) see the guru figure in different ways. Sometimes he is simply considered to have the particular gifts and spiritual experience to make him a competent guide in leading his disciples' search for the Absolute. In those religious traditions which accept the Absolute as a person, God is said to be the *Satguru* (supreme guru) the only true one, towards whom the human guru must lead his followers, the one who must be invoked in times of spiritual distress.[1]

By contrast, in places where a philosophy with monist or pantheist trends prevails, the human guru is often considered the direct means of communication with the divinity that is present in him, and which manifests itself by means of him.

We must serve the Lord with devotion, believing in the excellence of our guru, or even in his divinity.[2]

So says the *Bhagavata Purana*. In the same vein, among certain groups of Sufis, the holy one is called '*Quth, axis of the world*' and is considered as a manifestation of the divine *Logos*.[3]

Whether he belongs to one or the other type, the guru usually does not occupy himself with material affairs but appoints some of his disciples to take care of such things. However, when an important question arises, they refer to him and, at least in Indian ashrams, no appeal can be made against his decision.

The second type of superior, which grew out of the context of a pre-existent community, is typical of Buddhism. Buddha himself refused to nominate his successor and gave the assembly of monks the task of directing itself. It was first presided over by the most senior, his functions being limited to the assembly of the community. Later, under the pressure of internal difficulties requiring an intervention from the secular authorities, and because of the economic necessity of the competent administration of goods, the communities were forced to elect superiors.[4] While presiding at Chapters for temporal affairs, they gradually became involved in questions of discipline arising in that context. They thus became responsible not only for the material administration, but also for the general discipline of their monastery. Vows were pronounced in their presence, and they had to make judgements in disputes between the monks themselves or between monk and laity, and in cases of dismissal.

In cenobitic groups of this type, the young monks had a spiritual master who took care of their formation, in addition to their superior.[5]

---

[1] See for example the complaints of Kabir: 'I spend my night and days waiting for you, ... if I can't see you, how shall I survive, O Lord?' KABIR, *Au cabaret de l'Amour*, p. 141, French transl. C. VAUDEVILLE, Paris.

[2] BHAGAVATA PURANA 11: 2; 37; cf. MANU, 2: 225.

[3] J. SPENCER TRIMINGHAM, *Sufi*, pp. 161–164; R. CASPAR, *Cours de mystique musulmane*, pp. 102; 109, Rome I.P.E.A.

[4] SUKUMAR DUTT, *The Buddha and five after centuries*.

[5] One of the roles of the superior, at least among the Tibetans, is to help the postulant to choose his spiritual master.

Therefore, we can see that the role of the superior is considered essential in all types of monasticism, and is abundantly described in their literature.

2. TWO PARALLEL TRADITIONS IN PRIMITIVE CHRISTIAN MONASTICISM

The origins of Christian monasticism also show a dual process leading towards the institution of superiors.[6]

As in the other religions, the superior was considered primarily as a spiritual master. His role was described, in the earliest period, by Clement of Alexandria, who devoted a whole Chapter of his *Stromata* to this subject:[7]

> *He must excel in virtue; . . . his special dignity derives from the fact that he represents God and leads people to him.*

Origen continues the theme. For him also, the role of the master consisted mainly in leading souls to the only true teacher, the Divine Master.[8] The Fathers of the Desert and Cassian took these ideas for granted and catered for the practical consequences in the formation of those who came to them, thus creating a Christian type of monastic life. Nevertheless, as their disciples increased in number, they felt the need to organise them in communities. Pachomius,[9] although further from the influence of Alexandria, followed the same way of development in creating his first communities, in which all the authority of the superior was considered as coming from God, by means of a charism comparable to that of the prophets and Apostles. Later, the author of *RM* took up the same line of thought, and is noteworthy in that he organised the scattered

---

[6]   Cf. T. KEATING, 'The Two Streams of Cenobitic Tradition in the Rule of Saint Benedict' in CIST STUD 4, 1976.

[7]   CLEMENT OF ALEXANDRIA, *Stromata*, 7, 9.

[8]   ORIGEN, *Com. in 1 Cor. Sch. on Apocalypse*, cf. Mt. 23: 10.

[9]   Pachomius's case is complicated. From a sociological point of view, his monastic way began like the Desert Fathers, but his teaching and (even more) that of his successor, Orsisius, with their insistence on *Koinonia* or the common life and the way of finding God in fraternal relationships, put it with the second type. Here we find the beginnings of a synthesis which probably inspired Saint Benedict. Cf AV *Saint Pachôme et son oeuvre, d'après plusieurs études récentes*, RHE LXIX, 1974. No. 1; *RB* 7, pp. 100–110. Pachomius's system is the first in Christian monasticism to be created by a charismatic personality, and having subsequently to organise itself without him. This was the challenge that Orsisius had to face.

recommendations of his predecessors around the principle that the Abbot represents Christ.

By following the development of the Rules of Saint Basil we can discover the other part of the process of instituting monastic superiors: in which groups of brother ascetics gradually organised themselves, and chose a leader who, says Saint Basil:

> *Ought to carry out the function of the eye . . . He must be prudent, know how to speak, be sober, merciful, search for justice from a perfect heart, and always be there to console his brothers.*[10]

The communities for which Saint Augustine was responsible seem to have followed a similar evolutionary pattern. Orsisius and Gregory of Nyssa[11] were involved with houses that were already organised, and they emphasise that fraternal relations are the source of union with God, in their addresses to the monks. They see the superior as one who carries out a service of unity and charity in the monastery. He ought therefore to promote everything which favours these dispositions: fraternal service, sharing of goods, mutual obedience, adaptation of work and food to the needs of each individual, and care of the sick, the weak and the guests.

Although they differ in their conception of the role of the superior, Christian authors share many points in common on the subject, and

---

[10] BASIL, *LR*, 35; *SR*, 103.

[11] ORSISIUS, by various counsels spread throughout his *Testament* (ch. 7; 18; 39; 40) perfects what PACHOMIUS had written (*Institutions*, 18): the Abbot must avoid negligence and severity, indifference to faults and injustice; he must, in effect, render an account to God of the souls of his monks; he must therefore take care of them, especially if they are sick or afflicted. BASIL describes the orientation of the superior as regards God (fear of departing from his law, which he must teach) and towards the brothers (devotion without measure, until death, just like Christ). In *LR* 30, 45, 50, 51, he compares the Abbot to a doctor who takes care of people with charity and tenderness; *LR* 43 insists on humility, following the example of Christ. The *De Instituto Christiano* (ch. 70), attributed to GREGORY OF NYSSA, develops Basil's *LR* 43: the superior must be humble, must adapt himself to the brothers with wisdom and charity because they are a charge which God has left to him. These texts, unknown to Saint Benedict but setting out the same ideas as *RB*, show clearly the unity of the Christian tradition on this subject. The *Rule of Saint Augustine* has a chapter on the superior (ch. 15). He assumes Saint Gregory of Nyssa's ideas on the humility and responsibility of superiors, adding that they must incite the monks to practise the regular discipline more by love than by fear. The little Western Rules: *Regula Orientalis, Regula Quattuor Patrum* and the *Regula Virginum* of CAESARIUS OF ARLES also give some indications on the role of the Abbot or superior. CASSIAN does not have a special chapter on the Abbot. He does, however, delineate a treatise on the formation of future Abbots in *Inst.* 2: 3.

base their teaching on the same texts of Scripture. Their principal themes include the right and duty of the Abbot to teach, while remaining humble and submitting his doctrine to the bishop. He should also adapt himself to different characters and show equal love towards everyone. He has a duty to correct the brethren, being responsible before God for their conduct. He must follow the example of the Good Shepherd and be in possession of the qualities outlined in the Pastoral Letters.[12]

As it develops, Christian monasticism presents us with a dual sociological phenomenon that is very similar to what happened in the other religions. Either a charismatic personality draws disciples, who must subsequently face the task of organising themselves without him; alternatively, a group of brothers gradually invents a structure for itself, thus ensuring a peaceful survival. This common basis gave rise to other similarities that we will consider later – in particular, those regarding formation of disciples.

From a religious point of view, these two tendencies of Christian monasticism can be seen as part of the logic of faith in a personal God as the only true master, of whom the human superior is merely the representative. It has its own special flavour. As we have said, the first point is that a monk meets God in his neighbour. Secondly, a teaching authority supervises the instruction. Lastly, the community itself has a spiritual value complementary to that of its superior.

Saint Benedict was to make a synthesis of these common elements, one that is of special interest to our own era, in which the roles of the spiritual father and of the community in running and animating the monastery are being brought to the fore.

3. THE *RB* TEXTS CONCERNING THE ABBOT

The Abbot is very often mentioned in the Rule.[13] But some chapters are specially dedicated to him, such as chapter 2 (with its corresponding chapter in *RM* 2), chapters 23–30 and 43–46 on correction and satisfaction (partly inspired by *RM* 12–15 and 73), and chapter 64, which is peculiar to *RB*.

In chapter 2, Saint Benedict uses the text of *RM* 2, modifying it with additions and omissions, infiltrating his own cherished ideas.

---

12 The texts most often cited are: 1 *Thess*, 5: 14; 2 *Tim*. 4: 2; *Tit*. 2: 7. Several allusions are made to the example of Christ, giving his life for humanity and entrusting to his disciples the mission to preach his doctrine: *Lk*. 10: 16; *Jn* 21: 15–18; cf. *Jer*. 3: 11–15.

13 The Abbot or superior is mentioned about ninety times in *RB*.

He reproduces the first part of the text which describes the Abbot as representing Christ, the shepherd responsible for the flock before the Father of the family, the one who sets forth the gospel teaching by word and example (*RB* 2: 1–18).

The text then considers the Abbot's duty to love all the brothers with an equal love. Saint Benedict applies this principle to the question of rank within the community (a subject ignored by *RM*) giving it a special nuance of meaning, as, for example, when he asks the Abbot to take account of the merits and personality of each one (*RB* 2: 19–22).

The Master continues by discussing the duty of the Abbot to receive back a brother who has left (*RB* 2: 23–25). Saint Benedict insists on the need for the superior to help the monks to amend by adapting his remarks to the temperament of each one (*RB* 2: 23–29), and leaves out a passage comparing the Abbot by turns to a father, mother and child (*RB* 2: 26–29).

The Master returns to the subject of the responsibility of the Abbot before God (*RB* 2: 30). Saint Benedict's clarifications for difficult cases (in which the superior needs to show a special kind of courage, adapting himself to different characters) and for the problems posed by a recruitment which is either too feeble or excessive are, however, different. The Abbot ought to be more concerned for the good of souls than for material advantages, since *'nothing is lacking to those who fear [God]'* (*RB* 2: 31–36). Leaving out a passage of *RM* which does not contain any new ideas, *RB* ends with the text of *RM* recalling the account which the superior will have to give to God concerning all those who are confided to his care (*RB* 2: 37–40).[14] Later, we shall study the chapters about correction in themselves.

Chapter 64 is divided into two parts: the first, describing the manner of choosing a new Abbot, the second (a complement to chapter 2) describing the qualities required in the superior. This part is more developed but its plan is simple. The introduction and conclusion repeat the idea of the account to be rendered to God. A first paragraph gives the list of the positive qualities with a note on the method of making corrections, while a second gives the possible negative ones, adding a word on discretion in the giving of commands.

The tone of the chapter, with its insistence on love and prudence, seems to be the reflection of a man of experience and contrasts with the severe feeling of chapter 2, which appears more like the reaction of a young Abbot to abuses which have caused him trouble.

[14] The parallel text of *RM* 2 and *RB* 2 are given in AV *Communauté*, pp. 93–97; and AV *RB* I, pp. 440–453.

Nevertheless, at base, all these chapters set out a coherent sort of teaching.

4. THE ABBOT: HIS QUALITIES AND ROLE IN THE MONASTERY

The beginning of chapter 2 of *RB*, borrowed from *RM*, expresses clearly the role of the Abbot in the Christian tradition:

[The Abbot] is believed to act in the place of Christ in the monastery.

Like him, he is called 'Abba – Father', because of the gift of the Spirit who 'makes us children of God'. The role of the Abbot is to make his sons into sons of God. Participating in the mystery of the transmission of the divine life to the Church, through Christ and in the Spirit, this role can be described only in various successive and complementary layers, all of them inadequate.

Saint Benedict, developing *RM*, uses the same images that Christ himself used to define his mission. We will follow these biblical themes rather than study the chapters in the order they appear in *RB*, which is sometimes haphazard.[15]

THE STEWARD

The first image is that of a steward, thus qualifying the idea of fatherhood that will follow, showing that the father is only a delegate.

An Abbot who is worthy to be in charge of a monastery must always bear in mind what he is called and fulfil in his actions the name of superior.

The word *major* is often translated by 'superior', but reminds us also of a *major-domo*, the steward of the household, that is to say, the servant who represents the master before the other employees.

For he is believed to act in the place of Christ in the monastery, since he is called by his title, ... Abba, Father.[16]

The superior bears the very name of Christ because he represents him. As we said earlier, this gives the principal focus of the teaching in the two Rules about the Abbot. The image of the steward is the frame-

---

[15] Cf. AV 7, p. 264.
[16] Cf. *RB* 2: 3–4.

work of chapter 2, an image which it repeats, towards the end, in an almost identical phrase: *The Abbot should bear in mind what he is called.* It is then repeated twice more in chapter 64, reminding the Abbot that he must give an account of his 'stewardship' and concluding with the citation of Luke 12: 44 on the faithful steward.

In the course of these chapters, other biblical comparisons are made: the teacher, the father, the shepherd, and the doctor. Each in turn sheds its light on the diverse ways in which the Abbot represents Christ, but the essential characteristic is fixed right at the beginning: the Abbot has an authority subordinate to that of Christ, who will require an account from him – a familiar idea in Christian tradition.[17]

The Rule reminds the superior not just of his responsibility but of the biblical tradition of the steward,[18] which requires the superior to be humble, respectful of Christ in his 'fellow-servants', whom he must 'serve rather than preside over'. Saint Benedict emphasises this by repeating that Christ is present in each of his members.[19] The Abbot is thus at once the representative of Christ, and his servant.

Thus, the superior fulfils a double role in the monastery. Yet each of the monks has to do likewise, from the moment he takes on the least responsibility in the house. In this perspective, the Abbot ought to be considered not as an exceptional case, but rather as the typical monk, since almost all that is said about him may be applied to every monk in his relations with the brethren. In fact, the recommendations made to the Abbot are also repeated in the case of the cellarer, and for each of the other officials of the monastery.

THE TEACHER

In chapter 2, the authority given to the Abbot in the name of Christ is immediately applied to his duty of teaching:

---

[17] The responsibility of superiors before God is frequently mentioned in the tradition, see for example: ORSISIUS, *Testament*, ch 12; 18; 19; 39; 40; *De Inst.* C.70; AUGUSTINE, *Reg.* 15; CAESARIUS, *Reg.* V.

[18] Here is the biblical context of the steward: *Mt.* 24: 45–51; 25: 14–30; *Lk* 12: 37–48; 19: 12–28; 1 *Pet.* 4: 9–10; 1 *Cor.* 4: 1–2. In the tradition: BASIL, *SR* 98; AUGUSTINE, *Reg.* 'Do not offend God in the person of the superior'; ORSISIUS, *Testament* 40, 11, 14–15; cf. AV *Communauté*, p. 141.

[19] *RB* 64: 8; 21. Here we see how Saint Benedict introduced relations among the community members as part of the role of the Abbot, doing so under the influence of AUGUSTINE: *Serm.* 340. 1; *De Civ. Dei*, 19.19. Cf. ORSISIUS, *Testament*, 14: fellow-servants, PACHOMIUS, VC *Bo.* 63; 72; BASIL, *LR* 11: 43. Christ present in the brethren: *RB* 3; 36; 53; 58; 59. It is Christ whom the monk follows in every action, especially the most difficult: *Prol.*: 4; 5; 7; 68; 72.

He is believed to act in the place of Christ in the monastery, since he is called by his title, as the Apostle says, 'You have received the Spirit of adoption as sons, through whom we cry, Abba! Father! Therefore the Abbot should not teach or ordain or command anything that lies outside the Lord's commands, far from it; but his commands and his teaching should mingle like the leaven of divine justice in the mind of his disciples (RB 2: 2–6).

Here we see an echo of a long tradition that considers abbots and, above all, founders, as men guided by the Spirit, leading their brethren in the manner of the apostles and leaders of the people of God in the Old Testament.[20]

Cassian consolidated the monastic practice of the early church, by making a link between the teaching authority of the Abbot and that of the Apostles. The Master links this authority with the charisms given to the Church, quoting *Eph.* 4: 11: '*He chose some as apostles, others as prophets, others as evangelists or pastors or teachers'.* But *RM* puts the prophets before the apostles, thus suggesting the chronological succession.

The relationship established between pastors and teachers dependent on the Church gave rise to distinctions between the monastery on the one hand, and the Church[21] on the other, thus creating a prophetic role for the monastic life among the people of God. The monastery is not an independent society, on the margins of the Church. It is, rather, a body within the Church, an eschatological sign, pointing to the perfection of a life of holiness and praise in the presence of God, as the Second Vatican Council has made clear.[22]

Despite all these demands on the superior, Saint Benedict seems to imply that he needs not an extraordinary charism, but rather a sense of duty, so that he can activate the grace which derives from his role as teacher, adapting himself to each one in the particular situation:

The Abbot should not teach or ordain or command anything that lies outside the Lord's commands, far from it ... In his teaching the Abbot should always observe the method of the Apostle, 'Employ arguments, appeals and rebukes.' He must behave differently at different times, sometimes using threats, sometimes encouragement. He must show the

---

[20] Abbots guided by the Spirit like the apostles and the leaders of the People of God: ORSISIUS *Testament,* 12; 13; 15; 17; 40; 47; PACHOMIUS VC *Bo.* 24, 194; PALLADIUS, *Hist. Laus.* 38; cf. AV *Communauté,* p. 156, n. 2; HAUSHERR, *La Direction spirituelle en Orient autrefois,* p. 242.

[21] Cf. AV *Monastère–Eglise,* p. 39; AV *RB* 7, ch. 1.

[22] Vatican II, *Perfectae Caritatis,* 6; 7; 9.

tough attitude of a master, and also the loving affection of a father (RB 2: 4, 23–24).

He ought, therefore, to be learned in the divine law, so that he may know it well, and that it may be for him a store whence he draws forth new things and old ... as seems best in each case (RB 64: 9, 14).

The role of the Abbot is to make the word of God living and active in the heart of his monks, so that they allow themselves to be transformed by the Holy Spirit. Here we see a most important part of the Abbot's role as the one who initiates – something which is emphasised in many religions. He must also make sure that his words correspond with those of the 'inner Master':

His teaching should mingle like the leaven of divine justice in the mind of his disciples (RB 2: 5).

His doctrine should be solid, in conformity with sacred Scripture and the teaching of 'orthodox fathers'.[23] Here again, *RB* is in line with a constant tradition that makes Scripture the basis of monastic teaching which, in turn, is placed under the control of the Church's magisterium.[24]

The concern for orthodoxy is one of the distinctive marks of *RB*, which carefully avoids the doubtful passages of *RM* and Cassian.[25] This surety in doctrine and in the choice of texts is one of the most remarkable examples of the genius and sanctity of Saint Benedict.

The author of *RB* also shows the spirit of the gospel in asking the Abbot to teach not only by his words but by his example. This point had often been made by the Fathers. Following Scripture, they emphasised that the Abbot must be the *forma gregis*, the model for his flock,

[23] *RB* 9: 8; 73: 2–5.
[24] Cf. *RB Prologue* 'under the guidance of the Gospel'; JOHN MOSCHUS, *Le pré spirituel*, I: *Apophthegmata*, Daniel, 8; PACHOMIUS *VC Bo*. 201–203 and *passim*, see index 'Athanasius'. Frictions were frequent in Egypt (p. 120) and sometimes went as far as becoming violent, as in the case of the 'Long Brothers'. Later in the East, one of the officials of the diocesan Curia was a monk whose task it was to refer his confrères' problems to the bishop. In the West, Pope Gregory the Great remonstrated with a bishop who prevented an Abbot from preaching (*Dial*. I, 4). A certain teaching role was also recognised among the superiors of female monasteries, cf. HAUSHERR, *Dir. Sp*. 271; AV *Communauté*, p. 157, n. 1.
[25] Saint Benedict omits the apocryphal quotations given by *RM*, as well as its erroneous teaching on the non-responsibility of the obedient monk. He also avoids the semi-Pelagian tendencies of Cassian by emphasising that the effort made by the monk is a response to the call of grace, to the action of Christ or of the Holy Spirit, *RB Prol*.; ch. 4; 5; 7; 20; 49; 72; 73.

the one who builds up the unity of the community by his example, his humility and his kindness. In company with the Hindus and Buddhists, they also note that, in spiritual matters, one learns as much by watching the master as by listening to him.[26]

RB gives its teaching a positive note, like the early fathers of monasticism. All of them sought to inspire their disciples with a living ideal of following Christ. The inevitable renunciations[27] were made with a good grace, without over-dramatisation, as would be done a few centuries later. We need to rediscover today this early thread of generosity and enthusiasm.

Saint Benedict has his own particular motives for asking the superior to give a good example. While *RM* considered the Abbot as an irreproachable model, *RB* notes that the superiors are themselves fallible and even 'fragile' (*RB* 64: 13). So Benedict takes pains to put them on guard against a pharisaic kind of divorce between words and deeds. In chapter 4, on the Tools of Good Works, Benedict reminds the monk that they should obey

> *the Abbot's commands in everything, even though he himself (which God forbid) acts otherwise, remembering always that command of the Lord's, 'Do what they tell you, but do not do the things that they do'* (*RB* **4: 61**).

This assertion of human frailty in both superiors and monks leads Saint Benedict to emphasise two aspects of the teaching function of the Abbot. These were, the duty of correction, which we shall discuss in the chapter on formation, and the responsibility of the superior before God as regards his teaching, his behaviour and that of his disciples. These themes return like a refrain in the course of the Rule, each time an important decision is left to the discretion of the Abbot. Besides warning him to be objective in making judgements, this preoccupation takes us back to the central theme of the Rule, which asks all the monks to make a constant effort to put their will in harmony with '*God's Kingdom ... and his righteousness*' (*RB* 2: 35).

---

[26] *Apophthegmata*, Antony, 27; Isaac, 1; Poemen, 24, 25, 66, 188; Sisoes 43–44; Syncletica, 1; Martin of Dumes, 61; 66; 106; ORSISIUS, *Testament*, ch. 7; 13; 18; PACHOMIUS *VC Bo.* 23; *Instit.* 18; BASIL, *LR* 11; 43 (quoting 1 *Cor.* 11: 1; *Mt.* 11: 29; *Lk.* 22: 27; 2 *Tim.* 2: 24–25; 1 *Tim.* 3: 10); AUGUSTINE, *Reg.* 15, etc. Hindus and Buddhists insist on teaching by means of observation because the experience to be transmitted is beyond words.

[27] Cf. ATHANASIUS *VA* 14; CASSIAN, *Conf.* 2: 1; 3: 7–10.

THE SHEPHERD

This image, traditional in Christian monasticism,[28] comes back several times in chapters 2 and 64, while chapter 27 invites the Abbot, yet again, to follow the example of compassion given by the Good Shepherd.

In chapter 2, the first mention of the shepherd is made concerning his responsibility towards God, the head of the family who will demand an account of his sheep. This theme is practically identical with that of the steward. Nevertheless, chapter 64 adds several important qualities. First, *'discretion'*, which is a particular way of being attentive to people, leading them to respond to the grace they are being offered. It consists in avoiding excess in orders, work, and correction, while leaving room for generosity:

> *[so] that the strong may desire to carry more, and the weak are not afraid (RB 64: 19).*

This moderation is commonplace in monastic literature, especially in the Fathers of the Desert, for whom:

> *All excess comes from the devil.*[29]

Cassian devotes the whole of his second Conference to discretion, calling it the 'mother of virtue'.[30] This presupposes that the superior has the kind of tranquillity described in the second list of qualities (*RB* 64):

> *Let him not be restless or anxious, not over-demanding and obstinate, not a perfectionist or full of suspicion, or he will never have any peace (RB 64: 16).*

The vocabulary used here shows the underlying model of the Suffering Servant of Yahweh (Isa. 42: 1–4) which was applied to Christ in the Gospel of Saint Matthew.[31]

Discernment is yet another quality needed by the shepherd to lead his flock to the Lord. The Abbot should help each monk to see his problems objectively and to discover the will of God for him. In the

---

[28] Cf. Orsisius, *Testament*, ch. 13; 17; 39; 40: Pachomius *VC Bo.* 55; *Apophthegmata*, Ammonas 10; Achilles. 3; Basil, *LR* 43; *SR* 98.

[29] *Apophthgmata* Poemen 129. This idea is the subject of Chapter 10 of the 'Systematic Collection'.

[30] Cassian, *Conf.* 2: 4; cf. Dorotheus, *OS Lettre 2 aux Supérieurs.*

[31] *Mt.* 12: 18–21; cf. AV *Communauté* pp. 372–374.

second chapter of the Rule, Saint Benedict adds a paragraph in which he asks the Abbot to adapt himself to different characters, providing each one with the kind of help he needs:

Thus he must adapt and fit himself to all, so that not only will he not lose any of the flock entrusted to him, but he will rejoice as his good flock increases **(RB 2: 32).**

Regarding the community as a whole, Saint Benedict several times uses the words *'have forethought'* and *'be discerning'*,[32] to indicate that the superior should look for what leads towards God, bearing in mind the ideal of the Gospel and the actual problems of the community. He should help the brethren to be aware of the situation, and confront it, while proposing something concrete to stabilise them in the way that seems to be indicated by Providence.

The role of the shepherd also reveals the dynamic function of the Abbot as the one who listens to the Spirit and guides the community towards what God wants for it in its actual situation. However, it is difficult for all to move at the same pace – some grow weary while others have other weaknesses – so the Abbot must be a doctor as well as a shepherd.

THE DOCTOR

This image, suggested in chapters 2 and 64 of *RB* in connection with the shepherd taking care of his sickly sheep, is dealt with specifically in chapters 27 and 28 about recalcitrant monks, although it is mixed here with the idea of the Good Shepherd.

We see the Abbot acting as a doctor in the way that he deals with brothers in difficulties. The monks need their Abbot because they are sinners.[33] The Abbot is the one who reconciles the monk to Christ. He must open the monk to repentance, so that he can find peace in his heart which, in turn, will renew his integrity as a person and restore him to an ever-deeper communion with God and his brethren.

Let us also note a passage of *RM* that speaks about the Abbot, a section that Benedict places at the end of chapter 2 as a conclusion – and conclusions are always important in *RB*:

---

[32] *Sit providus et consideratus ... discernat et temperet* – 'He should have forethought and consideration ... let him be discerning and moderate' (*RB* 64: 17); *provide et juste condecet cuncta disponere* – 'he should settle everything with foresight and justice' (*RB* 3: 6).

[33] Cf. Dom Rembert Weakland, *Congrès Monastique d'Asie*, Bangalore 1973.

the thought that he takes concerning the accounts to be rendered for others will make him careful of his own state. And so, while he provides by his instructions for the amendment of others, he will be brought also to the amendment of his own faults (RB 2: 39–40).

These words are full of wisdom and humility and they lend colour to the whole chapter, showing us the proper atmosphere for correction to take place. The Abbot should not think of himself as infallible but should, along with all the brethren, seek to heal his own faults, to progress in the ways of the Lord.

The 'medical' function of the Abbot is also dealt with in the chapter on the amendment of faults. However, correction is only possible and fruitful if the brother in question feels that he is loved and understood. The role of a father is to show such love and understanding, a role that includes all the other aspects of the abbatial charism.

THE LOVING-KINDNESS OF A FATHER

At the beginning of chapter 2 Saint Benedict linked the paternity of Christ and the Abbot's title of Father.

He is called by [a] title of Christ ... Abba, Father.

A little further on, in the same chapter, the orientation of a father is described as one of '*loving affection*' in the context of giving attention to the special characteristics of each person (*RB* 2: 3–24). Handing on the divine life is done by creating an atmosphere of trust that allows each one to grow personally and to fight generously *in the service of Christ (RB Prol.* 3), as well as by formal teaching.

However, it seems that Benedict was doubtful about identifying the monastery too easily with a normal human family, since he systematically suppressed in his own text all such allusions made by *RM*. In chapter 2, for example, he leaves out the comparison between the Abbot and a father and mother; likewise, in chapter 4, he replaces *RM*'s quotation of the Decalogue, '*Honour your father and mother*', with '*Honour all men*' (*RB* 4: 8).

RB's references to Christ prevent us from simply identifying the Abbot with the Roman *paterfamilias*; this word appears only once in *RB*, making a biblical allusion to the person of God. Benedict rooted the monastic life in the society of his time, but his ideal models are to be found mostly in Scripture.[34]

Besides the name of Abbot, the first mention of the word '*father*'

[34] AV *Communauté*, pp. 121–126. *Paterfamilias, RB* 2: 7; cf. *Ezek.* 34.

is the above quotation, on the need for equal love to be shown towards all the members of the community, and the attention to be given to each one's temperament:

He must behave differently at different times, sometimes using threats, sometimes the loving kindness of a father (RB 2: 24).

As well as natural affection, this phrase points to the fatherly tenderness of God, so often described in the Bible.[35]

In this passage which corresponds with the Master who, following tradition,[36] insisted on equality between the brothers who came from different social backgrounds, Saint Benedict adds (*RB* 2: 18–21) that one ought to take account of the personal characteristics of each monk:

... [their] obedience ... humble ... good works ... [their] merits ...

thus introducing that concern for each person which is one of the distinctive points of his Rule.

This same quality of personal love is also found in a more detailed form in chapter 64, although admittedly without an explicit reference to the idea of fatherhood. It is put in relation with prudence in correction and prudence in giving commands. The Abbot should

hate sin but love the brethren ... eliminate [vices] prudently and with charity ... [seeking] to be loved rather than feared (RB 64: 11–15).

His affection is not to be overwhelming but, on the contrary, full of humility and respect:

He ought to be of profit to his brethren rather than just preside (RB 64: 8).

Here again is the double aspect of the idea of the steward, an idea that colours these chapters: to represent Christ and serve him in the brethren.

Therefore, it is the image of the Lord that the Abbot should reproduce, as shown in chapter 64, recalling the example of the Fathers and the Sermon on the Mount:

He should be a chaste man, temperate and merciful. He should always prefer mercy to judgement (RB 64: 9–10).

The orientation of goodness and understanding mixed with firmness, which we find in many spiritual masters of other religions, is also a

---

[35] See, for example, *Ps.* 102; *Hos.* 11: 7–9.
[36] ORSISIUS *Testament*, ch. 9; 16; CAESARIUS, *Reg. Virg.*

stimulant for us Christians to imitate more closely 'our' Lord.

There is yet another way in which the Abbot can be compared to a father of a family: the way of managing the material affairs of the house. The cellarer assists the Abbot in this work and should himself *'be like a father'* towards the brethren.[38]

The monk renounces his right to own property because he wishes to consecrate himself entirely to God. The superior has the duty of guiding the brethren, through their daily toil of prayer and work, towards God. In his relationship with his Abbot, the monk has no private business. If we make a comparison between the monastery and the Church, this is one of the principal differences that exist between this kind of dependency, on the one hand, and the relationship of a member of the faithful to his bishop, on the other. As for teaching, correction, affection and attention to persons, all the care of *'transient earthly things'* is dominated, as far as the Abbot is concerned, by *'the salvation of the souls entrusted to him'*. In everything, he must look for *'God's kingdom and his righteousness'*. This is the meaning of Benedict's addition in 2: 31–36. Nevertheless, here he is not an innovator: the Pachomians had already given this teaching.

The Abbot need not take direct charge of business in order to give a spiritual tone to the manner of life in the house; rather, he brings this about more effectively by the general guidance given to the community, and by his choice of officials. His role is to keep an eye on the organisation of the various services so that conflict may be avoided, and he must safeguard *'peace and charity ... in the monastery'* (*RB* 65: 11). He should pray for those who are confided to his care.[39]

---

[37] Cf. *Mt.* 5: 7; *Jn.* 8: 3–11; *Jas.* 2: 13. The Fathers of the Desert expressed this in a similar way: 'To each of the brethren who surrounded him he [Macarius of Egypt] gave encouragement, according to his conduct. He would say: "All this time that I have been with you, the Lord knows that I have not neglected the duty of announcing to you what is profitable for your souls and for your instruction ... giving you an example of love for God and for one's neighbour"'. After his death the brethren lamented because 'their father had been taken away, a father who was both a stimulus and an encouragement towards the eremitical life and all the other good works ... they were in a state of deep mourning because of the loss of him who nourished their souls in the fear of the Lord'. AV *Palladiana*, MON STUD 34, 1992.

[38] *RB* 31: 2. CASSIAN also shows the relationship between the way of dealing with material concerns and the spiritual life of the monks; he emphasises that the Abbot has a responsibility in both these domains. Cf. *Inst.* 4: 5, 14; 7; 12: 25; *Conf.* 18: 7; 19: 6–9; 24: 23.

[39] Cf. *Apophthegmata*, Sisoes, 12; Amoun, 6; anon., 160. DOROTHEUS OF GAZA often reverts to this theme (*O.S. introd* p. 73; *Instr.* 23) he cites the famous story, told in various forms by the Fathers of the Desert, of the monk who is tempted, but saved by the prayer of his Father (cf. *PL* 73, 788; 951).

In conclusion, the monk needs to be loved by his Abbot in the way that Christ loves. He needs to know that his superior wants the best for him and seeks to guide him towards God. The Abbot's concern for each person leads him to promote an atmosphere of peace and unity in the community, in which each can give of his best in the search for God, for charity and mutual respect.

The originality of Saint Benedict is seen in the way that he united two different currents, already existing before his time in the Christian tradition, thus giving the Abbot both the pastoral responsibility for the community and for organising the brethren in the management of the monastery.[40]

In these different roles, spiritual and material, the Abbot, as we shall see, is helped by his officials. Though it can happen that he is involved personally in the spiritual direction of some of the brethren, or in some work of the monastery, his function is rather to make sure that his overall supervision assures the harmony of the whole, carrying both strong and weak towards God.

5. THE CHOICE OF AN ABBOT

Monastic Christian tradition, as that of other religions, knows of two principal ways to choose a superior: a choice made by the predecessor (or by an authority which represents his spirit), or an election by the members of the community. It is quite natural that the first method is usual in the guru tradition, while the second is found in community groups.

Election has always been the rule for succession in Buddhist monasteries. Among Hindus, on the contrary, the guru chooses and forms his successor. Monasteries of celibate Sufis use the election method, but the sheikhs choose their successors, often from among their sons or nephews.[41] In modern Hindu orders there is now an election. We can find examples of institutions created by a famous personality which, once the founder disappears, organise themselves with a more 'horizontal' kind of structure.

The same phenomenon is found among Christians: the first

---

[40] In eastern monachism prior to Saint Benedict, Saint Theodore the Studite (d. 826) has the same mixture of the two currents: before him, the Hesychastic superiors concerned themselves only with the spiritual, leaving the care of material things to the cellarer. Saint Theodore kept the organisation of the monastery all in his own hands and makes frequent allusions to this fact in his catecheses. Cf. J. LEROY, 'La Réforme Studite' *Orient. Christ. Anal.* 153, p. 181 ff.

[41] R. CASPAR, *Cours*, p. 126.

Pachomian abbots designated their successors; in Palestine, Euthymius and Sabas did the same and, in default of a choice by the predecessor, the monks asked the bishop to appoint the *hegoumen*[42] (superior). The same thing happened in the West – *RM* moves quite naturally in this direction. However, these cases remain exceptional and election seems to have been the more common procedure, recommended by both ecclesiastical and secular law in West and East.[43] During the first centuries of the Christian era, the procedure for election and the choice by a predecessor were practised simultaneously in Christian monasticism, although in very different proportions.

Saint Benedict stands at the mid-point of the two groups: he recommends election by the community, but without putting his entire confidence in the system. He actually foresees that there might be a need for an intervention by people who have '*a sounder judgement*', being either within or outside the community, and the possibility of recourse to the bishop. Fundamentally, the *way* of choosing matters little to him; his only wish is that a suitable candidate be found. He indicates this in an original phrase, making the criteria of choice quite distinct from the usage of the time:

> **He who is to be appointed must be chosen on account of his virtuous life and wise teaching, even if he is the last in order in the community (RB 64: 2).**

Cassian and the *Laws of Justinian* recommend that the merits of the person and his seniority be considered.[44] Saint Benedict, perhaps following *RM*, takes no account of his rank but only of his personal worth. The following part of the chapter describes the qualities the Abbot ought to possess. It is not necessary to return to these as we have already discussed them while examining the various functions of the superior.

We have spoken much about the qualities of the Abbot. Perhaps it would be a good idea to say a word about his faults, or rather, about the difficulties that they can cause for his monks. *RB* does not ignore them; we saw that chapter 64 gives a list of negative qualities, that is

---

[42] PACHOMIUS *VC Bo.* 124.

[43] 'It seems that designation by the predecessor was less what happened in a particular epoch and more a kind of marginal variant on the common practice according to law ... it is found in a certain type of situation which occurs in every age ... usually there has been a particularly famous Abbot, either as founder (like Pachomius, Honoratus, Lupicinus, Colomban, Jean de Réomé, Landelinus) or someone of renowed sanctity (like Pinufius, Paphnutius)'. AV *Communauté*, pp. 352–353; other examples are given on pp. 363–364.

[44] CASSIAN, *Conf.* 21: 1; AV *Communauté* p. 265.

to say, possible defects. Chapter 4 also foresees that the superior may not give a good example,[45] indicating the spirit of obedience in faith that the monk must continue to observe. This spiritual orientation, however, should not leave the monks hoping for the utopia of a perfect superior, while neglecting the means to improve the situation.

The Buddhists have some reflections on this situation which it would be good for us to consider. The situation is actually even more delicate for them, since a monk in disagreement with his spiritual father has the right to leave and find another. He is first recommended to persevere in his attempt to develop a positive relationship with his master, until a good rapport has been re-established. Then he is asked to consider whether his problem might possibly come from obstacles that are in his own heart. In this case, difficulties with superiors are useful to show him his own personal deficiencies and give him the chance to remedy them, with their help.[46]

To come to a kind of synthesis about the role of the Abbot, one could say that he works on two levels, being both father and brother in his community. He gives it life, animates it spiritually, and guides it towards God by his teaching, discernment, and the unity that he creates, brought about by the harmony of the whole body and through a shared vision. At the personal level, the monk cannot live happily in his monastery if he does not find the charity of Christ for each person in his Abbot and '*the loving affection of a father*' who exemplifies '*Let him hate sin: let him love the brethren*'.

However, the Abbot is also a brother among brothers, sharing the same spiritual combat, '*fellow servant*' of God with all the rest. Seeking to '*be of profit to his brother rather than just preside*', he favours fraternal relations, service and exchanges in which Christ is found in one's neighbour and in the midst of those who are gathered together.

We can summarise all this by looking at the image of the *coryphaeus* or '*animateur* of the orchestra', applied to Christ by the Greek Fathers: though himself part of the orchestra, it is he who gives it life and harmony.

6. THE GURU AND THE ABBOT[47]

In the foundation of monastic groups, all religions show some comparable sociological phenomena:

[45] *RB* 4: 61; PACHOMIUS gives a long lists of faults to be avoided in the *Praec. et Inst.*
[46] THARTANG, *Gesture.*
[47] Due to lack of another generic word, we use 'guru' here to describe the superior and spiritual leader of a group of *non-Christian* monks and 'abbot' to describe a *Christian* superior.

- Grouping of disciples around a spiritual master, or
- A fraternal group which invents its own structure.
- The role of the superior takes in a certain responsibility over the religious life and the material organisation of the group. Nevertheless, depending on the various different trends, one or other of these aspects will be highlighted in an almost exclusive way.
- A spiritual master usually attaches himself to a line of spiritual antecedents whose spirit he transmits, or to a religious school into which he causes his disciples to enter, using his method of leading them towards union with the Infinite.
- If the religion is theist, the master is considered as the spokesman of God and the guide who leads people to him; if not, he is at least an experience guide for discovering the presence of the Infinite.
- The master always feels a certain responsibility regarding the spiritual path of each of his disciples and towards the group which they have formed, even as far as removing those who do not enter into its spirit.

Each religion brings its particular characteristic to this general schema. The note of Christianity is to see the master at once as the representative of Christ, to whom he must render account of the monks confided to him, and as servant of Christ, present in each of the members of the community. For all of them, the supreme rule is the Gospel, and the road to God is found in conforming oneself to the example given by Christ.

Within this Christian tradition, Saint Benedict adds his own special note, insisting on

- The paramount importance given to an interior orientation of listening and of docility to the word of God transmitted by the Abbot, to follow Christ with courage and generosity.
- The loving attention given to each person, and especially to the weak, by the superior, who adapts himself to their temperament and needs.
- *Discretion*, or the spirit of proportion, so to arrange things that '*the strong may desire to carry more and the weak are not afraid*'.

From an institutional point of view, Saint Benedict synthesised the thought of those who preceded him, making the Abbot equally responsible for the movement of the brothers towards God and for the economy of the monastery. He thus gave equal importance to the 'vertical' Godward dimension in the person of the superior, and the 'horizontal' dimension in which Christ is discovered in fraternal relations.

Saint Benedict makes the Abbot's role clear. He is both a father who gives life, vitality, unity and harmony to the community by his teaching and decisions, and a father for each monk in the responsibility which he has for him before God and by the attention which he gives him in the love of Christ. He is also a brother among brothers, fellow servant of Christ, struggling personally in the same spiritual combat, finding and serving the Lord in each person and, like everyone else, fulfilling a role in the community. What is said about him goes equally for each one of the brethren.

In the choice of the Abbot, *RB* opens the door to the future, envisaging a supervisory process for the election by a higher ecclesiastical authority.

Saint Benedict enriches the tradition by his personal experience, which seems to have led to a double affirmation that appears often in the text. Superiors are fallible men, rather than persons endowed with extraordinary charisms. In contrast, their sharing in the community's orientation towards things of the spirit allows both him and them to succeed in their task. This collaboration is well described in the chapters on the councils of the Abbot and on the various officials of the monastery.

CHAPTER IV

CALLING THE BRETHREN TO COUNCIL (*RB* 3)

After the description of the Abbot's function in chapter 2 of his Rule, Saint Benedict complements the structure of the community in chapter 3 by speaking of the Council of the community. This chapter is of particular importance because it marks a definitive turn in the organisation of Christian monasticism, which from this point on makes use of Councils as a normal practice.

The questions raised by this text, written in the fifth century for a patriarchal society, are also interesting. First, what impact on the forms of monastic life did changes in the civil society have? Then, how can we discover, in the organisation of the Councils described by Saint Benedict, what is permanent, typically Christian, and able to guide our community discussions?

1. EVOLUTION OF MONASTIC STRUCTURES COMPARED WITH CONTEMPORARY SOCIETY

Religious institutions are by nature conservative, so the evolution of their structures is slow. Several centuries are sometimes needed to make a change visible. The thousands of years' experience in the monasticism of the Far East are thus particularly precious for making a comparison between the evolution of monastic structures and that of the civil society. A general view will allow us to observe their interdependence.

We shall first consider the Hindu and Buddhist monasticism, then the story of some monastic aspects of the Sufi Orders which, though subsequent to Christianity grew outside of it. Finally, we shall try to see if the successive forms of Christian monasticism follow the same pattern of evolution.

The forms of Hindu monastic life throughout the centuries

The ashram is probably the simplest and most ancient form of the monastic society. Essentially composed of a guru, or spiritual master, with his disciples, it was so similar to the schools of the time that sometimes the two institutions blended. The Sanskrit word *brahma-chari* means both the celibate student and the novice. Nevertheless the guru is not an ordinary master; his teaching is mainly spiritual. Some *brahmacharis*-for-life, carefully selected according to the caste system from among his disciples, dedicate themselves fully to the search for union with the Absolute. The ashram thus adopted special characteristics that came from both Indian society and religious tradition.[1]

Once trained under a master, some of the monks became *samnyasi* or *renunciants*, wandering solitaries begging for their food. Begging has always been one of the most common forms of poverty. To adopt it of one's own free will is the natural expression of total detachment. The *Laws of Manu* describe these two forms of monastic life,[2] with their customary rules; they are institutions of ancient Indian society, which still exist in our days.

Later, the monastic orders established by Shankara, Ramanuja and others, with a supreme master and dependent houses, found inspiration in the Buddhist universities, and from the feudal system of the kingdoms that were then arising within India. These monastic organisations followed the evolution of their secular model: in the same way as the big states were divided and the local governors became kings, so the monasteries of the different regions became independent, giving only a primacy of honour to the former head of the Order. These monasteries still exist today, while the regional kingdoms have disappeared.

In the nineteenth century, Vivekananda started a new monastic order, the Ramakrishna Mission, whose structure imitated the Christian missionary congregations that he witnessed at work in India.

In our own day, institutions coming from ashrams founded by contemporary spiritual masters prefer to model themselves on the multinational companies which are familiar to Indian traders. Several centres, dependent on the mother house, exercise considerable influence over a great audience, and a few monks are enough to animate

[1]   Cf. McMULLEN, *Guruship*, pp. 164–168.
[2]   On the primitive ashrams see *Laws of Manu* 2: 242–243; on the *Samnyasi*, ibid. 6: 25–79. VAN TROY, *Early Shiva ascetic movements* in ALL ASIA MONASTIC MEETING, Bangalore, 1973; G. F. GURUYE, *Indian Sadhus*, Bombay, Popular Prakasham.

them. These branches are periodically visited by the master or by one of his delegates.

The monastic institutions of Hinduism thus reflect the structures of Indian society throughout the ages. However, they never ceased to challenge them, remaining deliberately on the fringes. From the time of the great didactic epic poems like *Ramayana* and *Mahabharata*, until our own day, the monks stand as the moral conscience of the society; they endow human life with the significance of being an effort to foster a spiritual life leading to an eternal happiness after death.

On the other hand, when some monastic groups became rich and influential, interfering in politics and business, they soon fell into decline and disappeared.

The organisation of Buddhist monasticism

The Buddha lived in the fifth century BC. His new way was a reaction both against Hindu monasticism, then already thousands of years old and divided by quarrels between different schools of thought, and a society fully orientated towards the quest of money, glory and pleasure. The Buddha himself started by following the customs of the Hindu itinerant begging monks, who gathered their disciples together during the rainy season, taking advantage of the impossibility of travelling, to give them more profound instruction. Later he founded permanent monasteries. However, at the end of his days he did not want to appoint someone to replace him, and preferred to entrust the assembly of monks with the care of governing themselves. Each of their meetings was presided over by the eldest monk present.

His approach was not a surprise for his contemporaries since he merely passed on to his Order the way of government used by the Himalayan tribes from which he came.[3] There was no established hierarchy. The assembly of free men appointed a temporary chief to organise common works or lead an expedition of war. This democratic organisation differed from that of the kingdoms of the plains, but later, when the monks had to take care of important properties and urged by the State authorities, they were forced to elect superiors. Little by little, these leaders adopted progressively the forms of monarchic government in use in the country where they lived.

This change did not take place suddenly. In the history of Sri Lankan monasticism we note, for example, in the twelfth century the formation of a Council of elders charged with monastic affairs, requested by the royal authorities and approved by the king. In the

---

[3]   Cf. SUKUMAR DUTT, *The Buddha and five after centuries*, p. 13.

thirteenth century, a 'Supreme Pontiff' was appointed as the head of all monks, and in the fifteenth century, he was called *Sangharaja* (literally: prince of the monks' assembly). His counterpart in Thailand bore the same title. Little by little, in Sri Lanka, Thailand, Laos and probably elsewhere, the monastic institution developed a hierarchy of dignitaries parallel to that of the state. However, being more conservative than lay people, the monks retained titles that had long disappeared in civil society.[4]

In the course of its long history, Buddhist monasticism knew times of spiritual fervour and times of decline. However, periodical renewals allowed Buddhist monks, like their Hindu counterparts, to be a spiritual leaven in society. The Vietnamese Buddhist monks are witnesses of this since they recently preferred to burn themselves alive rather than yield to demands that would have been against their conscience.

The Sufi Orders and the society of their time

The history of Sufism shows once more how, in another religion, and at a distance of more than a thousand years, people who were seeking intimacy with God used contemporary institutions for their particular needs.

The first Sufi masters used the model of the early school, as the Hindus had done. The *Zawiya* or house where they taught their disciples was an urban counterpart of the ashram. But other institutions proper to the Muslim society of the Middle East as, for example, the *ribat*, hostel of the frontier posts, or the *khânâqah*, rest house and hospice, were also starting places of Sufi organisations. First used as transitory meeting places for prayer and songs, they subsequently became centres of Orders for missionary expansion.[5] In their internal organisation, the Sufi Orders followed the usages of the society in which they lived: the hereditary transmission of power, with a hierarchy similar to that of the clans.

The various forms of Christian monasticism

In a similar way, Christian monks borrowed the models given by the society in which they lived. When they formed small groups living in

---

[4] WALPOLA RAHULA, *History*; M. ZAGO, *Rites et cérémonies religieuses en milieu Lao*, pp. 40–51.

[5] Cf. J. SPENCER TRIMINGHAM, *The Sufi Orders in Islam*, Oxford, chs. 1 and 6. We should note however that governments often endowed the *khânâqah*, which sometimes became rich institutions, enslaved to power.

the countryside – like the first disciples of Antony, Basil or Benedict – they followed the forms of rural life, living as shepherds, farmers or villagers. When the Orders became organised – as under Pachomius and, later, in the European federations from Cluny and Cîteaux – their structures were inspired by the forms of government usual in their times. This is the case right up to the present day.

The monastic system of Saint Benedict thus underwent a progressive transformation: from Roman villa to the feudal system of isolated monasteries, grouping together various foundations; then the monarchic structure of Cluny, and onwards to the parliamentary regime which came with the modern monastic Congregations, each having its General Chapter. The manner of government of the 'great abbots' at the beginning of our century (due to conservatism among religious) resembles the kind of style used by the absolute monarchs or emperors of the previous centuries. Therefore, it should not now surprise us to see monastic institutions evolving towards democratic forms, in harmony with our contemporary society.

This brief historic outline allows us to draw some conclusions. First, it is obvious that monasticism used without hesitation all the forms of society it met: tribal life, democracy, the feudal system, monarchy, and great empires. The institutions used as starting points are equally diverse: school, hostel, hospice, commercial society, forest hut, village temple, town residential house and even the wandering beggar. This extreme diversity shows that it is pointless to try to define monasticism by one of the forms it has used or to make it the fruit of a particular form of society. We see also that monks of all times, whatever their religion, organised their life according to the forms of government used in their place and time. These forms of government evolved naturally in the course of time, allowing us to conclude that they do not affect the essence of monastic life.[6] The core of monasticism is elsewhere and the similarities with the secular world affect only its external forms.

There is another obvious point: though following the usages of the contemporary society, monks always challenged some of its aspects by stating the primacy of the spiritual quest above the affairs of this world. They have thus transformed the institutions they borrowed in order to adapt them to their own purpose. The monastic ideal is thus better manifested by the modifications it brought to the secular institutions than by the borrowings it made from them.

[6] We have already noted that this evolution was made with some delay, religious institutions being by nature conservative. This delay, in the past, could last more than a century, but tends to diminish with the acceleration of the pace of modern life.

These general statements find an interesting application in the case of the Councils or advisory bodies, institutions that exist both in the secular society and in the cenobitic monastic life of all religions.

2. THE COUNCILS

The communitarian type of monastic life was not highly structured in ancient Hinduism[7] or in Islam, and so only a little information can be found among them about the Councils of elders or community meetings. On the other hand, the documents describing the life of Buddhist monks or of Qumran groups give us very precise information on these points.

THE COUNCILS IN BUDDHIST CENOBITISM AND AT QUMRAN

The Buddhists

With regard to the Buddhists, here are the instructions given by the Buddha to his disciple Ananda for calling the brethren to Council:

> *If some monks say, during the discussion, 'This is according to the Dharma', while the others say 'No, it is not' – or 'This is the regular discipline' – 'No, it is not' – each and all the monks should assemble in good order. Once assembled they should discuss thoroughly what belongs, or does not belong, to the Dharma. Having discussed what belongs to the Dharma in the present situation, a legal decision is taken.*
>
> *But if, O Ananda, the monks are not able to solve the question at home in this way, they should go to a place where the body of monks is more numerous, and being again assembled in good order, the question should be discussed once more and the decision should follow the opinion of the majority.[8]*

Thus, an assembly follows precise rules aiming at avoiding disorder and fostering unity; each one speaks in his turn, and assent is marked by a silent gesture. The usages come probably from customs in use in tribal society, borrowed by primitive Buddhism.

At present, such village meetings still exist in Africa and in

---

[7] In the ashrams or institutions headed by a guru, above all when he is believed to be inspired by God, a human Council is not felt to be necessary and the decisions of the master are not subject to question. The modern monastic Orders have Councils. About these, however, I have been able to find but little information.

[8] *Samaguna Sutta* of the *Majjhina Nikaya*; cf. also WALPULA RAHULA, *Hist.* p. 172.

Madagascar.[9] There are rather strict regulations to govern the order of speaking, and what is to be said. The aim is to inculcate mastery of the self and mutual respect, in order to hear what is being said and to be able to offer pertinent advice. The questions are discussed until consensus is reached.

The disciples of Buddha added several elements, directly related to monastic life, to these inherited customs that tried to assure the cohesion of the group in the decision taken. The most important addition is the reference to a superior law or *Dharma* to which all individual and collective activities of the monks have to be conformed.

This Universal Law, which the Buddha discovered by intuition, was gradually made explicit in the practical precepts laid down by himself and by his disciples. From the beginning, monks assembled to learn the precepts from their elders, to accuse themselves of their shortcomings and receive a penance proportionate to their fault.

The general meetings of the monks, always structured in a democratic way, have continued right up to our own time, but when a hierarchic structure was established, the superior was assisted by a small Council which mirrored that of the kings of the time. These two Councils exist at present in most Buddhist monastic Orders, and their Rules lay down precisely how many members must be present, according to the nature of the questions to be dealt with.[10]

9   Here are, for example, the customs of the *fokonolona* (village community) meetings in Madagascar:
> After having waited for all people to sit according to the order of precedence, the presiding elder explains the question or asks somebody to do it. Then those who wish to do so may speak, beginning with the eldest. It is strictly forbidden to interrupt another. Further, when somebody begins to speak, he is required to start with a polite summary of what the others have already said on the question. Only then can he express his personal opinion. Many people, even the young, sometimes do so with surprising freedom.

10 In Sri Lanka, for example, in the fifteenth century, each monastery had its community meeting, and the 'Supreme Pontiff' had a Council made up of all the local superiors, who were appointed by him. Two of them were his assistants and their main role was to take care of the monastic discipline.
> At present monks are divided in several Orders, each one having a Superior General, assisted by a Council of twenty elders, appointed for life by him. This group acts as permanent Council of the Order. It elects the Superior General, and appoints the other officers, especially those who are in charge of training the novices. For questions of smaller importance, it is enough to call some of these elders. The rules of the different Orders determine precisely the necessary *quorum*: 4, 5 or 10 must be present, according to the matter to be dealt with. (This information was received from the Right Reverend *Sirimalwatta Anandhabidhana*, Superior General of the *Shiamapabi* Order, the most important of the country – about 10,000 monks, in 1972.)

A similar organisation is found among Tibetan monks.

These meetings aim also at strengthening the unity of the group by a common and freely accepted decision, and foster good understanding among its members, as well as with outsiders. One particular reason for such a meeting would be the admission of the young monks to vows. For this, a precise number of Council members have to be present.

Qumran

We find a similar organisation at the beginning of our era among the Jewish groups of Qumran, who expected the imminent coming of the Messiah and were preparing to be the nucleus of his army and government. The *Assembly of the Numerous* (professed members) was strictly regulated; here are the prescriptions of their rule on this topic:

> *They will range themselves according to rank. In this way, they shall consult one another to come to a decision. This is to be done in any deliberation and business referred to the Numerous, each one saying what he thinks in the deliberations of the community. Let no one interrupt when his neighbour speaks before his brother has finished; in the same way, let no one speak before his turn.*[11]

One of the main duties of the Assembly was to admit the members to the different stages of the life, which required three votes, separated by about a year from each other.

Seen as a whole, the texts on the Council show that this institution, borrowed from secular society, has also followed its pattern of evolution. Nevertheless, the monks modified it, giving it new characteristics that have a striking similarity in very different religions.

Reference to a Rule (expression of a supra-human order linked to the ideals of the community), discussions governed by precise regulations (in view of keeping good order and of establishing an atmosphere of trust in which each one could freely speak his mind), the progress of and recruitment for the community, the search for unanimity in decisions and concord in mutual relations – these are the specific values which, even before the coming of Christ, had been given great importance in monastic Councils.

What, then, did the Christian monks contribute?

---

[11] QUMRAN, *Règle*, c.6, 9–10; cf. also 16–23.

THE COUNCILS IN CHRISTIAN MONASTICISM BEFORE SAINT BENEDICT

In the Christian primitive cenobitic life, we notice the existence of elders who, from time to time, are brought together by the superior. Among the disciples of Pachomius, where the authority of the founder was strongly felt, the elders seem to be more witnesses of decisions taken than true counsellors.[12]

The situation was very different among the monks of Saint Basil. Here, we see groups of brothers, among whom the superior was hardly noticeable. The elders' duty was to advise the superior, thus strengthening his authority and reinforcing the trust the brethren have in him. Sometimes they had to express their opinion by voting, especially for the appointment of officers. In doing so they *'avoided destroying the good order'* and peace of the community.[13] For the superior himself, the group of elders is also a security:

> *Their rank and prudence make them worthy to be close to him, so that he can take their advice and counsel in all the affairs of the community, and so comply with the Scripture which says: 'Do everything with counsel'.*[14]

This quotation shows how the Word of God is, for Basil, the norm of life, which monks and superiors should obey. He quotes it constantly, above all when there is a decision to be taken by any person in charge. His *Short Rule* No. 1 dealing with that topic concludes:

> *Man needs to be led with kindness by the Holy Spirit, to follow the way of truth ... So we should submit to God, according to his commandments, or submit to others because of his commandments ... This means, obviously, to renounce one's own will and imitate Christ.*

Saint Pachomius also grounded his teaching very strongly on the Bible. His precepts were so much considered as its application to the daily circumstances of monastic life that, after his death, his disciples refer to his Rules as the expression of God's will for them. The monastic Rule thus took on an importance, in this realm, almost equal to that of the Scripture itself, which was its origin.

As a whole, Christian monasticism quite instinctively rediscovered, in the consultation of the elders by the superiors, some of the values developed by monks of other religions in their community meetings: it was a reference to a supra-human norm of action, unity, order and peace among the brethren.

---

[12] PACHOMIUS, *VC S.* 7; *Bo.* 73; 92.
[13] BASIL, *SR* 104; *LR* 27.
[14] BASIL, *SR* 48; cf. also 27 and 45.

For Christians, the supreme norm is the Word of God, to which the disciples of Pachomius added the founder's Rule. However, the Bible transforms the idea of an abstract norm into that of a loving God who guides human beings through his commandments, and by the Spirit given by Jesus to his disciples. The aim of consulting the Councils, then, is not only to find an acceptable solution for the problems which come up, but to discover God's will, and fulfil it in following Christ.

If the Council of the elders is well attested from the beginning of Christian monasticism, meetings of the community as a whole seem to have been very rare. Pachomius does not speak of them, and Basil was opposed to the calling of all the brethren together, probably because he feared disorder and confusion.[15]

Community meetings appear as an institution only in the fifth century with the *Rules* of Caesarius of Arles and of the Master.[16] In their time, there was a rather painful situation of tension between abbots and their communities, concerning the goods of the monastery. It seems that, in those times disturbed by barbarian invasions, some superiors disposed of the wealth of their house (selling properties or liberating slaves) without informing the brethren. It was because of this that the Emperor Justinian made compulsory the consultation of the community, before selling or renting what belonged to the monastery.[17] These community meetings therefore seem like a limitation of the Abbot's power and a means of ensuring the monks' right to scrutinise his administration.

This situation reflects the antagonist tendencies of a time of transition. On one side, there is an insistence of the Abbot's function as spiritual father, taking charge of all the material needs of the monks; on the other hand, we see a move towards giving the monks a share in the temporal administration of the monastery.[18]

THE COUNCILS IN THE RULE OF SAINT BENEDICT

Even in the title of the chapter Saint Benedict speaks of calling together all the brethren. Benedict develops this to the full, though it did exist before him. The fact is all the more remarkable because, in his environment, the authority of the superior remained predominant; its basis was a religious tradition coming from Cassian and from the Master, and

[15] BASIL, *SR* 27; 48.

[16] *Reg. Caes.* 5: 65; *RM* 2.

[17] *Cod. Lib.* I, *Tit.* 2, No. 17; *Nov.* 120, 6–7; 123, 6. Cf. AV *Communauté*, pp. 185–198, quotations, p. 196.

[18] The right of the monks to control the administration of the superior is affirmed above all in the Rules of Gaul and Spain of the sixth and seventh centuries, like Aurelian of Arles, Ferreolus of Uzès and Isidore of Seville; cf. AV *Communauté*, pp. 195–198.

was seen also in secular life. The Roman *paterfamilias*, like the emperor of Constantinople and the chiefs of barbarian tribes, enjoyed absolute power over their subordinates, and their decisions were final.

Cassian states that the monk should abdicate all concern for himself, and leave it in the hands of his Abbot.[19] The *Rule of the Master* tries to find a more delicate solution, in calling the community to deal with temporal matters for '*the goods of the monastery belong to all and to nobody*'.[20] To emphasise this detachment on the part of the monks, it reserves to the Abbot all authority, and in fact considers him as the only owner of the goods of the monastery, for he has to hand them over to his successor by means of a will.[21]

Though keeping the contemporary framework that makes him entrust the decisions to the Abbot, Saint Benedict changes the institution by introducing several modifications. He is the first to give the Abbot both the Council of the community and that of the elders. Then he extends the competence of the community Council: it does not meet any more to discuss the transfer of monastic goods, but to be consulted on '*anything important*'.

In the same way, the elders' Council deals with '*less important matters*'.[22] The question is no longer how to supervise the Abbot's administration: these are true Councils, from which the Abbot can ask advice in any circumstances.

Another novelty introduced by *RB* is the part given to the young monks in the Councils. Before its time, among Christian monks as well as in other religions, the elders spoke first, and their opinions carried the most weight in the discussions. Saint Benedict feels, on the contrary, that the younger ones, who arrive without experience or prejudices, were more open to receive inspiration from the Holy Spirit:

The reason why we say that all should be called to council is this: It is often to a younger brother that the Lord reveals the best course.[23]

---

[19] CASSIAN, *Inst.* 4; 5; *passim*; 12: 25; *Conf.* 18: 7; 19: 6–9.
[20] *RM* 16: 97–102.
[21] *RM* 78: 60–68; 93: 25–30.
[22] *RB* 3: 12 says exactly '*less important matters for the interest of the monastery*' (*in monasterii utilitatibus*). The words '*utilitas monasterii*' designate (in the following chapters, 21, 35, 65) what is of the competence of the elders (deans, cellarer, prior), that is, material business and questions regarding persons.
[23] *RB* 3: 3. The importance given to the young members of the community is unprecedented among Christian monks as well as in those of other religions. In their meetings the most important part is given to the elders, who are the guardians of experience and tradition. The attitude of Saint Benedict shows a great concern for openness to God, and perhaps also, in the changing circumstances of his era, to the new point of view brought by each young generation. Even now, in Chapter meetings, it is often the custom to ask the youngest to speak first. The same supernatural spirit is seen in *RB* 63, concerning a brother's rank in the monastery.

This sentence shows clearly that the aim of the Councils is to allow the Abbot and the brethren to search together for God's will: no more tensions, no more rights to defend, but a common effort of the community, united with its superior, to discover the desire of the Lord and to fulfil it. The partners in the discussion are no longer just the Abbot and the monks, but God and the whole community, all united from the youngest monk to the Abbot.

This supernatural point of view dominates the whole chapter, indicates the procedure to be followed and the attitude that each member should adopt during the meeting.

How to find God's will in community meetings (*RB* 3)

Saint Benedict puts various actors into the scene, when he describes how the conventual chapter should be put into operation; these are: the brethren, the Abbot, the Lord, and the Rule.

The Brethren

On summoning the Brethren to Council is the title of *RB* 3. Further,

> *the brethren must give their counsel submissively and humbly and not presume stubbornly to defend their opinions.*

Moving beyond what can change according to the circumstances, Saint Benedict's basis is the spiritual life and human psychology, which remains the same in every age. He speaks to the monk as such, showing him how to conform his heart to the Gospel through humility, mutual respect, an attitude of willing listening, with a desire to follow God's will. All this is suggested in the few words used to describe the meeting.

He also specifies its aim. The monks do not meet to criticise or to judge, but to '*give their counsel*', that is, to offer facts, or explain situations. It is not a question of defending one's opinion, but of mutual exchange of information, in order to gain a better understanding of the different aspects of the problem under discussion.

A comparison here might shed some light. Near our monastery in Madagascar, there is a mountain called *Andringitra*. Seen from the house, it seems like a black peak, standing against the sky. When we go to the town, passing round its southern flank, it appears like a cliff, falling sheer down to the plain. If, on the other hand, we approach it from the west, we see a grassy slope, decorated with woods and villages. Three persons, each of whom knew only one of these sides, could discuss endlessly what the nature of the mountain was, without coming to an agreement. But, by listening to each other's account, they would discover that the *Andringitra* is a mountain with a north–south axis, having a gentle slope on one side and an abrupt precipice on the other, which ends by tapering to a point like a knife-blade that looks like a peak, from the south.

Therefore, the brethren come together to give information to one another, each giving his frank opinion of how he sees the question (influenced, for example, by his work, his experience, or his character). If this is done peacefully, it opens the road to new insights, clears up misunderstandings, and leads to mutual esteem. The essential disposition is thus a benevolent listening, creating a friendly atmosphere which facilitates self-expression.

Solutions to the problem in hand may also be proposed, but only as tentative suggestions, meant to be complemented by others' opinions. A spirit of *submission* to the decision that will finally be taken gives a great freedom of expression and allows them to search objectively for the will of God, for the good of all concerned. Mutual information is also conducive to a change of opinion, and generally helps the group to move towards consensus, which offers the best guarantee possible for human and spiritual wisdom.

These dispositions of mutual listening and information are useful for any dialogue. However, dialogue often becomes blocked, because the partners want to impose their point of view, without realising that they have something to learn from the others.

What does Saint Benedict say about the role of the father in the monastery?

The Abbot

As shepherd and guide of his brethren '*the Abbot must assemble the whole community and explain what is under consideration*' (*RB* 3: 1).

His first duty is to inform the community of the challenges that it faces, so that the brethren may bear them in mind. Thus, he initiates a common reflection, made in the presence of God, to discover his will. Then he has to unite the brethren in making a decision that will be the response of the community to that will.

This process may take time, because unanimity is not necessarily reached in the first meeting. It is thus the Abbot's duty to allow the problem to mature in order to bring the community to a quasi-unanimity, which will be expressed in a meaningful vote.[24]

When there is hesitation, or division of opinions, it is often because one of the aspects of the question has not been clarified. It is thus

---

[24] The two-thirds majority required by law for important decisions underlines this care for unity. It is worth noting that today, in many countries, voting becomes rare and instead there is a prolonged discussion leading to unanimity.

necessary to take sufficient time to study the problematic point and, if necessary, to delegate some brothers for such a study. This done, the community meeting becomes more fruitful, calming any fears that may have existed, or proposing an intermediary step which would be acceptable at all.[25]

As far as the Abbot is concerned, all this process may be rather trying. Saint Benedict thus advises him:

When he has heard the counsel of the brethren, he should give it consideration (RB 3: 2).

These words refer to a scene of the Gospel (Luke 2: 41–52), which is also a model of dialogue in the family. When Jesus was twelve years

---

[25] When the questions have been sufficiently discussed, it is the Abbot's job to give a good start. He should avoid giving the impression that everything is already decided, for then any intervention will be seen as a challenge to his authority. Such a way of proceeding prevents the brethren from speaking according to their conscience and stops any creativity.

Some recent developments in the procedure of monastic Chapters are also worth noting. When the Abbot and his Council or the community Chapter find a particular subject worth pursuing, a commission is appointed to study the project. It makes the necessary consultations and presents a suggestion to the Abbot. He examines it with his Council and either approves it or returns it to the commission with the objections raised and the modifications requested.

Once the superior and the deans accept the project, it is presented to the community and, if necessary, a trial for a limited time is proposed. It is much easier to gain the consent of all for a trial period that can be modified after a precise date, than for a definitive project where there is no possibility of ongoing evaluation.

To facilitate the discussion and give all participants the possibility of expressing themselves, written answers are sometimes requested, or meetings in small groups are proposed, with a member of the commission present to answer the questions. Eventually the report of the group discussion is brought to the community Chapter.

At the end of the trial period there is an evaluation at a Chapter meeting, or sometimes in small groups, and necessary modifications can be made. It is often good to plan several trial periods with successive modifications. The repeated refusal of a project has a depressive effect on the community.

By contrast, successive improvements allow for progress by stages, acceptable to all concerned, thus preserving unity in the community. This gives a sense of moving forward, while fostering a fervent atmosphere in the community.

In some places, another means is used to give to each one the occasion of asking questions and expressing his point of view. All the brethren, even the non-professed, are frequently called together (even every week, in some monasteries), so that they can be given questions for reflection arising from what is going on in the house. Most of the time there is no decision to take, but the monks are informed and can give their opinion.

When it is question of a change in the observance, it is good to begin by looking for the human and Christian values that the 'old way' embodied, while seeing how to express them in the present context.

old, he had a surprising lapse of behaviour in abandoning his parents, to stay in the Temple. His mother had reason to be unhappy. Nevertheless, she asked calmly: *'My son, why did you do that?'* Not immediately understanding his answer, she pondered on it at length, to be able to help her son later. Mary gives us the model of an attentive and benevolent listening that fosters trust, and facilitates a solution that leads to unity.

> *The decision should, however, depend mainly on the Abbot's judgement, and all should be joined in obedience to what he considers the soundest course (RB 3: 5).*

In the sociological context of Saint Benedict's time, the word of the chief was, as we have seen, the natural expression of the community's consensus. In our own time, this consensus is manifested in some areas by a vote, which is a support for the Abbot when putting into action the decision that has been taken. Here we see a sociological evolution which, however, does not modify the essential spirit of the arrangement.

> *But just as it is fitting that disciples should obey their master, so it is incumbent on [the Abbot] to settle everything with foresight and justice (RB 3: 6).*

We are still in the atmosphere of Nazareth: the child *'was obedient to'* his parents who *'kept the memory of this in [their] heart'*, reflecting on how to deal with him. Saint Benedict's phrase is all the more remarkable, in that it reverses a passage of *RM* that had emphasised the obedience of the disciples. Here, this obedience is taken for granted; there is no tension. The Abbot has only to face his responsibility as shepherd. The superior and the community are united in common search for the good, before God.

Nevertheless, even today, it falls to the Abbot to take the decision in many areas, but not, however, entirely at his own whim. There are two other interlocutors: the Lord and the Rule.

The Lord and the Rule

These two are in fact one, for the Rule is considered as the echo of God's word. The Rule gives general norms that all, Abbot and community, should respect, because these norms are the application of Scripture to their daily life. Here, Saint Benedict adopts the view of Pachomius's disciples, uniting more closely the fear of God with the observance of the Rule (*RB* 3: 11). With Saint Basil, he considers faithfulness to the word of God as a protection against self-will, which

might influence either the reaction of the brethren or the decisions of the superior.
s

In every circumstance, therefore, all should follow the authority of the Rule, nor is it to be rashly abandoned by anyone. No one in the monastery is to follow the prompting of his own heart ... The Abbot himself, however, in all his actions must fear God and keep the Rule (RB 3: 7–9).

Still, as in Saint Basil, Saint Benedict's Rule refers most of all to Christ. The Lord is listened to in the brethren. As they speak in all sincerity, his Spirit *reveals the best course* even, and especially, if they are young. We have all noticed how the children of a family, with their natural straightforwardness, can sometimes speak a word that seems to come directly from God. The Lord has his loving plan for humanity and for communities, and wants to lead them to perfection and happiness. His Spirit shows them how to follow Christ, in the details of daily life as much as in the big decisions. Saint Benedict uses all possible means to promote their listening to this Spirit.

If we place the *RB* in the general setting of history, we see that in establishing the two Councils, Saint Benedict makes a sociological development, which is found in the secular world and in the main monastic Orders of all the world religions. In the same way, after Saint Benedict (and perhaps also in his time) the admission of new candidates to monastic profession is among the main items on the agenda of community meetings.

Good order in the Council, an attitude of mutual listening to find a constructive solution, and reference to a Rule as the objective norm to be respected are traditional in all monastic systems. However, listening to the Spirit to discover God's will for the community, seems peculiar to the Christian form. Saint Benedict gives it more emphasis by highlighting the importance of the young.

The history of the different monastic ways has shown us, in this chapter, how the expression of the community's consensus varies, according to the time and mode of government of the society in which the monastery lives. *RB* goes beyond these contingencies, so as to reach the human heart and bring it into line with the Gospel, by fostering humility, kindness, mutual respect and submission to God, virtues which allow us to discover his will.

The most remarkable contribution of Saint Benedict in this field is his way of getting everyone to collaborate, monks and superior, each one with his proper function, so that voice of the Spirit can be followed and recognised, by mutual listening, in the light of Scripture and of the Rule.

CHAPTER V

THE TOOLS OF GOOD WORKS (*RB* 4)

The first three chapters of *RB* defined the monastery and its essential structures; the following ones, 4 to 7, try to describe the fundamental points of monastic spirituality.

Chapter 4 is quite different in style from the rest of the Rule. Made up of maxims, placed one after the other, it might appear as alien to the rest of the text. However, its doctrine is quite in harmony with *RB* as a whole and is so rich in content that some writers have taken it as a base to describe the whole of monastic spirituality.[1]

We will return to these tools of good works later, speaking of them individually while treating the subjects to which they refer. At present, we shall be content to look at the chapter and its structure as a whole. These alone can teach us many things.

The plan of the text is not very apparent at first, but becomes clearer by comparison with similar passages in the monastic writings of other religions.

1. PARALLEL TEXTS IN HINDUISM AND BUDDHISM

The Buddhist *Vinaya* and the Hindu Books 2 and 6 of the *Laws of Manu* have some parallels with this chapter.

First, the passages concerned are placed towards the beginning of these books, as is the case also with *RB*. The order of material follows a similar schema in both these religions. They begin by describing what the fundamental attitude of the monk ought to be, in view of the

---

[1] See, for example, JEAN DE MONLÉON, *Les Instruments de perfection.*

way he has chosen. It then sets out, often in the form of precepts, the great virtues which he must practise to attain his spiritual goal: non-violence, and what we could call 'non-sensuality' or, in other words, good will towards other people, and mastery of the desires of the senses or the passions.

The *Vinaya* deals with these virtues in speaking of the vows. The ceremony is described at the beginning of book 4. It begins by explaining the essential attitude of the Buddhist monk which is to 'take refuge', that is, affirm his faith in the way shown by the Buddha:

> *I, such and such a one, take refuge in the Buddha, in his Law and in his Order. In imitation of the Buddha, I leave my family.*[2]

After this declaration of principle, which is repeated six times, the monk promises the practice of the virtues of his state, in the form of ten precepts, given out, one by one, by his Spiritual Master.

> 1. *Never to kill, this is the first precept of novices. Do you have the strength to observe it? The postulant replies: I will observe it.*
> 2. *Never to steal, this is the second precept of novices. Are you capable of observing it? . . . I will observe it.*

The same formula is used for the following precepts:

> *Never commit impurity. Never lie. Never drink wine. Never to adorn one's head with flowers nor anoint one's body with perfumes. Never chant or dance, as do the actors and prostitutes. Never look upon such a spectacle, nor listen to such chants. Never sit on a raised chair nor on a spacious divan. Never to eat outside the permitted times* [dawn to midday] *and never to touch gold nor silver.*

The Master concludes:

> *Since you have made your submission to the precepts, your duty is henceforth to honour and make honoured the Three Treasures: the Buddha, his Law, and his Order. You must apply yourself diligently to the task of mortifying your thoughts, words, and actions. You must meditate, study, and take your place in the common work.*[3]

The formulation of these ten precepts or vows varies a little from school to school. Some of them place much emphasis on the verbal

---

[2] *LW, Vinaya*, p. 151. The texts quoted in this book belong to various schools of the *Hinayana*. The texts and rituals of the *Mahayana* insist on detachment and on offering one's own merits for the liberation of all beings.

[3] Ibid. p. 123.

aspect of non-violence, which consists in avoiding bringing harm to one's neighbour, by fraudulent or lying words, by injuries or even by malevolent thoughts. A series of about 250 minor prescriptions applies these vows to the everyday situations of life.[4]

On the subject of non-violence and non-sensuality among the Hindus, book 2 of the *Laws of Manu* has the same goal in mind when it gives the following essential principle of their monastic life:

> *love of self is not a praiseworthy thing.*[5]

A pernicious self-love can be concealed beneath even the most holy practices.

The monk must also practise perfect detachment, a liberating kind of attitude, which alone allows him to attain everlasting happiness:

> *In fulfilling perfectly his prescribed duties, without looking to the reward, a man can arrive at immortality and, even in this world, rejoice in the accomplishment of all the desires that his mind felt able to conceive.*[6]

The *Laws of Manu* come from a legalistic Brahmin milieu, and are intended either for hermits or for young monks living with their spiritual master. The absence of contacts with a community and with the world concentrates the attention of the ascetic on the study of the Scriptures and ritual observances. As regards benevolence, the young monk will practise it above all in the veneration of his guru and in respect for his family.

> *A the time of study, the young novice, having made his ablution in conformity with the law, should venerate the holy book with a reverence [anjali] and receive his lesson, covered with a pure garment, while controlling his senses.*
>
> *In beginning and finishing his reading of the* Veda, *he must always touch the feet of his guru with reverence; let him read with joined hands, for this is the homage due to the Sacred Texts.*[7]

A little further on, it is explained that the novice must keep watch over his senses, so that they may not lead him astray into selfish desires, alien to the goal he is seeking:

[4] We will return to this subject in speaking of the vows.

[5] MANU, 2: 2.

[6] MANU, 2: 5. This attitude of detachment is considered by the *Bhagavad Gita* as fundamental, not only for monks but for all those who aspire to eternal life. (Cf. 2: 117–158.

[7] MANU, 2: 71. The marks of respect for the guru and his family are subsequently described at length. Cf. 2: 117–158.

Since the senses are always seeking attractive objects, the experienced man must make every effort to conquer them, as a charioteer would restrain his horses ... [Then follows the list of eleven organs of perception and action] ... *For in abandoning himself to sensory desires, he would not be able to avoid falling into error, whereas their restraint will bring him supreme happiness.*[8]

The hermit and wandering monk have similar duties:

Leaving the village so as to retire into the forest, let the ascetic dwell there, mastering his sensory organs ... *As far as is in his power, let him make offerings to animate beings, let him give alms from what is destined for his nourishment, let him honour those who come to his hermitage, presenting them with water, roots and fruits.*

He must apply himself without ceasing to the reading of the Veda, *endure everything with patience, be benevolent and perfectly recollected, give always, never receive, and show himself compassionate towards all creatures.*[9]

The texts of the vows used by some Hindu schools and by the Jains gives the same emphasis as the Buddhists do to these ideas. Here, for example, is a formula with five vows. An act of repentance and a gloss (which we shall reproduce only when it offers some interesting detail) follows each one:

1. I execrate all killing of living beings, great or small, endowed with movement or not. I shall never kill, nor shall I induce someone else to kill, nor consent to any killing.
I repent of any faults that I may have committed in this regard in mind, word, or deed.
    GLOSS: *walk with care so as not to kill or harm a living thing. Avoid all thoughts and words that might provoke offence, a quarrel and, as a consequence, lead to the wounding of a living being* ...

2. I execrate all lying, and the causes of lying, which are anger, avarice, fear and jesting. I shall never lie, nor shall I induce a person to lie nor consent to any lying. I repent of my faults ...

3. I execrate all making my own what has not been given me by the owner – be it in town, village, forest, be it a little or great thing, living or inanimate. Never shall I appropriate what I have not been given, nor induce anyone to do so, nor consent to it. I repent ...

[8]   Ibid. 2: 88–93.
[9]   Ibid. 6: 4; 7–8.

4. *I execrate all sexual relations with either gods, men or animals. I shall not enter into such relations, nor permit them, nor consent to them. I repent . . .*

> GLOSS: *never speak of women, nor look at them, nor recall the memory of those one has known previously. Do not satisfy oneself in eating and drinking, but always eat less than one's full appetite. Do not drink any fermented liquor, or eat spiced foods.*

5. *I execrate every link, attachment, affection and pleasure, be it little or much, great or small, living or inanimate. Never shall I form an attachment in any way whatsoever, nor induce others to do so, nor consent to such things. I repent . . .*

> GLOSS: *This means privation and flight from all pleasures of hearing, smell, and touch. In cases where the sensory perception cannot be avoided, one should repress and extinguish all interior feeling.*[10]

These passages show that monastic legislation instinctively puts the ideal of seeking the Absolute in first place. It then develops the practical consequences, by demonstrating how we must try to overcome both the innate aggression of human nature by non-violence, and the sensuality that makes a person languid.

A comparison with *RB* 4 shows a fairly similar order of material.

2. THE STRUCTURE OF *RB* CHAPTER 4

The text begins by affirming an essential point of doctrine: the great commandment to love God and one's neighbour.

1. **In the first place to love the Lord God with all one's heart, with all one's soul and with all one's strength.**
2. **Then to love one's neighbour as oneself.**

The passage of *RM* (the immediate source of this chapter) puts a Trinitarian confession of faith first, and follows it with the double commandment,[11] which, of course, is perfectly logical in the context. But this confession is not reproduced in *RB*, either because the text of *RM* which Benedict had at his disposal did not give it, or because of his habitual tendency towards brevity.

---

[10] *Acâranga Sûtra*, cited by *LW*, *Vinaya*, pp. 81–82. In the formulation of the vows, we notice the numerous influences between Jains, Hindus and Buddhists; their chronology is difficult to establish. Another text of Hindu vows is given in *Studia Missionalia*, 28, p. 331.

[11] *RM* 3; cf. AV *RB* 4, pp. 190–192.

Next, we have the theme of non-violence:

3.   **Then not to kill.**
4.   **Nor to commit adultery.**
5.   **Not to steal.**
6.   **Not to covet.**
7.   **Not to bear false witness.**
8.   **To honour all men.**[12]
9.   **Not to do to another what one would not wish to have done to oneself.**
10. **To deny oneself in order to follow Christ.**

Almost all the tools up to No. 34 describe traditional themes, found in other forms of monasticism: respect for the life, property, reputation and peace of one's neighbour. The most notable exception is in Nos. 10–13, speaking of mortification. These were put here probably because of the idea of self-renunciation in seeking Christ and the good of one's neighbour, found in the preceding numbers.

11. **To punish one's body.**
12. **Not to seek pleasures.**
13. **To love fasting.**

But Saint Benedict soon comes back to the theme of charity, which is expressed most in exterior actions:

14. **To relieve the poor.**
15. **To clothe the naked.**
16. **To visit the sick.**
17. **To bury the dead.**
18. **To give help in trouble.**
19. **To console the sorrowful.**
20. **To avoid worldly behaviour.**
21. **To set nothing before the love of Christ.**
22. **Not to give way to anger.**
23. **Not to yield to anger**

Charity then enters the depths of the person:

24. **Not to preserve deceit in one's heart.**
25. **Not to give a false peace.**
26. **Not to abandon charity.**
27. **Not to swear, for fear of perjury.**
28. **To speak with one's mouth the truth that lies in one's heart.**

---

[12] The words proper to Saint Benedict are in bold print.

29. *Not to return evil for evil.*
30. *Not to inflict any injury, but to suffer injuries patiently.*
31. *To love one's enemies.*
32. *Not to curse anyone who curses us, but instead to return a blessing.*
33. *To suffer persecution for righteousness' sake.*
34. *Not to be arrogant.*

We then move to the struggle against sensuality: the desires of the body, the passions, evil thoughts, and words that dissipate the mind:

35. *Not given to drinking.*
36. *Not a heavy eater.*
37. *Not given to much sleeping.*
38. *Not lazy.*
39. *Not a grumbler.*
40. *Not a detractor.*

Then there are some tools dealing with humility and the fear of God, which we will return to later. The list continues:

51. *To guard one's mouth against evil and vicious speech.*
52. *Not to love much talking.*
53. *Not to utter words that are foolish and provoke laughter.*
54. *Not to love much or unrestrained laughter.*
55. *To listen willingly to devout reading.*
56. *To fall often to prayer.*
57. *In our daily prayer to God to confess with tears and groans the wrong-doing in our past life.*
58. *To amend these wrong ways in the future.*
59. *To reject carnal desires.*
60. *To hate one's own will.*
61. *To obey the Abbot's commands in everything, even though he himself (which God forbid) acts otherwise, remembering always that command of the Lord's, 'Do what they tell you, but do not do the things that they do'.*
62. *To be unwilling to be called holy before one is so, but to be holy first so that it may be truly said of one.*
63. *To carry out God's commands daily in one's actions.*
64. *To love chastity.*
65. *To hate no one.*
66. *Not to cherish bitterness.*
67. *Not to indulge in envy.*
68. *Not to love quarrelling.*
69. *To flee vainglory.*
70. *To revere the elders.*

71. To love the young.
72. To pray for one's enemies in the love of Christ.
73. After a quarrel to make peace with the other before sunset.
74. And never to despair of God's mercy.

This list contains several tools which, we might think, ought to have been placed in the first group: for example No. 40, *Not a detractor*, or Nos. 70–73, on charity and mutual respect between elders and youngsters. These tools were added here by Saint Benedict because of their psychological relationship with the neighbouring ones. Grumbling leads to speaking untruths about other people, something that we find before No. 26 in *RM*: *not to abandon charity*. The struggle against anger and pride needs the antidote of mutual respect and fraternal love. These additions also show how the division of the text into matters concerning non-violence, and those concerning non-sensuality, dates from the time before Saint Benedict, who seems unaware of this particular point.

So, despite the apparent lack of order, this chapter keeps the schema used by the monks of Asia. Does this mean there is some kind of remote dependence? I am inclined to think that these various monastic writings are a way of expressing the same psychological intuition and the same lived experience: good will towards others and mastery of the passions are the indispensable conditions for the spiritual search.[13]

Finally, we should remember that these teachings are valid for all states of life, since the list given by Saint Benedict and the Master has its source in a Christian catechesis intended for *lay* people.[14] These fundamental principles are also valid for lay people of the other world religions.

3. A CHRISTIAN TEXT

The similarities between the parallel texts of the various religions serve to highlight all the more the Christian originality of the list set out by *RB*.

We should note first the great principle that he uses as a point of departure: to love God and one's neighbour. The God of Jesus Christ

---

[13] There is certainly a mutual influence between certain Jain, Hindu and Buddhist texts. Here, however, we are thinking of the overall relationship between these religions and Christianity.

[14] We see other examples in the *Didache*, the *Passio Juliani* and in some of the *Apophthegmata* such as MARTIN OF DUMES, 109.

is a God of love. Father, Son and Holy Spirit, and the entire life of a Christian monk cannot help but be a response to that love, by following Christ. Even the text of *RB* itself leads us back to the Gospel in the first few lines.

The two great commandments, taken from Luke 10: 27, are followed by six precepts from the Decalogue, of which five are given in the form in which Jesus quoted them (*Luke* 12: 18–20). In No. 9, we have the Golden Rule, taken from the Sermon on the Mount:[15]

Not to do to another what one would not wish to have done to oneself.

In No. 10, Christ is presented as the model to follow. All self-renunciation is intended to make us like him and, in this service rendered to others, it is him whom we love above all else, as No. 12 tells us. The last maxims of this section (Nos. 29–34) herald the fourth step of humility, and we can glimpse the image of the suffering Christ, since each one of these tools evokes some part of the Passion narrative.

With No. 34, we begin another series which deals with the mortification of sensuality and pride (34–40), selfish desires which are balanced by the idea of hope in God, source of all good, and the eternal life which he promises us.

41. *To rest one's hope in God.*
42. *Whenever one perceives any good in oneself to attribute it to God, not to one's self.*
43. *But to recognise that whatever is evil is always one's own doing, and to blame one's self.*
44. *To fear the Day of Judgement.*
45. *To dread hell.*
46. *To yearn for eternal life with all possible spiritual desire.*
47. *To keep death daily before one's eyes.*
48. *At every moment to keep watch over the actions of one's life.*
49. *In every place to know that God most surely beholds one.*
50. *To dash the evil thoughts that invade one's heart immediately upon Christ, as upon a rock, and to reveal them to one's spiritual father.*

Here, as in the first degree of humility, which has the same ideas, the purifying presence of God is not an impersonal Absolute. It is Christ who breaks the evil thoughts (No. 50), it is he who is obeyed in the superiors (No. 61), for his sake we are to love even our enemies (No. 72) and, finally, it is he who gives his rewards to those who have loved him (Nos. 76–77).

[15] *Mt.* 7: 12; this rule already existed in *Tob.* 4: 16.

Notice that, in the chapter as a whole, Christ or *the Lord* is named six times, of which four are proper to Saint Benedict. This clearly shows how his thought is centred on Christ.

4. SAINT BENEDICT'S OWN TOUCHES

Other changes, introduced into the list given in *RM* by Saint Benedict, show us some of the main themes of his Rule.

In general, he wants to make a better adaptation of these tools for the monastic life. *To honour one's father and mother* becomes to *honour all men*; the tools dealing with loans of money, almsgiving, and fidelity to the promises are left out, because monks have few opportunities to practise these virtues.

Instead, Saint Benedict added other tools so as to underline the aspects of monastic life which were dear to him. The first concerns the Abbot. Far from making him into a superman, Saint Benedict is aware that he has his limits and weaknesses, like every other person. The Abbot should be obeyed, even if he himself does not always give a good example (No. 61). It is also quite normal that he should be assisted, even in the spiritual realm, by other officials (No. 50).

Saint Benedict then goes on to emphasise the importance of relations that are marked by charity, whether inside the community or outside. Tools 69 to 72 refer to this subject:

69. *To flee vainglory.*
70. *To revere the elders.*
71. *To love the young.*
72. *To pray for one's enemies in the love of Christ.*

He continues, in line with *RM*:

73. *After a quarrel to make peace with the other* before sunset.

He gives an affectionate and personal note to the last tool.

74. *Never to despair of God's **mercy**.*

The addition of the word **mercy** recalls the paternal goodness of God, mentioned in the Prologue.

The last phrases of the chapter are also proper to Saint Benedict; they replace the long description of the joys of heaven given by *RM*.

75. *These then are the **tools of the spiritual craft**.*

76. *If we make full use of them unceasingly day and night, then, when
    we give them back on the Day of Judgement, we shall in return
    receive from the Lord that **reward** which he himself has promised:*
77. *'**The things that no eye has seen, and no ear has heard, which
    God has prepared for those who love him.**'*
78. *Now the workshop in which we make diligent use of all these tools
    is **the enclosure of the monastery combined with stability in the
    community.***

These lines also indicate important themes that will return, from time
to time, in the course of the Rule: the love of the Lord and stability
in the community. The attraction that God exercises over the monk is
already felt in No. 46: *to yearn for eternal life **with all possible spiritual desire***. The love of Christ underlies the whole Rule, creating
harmony in the community that is expressed each time a particular
effort is required from the monk. Personal love for Christ is also one
of the most remarkable traits of early Christian monasticism, a tradition which Saint Benedict here adopts.[16]

The concluding phrase builds a bridge between ascetic effort and
stability in the monastery, as was made in the final addition to chapter
1. These ideas will occur once more in chapters 53 and 61 on religious profession.

5. A METHOD OF PRAYER

The comparison we have made between the religions of Asia and *RB*
is made still clearer by another aspect. Most of the spiritual masters
of the East give their disciples a few words or a *mantra* to be repeated
constantly, to create in them, by stages, the kind of spiritual attitudes
they desire.

Saint Benedict's *tools* are also pithy sentences, not chosen at
random, but taken from passages of Scripture frequently quoted by the
Fathers. They are a condensed version of a spiritual experience, made
to be remembered easily. Benedict often mentions scriptural words in
the Rule, words that the disciple ought to repeat *without ceasing* so as
to develop the attitude of heart that is required in his current situation.[17] The *Tools of Good Works* are like a catalogue of phrases
which, when repeated knowingly, become like a kind of hammer to

---

[16] Cf. Athanasius, VA, 3; 5; 8; 13. *Apophthegmata*, Lucius, 1; Macarius, 19;
Basil, *LR, Prologue*; 1–3; 5; 6; 8; *SR*, 115; 116; 160; 162; 163; 170; 175–179;
186; 199; 200; 284.

[17] This recommendation is repeated twice in *RB* 7, the first degree of humility,
whose text, as we have seen, is partly paralleled in the present chapter.

break the bad thoughts against the person of Christ, or like a chisel, which engraves the image of the Redeemer on our hearts.

Another indication in the same vein is given by the manuscript tradition of *RM*, which sees this chapter as kind of directory for the superior.[18] The superior should give the disciple the kind of *mantra* he needs. If Saint Benedict regards this list as not exclusively reserved to the superior, that is because, in Christianity, there is no need of secrecy to lend an air of magic to the list. The goal envisaged – to become like Christ, the inner Master – is known to everyone. It is Christ who endows certain words with the fragrance of his life[19] and draws the disciple to conform his own life to them. The role of the Christian spiritual father is most of all to help his brothers to discern what comes from God, so as not to let themselves be drawn astray by selfish sensual attractions.

Thus, like the sages of other world religions, the Fathers invented these key words as a means of getting rid of self-love so that they could abandon themselves entirely to the spiritual search. For the Christian, however, this search is focused on union with Christ. The Fathers thus propose that we adopt his example and life, using the words of Scripture chosen by the Abbot or chosen under the influence of the Holy Spirit, words that will be repeated and savoured in the most intimate part of the self.

Seen as a whole, and compared with the texts of other world religions, this chapter once again highlights the indispensable qualities of every form of monastic life: namely, good will towards everyone and mastery over the passions. This comparison emphasises the love of God and neighbour as a Gospel principle, and one that is essential to Christian monasticism. Saint Benedict refers constantly to Christ, even more than his immediate predecessors. The example of the Lord induces the monk to love, in a way that will enable him to surmount all the obstacles blocking him from union with God and charity towards his neighbour.

The following chapters will develop this theme, showing how interior progress is the work of the Holy Spirit.

---

[18] Cf. AV *RB* IV, pp. 120–121; 125.
[19] The Fathers speak of *words of life*.

CHAPTER VI

AUTHORITY AND OBEDIENCE

Relations with authority and the kind of obedience due to authority are important questions in all societies. They are, however, even more acute in religious life, where the superior often acts in the name of a divine or superhuman law. All the world's monastic systems deal with this topic, each emphasising a different aspect that helps us to understand the Christian tradition and Saint Benedict.

1. THE MASTER–DISCIPLE RELATIONSHIP IN HINDUISM

THE GURU

The obedience of the disciple is directed first towards a guru or spiritual master. It is well known[1] that the institution of the guru has its roots in Indian prehistory, where upper-caste families entrusted the education of their children to a wise elder among their relatives. Gradually, this master began to be a specialist in the ways that lead to the supreme goal of human life: union with the Absolute.

Because of this, the master–disciple relationship is the sharing of an experience as well as a method of teaching. The guru makes it his duty to love his disciples,[2] because he must be able to have full confidence in them, to be able to show them the secret of his life, and share

---

[1] SR VANDANA, *The guru as present reality*, in CLARENCE O. MCMULLEN, *The nature of guruship*, p. 163 ff. Cf. MANU 2.
[2] We have seen it in connection with *RB* 2.

with them his deepest aspirations. He thus expects each of his disciples to have a respectful openness of heart, together with the readiness to co-operate, which comes about through affection.

THE DUTIES OF THE DISCIPLE

This atmosphere of mutual understanding is shown by texts explaining the duties of the disciples: Here, for example, is what the sage Kapila says in the *Bhagavata Purana*:

> *This wisdom should not be handed over to a man who is sanctimonious, unbelieving, dishonest, or wanting in obedience, devotion, and humility.*[3]

Obedience to the guru is very strict during the time of formation. It becomes less so when the disciple has received the wisdom inherited from the line of the masters who preceded him, and is himself able to transmit it.[4] Nevertheless, the guru continues to be venerated by his disciples, even after his death. In our own time, most ashrams keep a picture of the former guru in a place honour, and it is greeted with the same signs of respect as the living master. Throughout his entire life, the disciple holds his master in veneration, which always includes some kind of obedience. Similarly, the *Laws of Manu* praise submission, which lasts until death:

> *One who submits himself willingly to the wishes of his guru, right to the end of his life, shall rise, immediately after, to the eternal abode of the Divine Being.*[5]

THE MOTIVES OF OBEDIENCE

These would appear to be the same throughout the diverse branches of Hinduism. One person follows his guru as an experienced guide in the spiritual way into which he wants to enter. The function of the master is to help his disciple to avoid false moves and to rid him of all that would delay his union with the Absolute.

The Hindus are almost unanimous, too, in teaching that, by obeying the guru, one submits oneself to God, who is present in him. The ways in which the guru is deemed to be united to the inner Presence differ according to the schools, but all show their disciples a way

[3] *Bhagavata Purana* 3: 32, 41–42, quoted by SUBASH ANAND in *Discipleship in Bhagavata Purana*, CHRISTIAN SPIRITUALITY FOR INDIA, I, Bangalore, 1978.
[4] It is characteristic, for example, that book 6 of the *Laws of Manu*, dedicated to elderly ascetics, does not mention the obedience to a guru.
[5] MANU, 2: 244; cf. 243 and 249.

towards union with this Presence. Hence, the source of their authority is found in the intensity of their personal experience.

These prescriptions regarding the Master and his disciples are well described in the first lines of the *Bhagavata Purana*:

> *Desiring to reach the dwelling of the One whose praise is sung in heavens, Saukana and other sages met in a sacred place to offer a sacrifice ... One morning they welcomed [their master] Suta and asked him respectfully: O sinless Suta, you have studied and even expounded [the Sacred Books and the writings by holy men]. By their grace, you too, O dear One, know all that thoroughly ... for a master holds nothing secret from a disciple who loves him. From all that, you discern what is useful for us. So we request that you too explain it to us, O you who have lived so long. O you who are lovely – in this world man's life is short, many are lethargic and dull-witted, not favoured by fortune and troubled by many things. The branches of learning are numerous, painful and long to learn.*
>
> *O you who are holy, through your discernment, draw out for us the quintessence of all that, and speak to us who are full of faith, so that our mind may find rest ... Please, to us who are attentive, tell [the story] of Lord Krishna ...*
>
> *Suta answered: 'O sages, in desiring to know what regards Krishna, you have asked me the right question on the source of happiness for the world, where man's mind finds peace ... It is in [the Lord's] love that man finds peace.*[6]

The way indicated here is that of *Bhakti* or devotion and love. Other gurus teach non-duality as the supreme way; still others prepare their disciples to listen to the interior voice of the *Sat-guru*, God, who alone can lead to the fullest union with himself.

MASTER AND DISCIPLE

The diversity of the relations with the Absolute introduces other similar differences in the understanding of the master's function and in the obedience due to him. The *bhakti* current insists on love, with all its tactfulness, but also with all its violence and, sometimes, its excess. On his side, the guru who believes that he has reached identification with the Absolute expects all his words to be considered as the very expression of the Most High.[7] On the other hand, he who believes that he is

---

[6] *Bhagavata Purana* 1: 1; 4–13; 1: 2; 5–6. Cf. Subash Anand, art. cit.

[7] The two tendencies are not excluding each other. The *Bhagavata Purana* say for example: *One should love the Lord with devotion, believing in the excellence of his guru, indeed, even in his divinity* (11: 2; 37).

merely the guide towards the *Sat-guru* strives to lead his disciples to the point where the Lord himself takes the initiative.

Each of these positions requires on the part of the disciple a proper interior attitude which will direct his whole life. Regarding external matters, however, the master expects from his followers a submission full of respect and faith;[8] it is a necessary precondition to benefit from his directions, and to share progressively his spiritual experience. If the disciple is not satisfied, he can go to another guru, but the attitude towards the new master has to be the same as it was with his predecessor. It is necessarily so; that is why the Hindu spiritual texts speak rarely of obedience as such.[9] They consider it as a quality necessary for any disciple who wants to benefit from his master's teaching, as we have seen in the above-mentioned texts.

SOCIAL OBEDIENCE

Book 2 of the *Laws of Manu* introduces another dimension of obedience: the kind that affects one's social life. Indeed, in this perspective, there is almost no distinction between the novice and the student, as they are both under the same master. Obedience to the guru is like obedience to one's parents:

> *The young man should do, on every occasion, what is pleasing to his parents and to his guru. When these three persons are satisfied, all the practices of devotion are happily fulfilled and receive their reward. A respectful submission to what pleases these three persons is declared the most eminent perfection, and the disciple should not undertake any other pious duty, without their permission.*[10]

The aim of this submission is the good order of society, order which is itself a condition of well-being here below, and of immortality:

> *In accomplishing perfectly the prescribed duties, without aiming at a reward, a man reaches immortality, and, even in this world, fulfils all the desires that his mind could conceive.*[11]

---

[8] This submission is sometimes nearly blind and becomes the cause of serious abuse with unscrupulous gurus. Cf. C. O. McMullen, op. cit. p. 163.

[9] It is worth notice that the word *obedience* is hardly mentioned in the book *The nature of guruship* and in the articles on the same subject of Subash Anand and Van Troy in *Christian spirituality for India*, I.

[10] Manu, 2: 228-229; these laws also settle all the details about precedence in society, the customs of respect and politeness in the mutual relations between its members. Cf. 2: 119-139; 200-208.

[11] Ibid., 2: 5.

2. THE MASTER, THE *DHARMA* AND THE *SANGHA* IN BUDDHISM

THE MASTER AND THE *DHARMA*

As we have seen, all Buddhist monks, masters and disciples, follow the *Dharma*, the supreme law taught by the Buddha. In his relations with the community, the monk is subject to the Abbot of the monastery, but from the moment of his arrival, the young man is entrusted to a master (*Upajhaya*) helped by an assistant (*Acharya*). He remains under them for five to ten years, depending on the school, and vows obedience to them. The ceremony of entering the novitiate includes the acknowledgement of their authority, and the ceremony for becoming a monk is still more explicit. The novice begins by asking an elder monk to receive him as disciple:

> *Venerable Father, please listen to me favourably. I, so and so, ask you, Venerable Father, to be my Upajhaya. I submit myself to you, to be received as a monk, for charity's sake.*[12]

Before the assembled monks, he says:

> *I, N.N., take refuge in the Buddha, the Dharma, and the Sangha. In imitation of the Buddha, I leave my family, and acknowledge X as my Upajhaya. The One who came, the Truthful [the Buddha] and all the Enlightened [monks of the Sangha] are the objects of my veneration.*[13]

The ceremony is concluded by this piece of advice to the new monk:

> *You are now a monk, and have been informed of the grounds for expulsion. If you behave well, it will be your benefit. Give to your Upajhaya, to your Acharya, to the whole community [Sangha] what you owe them, according to the Rule [Dharma]. Accept willingly their instructions, work for your happiness, and be an honour to your monastery. Ask, meditate, study, and find your good in the doctrine of the Buddha ... In your doubts and difficulties turn to your Upajhaya and to your Acharya. Now you may leave.*[14]

In some traditions, as for example, in Korea, and among Tibetans, submission to the spiritual master lasts for life.[15] In general,

---

[12] LW. *Vinaya* 4 (our translation), cf. text already quoted about *RB* 4.
[13] LW. *Vinaya* 10, p. 195. Cf. M. ZAGO, *Rites et cérémonies en milieu bouddhiste Lao*, pp. 52 ff.
[14] LW.*Vinaya* 10, p. 201.

however, submission depends on the benefit one gets from his teaching. If the disciple is not satisfied, he can change masters. He desires before all to be led to the perception of the Total Truth, and a change of master is a matter of indifference, for the true guide is the *Dharma*, the Law set forth by the Buddha. This law is a reflection, made in human words, of this Eternal Truth already present in the heart. The function of the master is to help the disciple to discover it:

> *Withdraw your eyes from the illusions of the world. Do not trust your senses, they deceive you. However, inside the body, in the sanctuary of the feelings, look for the Eternal Man in the impersonal, and after finding it, look inside: you are the Buddha.*[16]

Buddhism includes many branches that have explored various ways of attaining to this supreme perception. These branches are often parallel to those of Hinduism, and each one requires a particular interior attitude, which the master hands over to his disciple through appropriate methods. The forms of obedience of the disciple thus depend on the aim to be reached and on the kind of formation he receives.

THE RULES OF THE *SANGHA*

One of the master's functions is to teach the novice the Rules of monastic life. There are two levels: the first links the monk directly to his ideal (which means that, if he breaks it, he does not have the qualities required to be a monk).[17] The second level deals with the numerous details of observance, which aim to train the monk in self-control. The novice has, for example, to learn to bow the knee, to raise his folded hands, to walk 'with solemnity', to adopt postures for meditation, to speak in a low voice, and to handle each object in the proper way.

Obedience to these rules also has a social aspect (more so than in

---

[15] I have seen Korean monk–students in France, writing regularly to their spiritual master and giving an account of themselves. A Tibetan monk journeyed right across the world to consult his spiritual master in a difficult case. On the relationship master–disciple in Tibetan monasticism, see LAMA DENIS TENDROUP, *Maître spirituel et maître intérieur dans le monachisme tibétain* in QUESTIONS DE, 84, p. 43 ff. for the Zen: P. DE BETHUNE, *Le Maître selon la tradition Zen*, ibid. p. 61 ff.

[16] Cf. *The voice of the silence* in C. HUMPHREYS, *The Wisdom of Buddhism*, 10.

[17] The essential rules of monastic life are defined by the ten vows and the four cases of expulsion (LW, *Vinaya* 4 and 10); they will be mentioned later about the vows.

Hinduism). Living in communities that are in constant contact with lay people, monks need to adopt a way of behaviour that avoids quarrels and creates an atmosphere of peace and good will, things that are necessary for the spiritual quest. This ideal of harmonious living is well described in the legend of *Anuruddha* who says:

> *It is indeed for me an advantage, it is a great fortune to live with*
> *such religious men. I have been attracted toward these venerable men,*
> *because they live in good understanding, in private and in public, in*
> *deeds and in words. Thus, having left aside my own views, I adopted*
> *their way of life. We have different bodies, but indeed one spirit.*
> *Living together in the same house, we help each other to ensure the*
> *cleanliness of the place, and we keep silence. Every five nights we*
> *meet to speak of the* Dharma. *This is how we live, full of ardour,*
> *zealous, and resolute.*[18]

The community as such, the *Sangha*, plays the role of the master. The supervision of the observance is usually made in the fortnightly meetings of the *Uposatha*, where the monks accuse themselves of their faults, not against the superior, but against the *Dharma*, the Universal Order concretely expressed in the details of the 'vows'.

3. MASTER AND DISCIPLE IN SUFISM[19]

THE MASTER

Obedience to the *sheikh*, or spiritual master, is considered by Sufis as one of the essential duties of any disciple. The ceremony of initiation, which is more or less the same in all orders, highlights this aspect:

> *It was called the* ahd *and the essential aspect was the* bai'a *or vow of*
> *allegiance . . . The formula of a simple* bai'a *given to me by the* shaikh
> *of a small* Shadhili ta'ifa *runs:*
> *'O God, I have repented before Thee, and accept as my teacher,* Shaikh
> X *as my shaikh in this world and in the next, as guide and leader to Thy*
> *Presence, and as director* (murshid) *in Thy Path. I will disobey him*
> *neither in word nor in deed, neither overtly nor covertly. Confirm me,*
> *O God, in obedience to him and his* tariqa, *in this world and the next,*
> *and in the* tariqa *of the shaikh of shaikhs and* imam *of imams, the* Qutb

---

[18] *Legend of Anuruddha*, in the *Calla Cosinga Sutra* of the *Mahajina Nikaya*.

[19] Though not belonging to monasticism, the Sufi Orders have developed the relationship master–disciple, and their experience can be useful for others.

of the community, my Lord Abu'l-Hasa ash-Shadhili – *God be pleased with him!*[20]

The gestures and ceremonies that accompany this pledge are equally significant. The disciple sits close to his master and they clasp their right hands. The *sheikh* dictates prayers to be repeated, sentence by sentence, asking for God's forgiveness, testifying that the initiation given is that of God and his Prophet, and that the hand of the *sheikh* is that of the founder of the Order. The disciple promises to recite the prayers (*Dhirk*) given by the *sheikh*.

When all these conditions have been accepted, the *sheikh* says, by way of conclusion, '*I accept you as my son*'. After a prayer, the *sheikh* gives him a ritual cup to drink, as a sign of his integration into the Order. He then receives the religious habit, the rosary, and the prayer book. The newly initiated is henceforth attached to a convent, and leads a life according to rule, at least during his time of formation.[21]

GOD

Though this absolute submission to the *sheikh* has sometimes led to abuse of authority, or has been an exploitation of popular credulity, we must remember that it is primarily *directed towards God*, as is clearly seen by the full formula of the *ahd*. Here is a characteristic passage:

> *Be with your* shaikh *like a corpse in the hands of the one who washes it. Obey him in all his commands, for it is God himself who commands, through his voice. To disobey him is to incur God's anger. Do not forget that you are his slave and that you should do nothing without his order.*
>
> *The* shaikh *is a man loved by God; he is superior to all other creatures and takes rank after the Prophets. Therefore, you should see him everywhere. Discard from your heart any other thought than those that have God or the* shaikh *for their object.*
>
> *As a sick person should not hide anything from the physician of his body, in the same way, you must not hide any of your thoughts from the* shaikh – *not a single word, nor a single action – for the* shaikh *is the physician of your soul. You should keep your heart chained to your*

[20] J. SPENCER TRIMINGHAM, *The Sufi Orders in Islam*, pp. 186–187. The initiation comprises several degrees, the above formula is used for the simple affiliation to the Order. The ceremony for the initiation of a dervish is more elaborate; it is made at the end of the novitiate and the instructions given during the *ahd* end with the famous sentence *Be with your shaikh like a corpse in the hands of the washer*, quoted below.

[21] Ibid.

shaikh. *Discard from your mind any reasoning, good or bad, without analysing it or seeing where it is leading, for fear that a loose thought may lead to error.*[22]

THE CURE OF VICES

One of the most important tasks of the *sheikh* towards his disciple is to cure him of his vices, especially pride, which separates from God. Here, for example, is what *Al Arabi ad-Derqawi*, a famous nineteenth-century *sheikh* of the Maghreb tells us about his own formation:

The first thing I learned from my master (God be pleased with him!) was that he loaded me with two baskets full of prunes. Instead of putting them on my neck, as he had told me, I took them in my hands. Nevertheless, despite that, it was a very hard task for me, so painful, in fact, that my soul seemed to shrivel up.

I was in deep distress, and extremely confused – so much so that I was nearly weeping – and, by God, I had still to weep because of all the humiliations, scorn and vexation that I was to undergo in this situation.[23] *For my soul had not yet accepted such a thing, nor had I bowed my head. Up to this point, I had been unconscious of my pride, its revolt and corruption ... Then, when I was in this perplexity and pain, the master came to me and, with his great insight, took the two baskets from my hands and loaded them on my neck, saying, 'Now undergo this test for your good, to drive out some of your pride.' By these words, he opened me the door of righteousness.*[24]

THE SPIRITUAL LINEAGE

Once the disciple is purified, the *sheikh* can introduce him to the spiritual lineage that links him with the Prophet and hand over to him the special charism or attached blessing (*barakah*) with its secret power. However, this is God's gift, to draw people towards him.

One of the effects of divine grace, of divine goodness and generosity, is the existence of a master who educates us in spiritual ways. For without divine grace, nobody would find him, nor know him: it is more difficult

---

[22] Quoted in French by P. CASPAR, *Cours de mystique musulmane*, p. 128; cf. L. RINN, *Marabouts et Khouan*, p. 92.

[23] For a well-read person of noble family as Al Arabi ad-Derqawi, it was very humiliating to be treated as a market porter, going through the city in front of his friends and acquaintances.

[24] Letter of sheikh Al Arabi Ben Ahmed ad-Derqawi (d. 1828) to his disciples, quoted by TITUS BURCHARDT in *Chaine d'Or, Maîtres et disciples dans l'Islam Maghrébin*, HERMES IV, *Le Maître Spirituel*, pp. 134–135.

to know a saint than to know God, as Abul'-Abbas al Mursi *said. In the
same way,* Ibn'tâï-Ilan *said: may he be exalted, who shows us his saints
so as to show us himself, and attracts to them those whom he wants to
lead to himself.*[25]

Like the ascetics of other religions, the Sufis were divided into
various schools of thought. One of the strongest was Monism, which
suppressed the distinctions between beings, and tended to consider the
words of the spiritual master as if they were God's words.[26] Another
school is linked with the devotional current, which seeks union with
God by love. It requires a spontaneous and constant faithfulness to
God's will.[27]

The survey we have made of the relations between superiors and
ascetics in Eastern religions shows several common points. We shall
consider these at the end of the chapter and compare them with the
Christian tradition.

4. AUTHORITY AND OBEDIENCE IN THE CHRISTIAN TRADITION BEFORE SAINT BENEDICT

THE BIBLE

The first monastic rules refer constantly to the example of Christ, who
always fulfilled the will of his Father[28] to show his love for him,[29]
and who invited his disciples to imitate him in mutual service, even
as far as giving up their lives.[30] Jesus founded a Church, through
which he continues to speak and act.[31] The Letters of the New
Testament, above all those of Saint Paul and Saint John, constantly
refer to his teachings.[32]

The first Fathers of the Church began the discussion of obedience
in their commentaries on Scripture. As an example, we have the

---

[25] Ibid. p. 140.
[26] Ibn 'Arabi is one of the most famous representatives of this tendency.
[27] Hallaj is the pre-eminent bard of the love of God. His entire life and death witness
this heroic fidelity to his ideal.
[28] *Jn* 4: 34.
[29] *Jn* 15: 10.
[30] *Jn* 15: 13.
[31] *Lk*. 10: 16.
[32] The texts which are used more frequently by the monastic tradition will be indicated below, in connection with the passages in which they are quoted.

Commentary of Saint Cyprian on the words of the Our Father: 'Your will be done', which has been used by several monastic Rules.[33]

THE DESERT FATHERS

The spiritual father

We see that, among the Desert Fathers,[34] individual monks have a spiritual father, whom they obey as naturally as the young Indians obey their guru – and for similar motives. The Abba is the *saint whose wisdom knows how to find God's will.*[35] He is able to point out the right path to his disciple and he considers it his duty to help him rid himself on his defects, above all, those of pride and self-will:

> *Amma Syncletica said: 'We have to behave with discernment, not seeking our own advantage, nor being a slave of our own will, but trusting the one who, in the eyes of faith, is our father'.*[36]

The function of the spiritual father is to apply what God says in the Scriptures to his disciple:

> *An elder said: 'God asks the Christian to obey the Divine Scriptures (for he will find there the model of what he should do or say) and to rely on the superiors and the spiritual fathers'.*[37]

This obedience is without limitations. The disciple is to obey without discussion or reservation:

> *To obey is to exclude discernment, by superabundance of discernment.*[38]

Examples abound of extraordinary obedience or obedience regarding seemingly stupid things.[39] The reason for this is, that the Abba knows what to ask from the brethren, so that they may make spiritual progress, and also that:

---

[33] Cf. AV *RB* VII, pp. 151 ff.

[34] Obedience among the Desert Fathers is described in *Apophthegmata*, Syst Col. ch. 14 and *Apoph.* Zachariah 4, Isaiah 2; 7; Isidore, 10; Macarius, 33.

[35] *Apophthegmata*, Isidore, 10.

[36] Ibid. Syncletica, 26; Syst. Col. 14: 10.

[37] Ibid. 14: 13.

[38] JOHN CLIMACUS, quoted by I. HAUSHERR, *La direction spirituelle en Orient autrefois*, p. 19. In this chapter on the disciple's faith and submission, he gives many examples, and also attempts to justify its abuses.

[39] *Apophthegmata*, Syst. Col. 14: 1; 3; 4; 5; 7.

It is not always unreasonable to ask unreasonable things, to be done by people who are too attached to their own reasoning.[40]

If we want to understand the absolute tone of these texts, we should view them from the standpoint of the Desert Fathers. Newcomers could freely choose their spiritual father and change him, as they liked.[41] They could also ask advice from other fathers, but remained free to follow them or not, as they saw fit. We can appreciate that, in this atmosphere of freedom, the elders felt the need to give striking examples to encourage their disciples.

Collegiality

The Fathers were also aware of being merely the interpreters of the same Spirit, hence their guidance assumed something of a collegial character. As the brethren were in the habit of consulting several fathers, the elders were careful not to contradict each other. If someone felt obliged to rectify a less than wise directive given by another, he did so with tact, and often with humour.[42]

To obey like Christ

Nevertheless, the real model of the obedient disciple is Christ himself.

Abba Hyperechios said: 'The jewel of the monk is obedience. A person who possesses obedience will see his requests granted and will stay trustfully near the Crucified One. For the Lord who was nailed to the cross made himself obedient even unto death'.[43]

The obedient monk is as much a witness of Christ as is the martyr, not because obedience would necessarily cause suffering, but because it is a perfect example of faithfulness to the Lord:

---

[40] I. HAUSHERR, op. cit. pp. 198 ff. These explain many eccentricities of the Desert Fathers: e.g. planting a dead stick and asking a monk to water it. Tales of this kind are sometimes only pious stories, destined to help novices to understand the totality of obedience.

[41] I. HAUSHERR, op. cit. pp. 188–189, giving several examples.

[42] Cf. P. DESEILLE, *Regards sur la tradition monastique*, pp. 93; 203; *Apophthegmata*, Anonymous, 85; 91; 97; 113; etc.

[43] *Apophthegmata*, Anonymous, 11; Hyperechios, 8. The imitation of Christ in everything was indeed one of the fundamental rules of the primitive monasticism, cf. ATHANASIUS, *VA*, 4; *Théologie de la vie monastique*, Saint JOHN CHRYSOSTOM, p. 166; THEODORET, pp. 265–266.

[The obedient monk] *renounces his own will to do that of another: people of this kind are martyrs, if they persevere up to the end.*[44]

Thus, relying on his Abba as an experienced guide, the monk of the desert obeyed God by following Christ's example. All this seems to be obvious for the Fathers: they do not seek to justify it, they offer no scriptural proof; they simply give examples to inculcate these truths in the heart of the beginner.

CASSIAN

The role of the spiritual father

In his youth, Cassian came to know the Desert Fathers. In his writings, he quotes the example of Saint Antony who:

recommended discretion, the source of intelligence, judgement and wisdom, and found in Scripture an effective remedy for the temptations of the brethren.[45]

For Cassian, one of the first reasons for obedience to the elder was to rid the disciple of his own will:

The duty and the skill of the elder consist, above all, in training the young monk, so that he will be able to reach the highest summit of perfection. He should, first, teach him to master his own will, by frequent and persevering exercises, deliberately ordering him to do what is contrary to his feelings ... The tradition of the elders is that monks, especially the youngest, will not be able to curb their concupiscence, if they have not learned first to mortify their will through obedience.[46]

Examples of heroic obedience are then given, as models to be copied.[47] These hard principles are softened by the affection recommended for superiors in *Conference* 2:

[44] *Apophthegmata*, Pambo, 3; cf. Macarius, 33.
[45] CASSIAN, *Conf.* 2: 4; 11; cf. *Inst.* 2: 3, where he insists that a future superior needs, himself, to learn to obey. Among the Desert Fathers the superior was considered as a spiritual father. Beside the case of Pachomius, it was so, for example, at Nitria, cf. *Lausiac History*, VII.
[46] CASSIAN, *Inst.* 4: 8. These ideas were not followed by Saint Benedict.
[47] Ibid. 4: 23–30. The examples given come from the Desert Fathers, and are used by Cassian in the same way (cf. n. 39). Curiously, the example given in ch. 29 about a brother of noble family sent to sell baskets in the market is similar to the case of the Sufi Sheikh al Arabi, quoted above.

... to take pity on the afflicted ... to comfort with consolations full of sweetness and kindness.[48]

Obedience for the love of Christ

For Cassian, as for the Desert Fathers, obedience to the Abbot, who is both kind and strict, is ultimately given to God:

> *The brethren carry out his orders with alacrity, and without discussion, as if they came from God.*[49]

This perpetual holocaust makes the monks into martyrs:

> *... their patience and their strict faithfulness ... – never doing their own will – daily renders them crucified to the world, and living martyrs.*[50]

Elsewhere he reminds us that all these renunciations are made *for the love of Christ.*[51]

The good of obedience

Obedience in the monastery is the imitation of Christ, according to Cassian, who sees it not only as a means of education, but as a permanent value, and a source of humility and union with God:

> *The good of obedience, which holds the first rank among all the virtues.*[52]

This virtue is necessary for those who want:

> *to gain the humility of Christ through the grace of obedience, which is true nobility.*[53]

In *Conference* 24, after citing the example and words of the Lord,[54] he continues:

[48] CASSIAN, *Conf.* 2: 13.
[49] CASSIAN, *Inst.* 4: 10.
[50] CASSIAN, *Conf.* 18: 7.
[51] CASSIAN, *Inst.* 4: 27; cf. AV, *La communauté*, pp. 266–268 and CASSIAN, *Conf.* 19: 6, quoting *Phil.* 2: 8 and *Jn.* 6: 38; *Inst.* 12, 28, quoting also *Phil.* 2: 6–8 in the same context of obedience like Christ's.
[52] CASSIAN, *Inst.* 4: 30.
[53] Ibid. 29.

Monks practise this virtue especially in the cenobitic houses. The author-
ity of an elder guides them, and they do nothing of their own will, but
rather depend on the abbot's.[55]

All these texts make the Abbot into a figure like the spiritual masters
of the Desert. His authority is as unquestioned as theirs is and Cassian
praises it, without seeking to justify it. The texts of Scripture quoted
are presented more as models to follow than as proofs supporting the
superior's authority.[56]

SAINT PACHOMIUS

The superior and the community

Pachomius was considered by his successors as the model and spiritual father of all his monks:

The man we celebrate is, after God, the father of us all ... God saved
us, thanks to his holy prayers. For he also – I mean our Father
Pachomius – is one of the saints of God, one of those who have accom-
plished his will, always and everywhere.[57]

Pachomius himself did not expand the theory of spiritual fatherhood
any more than did his contemporaries. Rather he made the role
continue, without feeling the need of justifying it. He did, however,
bring his own particular flavour to it. Pachomius is not only the father
of the monks, but also the father of the *community* as such, the
koinonia, united in the love of Christ.[58] Here, once more, is the spiritual collegiality of the Desert Fathers, presented in a more
hierarchical manner. His successor, Orsisius, thus describes obedience to the elders and their special role:

Be subject to the Fathers in all obedience, without murmuring or reluc-
tance ... Listen to what Saint Paul says: 'Children, obey your parents
and find your salvation through those who are in charge of you ... Obey

---

[54] *Jn* 6: 38 and *Mt.* 26: 39.

[55] CASSIAN, *Conf.* 24: 26.

[56] Cf. *Jn* 6: 38 and *Mt.* 26: 39, quoted in *Conf.* 16: 6 and 24: 26; *Jn* 6: 38 and *Phil.*
2: 8, quoted in *Conf.* 19: 6. The authority of the elders is magnified in *Conf.* 2:
5 and 18: 5–8. Cf. AV *RB VH*, p. 155 and n. 68. *Théologie de la vie monastique*,
CASSIEN, pp. 219–222.

[57] PACHOMIUS, *VC Bo.* 194.

[58] *VC Bo*, 26. Cf. P. DESEILLE, *L'esprit du monachisme pachômien*, pp. xv–xix;
Liber Orsiesii, 7; 15.

your leaders, and be docile, for they have care of your souls, and will have to render an account of them.[59]

This submission to the various persons in charge is compared to obedience to one's parents, and to the social structures of the people of God, rather than to the spiritual authority of Christ. The followers of Pachomius seem instinctively to make a distinction between the natural domain of the organisation of the monastery and that of its spiritual direction, though they remain closely linked.

The Rule

Another new aspect of the Pachomian organisation is its submission to written Rules and a timetable. All that had seemed to be flexible in Pachomius's time,[60] and the opening words of the *Praecepta atque Judicia* indicate the spirit of the Rules:

> *The fullness of the Law is love. (Rom.* 13: 10)

Within this firm yet supple framework, there is no need to stress obedience, as the *Apophthegmata* had done. The different books of the Pachomian *Precepts* hardly speak of it. Instead, they condemn murmuring, duplicity, and reluctance to do the work requested.

Obedience to the Rules and to the superior thus goes beyond the personal dimension of spiritual progress, and becomes a participation in the Spirit, who unites the different members of the community in Christ:

> *Let us love humanity, and we shall be friends of Jesus, the friend of humanity.*[61]

SAINT BASIL

The spiritual father

The aim of those in authority, for Saint Basil, is to lead souls towards God:

---

[59] *Liber Orsiesii*, 19.

[60] Cf. P. DESEILLE, *Regards sur la tradition monastique*, pp. 129–131. A. VEILLEUX, *L'esprit du monachisme pachomien*, pp. xliv and 13. The texts quoted show a diversity of observance and some personal freedom inside the community, especially concerning meals. But it seems that the brethren were above all free to do more than the common rule.

[61] CSCO 160, p. 21.

> *If we have handed over the direction of our life to a brother, knowing well that he will have to render an account for it to God, it is quite unreasonable to refuse him our trust in the most ordinary circumstances.*[62]

His role is compared to that of a father, guide, and physician.[63] He should help the weak to *progress, by becoming like Christ.*[64] Indeed a person who

> *because of his incapacity, tries to find for himself what is good, will often make a bad choice, if he is left to his own devices.*[65]

Saint Gregory of Nyssa, in his *Treatise on Virginity*,[66] gives Basil as a living model of a spiritual master. In chapter 23, he explains the necessity of such a guide to avoid *going astray from the right way.* He describes his function as *leading to the summit of perfection* the souls attracted by the *good scent of Christ.* Around him they are like:

> *a choir of saints, assembled under the direction of this master* [coryphaeus], *imitating him who has practised virtue with success.*[67]

The superior's assistants

Saint Basil (*LR* 48) invites the superior to share his charge with an assistant, who will replace him in case of absence,[68] with a bursar, who gives to each one according to his needs,[69] and with other Elders, *who have given proofs of their faith and their prudence.* The brethren choose confidants – those whom they feel are *best able to understand them* and whose advice they will accept:

> *... in this way, what in us is twisted will be straightened, what is good, strengthened, and so we shall avoid being condemned with those who are prudent only in their own estimation.*[70]

These texts show us an evolution rather like that of primitive

---

[62] BASIL, *LR* 48.
[63] BASIL, *SR* 98; 99; 113; *LR* 28–30; 43.
[64] BASIL, *LR* 43.
[65] BASIL, *SR* 119, cf. *SR* 60.
[66] GREGORY OF NYSSA, *De Virgin.* SC 119, Introduction of M. AUBINEAU, pp. 58–59.
[67] GREGORY OF NYSSA, ibid. 23: 3; 5; 6.
[68] BASIL, *LR* 45 and 48.
[69] BASIL, *LR* 34; *SR* 135; 148.
[70] BASIL, *SR* 227; cf. *SR* 104; *LR* 53.

Buddhism. In both cases, we have a group of monks choosing a superior from among its members, who will, in turn, be helped by a council of elders.[71] We can also recognise the hierarchical collegiality of Saint Pachomius, where everyone tries to be faithful to the same Spirit.[72]

Obedience to the divine commandments

In carrying out their duty, the officers should be faithful to God. Basil is not bothered about finding a justification for their authority, but rather about the conformity of their life and their teaching to the word of God.[73] Obedience to the *divine commandments* is thus one of his favourite themes. The orders of the superiors should always conform to Scripture.[74]

The superior, a man of *faith and prudence*, shows each monk how to follow Christ, doing *what is pleasing to God*.[75] The monk, for his part, obeys because of a personal love for Christ.[76]

Speaking of the brethren, Basil underlines the dispositions of heart which are necessary for making progress towards God. The first is an attitude of faith. The monk:

> *ought to be completely convinced that he is obeying, or resisting, not a man, but the Lord, for He himself said: 'The one who listens to you, listens to Me; the one who despises you, despises Me'.*[77]

In following Christ, the monk should fight against his own will.[78] This means he should obey willingly and avoid grumbling, as is recom-

---

[71] Cf. BASIL, *SR* 104; *LR* 27. In *SR* 304 the expression: *Those who are superiors with him is* used about the bursar. Cf. J. GRIBOMONT, *Saint Basile* in *Theologie de la vie Monastique*, pp. 99–113; P. DESEILLE, *Regards sur la tradition monastique*, pp. 106–163.

[72] This evolution explains also that most of the rules concerning obedience or correction speak less often of the superior of the monastery than of 'the superiors'. BASIL, *LR* 41; *SR* 96; 105; 106; 119, or do not specify who is correcting or commanding *SR* 38; 81; 82; 99; 122; 123.

[73] BASIL, *SR* 98; *LR* 47; 50.

[74] Cf. BASIL, *SR* 38; 119; *LR* 24; 47. In his Rules Basil does not quote the Scripture to support his proposal. Instead, he refers to Scripture, to find in it what is to be done.

[75] Cf. Monique Simon, *Plaire à Dieu selon les Règles de saint Basile*, COLL CIST 39, 1977, 4.

[76] BASIL, *LR* 2; 3; *SR* 115; 116; 121.

[77] *Lk.* 10: 16; *SR* 38.

[78] The question of fighting against one's own will, especially against pride, comes very often, particularly about the choice of a work or of any obedience. Cf. BASIL, *SR* 74; 96; 120; 122; 123; 125; 128; *LR* 5; 21; 29.

mended by Saint Paul.[79] Moreover, *He who loves in truth* strives to obey, *even if the work seems to be beyond his strength*.[80]

Moderation and dialogue

The superior should take care not to impose too heavy a burden[81] and, if the obedience is difficult for *some valid reason*, Saint Basil advises dialogue with the superior. He even says that *if the brother does not dare to speak, he may do it by the intermediary of another*.[82] Obedience thus takes on a community dimension, and even when he speaks of each monk, Basil always has in mind the repercussion of individual acts on the whole community.[83] He fears the disastrous consequences of a bad example,[84] and desires to foster charity, peace, and good order.[85]

Alongside the elders, who help the superior in his *care of souls*,[86] Basil gives an important role to the bursar and his helpers, thus building up fraternal concord. He asks them not only *to care for order and faithfulness to the Rule*[87] but also to be *merciful and kind to all*, to foster *concord, the fruit of fraternal love*.[88] Hence, all the brethren should:

> Obey each other, like servants to their masters. This is the desire of the Lord, . . . who says: '. . . The Son of man did not come to be served, but to serve'.[89]

Mutual obedience has no other limit than the one quoted by Saint Paul, who:

[79] BASIL, *SR* 39; 133, quoting 2 *Cor.* 7: 9 and 1 *Cor.* 10: 10.

[80] BASIL, *LR* 28; *SR* 121; 152; 199; 206. This last rule is characteristic of Basil's attitude. To an interrogation on how to observe the Lord's commandment saying not to worry about food and drink, he answers: *This commandment, like the others, goes up to death, for the Lord has been obedient up to death . . . That which makes easier this disposition is an ardent zeal for the Lord's commandments and a desire so strong that we do not even have leisure to worry about the body's necessities.*

[81] BASIL, *SR* 152; 276.

[82] BASIL, *LR* 47.

[83] In the same way in *LR* 30, the superior is called *He to whom has been entrusted the care of nursing the community*, and Basil adds: *Let him be convinced that to govern is to serve.*

[84] BASIL, *SR* 98; 114.

[85] BASIL, *LR* 9; *SR* 98; 119.

[86] BASIL, *SR* 113.

[87] BASIL, *SR* 156.

[88] BASIL, *LR* 34; cf. *SR* 91; 93; 100; 135; 148–150.

[89] BASIL, *SR* 115; *Mk.* 10: 45.

cites as an example the obedience of Christ *'who was obedient unto death, death on a cross' (Phil. 2: 8); and he added, 'have the same mind, the mind of Christ Jesus' (Phil. 2: 5).*[90]

In this way

the rule of pleasing God is observed and each one takes part in the building up of one body in the Spirit, by means of concord.[91]

SAINT AUGUSTINE

The superior serves Christ in his brethren

Saint Augustine's Rule ends with a chapter on obedience:

The superior should be obeyed as a father and duly honoured, so that God be not offended in his person . . . It is his special duty to watch over these prescriptions, not overlooking infractions because of negligence, but making the necessary corrections.[92]

These words refer to *Heb.* 13: 17, where Saint Paul recommends the faithful to obey the leaders of the Christian community who *watch over it*. The same passage also refers to the Decalogue (*Exod.* 20: 12), where honour due to parents is given to God.[93]

Saint Augustine considers the superior, the head and father of the community, as the servant of Christ in his brethren. This is a complex duty, in which authority always implies respect and tactfulness towards the brethren. On the one hand, he has to see that the Rule is followed. On the other, he has also to adapt himself to each person, with love and humility.

He should not take pleasure in subduing others to his authority, but rather find it in the services he renders them through charity. Because of his dignity, you must consider him your Head, but by his fear of God may he stay at your feet. Let him be a model of good works for everyone, taking pain to correct the unstable, revive those who lack courage, support the weak, and be patient with all. He should observe these rules willingly, and make the others respect them, and though both are necessary, he will strive to be loved rather than to be feared, always thinking of the account he will have to render.[94]

[90] BASIL, *SR* 116.
[91] BASIL, *SR* 116; *LR* 7.
[92] Cf. L. VERHEIJEN, *Nouvelle approche de la Règle de saint Augustin, Reg.* VII 1.
[93] Cf. AUGUSTINE, *Ep.* 6, 1–2, AV *RB* VII, pp. 156–158.
[94] AUGUSTINE, *Reg.* VII, 8.

The Rule and the community

In the above text we hear an echo, albeit weak, of the spiritual father's task of adapting the prescriptions of the Rule to individual needs. Elsewhere, Augustine introduces a new comparison: the Rule is like a mirror, in which the religious may notice their defects. This image would later have great influence in the West. The Rule is considered as a model of perfection, taking the place of the spiritual master.

For Augustine, as for Basil and Pachomius, these recommendations find their milieu in the life of the community. The Rule is addressed to the community as a whole, united by the ideal of the primitive Church described by the text of *Acts* 4: 32:

> Before all, as such is the reason of your coming together, you should live in the house, having the same mind, with one heart and soul, directed towards God. Let there be no talk among you of private property.[95]

The chapter ends with a kind of summary:

> Live in unity of heart and soul, and honour, in each other, the one whose temple you are: God.[96]

Charity unites the body of Christ

The rest of the Rule describes the daily life of the monastery, in the light of these principles. The community comes first; the superior is merely one of its parts and obedience is intended to create unity of heart according to God, that is to say, in charity. This theme of charity that comes from God and unites all Christians in the body of Christ,[97] so important for Augustine, thus finds its application in the strict relationship he establishes between obedience and charity. The idea would have great influence on subsequent Rules, especially Saint Benedict's.

THE RULE OF THE MASTER

To obey Christ. To obey like Christ

The Master was influenced by Cassian, Pachomius and Basil,[98] and firmly adopts Cassian's thought when he considers community rela-

---

[95] AUGUSTINE, *Reg*: I, 2.
[96] Ibid.
[97] Cf. VERHEIJEN, in *Théologie de la vie monastique*. pp. 206–208.
[98] The Master, like Saint Benedict, knew only the part of Saint Basil's Rules known as the *Small Asceticon*, and translated into Latin by Rufinus.

tions only in the vertical direction, from the brethren to the Abbot and, through him, to God. He presents the disciple's obedience under its twofold relation to Christ: the disciple obeys Christ, by Christ's example. *RM* often quotes texts on Jesus' obedience, such as:

> *It is the will of him who sent me, not my own will, that I have come down from heaven to do* (*Jn* 6: 38) or *He accepted an obedience which brought him death* (*Phil.* 2: 8) and *Thy will, not mine, be done* (*Matt.* 26: 39).

This concern to make the text Christian is one of the most interesting aspects of *RM*. Less laudable is its manner of carrying to extremes the idea of Cassian, according to which the disciple should obey without examining the order received, since the Abbot carries alone all the responsibility of the disciple's act, done in obedience.[99]

RM sees the Abbot as the leader of the community, in charge of teaching the brethren and enforcing the Rule. But the notion of spiritual father is lost[100] and the Master has to find another base for the Abbot's authority. Therefore, he uses his predecessors' quotations of Scripture, showing that the Abbot participates in some way in the authority of the Church's hierarchy. In this way, he may be considered to represent Christ for the brethren. The Abbot is a *teacher*, successor of the Apostles, and entitled to speak in the name of God.[101] In this sense, he quotes the text of *Luke* 10: 16: *He who listens to you, listens to me.*

The Rule

This authoritarian tendency, along with his taste for detailed regulations, makes the Master a staunch adherent of a trend of thought that has accompanied the monastic movement throughout its history. This concept comes from a confusion of spiritual principles, based on Scripture, with the good order necessary for the smooth running of the community. Consequently, there has often been an abuse in the

---

[99] The irresponsibility of the obedient monk is also found in the Rule of Saint Colomban. Cf. AV *Communauté*, pp. 231–232.

[100] Cf. AV, ibid. p. 275 and *L'abbé vicaire du Christ* in COLL CIST 2, 1982. The weakening of the notion of spiritual father is found in the whole of Latin monasticism at that period. The influence of Saint Augustine may not be foreign to this evolution.

[101] *RM* 1; 2; 11; 14. Cf. AV *RB* I, pp. 153–154, and *La communauté et l'abbé*, p. 167.

use of Scripture, quoting it as justification for small regulations.[102] In the field of formation, the role of the spiritual father disappears, being superseded by the conformity to detailed rules.

The Master himself seems to have had an inkling of these difficulties. To remedy them, he allows the observance to be more or less strict, according to the degree of the monks' fervour, and he asks the Abbot to adapt himself to their different temperaments when he corrects them.

5. AUTHORITY AND OBEDIENCE IN SAINT BENEDICT'S RULE

Saint Benedict, as we have seen, has several chapters on the Abbot, his qualities, and the manner of his election. He touches the question of the relationship between monks and superiors mostly in regard to obedience, where he speaks alternately about the attitudes needed for the monks and those for superiors.

The common search for God's will (*RB Prologue* and ch. 3)

In its first words, the Prologue presents a dialogue between the disciple and his '*Master*':

> *Listen, my son, to the precepts of your master and incline the ear of your heart. Willingly accept and effectively carry out the advice of your loving father so that, through the toil of obedience you may return to him from whom you have separated by the sloth of disobedience. To you, then, whoever you may be, my words are addressed who renouncing your own will to do battle under the Lord Christ, the true King take up the strong and bright weapons of obedience.*

The authority is that of a *loving father* and obedience is a weapon in the fight for Christ and against one's *own will*, that is to say, against all within us that is opposed to God. This attitude of constant striving to conform one's thoughts and acts to Christ defines the monk. Chapter 3 then goes on to show that the search for God's will is made into an institution: the whole community, or the elders' council, is regularly called to make that search together.[103] *RB* thus considers the

[102] It is understandable, for example, to have rules for the behaviour in choir, but is it necessary to refer to Scripture for indicating how to blow one's nose (*RM* 48, 7-9) or to quote *Lk*. 10: 16 to ask the brethren to go on an errand outside the monastery? (*RM* 57, 14-16). Examples of this kind could also be found in Pachomian texts.

[103] *RB* 3: 12-13.

Abbot as responsible for the whole of the monastery, assisted, in spiritual direction and temporal affairs, by elders, who are competent and *God-fearing*. For this reason, following Basil and Pachomius, Benedict also adopts the notion of hierarchical collegiality among the spiritual fathers.

Saint Benedict, however, presents his Rule not as a mirror or a model for the monk, but as a *guide*, leading him to God.[104] The Rule is not closed in on itself, but refers constantly to the Word of God.[105]

The Rule tries also to be an echo of the entire Christian monastic tradition, borrowing from it and referring explicitly, in its last chapter, to the examples and writings of the Fathers.[106]

Obedience and love (*RB* 5)

The text of *RB* 5 is borrowed, for the most part, from chapter 7 of *RM*.[107] Saint Benedict leaves out the parts referring to imperfect obedience, the 'broad way', and the fact that the obedient monk is considered not to be responsible for actions done under obedience. For Benedict, the monk should be fervent (or at least want to be so) and be responsible for his own actions.

The chapter starts with joyful enthusiasm:

> *The first step in humility is prompt obedience. This is fitting for those who hold nothing more dear to them than Christ.*[108]

This love results in a consecration of the self to God, a realistic appreciation of the Last Things, and a readiness to respond:

> *Because they have made profession of holy service or for fear of hell or to attain the glory of everlasting life, immediately when something has been commanded by a superior, it is for them as a divine command and they cannot allow any delay in its execution. The Lord says of them, 'As soon as he heard me, he obeyed me.' And he said also to those who are to teach, 'Whoever listens to you listens to me.'*[109]

[104] *RB* 3: 7.
[105] *RB* 73: 2. Let us notice that, at the example of Basil, Benedict, in his Rule, disposes himself to listen to Scripture, letting God's word give the guidance to be followed rather than utilising it to support a solution of his own.
[106] Cf, for example *RB* 9: 8; 48: 15; 73: 2-7.
[107] The chapter 7 of *RM* is made first of a parallel between the obedience of the perfect and that of the imperfect, followed by a second parallel between broad and narrow ways, and finally of a description of the interior qualities of the obedient monk.
[108] *RB* 5: 2.
[109] *Lk*. 10: 16; *RB* 5: 3-6.

This quotation from Luke, repeated a few lines further on, in *RB* 5: 15, appears only in this place in *RB*. Despite the allusion to the teachers which precedes it, *RB*, like Saint Basil, uses it more for underlining the spiritual motivation of the disciple than for strengthening the Abbot's authority.

As in the Prologue, the ardour of love is then expressed by the monk's desire to be rid of his own will to hasten towards eternal life, where Christ attracts him.[110] Obedience becomes thus the *narrow way that leads to life*, casting off selfishness and following Christ. So the monks

> *desire to have an Abbot ruling over them ... [and] imitate the mind of the Lord in his saying, 'I came to do not my own will, but that of him who sent me.'*[111]

Having described these qualities of willingness and zeal, the Rule goes on to list the defects to be avoided so that obedience may be *acceptable to God and agreeable to men*. Such obedience should be given:

> *without fearfulness, without slowness in performance, without half-heartedness or grumbling or an unwilling reply.*[112]

But the overall feeling of the passage is positive: we see the joy of the disciple who obeys *with good will*. For God *loves a cheerful giver.*[113]

The last paragraph speaks of failures. Here, Saint Benedict adds a sentence to the text of *RM*, showing that the way to overcome these is to acknowledge one's fault and do penance to correct it.[114]

> *For if a disciple obeys grudgingly, if he complains not only in words but even in thought, then, although he carries out the order it will not now be acceptable to God, who sees that his heart is grumbling; and for work like this he will get no reward – indeed, he incurs the penalty for grumblers, unless he make amends with penance.*

There is a considerable difference between the notion of obedience, as expressed in this chapter, and simply getting a job done. Saint

---

[110] The example of the unfinished work, sign of this zeal of love, comes probably from Cassian (*Inst.* 4: 12) where the monk Mark, a calligrapher, called by his Abbot, stopped writing, leaving a letter unfinished. But the text of *RB* may also refer to the example of the Apostles: *They dropped their nets immediately, and followed him* (*Mt.* 4: 20).

[111] *Jn* 6: 38, *RB* 5: 12–13.

[112] *RB* 5: 14.

[113] *RB* 5: 16; *Lk.* 10: 16

[114] *RB* 5: 17–19.

Benedict's idea requires a profound attitude of faith and love, which opens the monk to the action of God within him.

For this reason, the monks *live in monasteries and desire to have an Abbot ruling over them*, because they need a superior to obey, in union with Christ, just as the superior needs his brethren, so that he can love and serve Christ in them.[115]

Purification of the heart: Obedience like Christ's, through love (*RB* 7: steps 1–4)

In chapter 7, the first four steps of humility repeat the teaching of *RB* 5, with a more personal touch. The first and second steps deal with purification of the heart. They invite the monk to throw off all that is against God within him: his sins and vices, his own will, and the desires of the flesh. The monk:

> *by his actions will imitate the Lord in his saying, 'I came not to do my own will, but that of him who sent me.'*[116]

> *The third step of humility is that **for the love of God** one should be obedient to a superior in all things, imitating the Lord of whom the Apostle says: 'He was made obedient even unto death.'*[117]

The words *'for the love of God'*, added by Saint Benedict to the text of *RM*, are significant. The love of the Lord, and obedience, are two inseparable realities as far as the disciple is concerned.

The fourth step (*RB* 7: 35–43) deals with the difficulties, which might be found – or imagined – in religious obedience: *'trials, opposition and even abuse'*. The Rule recommends not only patience (like *RM*) but also *'a quiet mind'* which refuses to listen to the bad feelings that spring up naturally on such occasions. Effort is needed so that the monk may:

> *keep a firm grip on patience, and as he endures he should neither grow faint nor run away; even as Scripture says, 'He who stands firm to the end will be saved' (Matt. 10: 22) and again, 'Let your heart take courage and hope in the Lord' (Ps. 26: 14). Further, to show us how a faithful man should suffer all things, however painful, on the Lord's behalf, it gives voice to those who suffer in the words, 'For your sake we are afflicted by death all the day long' (Rom. 8: 36; RB 7: 36–38).*[118]

[115] Cf. D. REES, *Consider your call*, pp. 87–88.

[116] *RB* 7: 32; *Jn.* 6: 38.

[117] *RB* 7: 34; *Phil.* 2: 8.

[118] We find here the theme of the obedience–martyrdom, that *RM* develops at length in its ch. 5 on obedience, a passage omitted by *RB*.

In the context of *RB* 7, these trials are part of God's plan to purify the soul and lead it to the *'love of God which being perfect casts out all fear'*.[119]

The Rule and the customs (*RB* 7, step 8)

The eighth step of humility touches a different aspect of obedience: the observance of the Rule and of customs of the monastery.[120] These recommendations help the monk avoid singularity and conform himself to the common rule. This passage may be an allusion to the ascetic competitions of some Desert Fathers, but also to the recommendation of *RB* 49: 9, which requires that all special penances for Lent be submitted to the Abbot or to the spiritual father, lest they lead to *presumption and vainglory*.

On the other hand, all the monastic systems acknowledge that a way of life, whose details are fixed by experience, creates an environment of peace and self-control, which facilitates the spiritual quest. For that purpose, the customs established by tradition and the examples of the elders have a value that is beyond price.

Reading these steps, we find ourselves in the natural domain of social order. Perhaps Saint Benedict noted this difference from the previous steps, because he does not give any scriptural quotation at this point.[121]

In this chapter, the references to the superior are very rare. Some observances are shown merely as the kind of difficult situation the monks might have to face. We find here again the idea of the Prologue, where obedience is considered before all as a relationship with God, a response to his love of which the Abbot is only one of the mediators.

Dialogue and obedience (*RB* 68)

Dialogue
This short chapter, with its provocative title, *If a brother is set impossible tasks*, is a masterpiece of spiritual psychology, uniting a spirit of

---

[119] *RB* 7: 67.

[120] The text of this step is inspired by a passage of Cassian (*Inst.* 4: 39) concerning the customs established by the Fathers of monasticism and transmitted by the superiors. The *RM* restricted this obedience to the Rule of the monastery and to the teachings of the Abbot. Saint Benedict suppresses the mention of the abbot-teacher and thus comes nearer to Cassian in speaking of the customs in a general way.

[121] In this context also *RM* and Orsisius quote the Scripture only to support the natural authority of the parents and of the elders.

faith with human wisdom. Saint Benedict's answer to the problem of difficult commands is much more delicately shaded than that of Basil or Cassian.[122] *RB* takes the process at its beginning:

> *If it should happen that burdensome or impossible tasks are imposed on one of the brethren he should indeed accept with all meekness and obedience the command of the one who so orders (RB 68: 1).*

The order may have caused a reaction of anger or discouragement. The brother should then make a willing effort to examine the order without passion and even, if possible, try to carry it out. If the difficulty persists, dialogue should begin:

> *But if he sees that the weight of the burden quite exceeds the limits of his strength, he should quietly and at a suitable moment explain to his superior the reasons why he cannot do it, not in a proud way nor with the spirit of resistance, or contradiction (RB 68: 2–3).*

Such a dialogue can be fruitful only if those involved are able to speak together calmly, before God. On the monk's side, besides patience, meekness, and obedience, there should be an attitude of calm, humility, and right-mindedness. The superior should be approached *at a suitable moment*, that is, when it could be expected that he also might be suitably disposed, and not when he is tired, nervous, or in a hurry.

In dialogue, the monk does not have to judge or to criticise the order he has received, but simply to explain:

> *the reasons why he cannot do it, not in a proud way nor with the spirit of resistance, or contradiction (RB 68: 3).*

Saint Benedict, with his habitual desire to be succinct, touches only the difficult aspects of the question. He leaves the obvious unsaid. If one has to approach the superior *at a suitable moment*, it is not just because his way of listening enhances the good dispositions of the monk, but also to allow him to reflect calmly on the reasons given, and find a satisfactory solution to the problem. This is, in fact, the most frequent case.

---

[122] CASSIAN hardly envisaged the dialogue with the superiors. BASIL recommends the dialogue without describing it (*LR* 47: *SR* 119). The sentence ending this last text and a passage of the *Admonitio ad filium* (6) of the PSEUDO-BASIL seem to be the source of this chapter of *RB*. The first text leaves the decision to the Abbot and asks to avoid the *contradictio* (contending), in the second the disciple asks for a dispensation. Cf. AV, *Entre Basile et Benoît, l'Admonitio ad filium spiritualem* in *REG. BEN STUDIA*, 10/11, pp. 19–34.

Lovingly trust in God's aid

Nevertheless, on occasions, a change of decision will not be possible. Often, it happens that the superior cannot explain all his motives, without breaking charity or discretion:

> **But if after his explanations the one in authority remains firm in requiring what he has ordered, the junior must understand that this is good for him, and let him lovingly trust in God's aid, and so obey (*RB* 68: 4–5).**

The brother has to carry out the order given, knowing that this act of obedience is good *for him*, that is to say, he will not do any harm to his soul by obeying, even if, objectively, the decision is not the best possible. However, above all, he obeys *lovingly*, like Christ in his passion, *trust[ing] in God's aid*. Such help can sometimes obtain unhoped-for results, developing capabilities in the monk that he himself was unaware of. In all cases, this ought to bring him peace, and help him to progress in intimacy with the Lord.

Without touching on extreme or even fairly hard cases, it is sure that obedience does a great deal to help the monk go beyond his own limitations, and those which may come from his education or family background.

In this chapter, Saint Benedict gives an appropriate place to dialogue and to generosity, inspired by the love of Christ, both for the superior and for the monk who obeys. He thus gives a solution to the problem of obeying in difficult circumstances, a solution that seems to offer the best chance of being both wise, in a human sense, and according to the will of God.

That the brethren obey one another (*RB* 71)

This chapter of *RB* is made of two parts: the first describing the conditions of mutual obedience; the second, an appendix on the manner of receiving reprimands.

Saint Benedict begins by repeating Basil and Cassian's ideas on mutual obedience given because of the example of Christ.[123] He adds, with Cassian, that obedience is a *good*, because it leads to God:

> **The goodness of obedience is not to be shown only through obedience to the Abbot, but the brethren should also obey each other, in the knowledge that by this path of obedience they will draw nearer God (*RB* 71: 1–2).**

[123] Basil *SR* 115–116; Cassian, *Conf.* 16: 6–23.

The concept of mutual obedience seems to be self-evident, and Benedict, like his predecessors, does not linger over describing it. He takes for granted that it implies mutual attention to listen to others and follow their suggestions as far as possible. But experience has shown him that the application of this principle meets with problems, which he here tries to solve.

> *The commands of the Abbot or of the superiors[124] appointed by him must come first and we do not allow personal demands to be attended to before them, but otherwise all the younger monks should obey the older ones with all love and care. And if anyone is found to be contentious, he should be corrected (RB 71: 3–5).*

The rule asks, first, to take care that this exchange of obedience may not disturb the good order of the monastery, as laid down by the Abbot and his officers, and meant to help the brethren to search for God in peace. Hence, their orders should have precedence over all others. Then, in general,[125] everyone should submit to those in authority *with all love and care*, the juniors being disposed to obey, and those in charge, to listen to their helpers. Thus each one, without troubling the community, will be able to yield to the others, in the domain left to the initiative of each officer. All will then *forestall one another in paying honour* as the next short chapter puts it.[126]

The second part of the chapter seems to be a commentary, added as an afterthought to the warning that ends this passage. It aims at wiping out quickly the irritation that one may have caused, even unintentionally, to another, the way of expressing repentance and humility being adapted to places and times. The last lines refer to the usual process of corrections:

> *And if, for any reason at all, a brother is corrected in any way by the Abbot or by an elder, or if he perceives that the feelings of any elder have been roused to anger against him, even slightly, he should at once and without delay prostrate himself at his feet and lie there in sign of reparation until the rift is healed by a blessing.*

> *If anyone is too proud to do this, he must either undergo corporal punishment or, if he is contumacious, he must be put out of the monastery (RB 71: 6–9).*

---

[124] In *RB* '*praepositus*' always has the meaning of 'prior'; here it is probably talking about successive priors. Cf. AV *RB* II, p. 668.

[125] Along with several authors, I think that *de cetero* has here the sense of 'as a rule'.

[126] *RB* 72: 6. The same question was put to Saint Basil; he answers in a similar way in *SR* 303, and moreover insists on the conformity of the order given with the law of God.

Other passages of *RB* on the relations between monks and superiors

On the monks' side, obedience is seen as related to spiritual progress, as a means of renouncing one's own will, pride, or attachment to material things.[127] But, as a whole, these passages underline two important points:

Sharing of responsibility

Obedience is recommended to all officers, but is never presented as a minute control of their activity. Saint Benedict wants all officers to be *sound in judgement* and *God-fearing*, so that the Abbot can *share his burdens with them* and even his fatherhood.[128] Just as he desires that everything should be arranged in the way defined by the superiors, for the peace of the community, so he also gives each monk full responsibility for his work.

Saint Benedict's peace

PAX, peace, this Benedictine motto defines the atmosphere created by religious obedience in the monastery. The contrary vice is murmuring. Saint Benedict reminds the superiors to avoid giving *justification for grumbling*, just as often as he asks the brethren to abstain from it.[129] This requires a common effort to help and understand each other, to make peace and pray for each other. At Vespers and Lauds, all pray the Our Father together, precisely for this purpose. The monk also *is not to give way to anger, not to cherish an opportunity for displaying [his] anger, not to preserve deceit in [his] heart, and after a quarrel to make peace with the other before sunset.*[130] Such seeking of God's will together, in a spirit of love and collaboration (between the brethren themselves, and between them and the superior) is nothing less than the following of Christ in his obedience to his Father. This will create a family spirit and peace in the community, that peace which is one of the hallmarks of a Benedictine house.

[127] Obedience as opposed to own will: *RB* 58 (vow of obedience), 49 (Lent), 33 (clothes) etc.; to pride: 65 (prior), 31 (cellarer), 62 (priests); material goods 33 (depossession), 54–55 (gifts, clothes).

[128] *RB* 21: 3; 31: 2; 53: 22; 66: 1. The sharing in the Abbot's responsibility is not weakened by the fact that *RB* entrusts to the Abbot duties which now belong to other officers: giving the signal for prayer, or the distribution of clothes. According to the needs of each culture, some things have more or less importance. This example shows also how the Abbot's work can vary from one region to another.

[129] *RB* 41: 5. The recommendation to avoid murmuring is given five times to superiors and seven times for the brethren.

[130] *RB* 13: 12–13; 4: 22–25; 73.

6. AN OVERVIEW

Points common to all religions

In the beginnings of the different monastic systems, we find master–disciple relationships. The disciples willingly obey their spiritual master, as their guide and physician. They trust him to lead them to union with the Absolute by curing them of the vices that obstruct their progress, especially pride and sensuality.

Relations with the spiritual master vary according to the conception he has of the Absolute. Christians are among those who consider the human master as the person who leads them to the Supreme Master, the *Sat-guru*, the one who helps them to reach union with him, in a love and knowledge without limits. All masters belong to a tradition that defines their doctrine.

Another common point is that the diverse traditions refer to an Infinite, or to a beneficent supra-human order, the final destiny of human beings. The sages of all religions have put this order into concrete form, through codes of living that the master should both respect and teach.[131] The Rules of Christian monasticism thus refer to the *divine commandments*, expressed in Holy Scripture.

Beside this relationship between disciple and master, cenobitic life shows that there are also social duties to be performed towards a group or the authority in charge of its organisation. The motives for submission to these rules are the smooth progress of the community and harmony between its members. They are the necessary conditions for ensuring that each one has a suitable environment for his spiritual quest and a guarantee of respect for the law. It is worth noting that all masters, even the Christian ones, invoke the respect due to parents or to the leaders of society rather than a divine authority.

Nevertheless, the confusion of spiritual principles, based on divine law, with the order necessary for the smooth running of a group, is also a common fact. It is always an abuse if a divine authority is invoked to justify points of detail, or, conversely, when *divine commandments* are minimised, in service of human needs. It is comparatively easy to accept unpleasant material directions for the common good, but when one pretends to make divine law out of them, this can be damaging and hurtful. (This does not stop the Christian from doing every action out of love for God.) Another unhappy consequence of this confusion is the

---

[131] The West has a tendency to personalise everything (we speak of the bell which 'calls' us) and what with us is considered as a fault against obedience, is seen in the East as a breach of etiquette.

replacement of real formation through the spiritual master with mere conformity to regulations.

More specific to monastic life are the rules and customs of each religious group. The first motive for observing them is that, by conforming to detailed rules on a daily basis, one becomes trained in self-control. Such conformity also helps to promote an atmosphere of order, tranquillity, respect of persons and of things which, in turn, facilitates concentration. Similarity between observances in different monastic systems shows that these details were not settled haphazardly, but were rather the fruit of the experience and psychology of successive generations of spiritual masters, an experience often confirmed by modern psychologists.[132]

Authority and obedience in Christianity

The specificity of Christianity is in its reference to Christ, who is both God and man. As God, he is the authority; it is he, present in the superior and in the brethren, that the monk obeys. That is why the fathers insist that superiors' orders must conform to *the divine commandments*.[133] As man, Jesus is *the Way*: it is in imitation of him, and with him, that the monk obeys the Father. Joy, patience, and kindness come from him, but also boldness and strength, which find their limit only in a death on the cross. More than a mere ascetical exercise, obedience becomes for the Christian *a good*, an act of love for God and for humanity, a participation in the redemptive mission of Christ.

In Christianity, the master–disciple relationship is transformed into a tripartite one, where the most important person is the Lord. More than transmitting his own experience, the Christian master should help his disciple to discover where God is calling him. Nevertheless, Christ's incarnation makes the work and the organisation of the monastery into important elements of sanctification. The superior is thus also required to manage material things, which usually is not the case for spiritual masters in other religions.

Another difference concerns the relationships in community. All cenobitic forms of monastic life cultivate kindness and peace as

---

[132] Examples are given by J. E. BAMBERGER in his translation of the *Praktikos* of EVAGRIUS. Christians can note that many usages go back to Saint Pachomius and the Desert Fathers. So when a custom becomes out of date, it may be good to find out its origin and meaning, and thus find a new way of expressing it. An arbitrary suppression of a custom is often experienced as a loss for the life of the community.

[133] It is remarkable that when *RB* speaks of obedience, the greater number of the passages refer to God and not to the superior.

favourable conditions for the spiritual quest. For the Christian, it is of great importance that relations with authority should be coloured with mutual obedience, which acknowledges and loves Christ in each person.

Saint Benedict's special characteristics

What characterises Saint Benedict's Rule, in comparison with his predecessors', is the emphasis on the love of God as experienced in the relations of the monks with their superiors. Obedience is a duty common to all, and it is an expression of their love for the Lord. It is a virtue, a permanent disposition of the heart for all who want to respond to God's love following Christ's example. Scripture teaches such conformity to Christ, as does the Rule, which takes it as a pattern, and the superiors, who have to apply it. But it is above all the Holy Spirit, who shows each individual conscience the duty of the present moment.

Authority, for Saint Benedict, should try to align the community with the divine plan. It should take care of the harmony of the whole community, giving real responsibility to each member, at his own level, and taking care of the weak. In case of difficulty, dialogue is necessary, not just for finding a compromise between the desire of the superior and that of the monk, but to shed light on the situation so that they can see what the Lord wants. Then, even if it pains him, the monk is asked to *obey lovingly, trust[ing] in God's aid*, and knowing that it is often just as painful to the superior to ask difficult things, as it is to the monk to carry them out.

To summarise: Saint Benedict sees the relationship between the authority and the monk as a collaboration, in finding out and following God's will.

The submission of the disciple to his master, found in all religions, invites the Christian to acknowledge the illusions of his own will, and the necessity of a guide, if he is to make progress in the spiritual life.

CHAPTER VII

CONTROL OF SPEECH AND THOUGHTS

Silence, and control of one's thoughts, are monastic observances found, in various ways, in most religions. The common ground of these practices, and the differences between them, show how important the mastery of the tongue and the thoughts is in the spiritual journey, although each religion maintains its proper characteristics.

1. SILENCE IN HINDU MONASTICISM

Ancient texts and present practice show that silence holds an important place in the Hindu monk's life. Mastery of speech, fasting, and withdrawal from the world are important parts of a novice's ascetic discipline.[1] In the *Rig Veda*, the monk is even called *muni*, the silent one,[2] and silence is considered as an attainment of the final stage in the wandering ascetic's life:

> *Living without fire, without home, without pleasures or protection, he remains silent, opening the mouth only for reciting the Veda, going to villages to beg just enough to stay alive; he leads a wandering life, caring, yet free from all care.*[3]

The *Laws of Manu* give similar indictions, adding that:

> *His speech should be purified by truth, and his mind kept pure.*[4]

---

[1]   Cf. *Chandogya Up.* 8: 5.
[2]   *Rig Veda*, 10: 136.
[3]   *Apastamba Dharma Sutra*, 2, 9: 21, 10.
[4]   MANU. 6: 46–48.

He has also to bear insults without replying, controlling his anger, taking delight only in God's presence and in the desire of union with him, through the final liberation. The aim of this discipline is thus to avoid error in speech through anger or lies, which threaten to lead the disciple towards the world of illusion.

Thus the wise guru

> *wants to make his disciple more and more silent inside himself. He teaches him to withdraw from the objects perceived by the senses, or springing up from his imagination, and to fix his attention instead on a single point, repeating the name of God without ceasing. Later, when the disciple has become sufficiently free from desire, and has tasted something of this interior silence, the guru teaches him the supreme science of Brahman, so that he comes to know the Truth, the imperishable man beyond death.*[5]

This quest involves the whole person. Thus, many Hindu ascetics spend long periods either in solitude, in wandering, or as a hermit. Some even take a vow of silence, which lasts sometimes for several years. In fact, the *Brihadaranyaka Upanishad* says:

> *Let the wise, that is, those who know Brahman, demonstrate his presence in their actions, by their wisdom. Let them not use many words, for in speech is mere weariness.*[6]

In the *Upanishads* on the ascetic life, control of speech is required for concentration. Silence, as such, is rarely mentioned, but is considered to result from meditation:

> *[The ascetic], deeply meditating on his own self, keeps silence ... forgetting any other thing because of his absorption in the Self.*[7]

The final motive for silence is the quest of Ultimate Truth, that is, the Divine Presence hidden under the surface of things. Deep reflection is required to discover it; that is why silence is essentially linked with meditation:

> *One should meditate in silence on the Divine Presence, as on that in which everything is, lives, and dissolves. Jut as those who do not know where the treasure lies hidden in the field, pass over it repeatedly without discovering it, so all beings spend their life, day after day,*

[5] ABHISHIKTANANDA, quoted in *BULLETIN DE L'AIM*, 21, 1976.
[6] *Brihadaranyaka Up.* 4: 4, 21.
[7] *Turiyatitavadhuta Up.* transl. from UR, p. 268. Cf. *Narada-prarivrajaka Up.* 5: 21–22.

without finding in themselves the world of God, because they are wrapped in unreality ... The name of God is Truth.[8]

The Katha *Upanishad* describes this process:

Beyond the senses are their objects.
Beyond the objects is the intellect.
Beyond the intellect is the Great.
Beyond the Great is the Unmanifest ...[9]

Word or thought cannot reach it
Nor sight.
Nor does it allow itself to be perceived
Save by saying, 'It is'.[10]

This '*It is*' is not merely a spoken word, but signifies the experience, the *realisation*, of contact with the Infinite in the depth of the being. The vehicle used for entering the great interior silence is in general the repetition of a *mantra*, above all the syllable *Aum*, the divine name, summary of all sounds. *Aum* is the boat that allows a person to cross over to the *other shore*, to the cave, or lotus of the heart, the dwelling of the divinity.[11]

AUM is the bow: the atman is the arrow:
Brahman, they say, is the target, to be pierced
By concentration. Thus, one becomes
United with Brahman, as an arrow with the target.[12]

The image of the arrow and the target comes quite naturally when describing the quest for union with the Absolute. It is used in Zen and by Saint Gregory of Nyssa. It is probably the expression of a deep experience, quite similar in the different religious, though conceptualised in various ways according to the cultures and the creeds. We shall see it in Buddhism.

2. SILENCE IN BUDDHIST MONASTICISM

The mastery over speech is included in the ten rules of good behaviour required of the Buddhist novice when he joins the monastery; the

[8] *Chandogya Up*. 3: 14, 1; 8: 3, 1–4.
[9] The Unmanifest means *Prakriti*, the divine energy from which the world was born.
[10] *Katha Up*. 3: 10–11 ... 14. Cf. BG 6: 8–15.
[11] Cf. *Maitri Up*. 6: 28.
[12] *Mundaka Up*. 2: 2, 4.

monk also promises to avoid violence towards others in thoughts, words and actions, especially lies and deceit. All that is a part of the custody of the senses which prevents the body from becoming lax and helps to avoid what is against chastity.[13] The Rule even foresees that the master should teach the youngsters how to behave. According to the *Vinaya*, this rule was taken because some lay persons complained, saying:

> *They do not wear their robes in the correct manner. They walk in the village talking and laughing. They stay in the refectory, speaking and making noise during the meals.*[14]

Self-mastery is not only a matter of decency; rather it is intended to foster the spiritual quest by creating a suitable atmosphere. Many other texts belonging to the various Buddhist schools speak of this. The *Lotus of the Good Law* says, for example:

> *When he is alone, busy reading, in a place far from all men, in the forest or on the mountains, then I shall show him my luminous form, or I shall restore with my own mouth whatever he has passed over, by mistake, in his reading.*[15]

Like the Hindu, the Buddhist monk seeks indeed to control his thoughts in order to go beyond the senses. However, his strong feeling of belonging to a community leads him to seek above all the interior solitude. The Buddha considered that a stay in the forest could be useful for some monks, though not for all. It is said that he once told a hermit:

> *Thera, you live well in this solitary way. Nevertheless, I shall tell you of another method through which solitude can be accomplished in all its details: Here, all that is passed should be abandoned. All that can be done in the future should be abandoned. Desire and concupiscence, in the present state, should be well mastered. In this way, Thera, the true ideal of solitude can be accomplished in all its details.*[16]

Similarly, the Buddha prohibited his monks from taking the vow of silence, which seemed to him a foreign practice, coming from other groups and harmful for the unity of the community.[17]

[13] Cf. *Vinaya*, 1: 56, ff.

[14] *Vinaya*, 1: 44, *Mahavagga*.

[15] Transl. from *Lotus de la Bonne Loi*, p. 144. ed Maisonneuve, 1973.

[16] *Samyutta Nikaya*, 2: 232. *Theranama-Sutta*, transl. from M. WIJAYARATNA, *Le moine bouddhiste selon les textes du Theravada*, p. 127.

[17] *Vinaya*, 1: 159.

Instead, the various Buddhist schools have elaborated numerous forms of meditation which tend to purify the mind from the illusions of the sensible world, in order to awaken it to the true nature of being. This is brought about by pacifying mind and body, through a strict control of the thoughts, in order to go beyond intellectual reflection, and begin a silent contact with the deep Reality hidden in all beings. Using one of several methods, which often imply the recitation of a *mantra*, the attention is concentrated on an ever smaller field, which finally disappears, being replaced by *Nirvana*, the *Void*, the non-qualified, Supreme Reality, Ocean of Peace, in which the disciple wishes to be immersed for an eternity of happiness. This is the supreme fruit of silence.

Let us end with an old text that summarises well the attitude of Buddhist monks towards silence:

> *It is good to control the eye. It is good to control the ear. It is good to control the nose. It is good to control the tongue. It is good to control the body. It is good to control the speech. It is good to control the mind. In all these cases, control is good. The* Bikkhu *[monk] who controls himself in this way is free from suffering. The* Bikkhu *who controls his tongue and restrains his speech, is not swollen with pride, and interprets clearly the doctrine. His words are sweet ...*
>
> *The one who has no concentration has no wisdom either. The one who has both concentration and wisdom is really close to* Nirvana. *The* Bikkhu, *who pacifies his mind in solitude, tastes a superhuman joy, while clearly perceiving the doctrine.*
>
> *A man is his own protector. (Who else can be his protector?) So, control yourself, as the merchant controls his rearing horse. Full of joy, and carried by the Buddha's message, the* Bikkhu *reaches the tranquil state, the happy calm of those who have undergone such conditioning. Even a young* Bikkhu, *who dedicates himself to the doctrine of the Sublime Awakened, illuminates the world like the moon emerging from the clouds.*[18]

It is thus obvious that there are many points common to both Hindus and Buddhists, on the subject of silence. Mastery of the tongue is part of the ascesis necessary to control the passion, avoid the illusions of this world, and look for what is essential. Silence fosters an atmosphere favourable to the spiritual quest, and the finding of wisdom. Concentration, helped by the recitation of a *mantra*, leads to control of thoughts. By passing beyond them, the disciple is enabled to touch the Absolute and bask in its peace.

There are many schools of practice in both religions. Nevertheless,

---

[18] *Dhammapada*, 25.

silence in Hinduism is seen in a more personal way, and many ascetics take a vow of silence for longer or shorter periods.

The Buddhists, on the other hand, give greater importance to the community. Meditation is often prepared by psalmody in common, and helped by an atmosphere of silence, calm and order in the monastery.

3. SILENT PRAYER IN ANCIENT EGYPT

Before considering Christian monasticism, we should be aware that, in Egypt (the country where it started) many centuries before the coming of Christ, people used to spend time in the caves of the desert near Thebes. They were going into solitude *to see Ammon*, or the goddess Meret Seger, *who liked silence*. This custom derived from a long tradition: ancient papyri were already inviting people to silent prayer, coming from the heart:

> *Do not multiply words,*
> *Keep silent if you want to be happy,*
> *Do not raise your voice in the peaceful house of God,*
> *He hates shouting.*
>
> *When you pray with a loving heart,*
> *A prayer whose words are hidden,*
> *He gives you what you need,*
> *He hears what you say,*
> *And accepts your offering.*[19]

Let us conclude with this prayer to the God, *Tot*:

> *O Tot, you are a delicious well*
> *For those who are exhausted in the desert,*
> *A well that remains closed to the talkative,*
> *But which opens itself to the silent.*
> *When the silent man comes near,*
> *The well reveals its existence,*
> *When the noisy person arrives*
> *You stay hidden.*[20]

This tradition of silent retreat was continued through the centuries. According to Philo, the Jews had a similar practice, spending time in

---

[19] Papyrus Cairo, 4: 1–2, Transl. from *HERMES* 4, p. 17.
[20] Cf. A. SHORTER, *Prayer in the Religious Tradition of Africa*, No. 88.

silence, near Alexandria, at about the beginning of the Christian era. Having left the world:

> *They sought solitude, with fervour ... stirred up by a passionate desire of the eternal and blessed life.*[21]

Staying in their cells, they meditated on Scripture:

> *In order to apply continually their mind to God ... Therefore, during the week, they lived each one separate from the others, in their hermitages ... without crossing the threshold of the door, without even looking through the window.*[22]

On the Sabbath day, they came together for prayer.

It is important to see that, in retiring into the desert to pray, the first Christian monks of Egypt were not doing anything unusual in the eyes of their contemporaries. Nevertheless, they did have their own particular motive for doing it.

4. SILENCE IN CHRISTIAN MONASTICISM BEFORE SAINT BENEDICT

It seems likely that Christian monasticism received some of its characteristic forms from other religions, though its immediate source is the Gospel.

THE NEW TESTAMENT

It has been often remarked how Jesus' birth and childhood were shrouded in silence. Not a single word of Saint Joseph, his foster-father, has been recorded. Jesus was born in the middle of the night and, with the exception of the episode of the visit to the Temple in his twelfth year (*Luke* 2: 41–52), the Evangelists are totally silent about the first part of his life. It is stated that he started his ministry with a retreat of forty days in the desert, and during his public ministry all note that he retired in solitude to pray.[23] According to Luke (who mentions it at least five times) it is clear that it was the Lord's habitual way of life:

---

[21] Philo, *De Vita Contemplativa*, 24: 13.
[22] Philo, Ibid. 26: 30.
[23] Cf. *Mk*. 1: 35; *Mt*. 14: 24; *Lk*. 5: 15; 6: 2; 9: 18, 28–29; 11: 11; *Jn*. 6: 15: 20.

Talk of him spread increasingly ... but he would steal away from the multitudes into the desert, and pray there (Luke 5: 15).

Among Jesus' disciples, silent prayer is presented as a meditation on his words and example. Mary, his mother, *kept in her heart (Luke 2: 51)*, the words and mysterious actions of her son; and another Mary, sister of Martha:

has chosen the better part ... taking her place at the Lord's feet, she listened to his words. (Luke 10: 39–42).

Saint Paul prepared for his missionary journeys by a stay of three years in the desert of Arabia (*Gal. 1: 17–18*).

These few examples have been used, right up to our own days as models for Christian monastic life: the hidden life in Nazareth; Jesus praying on the mount; the Virgin Mary meditating on his words; and Mary, sister of Martha, who *chose the better part.*

A more thorough study of the two Testaments shows the ambivalence of these notions of silence, solitude, and desert. In some cases, they are considered as privileged places of encounter with God: theophanies in the presence of Moses or Elijah on the mountain; or the disciples on Mount Tabor, solitary places where God speaks to the heart.[24]

However, these places are also considered as a symbol of death, of chastisement, of desolation: the unfaithful towns become a desert, enemies are reduced to silence. The desert is still the abode of demons, a place of trial and suffering: the forty years of wandering in the desert; or the forty days of Jesus in solitude before his public life.

This double aspect (both ascetic and mystical) of silence, already found in non-Christian monasticism, continued in the Christian form, where the monk is considered not only as a contemplative, but as a *soldier*, a *fighter*. Words like these were dear to the Desert Fathers, as we shall see.

THE DESERT FATHERS

When the first Christian monks withdrew into the desert, they were seeking freedom from the worries of the world, and wanted to practise, to the letter, the Evangelical counsel to *pray continually*. Saint Arsenius's motto *Flee, keep quiet, seek peace*, is a typical example of this attitude.[25] Saint Antony, the 'Father' of monks, could both pray

[24] Hos. 2: 16; *Mt.* 6: 6.
[25] *Apophthegmata*, Arsenius 2.

continually and work the whole day, because he was very attentive to the word of God, read each Sunday at Mass, and had a good memory, which, for him, was a substitute for books.[26]

The Desert Fathers feared unguarded speech like a mortal enemy. Abba Agatho said about it:

> *It is like a violent and burning wind. When it rises, all flee before it, and it dries up all the fruits on the trees ... No passion is more dreadful than unguarded speech, for it is the source of all the passions.*[27]

Many *apophthegmata* (Sayings of the Fathers) talk of controlling speech: Abba Poemen, for example, said:

> *It is written: 'for those who answer before listening, foolishness and shame. If you are asked, speak, if not, keep silent.'*
> *To another brother, he said: 'If you are silent, you will find rest, wherever you live.'*[28]

Despite their silence, it is by their *Sayings*, the *Apophthegmata*, that the Desert Fathers are known to us, and are still useful. They give words of wisdom, inspired by the Scriptures, which point towards God. The hermits' silence was filled with these *words of life*, which bring the Word of God to bear on every life situation.

This silence, however, was not tense. Many stories praise the cordial hospitality of the Fathers. If Abba Arsenius, a Roman noble, was a model of austerity, the pleasant Abba Moses, a black Ethiopian and a former robber, was considered his equal. On one occasion, some brothers had visited both of them, one after the other: Arsenius remained absorbed in his prayer, and said nothing to the visitors. Abba Moses, on the other hand:

> *received them with joy and sent them back after having given them heartfelt hospitality ... One of the Fathers came to hear of this, and made this prayer: 'Lord, please explain to me why one of them shuns men, because of your name, while the other welcomes them with open arms, because of your name'. Then, in a dream, he saw two boats sailing side by side, on the river. In one, he saw Abba Arsenius, in contemplation with the Spirit of God. In the other, Abba Moses was with the angels of God, who served him honey cakes.*[29]

---

[26] ATHANASIUS, VA, 1.
[27] *Apophthegmata*, Agatho, 1.
[28] *Apophthegmata*, Poemen, 45; 85; cf. 37; 42; 47; Syncletica, 1; Epiphanius, 12.
[29] *Apophthegmata*, Arsenius, 38.

In general, the Fathers emphasised the necessity of controlling thoughts, for:

Malice springs out of letting go one's thoughts.[30]

The Fathers became famous because of the interior struggle that leads to silence. They wanted to reach union with God, and the main means was prayer, nourished by Scripture. Abba Isaiah said:

Do not despise the Psalms, for they expel the impure spirits from the soul, and introduce it to the Holy Spirit.[31]

In this way, the words of Scripture, pondered continually in the heart:

open it to the fear of God, as water, falling drop by drop, bores a hole in a stone.[32]

SAINT PACHOMIUS

Saint Pachomius founded several monasteries of cenobites. His Rules deal mostly with the relations between members of the community, and the ideals that ought to govern them. One of his first teachings, to his young disciple Theodore, is about the control of thoughts:

Make haste to produce the fruit described in the Gospel: 'Blessed are the pure in heart, for they shall see God'. If some bad thought comes in your heart, be it hatred, wickedness, jealousy, envy, contempt towards your brother, or human vainglory, be aware immediately, and say: 'If I consent to one of these things, I shall not see the Lord'.[33]

A similar control is required for actions and speech and for the custody of the eyes:

Do not look at another plaiting ropes or praying, but each one be attentive to his own work, keeping the eyes down ...
One should not look curiously at what the others are eating, nor serve oneself before the superior.[34]

When the brethren went from their house to the church, refectory, or

[30] *Apophthegmata*, Orsisius, 2; cf. Syst. Coll. 11: 4; 33–34; 43; 47; 50; 79.
[31] *Apophthegmata*, Syst. Coll. 11: 33.
[32] *Apophthegmata*, Poemen, 202. For the Fathers *'fear of God'* means a respectful love.
[33] PACHOMIUS, VC *Bo*, 33.
[34] PACHOMIUS, *Praec.* 7; 30.

their work, they had to *meditate something of the Scriptures*. The same thing was established for those who had to ring the bell (or sound the horn) and for those in charge of distribution to the brethren.[35] The Rules also say:

> One who laughs or speaks in the church ... or in the refectory, will receive a penance.[36]

The Rules indicate also the places and times where the silence is particularly needed: that is, during the choir office, during meals, at night, when going from one place to another, during the common work and in all the meeting places of the community.[37] It was also the case during conferences:

> When [Theodore] was sitting, giving a catechesis to the brethren [in small groups], they often asked him questions, because they did not understand them well on account of their depth of meaning. However, when he was standing, nobody asked a question, except the interpreter alone, according to the rule established since the beginning. This is the reason why they were conscientiously attentive to what he said.
>
> They were arranged before him in order of houses, according to the category and the rank of each one. The head of each house stood in front of his men, whereas his assistant was behind them, watching the brethren in case one were missing. They were standing, according to the rule, attentive to the word of God.[38]

Common work proved to be the most difficult occasion for keeping silence, especially at the bakery, when the dough was kneaded. Twice in the *Life of Pachomius*, he is seen to be angry with Theodore, the man in charge, because of breaches in the rules. Nevertheless, the fault continued, leading a young monk to ask Theodore (whom he believed to be a stranger) not to be scandalised.[39]

---

[35] PACHOMIUS, *Praec.* 3; 6; 28; 59; 36–37. It was the same when the brethren were going out in groups to welcome somebody or during work: *One day, when they were on their way back to the boat, all laden with reeds, following our Father Pachomius and reciting the Holy Scriptures, our father, having arrived at the half-way point, looked up to the sky, and received a great revelation. After that, he and the brethren let down their burden of reeds, stood up and prayed.* VC *Bo.* 66. Walking in groups, and singing Scriptures. *Bo.* 138; 202.

[36] PACHOMIUS, *Praec.* 8, 31.

[37] *Praec.* 8; 121 (Choir office); 31; 33 (meals); 88; 94 (nightly); 34 (going from one place to another); 68; 94; 116 (work); 56; 88 and *Praec. et Inst.* 18 (meeting places).

[38] PACHOMIUS, VC *Bo.* 188.

[39] PACHOMIUS, VC *Bo.* 74; 77; *S.* 5.

In all these texts, Pachomius aimed to stop the dissipation that would be caused by worldly conversation and laughter. Taken as a whole, we get the impression that silence was strict when the whole community was assembled, but small groups, at home or at work, could reflect together on Scripture, or exchange ideas on religious matters.[40]

The reason always given for keeping silence is the necessity for the monk to *meditate or recite some passages of the Scriptures.*[41] The importance given to the Scripture was such that a monk began to learn it by heart from the time of his postulancy:

> *If someone arrives at the monastery desiring to renounce the world in order to be admitted among the brethren . . . he will be taught the Lord's Prayer and what he is able to learn from the Psalms. He will stay in the doorkeeper's house for his probation.*[42]

The *Life* also notes that *the Holy Gospels of Christ were learnt by heart.*[43]

Scripture thus learned and recited, alone or in community, led quite naturally to silent contemplation. Nevertheless, in the *Life of Pachomius*, nearly all Scripture quotations are presented as models of a virtue to be practised, or an example to be followed.[44] The Word of God thus becomes a source of comfort and action. One of the main roles of the superior and officers was *to direct the Word of God to the brethren, using the Sacred Scriptures.*[45] If a Head of House detected some sadness in one of the brethren entrusted to his care, he had to meet him to see what was wrong.[46] Brother Titus comforts the sorrowing Theodore:

> *On his advice he stood, prayed, and took a book [of Scripture] . . . He was thus encouraged by the way the Lord had comforted him, through the intermediary of the prophet.*[47]

The officers should have their tongues *seasoned with salt*, that is,

---

[40] PACHOMIUS, *Praec.* 19; 60.
[41] PACHOMIUS, *Praec.* 28; 59–60; 119; 122.
[42] PACHOMIUS, *Praec.* 99; 139. That rule says '*20 Psalms, or two Epistles of the Apostle, or another part of Scripture.*'
[43] PACHOMIUS, VC *Bo.* 104.
[44] PACHOMIUS, VC *Bo.* 35, work for the poor; 48, charity; 64, obedience; 98 Humility and service; 100 ff. prayer for all the needs; 105, mutual service; 118; Saint Paul model of pastor, 125, trust in God, etc.
[45] PACHOMIUS, VC *Bo.* 193.
[46] PACHOMIUS, *Praec et Judi.* 11.
[47] PACHOMIUS, VC *Bo.* 94, cf. 187.

according to Saint Paul: *to be able to give the right answer (Col. 4: 6).*[48]

Similarly, superiors and their assistants should show *affability and compassion*, and give the word that *feeds the souls* and *cures the heart of those who suffer.*[49]

Pachomius's intention was thus that mastery of thoughts and tongue would lead to a silence filled with the memory of the Scripture; reflection on the word of God would be continued in silent contemplation, but also by words which convey God's grace and forgiveness. In this way, the relation of love that unites the community and leads to God is built up.

SAINT BASIL

In Saint Basil's Rules, silence is the usual atmosphere of the monastery.[50] It also results from control of speech, required from the novice from his entrance into the monastery:

> It is good for newcomers to practise silence. In giving tangible proof of their self-control by mastering their tongue, they will work zealously, keeping a perfect and constant silence, and learning how to ask and answer from those who know how to speak.
> Tone of voice, discretion in speech, knowing the opportune moment, and words suitable for religious life: all these are among the things they have to learn ... That is why, with the obvious exception of the psalmody, they have to keep silence and speak only when necessary, either for their personal need [spiritual direction], or if really required by an emergency during work, or when they are interrogated.[51]

Other rules give details on the way of speaking during spiritual direction, for the edification of guests, and for peace and charity in the community.[52] Several *Short Rules* condemn gossip and uncharitable words.[53] *Long Rule* 17 condemns loud laughter, but recommends a joyous smile, as a sign of peace and self-control.

In texts dealing directly with silence, Saint Basil links it rather to self-mastery and temperance. The joyful and peaceful atmosphere he aims at is meant to foster the prayer, which, for him, as for Saint Pachomius, should *constantly accompany* work.[54] Though this aspect

[48] PACHOMIUS, VC *Bo.* 26–27 (doorkeeper, and elder in charge of the nuns).
[49] PACHOMIUS, VC *Bo.* 32; 63; 70; 132–133; 140.
[50] BASIL, SR 173.
[51] BASIL, LR 13.
[52] BASIL, LR 45 (spiritual direction); 32 (guests); 47 (peace).
[53] BASIL, SR 25–29.
[54] BASIL, LR 37.

is always present in his thought, he does not develop it, because it had been overemphasised by the heretical tendencies of some ascetics of his time.[55] The true expression of his feelings is given in the writings of his friend and spokesman, Saint Gregory Nazianzen, or of his brother, Saint Gregory of Nyssa. Here are some verses of a well-known poem of Saint Gregory Nazianzen:

> *O you, who are beyond all –*
> *This is the only thing that we can sing about you.*
> *What hymn, what language could express you?*
> *No word can express you.*
> *Can the mind find anything to cling to?*
>
> *For you exceed all intelligence.*
> *You stand alone, inexpressible*
> *All that is said, comes from you ...*
> *All that is, prays to you.*
> *Towards you, all beings,*
> *Reflecting on your Universe,*
> *Lift up a hymn of silence.*[56]

SAINT AUGUSTINE

In Saint Augustine's Rule there are only a few allusions to silence. Nevertheless he recommends silence during meals, to focus attention on the reading, and silence during work. Gossip and murmur are condemned, whereas the monk ought to speak when necessary, either because his work demands it, or for the good of his own or of his brother's soul, especially in fraternal correction.[57] It is mostly in his spiritual teaching that Saint Augustine deals with silence and useless words. If there is need of speaking, it should refer to the Lord; anything else is mere useless gossip.

> *What do they say when they talk about You? And woe to those who are silent about You, for though they keep silent, they speak.*[58]

True Christian silence is filled with God's Word. Saint Augustine shows, in his commentaries on Scripture, how such a silence nourishes the soul of the Christian, and transforms his heart into Christ's

---

[55] The Eustathian and Messalian currents advocated continual prayer and rejected work. Saint Basil always resisted their ideas.
[56] Transl. from French *Prière du temps présent*.
[57] Cf. A. WATHEN, *Silence*, in *CIST STUD* 22, p. 141.
[58] AUGUSTINE, *Confessions*, I: V, 4.

image. Therefore, it is necessary gradually to cultivate silence in oneself, in order to reach the interior *tabernacle, God's sanctuary*. This progression is described in his commentary on Psalm 41:

> *It was while walking towards the tabernacle that the Psalmist arrived at God's house. Guided by a certain attraction, or an interior, mysterious and hidden pleasure, as if the sound of a very sweet music instrument were emanating from God's house, he, listening as to an interior sound, and leaving behind any noise coming from flesh or blood, reaches up to God's house.*[59]

The same theme is developed in Saint Augustine's *Confessions*, where he describes the experience of ecstasy, at Ostia, during his last conversation with his mother. Gradually quietening the created world, they arrived at a deep silence where, as in a flash, they touched *Eternal Wisdom*:

> *If a person were to silence the tumult of the flesh, to silence the images of earth, waters and air, to silence even the heavens; and if the soul itself were silent, going beyond itself, and thinking no more about itself; if dreams and visions of the imagination were likewise silent; if any tongue and any sign, and all which passes, or happens within a person, were shrouded in absolute silence, – for, if they can be heard, all things say: 'We have not made ourselves but the One who made us stands for ever' – if all these things were to happen: then henceforth they would keep silence, for they would have made our ears attentive to the One who made them, and if He spoke, He alone, and not through them, but by himself, and if He let us hear his word – not through a tongue of flesh nor an angel's voice, nor by a peal of thunder, nor in the enigma of parables – but that He himself, whom we love in them, made himself heard by us, without their aid, –*
> *– then, suddenly, for an instant, we were beyond ourselves, and in the space of a swift thought, we reached the Eternal Wisdom which is above all.*
> *Had this experience been prolonged, and the lesser visions withdrawn from us, and if this one alone were to bring the delight of interior joy to those who contemplate it, and if eternal life were like it was at that moment of understanding, the kind that we long for so, then, surely, this is what is meant, when it says, 'Enter into the joy of your Lord'.*[60]

For Saint Augustine, God is beyond speech, but the silent contact with

---

[59] AUGUSTINE, *In Ps.* 41, 9.
[60] AUGUSTINE, *Conf.* IX: X, 25.

him in prayer ends in jubilation. Beyond the words, there is an eternal 'Alleluia'.[61]

> *You were silent while you sought him, can you be silent after finding him? No, such a silence would be ungrateful. You will rather exult. After having tasted something of your God, you understand that it is impossible to express what you feel. Can you keep silent? No! For there is still the exultation.*[62]

Saint Augustine's experience of silence that led to contact with the unspeakable nature of God, in joy and love, echoes that of the Cappadocian Fathers, Saint Basil and his fellow bishops. Cassian describes the same experience, but in a more typical monastic setting.

CASSIAN

The teaching of Cassian on silence is very rich. He has no systematic account of it, but shows its strict connection with prayer in criticising the defects of its opposite. In the course of the *Institutes* and *Conferences*, he distinguishes a virtuous silence from a bad one. This latter type is found when a person refuses to enter a relationship with a neighbour because of anger, resentment or lack of humility.[63] In such a situation, he is not even willing to open himself to a spiritual father. The result of this type of silence is bitterness, sadness, and the refusal of responsibilities.[64]

Its opposite, virtuous silence, expresses the respect due to God. Silence is kept during meals and conferences, in order to create an atmosphere of recollection, helpful for listening to the reading. Silence is also a sign of humility when all orders, and even offensive remarks, are received in peace. This humility is still shown by the way of speaking and mastering laughter.[65]

Humility, self-mastery, and silence: all these Cassian views as a way towards prayer and meeting with God. After the divine office, each brother:

---

[61] Saint AUGUSTINE underlines the fact that God's nature cannot be expressed in words, in his *Commentary on Saint John*. He says, for example: '*We can say all kinds of things about God, and nothing of what is said fits him*' (*Tract. in Jn.* 5).

[62] AUGUSTINE, *In Ps. 99*, 5–6.

[63] CASSIAN, *Inst.* 8: 11–18; 11: 3–4; 12: 27; *Conf.* 4: 20; 16: 28.

[64] CASSIAN, *Conf.* 2: 11–13 (refusal to open oneself); *Inst.* 9: 1–7 (consequences of *mutism*, i.e. a false way of keeping silent).

[65] CASSIAN, *Inst.* 2: 10 (respect of God); *Inst.* 4: 17: 12: 27; *Conf.* 14: 9; 13 (atmosphere of recollection); *Inst.* 4: 41; *Conf.* 16: 26 (remarks); *Inst.* 4: 39; 12: 29 (laughing).

carries out his task, reciting by heart a Psalm, or a passage of Scripture ... without giving occasion for useless talk. Mouth and heart are constantly united, and busy with spiritual meditation.[66]

In the *Conference* 14, he explains how the refusal of useless thoughts and meditation of Scripture conform the soul to God and make it abide with him:

Having banished all worldly cares and thoughts, try by all means to apply yourself assiduously, or rather continually, to sacred reading, so that this meditation may finally imbue your soul and, so to say, refashion it in its image. It will make it, so to speak, like the Ark of the Covenant.[67]

To reach this concentration, Cassian proposes a method: the repetition of a simple and suggestive formula. He gives as a *model* the verse of *Psalm* 89: '*O God come to my aid, O Lord make haste to help me.*' The mind may feel impoverished by such limitation, but it becomes sharper, as it penetrates, from inside, the meaning of the Scripture, and reaches an ineffable union with God, in which:

The soul, bathed in light from above, makes no more use of human language, which is ever inadequate. Instead, something rises up in it, like a superabundant spring, which overflows from prayer and goes up towards God, in a way beyond all telling.[68]

Also in *Conference* 9, Cassian lets us understand that these sublime feelings are like arriving at the summit of a mountain, or receiving a reward unexpectedly from the Lord for those who constantly strive to repeat and keep the Word of God in their hearts. To avoid succumbing to distractions, such intense prayer should be *frequent and short*. It is to be made either after the recitation of the Divine Office, or during the work, or at night, but always in times of deep silence.

5. SILENCE IN SAINT BENEDICT'S RULE

Saint Benedict, heir of the whole Christian tradition took for granted Cassian's teaching, and makes frequent reference to it. We must keep this background in mind if we want to understand the meaning of the practical arrangements that his literary style imposed on the Rule.

[66] CASSIAN, *Inst.* 2: 15.
[67] CASSIAN, *Conf.* 14: 10.
[68] CASSIAN, *Conf.* 9: 25.

The texts of *RB* on silence

The Rule mentions silence, and control of speech in about twenty chapters.[69] In these instances, we can easily distinguish two groups of words describing silence.[70] Some come from the root that has given the word *silence* to the English language (Lat. *silentium, silere*): they are used in the practical part of the Rule and indicate merely the absence of noise. The other group comes from the Latin *tacere, taciturnitas*. Though used sometimes with the same meaning as the first (as in *RB* 42: 9), they usually designate the virtue of self-control in speech, and are used in *RB*'s first chapters, that is, in the doctrinal part of the Rule. Thus, in chapter 6, *we should refrain even from good conversation because of 'taciturnitas'* that is because of the virtue of control of speech.

The meaning of *'taciturnitas'*

The initial meaning of the Latin word *taciturnitas* for Saint Benedict was the effort made by the disciple to master tongue and thoughts:

At all times monks ought to strive to keep silence,

says the beginning of chapter 42. Progress in keeping silence is one of the points on which the monk is invited to make a special effort during Lent.[71] In the same way, the Prologue and chapter 4 instruct the disciple *to dash the evil thoughts that invade one's heart immediately upon Christ, as upon a rock.*[72]

This effort is intended to help create an atmosphere of peace and recollection in the monastery, which appears to be the main idea behind chapter 6 in which dissipation is condemned and gravity (*gravitas*) recommended, a word often found in this context. *Gravitas* means the kind of behaviour that is expected from a religious person, above all at sensitive moments, such as the necessity of speaking during the night, or with guests, or even the right way of hastening to the monastic choir.[73]

---

[69] Cf. for example *RB* ch. 4; 6; 7; 22; 31; 38; 42–43; 47–49; 52–53; 61; 64–66; 68–69.

[70] Cf. A. WATHEN, *Silence*, pp. 17–19.

[71] *RB* 49; 7.

[72] *RB Prol.* 28; 4: 50.

[73] *Gravitas* is sometimes translated as *the importance of silence*. A de Vogüé remarks, however, that this word in the Rule signifies *seriousness* or *gravity*, a meaning that fits very well here. Cf. AV *RB* II, ch. 6, note 3; *RB* 7; 22; 42; 43; 47; 53.

Such seriousness is not meant to become fraught and strained, but is rather seen as part and parcel of an ambience of charity and mutual kindness, which can be expressed just as well by keeping silence as by speaking, as circumstances may demand. So let us examine what Saint Benedict says about speaking to get a better understanding of the kind of silence he invites the monk to keep.

How to make good use of speaking

In the monastery, the person who normally would have the most to say is the Abbot. He has to teach, to advise, to encourage, to correct, and to give orders. However, he does not do so in his own name. He is *in the place of Christ in the monastery* (*RB* 2: 2) and the word of Jesus *'the one who listens to you, listens to me'* is applied to him (*RB* 5: 6). For his duty is *to take care for the brethren* (*RB* 27: 1), and direct souls towards God (*RB* 2: 31). *Therefore*, continues Saint Benedict, *he should not teach or ordain or command anything that lies outside the Lord's commands* (*RB* 2: 4) and must *in every respect keep this present Rule* (*RB* 64: 20).

Several officials assist the Abbot in his work. In their hands *let God's house be wisely cared for by wise men* (*RB* 53: 22). But the higher they are, the more they should be concerned to be the 'yeast' of charity and good interpersonal relations. Speaking of the prior of the monastery, Saint Benedict indicates that his task will be *the preservation of peace and charity* (*RB* 65: 11). In a similar way, the cellarer, or bursar, should see *that no one be upset or saddened in the household of God* (*RB* 31: 19). He should also speak in a way that promotes calm, courage and comfort. When he is not able to give what he is asked for *let him offer a kind word of reply, as it is written*: *'A good word surpasses the best gift'*.[74]

The brethren may speak among themselves for motives of service or charity, but each one should *set a muzzle over [his] mouth* (*RB* 6: 1) in order to avoid dissipation[75] or the sins of the tongue.[76] More positively, however, Saint Benedict invites all the brethren, and all the officials to know how to give a sensible word: *quietly, without laughter, with*

---

[74] *RB* 31: 13–14, cf. *Eph.* 4: 29: *No base talk must cross your lips; speak only good words, that will serve to build up the faith, and bring grace to those who are listening.*

[75] Gossip, and inappropriate lauhter, are condemned by Saint Benedict and by his predecessors: cf. *RB* 4: 53–54; 6: 8; 7: 59–60; 43: 2.

[76] *RB* 4 gives a full list of the faults to be avoided: anger, deceit, lack of charity, pride, etc. Murmuring is also frequently condemned, cf. *RB* 5: 17–19; 23: 1; 34: 6; 35: 13; 40: 8–9; 41: 5; 53: 18; etc.

humility, with restraint, making use of few words and reasonable ones (*RB* 7: 60). Kind words, given with a smile, and charitable manners, express respect for the seniors and love for the young,[77] and, at the same time, provide a cordial welcome for visitors.[78]

The brethren need also to be able to speak in a mature and fraternal way to elucidate and dispel any misunderstandings that may arise. They ought to be able to address one another so as to *make peace before sunset*, thus pacifying any irritation that they may have provoked.[79] The Rule requests them, above all, to explain to their Abbot or their spiritual father the difficulties they meet in practising obedience, or in their spiritual life.[80]

All these recommendations on control of speech seek to establish in the monastery, and in the soul of each monk, a climate of peace that will facilitate the search for God. They are complemented by other pieces of advice, whose aim is to create spaces of silence as an aid to prayer.

The practice of silence

To keep the atmosphere of gentle gravity fitting to the monastery, Saint Benedict advises times of deep silence placed at the moments where listening to God's words requires the full attention. They take place particularly during the choir office and the following minutes, reading during meals, the time allotted to *lectio divina*, and during the rest in the afternoon or at night, times always used for intense personal prayer.[81] The Rule also asks that the monk avoid giving or asking for things at times which may be inconvenient for others (*RB* 31: 19).

Times of silence are complemented by places of silence: the oratory (so that those who want can freely *go in and pray*); the dormitory (which was, in Saint Benedict's day, the place for *lectio* and rest); and the refectory (so that due attention may be given to the reading).[82]

Control of the tongue, and times of silence, always lead back to the central point of the encounter with God, which is found either in one's neighbour, through the practice of charity, or in listening to the divine word. We will explore more fully the role of silence in this encounter.

[77] *RB* 4: 70; 63: 3–13; 71: 4; 72: 2–11.
[78] *RB* 53: 1–6; 66: 3.
[79] *RB* 4: 73; 71: 6–8.
[80] *RB* 68: 2–3; 4: 50; 7: 44–48.
[81] *RB* 48: 18–20; 42: 1–8; 52: 2.
[82] *RB* 52 (oratory); 22: 6–8; 48: 13–18 (dormitory). In addition to these places mentioned in the Rule, we could add that each house has certain areas where silence should be especially cultivated, for the noise made there is heard everywhere.

Silence and prayer

The first reason for keeping silence, as indicated in *RB* 6 (probably under the influence of *RM*) is to avoid sin. Sin, obviously, leads a person away from God. However, the reason Saint Benedict gives most often for silence is so that we may listen to God. The monks' main dialogue is with God, rather than with the Abbot, officials, and brethren.

God is present in the depths of a person, so if we want to listen to him we have to make silence in ourselves, to *incline the ear of [the] heart* (*RB Prol.* 1), in an attitude of loving respect and humility. It is remarkable that Saint Benedict replaces the complicated ceremonial of the *RM* about asking or giving permission to speak with these attitudes of heart.[83] Thus, in his short chapter on prayer, he insists on *reverence*:

> *We should present our supplications to the Lord God of all things with complete humility and devout purity of mind. Indeed we must grasp that it is not by using many words that we shall get our prayers answered, but by purity of heart and repentance with tears. Prayer, therefore, should be short and pure, unless on occasion it be drawn out by the feeling of the inspiration of divine grace.*[84]

The ideas and vocabulary come from Cassian. Like him, Saint Benedict observes that Christian prayer begins with listening to God's word that can transform the heart. This word becomes ever more simple, finally leading to silent adoration. Such an attitude appears again in the chapter on the oratory of the monastery:

> *When the Work of God has been completed all are to go out noiselessly, ad let reverence for God reign there. So that if a brother should have a mind to pray by himself, he will not be disturbed by the ill-conduct of anyone else. Moreover, also on other occasions, if someone wishes to make a private prayer, let him go in without hesitation and pray, not, however, aloud, but with tears, and the attention of his heart.*[85]

Like Cassian, Saint Benedict knows that *attention of heart* is helped by the repetition of short sentences which concentrate the attention on God and mould the heart according to his Word. Twice in the Rule, he repeats a recommendation similar to that which he gives at the end of the chapter 7:

[83] *RB* 6: 7; cf. 20: 1–2.
[84] *RB* 20: 2–4.
[85] *RB* 52: 2–5.

He should always be saying in his heart what the tax-gatherer in the Gospel said ... or again with the prophet ... thus ... the monk will soon reach that love of God which, being perfect, drives out all fear.[86]

We shall deal with the question of prayer later in this book. For the moment, it is enough to point out here that silence is one of the necessary preconditions for it, and that the most sublime prayer:

springs up to God in a way that cannot be described.[87]

All monastic systems asked their disciples to control their speech and thoughts. They also established times of silence, and wanted to create an atmosphere of peace and mutual kindness, conducive to the spiritual quest.

Such control gives the disciple the opportunity to improve his concentration, so that, through silence, he may eventually reach the Absolute, which is beyond all words. One of the means commonly used to facilitate this concentration is the repetition of a *mantra*: simple words that can unify the mind and carry it towards its goal.

In this spiritual quest, Christianity's original contribution consists in finding God through the love of one's neighbour, as well as in the depths of one's being. It is seen, also, in the fact that concentration in prayer is brought about through meditation on the Word of God, which moulds the soul's internal attitude. The Holy Spirit brings the words of the Scriptures to life; and the soul which meditates on them is transformed by Christ, and united with him, so that he can carry it up towards the infinite and unspeakable love of the Trinity.

On the subject of silence, the Fathers of Christian monasticism, in their Rules, quite naturally stressed the concrete aspect of the observances, though briefly indicating their aim. What is remarkable in Saint Benedict's Rule is both the balance he establishes between silence and speech, and his insistence on the positive aspect of the good word, which makes peace and draws a person nearer to God. This all leads towards the silence of the heart, in which the words of Scripture, meditated and repeated, transform the soul and culminate in the ineffable experience of encounter with God's love.

---

[86] *RB* 7: 65–67; cf. *Prol.* 49; 7: 18.
[87] CASSIAN *Conf.* 9, 25; cf. *RB Prol.* 49.

CHAPTER VIII

HUMILITY: THE PATH OF THE MYSTICS

1. SPIRITUAL PROGRESS

Having dealt with the monastic virtues of obedience and silence individually, Saint Benedict groups them together, in his chapter 7 on Humility, under the form of a programme for the spiritual life. It is also a point of meeting with the great world religions, which always consider pride as one of the principal obstacles to be overcome on the journey towards union with the Absolute. Pride is very often contrasted with obedience and self-control, which are themselves two ways of conquering it.

THE HINDUS

The Hindu *Laws of Manu* had already prescribed that the ascetics:

> *should fear worldliness as if it were poison, and long to be despised as if it were the most delicious nectar.*[1]

Long before Christ, the *Bhagavad Gita* presented a disciplined way of life as the way of attaining divine fullness. That way began with mastery of the passions, and went on to inculcate detachment from the kind of egoistic advantages a person can receive from his actions. All this was to make it possible for the person to grow in the love of God:

> *We may deprive the senses of their object, but the desire still remains in us ... however, even the desire will vanish at the sight of the Supreme*

[1] MANU 2: 162.

One ... O! How willingly I would give myself to the one who does not cease from thinking about me.[2]

The text is punctuated with appeals to the Lord, like this one:

All that you do, all that you eat, all that you offer in sacrifice, whatever penitence you undertake: offer it all to me.[3]

Later, the *Bhakti* (or devotional movement) developed this tendency. Its mystics described their spiritual path in detail. They start with the prayer of petition. Then the devout person rises to a better moral condition, leading to good will towards others. Subsequently, he begins to praise God, finally attaining a humble love in which he confides himself to the Lord, desiring only to be dissolved in him, with peace and spiritual joy. The *Hymn of Tirumular* bears witness to this:

> *Only he who knows*
> *That Shiva is love*
> *And that love is Shiva*
> *Attains peace*
> *Once and for all*
> *With Shiva-Love.*[4]

The evidence suggests that this gift also includes humility, because:

God hates the pride of the one who has confidence in his own works and loves the humility of the one who feels feeble and trusts in God's goodness.[5]

Besides this devotional current, a more metaphysical research developed, following the great theologian Shankara. Nevertheless, the stages described remain substantially the same. Shankara gives eight fundamental precepts that lead to access to God (*Brahman*). These include: the discernment between the transitory and the Absolute; mastery over the passions, senses and mind; the peace of the soul; patience; faith in the sacred writings, and in the guru; and, finally, concentration on God, the one who is:

unchanging, the source of all being and the Reality that sustains the Universe; in him the perfect will always rest.[6]

---

[2] *Bhagavad Gita*, 2: 58, 61; 8: 14.
[3] Ibid. 9: 27; see also 2: 61; 6: 14; 7: 16; 7: 28; 8: 7; 8: 22 ...
[4] Quoted by ABHISHIKTANANDA: *Prayer*, p. 67, note 10.
[5] *Narada Bhakti Sutra*, 27.
[6] SHANKARA, translated in *Selected Works of Shankarasharya, Direct Realisation*, 113, by VANKATARAMANAN.

THE BUDDHISTS

From its origins, Buddhism appeared as a way towards infinite happiness in its attempt to suppress the *desire for transitory things* which cause suffering. The monastic rules of conduct strive to master the senses and the passions. Numerous types of meditation were invented to neutralise the different perceptions and emotions, so that the monk could achieve perfect calm allowing him to go beyond the impermanence of this world and attain *Nirvana*, the absolute quiet of the *Ocean of Peace*.

The best known of these methods follows a path of eight stages or *dyanas*, very close to the thought of Shankara:[7] by attending to the mental representation of an object which supports meditation, the spirit frees itself from sensible objects. Then one moves beyond discursive thought by means of faith, trust and the desire for something that is beyond the senses. The result is a feeling of interior peace and of compassion towards others. Nevertheless, one must move even beyond this sense of well-being, towards purity of spirit and equanimity of emotion; then one tries gradually to increase these feelings to the point where they have no limit. The soul thus becomes *empty*, and touches *Nirvana*, the supreme happiness, in an almost physical way, losing all contact with the physical world in a transitory ecstasy.[8]

The following quotation, from the *Theravada* tradition also called the *Small Vehicle (Hinayana)*, describes the monk who has courageously and perseveringly walked in this way, with perfect detachment, finding, even in this life, an infinite peace:

> *For the one who has finished the journey, who has no more cares, is free of everything, and has destroyed his bondage; for the one in whom the fever of passion is no more ... the pride of self has been eradicated, illusion is shattered. Free from passion, his spirit now shines in splendour ... By his perfect mastery of self, he is victorious over the world.*[9]

The way of the *Great Vehicle (Mahayana)* tries above all to cultivate compassion towards other people, and salutary confidence in the Buddha, as means of attaining supreme peace. At his profession, the novice proclaims:

> *In a world without refuge, without shelter, without safety, without an island, may I be the help, the refuge, the shelter, the safety, the island.*

[7] Shankara defended Hinduism against Buddhism. It is likely that he took the Buddhist elements, and revised them within his theist framework.
[8] A similar progression is described in CONZE, *Buddhism*, p. 100 ff.
[9] *Arahanta Vagga*, 90; *Samyatta Nikaya*, 3, 83–84.

May I help all beings, that have not yet crossed the ocean of existence, to cross it; may I bring to Nirvana all those who are not already there, consoling those who are desolate.[10]

THE SUFIS

The Sufi masters of Islam codified the stages of union with God in a similar way. They were perhaps among the first to attempt to classify both the moral aspects of this progression, and the stages of the mystical way. The two series of schemas also agree with one another. They say that the soul is covered with seventy thousand thin veils, which come between the individual and the Reality that these veils conceal. In order to perceive the infinite Light, one must undergo seven series of purifications, each of which destroys ten thousand veils at a time. Here is a summary of one of these schemas:

1. The unregenerate soul has the following attributes: ignorance, envy, pride, anger, sensuality . . .
2. The soul is still culpable of vanity, hypocrisy, and desire for glory and power . . .
3. The soul becomes inspired, and its attributes are worthy of praise: it is devout, humble, generous, and patient . . .
4. The soul becomes calm, full of gratitude and adoration . . .
5. The satisfied soul renounces all that is not God: it is faithful and content in every situation, because it is absorbed in the contemplation of Absolute Beauty.
6. This stage is characterised by the abandonment of all that is not God, and by goodness towards all creatures, inviting them to prayer, pardoning their faults, and loving them with compassion.
7. Having now arrived at the summit, all the preceding attributes are developed to perfection: joy, light and ecstasy.
   These states are due more to the grace of God than to the practices of the believers.[11]

A reading of these different programmes of spiritual life shows that they are strongly coloured by the idea that each religious group has of the Absolute. The Hindu ascetics of the *bhakti* movement seek a loving union with a personal God, to whom they submit without reserve. Those belonging to the *advaita*, look for the 'realisation' of their identification with an Absolute, who is considered present as the source of all beings. The Buddhists seek immersion in the Ocean of

---

[10] *Bodhisattva pratimoka suttra.*
[11] J. SPENCER TRIMINGHAM, *The Sufi Orders in Islam*, pp. 155–156, extract from the *Mirghanî* treatise: *Minhat al-ashâb*, by AHMAD IBN' ABD AR RAHMÂN AR-RUTBI.

Peace, either by the way of perfect detachment, or by that of 'compassion', while the Sufis aim for ecstatic joy in the Divine Presence by means of a long purification of the heart.

Despite all these differences, there are obvious similarities between these descriptions of the progress of the soul towards God.

All of them begin with the mastery of the senses and passions, pride being one of the principal ones. The disciple thus arrives at a certain peace, shown externally by benevolent relations with his neighbour, and patience in trials. However, one must go beyond this stage, to attain a Reality beyond the senses and concepts. The fullness of this Reality is irresistibly attractive, and makes him desire an intimate union beyond words, described as much in terms of love as in terms of knowledge, or simply in terms of peace and joy. The spiritual master holds an important place here. He must be the guide for the difficult ascending path. The disciple who wishes to succeed must have confidence in him, and follow his directives.

These stages are also found in the ladder of *RB* chapter 7, and we will examine them in more detail as we go through the various steps. But Saint Benedict himself made use of a long Christian tradition.

THE CHRISTIAN TRADITION

At the beginning of the third century, one of the first theologians of Christianity, **Clement of Alexandria**, thus described the stages of progress towards God:

> *From paganism to faith, from faith to knowledge, from knowledge to love, and from love to inheritance.*[12]

This progression has a moral aspect – knowledge – which implies the fulfilment of one's civic duties, and the keeping of God's law, along with repentance for faults, mildness, a profound calm (*apatheia*),[13] and virginity. All this finds it perfection in the love of God and neighbour.

Origen continued and improved the work of Clement. Using a theme that originated with the Stoics,[14] he distinguished three stages in the

---

[12] CLEMENT OF ALEXANDRIA, *Stromata*, 7: 10.

[13] *Apatheia* is a term that will be used, with various nuances, by the successors of Clement. It means, above all, a kind of calm of soul, which is the fruit of mastery over the passions.

[14] The Stoics divided the various disciplines into: moral, natural, and rational. Origen transposed these divisions, and applied them to the spiritual life.

ascent towards God. The first was called the *praktikē*, or purification, based on exercises. It starts with conversion, which restores the image of God in the soul. The disciple then tries to conquer the passions and practise the commandments. While doing this he begins to achieve purity of soul (*apatheia*), i.e. the suppression of passionate reactions (*pathē*) that come from the body. This process is symbolised by the Israelites during the Exodus, but Origen links it also with the book of Proverbs.[15]

The second stage is the *Physikē Theoria*, or contemplation of nature. This means the good use of things, in the light of eternity, realising the vanity of all that passes away. This is rather like the *correct vision* of Buddha, but Origen refers it to the book of Ecclesiastes (*Qoheleth: Vanity of vanities, all is vanity*). God progressively enlightens the soul by various spiritual trials, which teach it how to see things at their true value. The highest aspect of contemplation, in this stage, is the admiration of great and marvellous things, through contemplative prayer.

The summit in Origen is *theologia*: a theoretical state of perfect union of love, in the brilliant light that comes from God. He describes it in his *Commentary on the Song of Songs*:

> *The soul that has been purified in its habits is used to discernment, and is thus capable of being raised to contemplation of the Divinity, by spiritual love.*[16]

The soul loves the splendour of God, and receives from him a dart of love, which leaves it wounded.

A century later, **Evagrius** synthesised the experience of the Desert Fathers, and adopted Origen's classification. However, like those who taught him, his main interest lies in the *Praktikē*.[17] The Fathers had placed a very special emphasis on the need for vigilance (*nepsis*), which checks the thoughts that arise in the heart.

Another Greek Father, his contemporary, Saint **Gregory of Nyssa**, also uses the schema of Origen, and perfects it. The three stages are not successive steps for him, but parallel ways that can be used simultaneously. Each of them has a moral and a contemplative aspect.

The first one is related to the sacrament of Baptism. It brings purification from passions and false ideas, together with illumination; it is an opening to the invisible reality, and leads to *apatheia*. It is symbolised

---

[15] Origen describes this process in his homilies on Exodus and on Numbers.

[16] ORIGEN, *Commentary on the Song of Songs*, 78.

[17] See EVAGRIUS, *Praktikos*.

by the march of the Israelites towards Sinai, and by Moses' encounter with God at the burning bush.

The second is the ascent of the spirit by the ladder of beings. Here a detachment from sensory things is brought about, and the soul becomes accustomed to invisible realities through a gift of the Spirit (hence the link with the sacrament of Confirmation). The soul, at this stage, is like Moses, who enters the cloud as he ascends the mountain.

The third and final way is the contemplation of the invisible. This is outside sensory experience, hence its aspect of darkness, due to the incomprehensible nature of the divine infinity. Moses encounters God on the summit of the mountain, and in darkness. The other aspect of this way is the union of love, the mystical kiss, the obscure presence of God, and thus the relationship with the Eucharist.

Such progress is a continual discovery of new aspects, even after death, because God is infinite:

We go from beginning to beginning, by beginnings that have no end.[18]

Saint Benedict appears not to have had any direct contact with the thought of Saint Gregory of Nyssa. But this Cappadocian Father is interesting, because his teaching shows notable parallels with the way of the Buddhists.[19] It pinpoints further areas of development, to which the Spirit would lead Christian mystics in the following centuries. Saint Benedict himself was involved in these discoveries.

We must now look at the immediate sources of *RB* 7 in the writings of western mystics.

Saint **Augustine** described the stages of progress towards God, especially in his *Commentary on Psalm 41*. It all begins with a desire, both vague and yet intense, for a reality which is not clearly known, but which draws a soul towards contemplation and puts natural truths in a new light. At the same time, the destruction of vices and liberation from the passions appear as preliminary conditions for the approach to God. This thirst for him pushes Saint Augustine to reach him, in person, making his way up to him past the various forms of created things:

---

[18] GREGORY OF NYSSA, *VIIIth Homily on the Song*. He calls this continual progress *epectasis*.

[19] See *Actes du Colloque de Karma Ling*, Pentecost 1983: *Méditation chrétienne et méditation bouddhiste*, p. 176, MAYEUL DE DREUILLE, *Les voies de la prière chez Saint Grégoire de Nysse*.

We passed beyond all corporal creatures, step by step ... and were ascending further, outside of ourselves, fixing our thought on your works. Thus, we found our own souls – but went beyond them.[20]

He finds God neither in creatures, nor in his soul, but must rather go beyond all of these to find a truth and a being not subject to decline. Yet this truth would remain inaccessible to him, until the moment when he found that Christ was the way:

I sought the way, and found nothing, since I had not embraced the mediator between God and men, the man Christ Jesus, who is above all, God forever blessed. He calls us, and he says, 'I am the way, the truth and the life' (John 14: 6).[21]

Christ is also the one who purifies the soul from its sin, which must be humbly recognised:

He has descended to us, so that we might run to him. We were far from him, we were journeying away from him and, tired and weary, could no longer go forward. But he, like a doctor, came to us poor strays. He has saved us; we walk because of him.[22]

But where can one meet Christ? He lives in the depth of the heart:

You were within, and I was outside. I sought you there. You were with me, and I was not with you.[23]

In contrast to his predecessors, Saint Augustine does not idealise the experience of union with God. He simply states that any encounters with him, here below, are necessarily transitory:

I have seen these invisible things, but have not been able to fix my gaze on them. My weakness drew me back, and I returned to my normal experience, carrying with me the memory, the love, and the desire of the one whose fragrance I have perceived, without being able to feed from it.[24]

The faithful soul must seek the kingdom of God in the Church, as did the Apostles after the Transfiguration:

[20] AUGUSTINE, *Confessions*, IX, 20, 24, the ecstasy at Ostia.
[21] Ibid. VII, 18, 14.
[22] AUGUSTINE, *In Jn.*, Ep. 10, 1.
[23] AUGUSTINE, *Confessions*, X, 27, 38.
[24] AUGUSTINE, *Confessions*, VII, 23.

Come down, Peter. You were looking to stay on the mountain. Come down! ... Work in the sweat of your brow, suffer a little, and conquer, by love, that amazing beauty of good works, symbolised by the splendour of the Lord's vesture. Charity does not seek its own interest. It stops a man from looking for what pleases him. Come down! Work on the earth, be despised, be crucified, here on earth ... acquire charity ... thus you will come to eternity, and there you will find your security.[25]

In another place, he continues:

You should always have love as your goal. Whatever the subject you are speaking of, link all that you say with love.[26]

True contemplation, therefore, can be recognised by its fruit, which is charity towards all people. While taking up the themes of his predecessors, Saint Augustine underlines two points, which have left a strong impression on Christian thought, distinguishing it from other religions: the role of Christ as mediator between God and humanity, and humble charity towards everyone as a road to God.

Saint Benedict took most of the passages in his Rule in which he speaks about charity from Saint Augustine, but he inherited the *form* of his chapter on humility from Cassian and the Rule of the Master.

Cassian is the first author in the West who tried to organise a programme of perfection around the idea of humility. He does so in a chapter of his *Institutes*,[27] in which Abba Pinufius addresses a homily to a novice, who is to be clothed in the monastic habit. The point of departure is the fear of God, which urges a man to be converted and turn towards a Christian life, so as to avoid ending in Hell. This fear is transformed, by stages, into the *love that drives out all fear*.

The first step is made before entry into the monastery, by the renunciation of family and property.

The second is humility, which is recognised by ten signs, found in the different domains of the monastic life. The first three concern obedience, the following two are on patience, then there are three others on humiliations, and the last two on silence. By working at this, the monk renounces his inner possessions, that is, his vices. The first and principal way to achieve this is the rejection of self-will by manifesting all his thoughts to the spiritual father. In fact, by obeying him, he learns to obey God.

[25] AUGUSTINE, *Serm.* 78.
[26] AUGUSTINE, *De catechi. rud.*, 8.
[27] CASSIAN, *Institutes*, 4: 39.

Humility thus appears as an attitude of the heart that fights against vices by mortifying self-will and the desire to talk too much. This phase of the spiritual life is equivalent to the *praktikē* of Origen and Evagrius. It leads to self-mastery, purity of heart, and *apatheia*, a state in which he can obey the commandments almost naturally.

The perfection envisaged by Cassian, influenced by the Alexandrian Fathers, is realised here below in relations with other people: obedience and patience relate to one's neighbour.[28] The eschatological perspective of the fear of hell, mentioned at the beginning, does not return at the end.

The **Rule of the Master** transforms this programme of human perfection by placing it within the framework of the Gospel message. It introduces each verse with quotations from Scripture. We go up the ladder because God calls us. We obey *in imitation of the Lord*. It is *for him* that we endure everything, turning the other cheek to fulfil *his* commandment, confessing our faults *to him*. We are *near him*; we stand in *his* presence, in the midst of humiliations.

With the same Christian instinct, the transformation of the soul is attributed to the Holy Spirit. Similarly, the ascent ends, not with perfection on earth, but in heaven, and the chapter concludes with a long description of paradise.

The fear of God is introduced in the first and twelfth steps, being added to the ladder of Cassian. Since these two are directly related to God, they are given a lengthy development. The Master (and Saint Benedict) use the expression, the *fear of God*, in the biblical sense of a respectful love for God. The love of God and the fear of God are interchangeable phrases for them.[29] The Master does not make use of Cassian's progression from fear to love. Instead, he lays out a programme for the spiritual life based on humility, with its two branches: obedience, and the spirit of silence. This text of *RM* will be used by Saint Benedict his own chapter on humility.

2. THE STEPS OF HUMILITY IN *RB*

In chapter 7 of his Rule, Saint Benedict shortens the corresponding text of *RM*,[30] making a choice from among the quotations. He also introduces an important modification by suppressing the final description

---

[28] *Cf.* CLEMENT OF ALEXANDRIA, *Strom.*, 7: 10–11; EVAGRIUS, *Praktikos*, 1: 53: from faith to charity by means of *praktikē* and *apatheia*.

[29] Cf. *RM*, 2: 9–10 and *RB*, 72: 9: *to fear God by means of love*.

[30] *RM*, 10.

of heaven. He concludes the chapter with a phrase taken from Cassian and the Master about the love that casts out fear, making it clear that such love is in relation to Christ.

He thus insists that the goal of the monk is not merely to get to heaven, but to love the Lord from now on. Such disinterested love for God is one of the characteristics of the Rule of Saint Benedict, an idea that originated, perhaps, in Saint Augustine. We will notice its occurrence several times during the course of this chapter.

Introduction *(RB* 7: 1–9)

Following *RM* systematically, Saint Benedict begins with a meditation on *Luke* 14: 11: *Brothers, Holy Scripture cries aloud to us, saying, 'Whoever exalts himself will be humbled, and he who humbles himself will be exalted.'* *(RB* 7: 1). Everything comes from God, and the foundation of humility is the experience of human limitation:

> *Why thus? 'If I did not think humbly',*

since pride separates us from God, he would treat us *as a child on the mother's breast is weaned* *(RB* 7: 4). The image of the mother may lead us, in the present age, to think of Mary, the best example of Christian humility.

Saint Benedict insists that God is prepared to help the soul in its search. Taking the image of Jacob's ladder, he tells us that it is set up, not by the soul itself, but *by the Lord*, as *RM* also indicated. Such symbolism brings him close to the thought of Origen and Gregory of Nyssa, who compared spiritual progress with the journey of the people of Israel in the desert, and the ascent of Moses on Mount Sinai. Jacob's ladder subsequently became, in the East, a great symbol of spiritual progress. Many celebrated authors have used it, the most famous being Saint John Climacus.[31]

The first step of humility: the purifying presence of God *(RB* 7: 10–30)

We have already touched on the steps of humility when we spoke of obedience, but they have so much to offer that it is worth the trouble to study them further, on their own merits. Saint Benedict sees the first

---

[31] Many manuscripts of Saint *JOHN CLIMACUS* carry a miniature Jacob's ladder on their cover. The main authors who use the image of Jacob's ladder are APHRAHAT in *Le livre des degrés*, and JACOB OF SERUGH. The theme is much used in the hymns of the Jacobite Syrians. Cf. T. SPIDLIK, *La spiritualité de l'Orient Chrétien*, 3: 3.

step as a personal encounter with God. More than a mere point of departure, it should be the monk's fundamental and lasting attitude, controlling the whole of his life. Leaving behind the progression-by-stages of the Alexandrian Fathers, Saint Benedict gives us the global perspective of Saint Gregory of Nyssa. We are to live in the presence of God, attending to him with love and respect. This is precisely the sense of the phrase *the fear of God* in the Master and in Saint Benedict.

Here again, in the concern to centre all our attention on God and to *flee forgetfulness*, we see the concentration that we found among the Hindu and Buddhist ascetics. They tried to focus the soul on one point only: in order to distinguish the real from the unreal, the permanent from the transitory.

In developing the idea of control of one's thoughts, Saint Benedict adopts the *nepsis* or vigilance of the Eastern Fathers. The presence of God is purifying.[32] Saint Benedict considers several aspects of this, beginning with the purification of thoughts:

> *This is made clear to us by the prophet when he shows us that God is always present in our thoughts, 'God examines', he says, 'the heart and the mind.' And also, 'The Lord knows exactly how men think.' In order then to keep his perverse thoughts under careful control, the profitable brother should repeat in his heart, 'Then I shall be spotless in his sight, if I keep myself in check against my sinfulness.' (Ps. 7: 10; 93: 11; 17: 24).*[33]

The next stage, for one who refuses to follow his own will, is purification of the heart:

> *Scripture, indeed, forbids us to do our own will, saying to us, 'Turn away from your will' (Sir. 18: 30). Moreover, we ask God in our prayers that his will may be done in us (Matt. 6: 10).*[34]

Lastly, bodily purity comes through control of desire:

> *Indeed in what concerns the desires of the flesh, we must believe that God is ever present to us, ... We must, therefore, be on our guard against any evil desire, because death is stationed beside the entrance to delight, as Scripture teaches in the words, 'Do not go after your lusts' (Sir. 18: 30).*[35]

---

[32] The purifying presence of God is a biblical theme, well exemplified in *Is.* 6: 1–8.

[33] *RB* 7: 14–18. The theme of the purifying gaze of God has already been approached in *RB* 4: 48–50: *to know that God most surely beholds one ... to dash the evil thoughts upon Christ.*

[34] *RB* 7: 19–20.

[35] *RB* 7: 24–25. This text takes us back to *RB* 4: 10–13: *to deny oneself in order to follow Christ. To punish one's body. Not to seek pleasures ...*

The conclusion of this step (*RB* 7: 26–30) adopts the general theme of vigilance: since we live under the gaze of God, we must take care:

> *lest one day God beholds us falling into sin and becoming unprofitable* (*RB* **7: 29**).

The last word contrasts with the *profitable brother, [who] should repeat in his heart, 'I shall be spotless'* (*RB* 7: 18). This opposition recalls what Saint Paul said in his Letter to Philemon, where Onesimus became 'useful' after being 'useless'.[36] Here, it is attention to God that renders a man useful in his service.

The second step of humility: the renunciation of self-will (*RB* 7: 31–33)

The second step continues the purification of heart that was initiated in the first, and underlines its importance.

> *The second step of humility is that a man should not love his own will nor take pleasure in carrying out his desires* (*RB* **7: 31**).

In monastic language, *self-will* does not refer to the personality of each monk, but rather to whatever in him is in opposition to God, following the word of Christ which the Rule goes on to use: *I came not to do my own will, but that of him who sent me* (*John* 6: 38). As Saint Paul says, *Seek the things that are above, where Christ is, . . . and, in order to destroy your evil tendencies, take off the old man and be clothed in the new, which is constantly being renewed in the image of its Creator.*[37]

Here we are reminded of the Hindus' detachment from selfish action, and the Buddhists' renunciation of desires. This means a detachment from anything that, insofar as it is transitory, keeps us away from the Permanent. However, the difference, for the Christian, is that Christ is both the model and the way:

> *[The monk] by his actions imitate[s] the Lord in his saying, 'I came not to do my own will'.*[38]

So it is not a question of a rejection of human development, but rather

---

[36] *Philem.* 11. See also *Sir.* 10: 4: God will raise up a useful man, at the appointed time.
[37] Cf. *Col.* 3: 1–10.
[38] *RB* 7: 32; *Jn.* 6: 28.

of clinging to Christ, who makes us choose a life like his own, as a way of moving towards God.[39]

The third step of humility: obedience in imitation of Christ (*RB* 7: 34)

The text of this step is very short, but none the less quite striking. It applies what has been said before to the domain of obedience:

> *The third step of humility is that for the love of God one should be obedient to a superior in all things, imitating the Lord of whom the Apostle says, 'He was made obedient even unto death' (**RB** 7: 34; Phil 2: 8).*

Its absolute tone reminds us of Saint Basil, who also quotes the example of Christ from *Phil.* 2: 8.[40]

Saint Benedict's distinguishing feature, however, is that he adds to the text of *RM* the words, *for the love of God*. The monk, then, is to obey, not just because he wishes to imitate the Lord, but because he wants to be conformed to him, in the depths of his heart. Like Christ, he obeys through love: *if you keep my commandments, you will remain in my love, just as I have kept my Father's commandments and remain in his love* (*John* 15: 10).

The notion of the love of God is a trait of the Rule which Saint Benedict has taken mainly from Saint Augustine, although he is not quoted explicitly here. With this step, we arrive at the heart of Christian monasticism, whose only goal is to follow Christ by love.

The fourth step of humility: patience (*RB* 7: 35-43)

Following the Master, Saint Benedict here combines the fourth and fifth steps of Cassian: patience in obedience and in adversity.

In the first part, dealing with how to put up with unpleasant orders (*RB* 7: 35-41), there is an insistence on *inner* silence, a nuance which Saint Benedict adds by using the word '*conscientia*': ... let him *keep a firm grip on patience **in his conscience** (with an uncomplaining spirit)*. In other words, at such difficult moments, the monk has not only to keep silence externally, but to be silent *in his heart*, replacing his murmuring with the inner repetition of the strong words of Scripture, like these which are given in the text:

---

[39] In the last phrase, Saint Benedict copies the text of *RM*, which calls any pious book 'Scripture'. In fact, he is using the life of a saint: the *Passio Anastasiae*, 17.

[40] BASIL, *LR* 28; *SR* 116.

'He who stands firm to the end will be saved' (Matt. **10: 22**), *and again, 'Let your heart take courage and hope in the Lord' (Ps.* **26: 14**).

In the midst of the trial, as in the preceding step, the love of the Lord fills the monks with hope, and even with joy:

Yet unmoved, through their hope of divine reward they joyfully persevere, saying, 'These are the trials through which we triumph on account of him who has loved us'.[41]

We should take note of the quotations from the psalms that follow: *Ps.* 43: 22 in *RB* 7: 38: *for your sake we are afflicted by death, all the day long,* and *Ps.* 65: 10–11 in *RB* 7: 40: *you refined us in the fire.* These are borrowed from *RM*, which uses them again further on in the text, in relation to martyrdom, of which obedience is the equivalent. In shortening the text, Saint Benedict decided not to use the comparison of obedience and martyrdom, which is classic in Christian monasticism.[42]

The second part, patience in trials, is a paraphrase of the model given by the Lord himself in *Matt.* 5: 39–41: *struck on one cheek, they offer the other ...*

We should put this text beside other passages of the Rule, proper to Saint Benedict, where he speaks of patience. This virtue is necessary for everyone: for the Abbot, as the Good Shepherd; for the cellarer, as a father to the community; but also for each monk, in his relations with the brethren, since *they should with the greatest patience make allowance for one another's weaknesses, whether physical or moral (RB* 72: 5). It is characteristic of Saint Benedict to give particular attention to the subjective difficulties that a monk might encounter, difficulties that might lead to murmuring.[43]

Throughout this step, as in other passages of the Rule about patience, we are constantly confronted with Christ who was *obedient unto death, death on a cross.* The monk is invited to adopt Christ's patience, and manifest it towards others.

The fifth step of humility: Opening the heart *(RB* 7: 49–50)

According to the tradition of the Desert Fathers, this step in Cassian meant the opening of one's heart to the spiritual father. All actions

[41] *RB* 7: 38; *Rom.* 8: 37.
[42] The theme of obedience as martyrdom is found in the *Vita Patr.*, 5, 14, 17; SULPICIUS SEVERUS, *Dial.* 1: 18; CASSIAN, *Inst.,* 13: 33; *Conf.* 9: 14; 18: 7. Cf. AV *La communauté et l'abbé*, pp. 233–234.
[43] *RB* 34; 35; 36; 39; 41; 68; cf. A. BORIAS, 'Saint Benoît maître en patience,' *Lettre de Ligugé* 225, 1984, 3.

and thoughts, whether good or bad, had to be revealed to him, so that he could give a sure direction.

The Master had reduced this step to the mere accusation of faults. However, he did put the accent on mercy and hope, by means of quotations from the psalms:

> *'Reveal your course to the Lord, and hope in him,' and again, 'Make confession to the Lord for he is good, and his mercy is everlasting'* (*Ps.* 36: 5; 11: 1).

Saint Benedict uses the same text. But in two other chapters, he completes its sense with his own additions. In chapter 4: 50, he notes that confession need not be made exclusively to the Abbot: another elder could become a spiritual father:

> *To dash the evil thoughts that invade one's heart immediately upon Christ, as upon a rock, and to reveal them to one's spiritual father.*

In chapter 49: 8, openness of heart is extended to every good action: each monk must make known to his Abbot what he wants to do (especially during Lent), since everything must be done *with his blessing and approval.*

Saint Benedict here adopts the traditional idea of spiritual direction: an openness of heart that is both humble and simple, allowing the light of the Lord, mediated by the spiritual father, to penetrate the soul.

The sixth step of humility: the useless servant (*RB* 7, 49–50)

This step begins by asking the monk to be prepared to accept the material things he may be given – objects, habits, utensils, work – regardless of whether or not they are suited to his taste and preferences:

> *The sixth step of humility is that a monk should be satisfied with whatever is of lowest value or quality ...*

However, by the fact that he is asked to *be satisfied* with these things, the monk is invited to seek humility at a deeper level, accepting his personal limitations and, above all, his sinful state before God. He is asked to be like Saint John the Baptist, content with *what is given from heaven* (*John* 3: 27).

Here, we can distinguish true humility, which recognises the gifts we receive as coming from God, from the false humility that will not thus recognise them, and from the kind of pride that attributes such gifts to oneself:

With regard to the tasks laid on him [the monk] should think of himself as a bad and unworthy workman.

Note that the text does not speak of incapable workers, but rather of bad and unworthy ones. The monk is not called to deny his natural qualities but to use them, in spite of the unworthiness caused by his sin. This attitude is also recommended in the Gospel: *'When you have done everything required, say, "We are but useless servants"'* (*Luke* 17: 7–10). We will always be the workmen of the eleventh hour, employed by the Father not because he needs us, but because his mercy wants the best for us (*Matt.* 20: 1–16). The opposite attitude, implicitly condemned by Saint Benedict, would be to do badly any work that was not congenial to us.

Nevertheless, this cannot be achieved without suffering. For this reason, the last words of the text take us back to Christ in his Passion:

I have been brought to nothing; I have known nothing; I am like a pack-animal before you ... and yet I am always with you.

The seventh step of humility: to reckon oneself to be the last of all (*RB* 7: 51–54)

The seventh step of humility is that he should not only say in words that he is inferior and less virtuous than all other men, but that he should really believe it in the depth of his heart ...

This might seem unreasonable, were it not for the fact that the idea is found among the majority of mystics, either Christian[44] or non-Christian. With them, such an attitude of heart is the fruit of knowing our own nothingness before God. If my entire nature, right down to its deepest roots, comes from God, I am nothing, in and of myself. How, then, can I pretend to be greater than another, or raise myself above him?

It is easy to understand the intellectual reasoning behind such an argument, but *believing it in the depth of one's heart* is a gift from God, who alone can make us experience it.

The text of this step follows a path similar to that of *Phil.* 2: 3–11. Saint Paul invites the Christians to *think of others as superior to them-*

---

[44] Saint Benedict, and the Master, might have found such expressions in the *Vita Patr.*, 7, 43, 2; BASIL *LR*, e.g. 62. CASSIAN does not have this degree of humility, but the same notion is found in his *Inst.* 4: 39, 2; 12: 33. Later Christian mystics would develop this theme abundantly.

selves, giving them the example of Christ who emptied himself by his Incarnation and Passion. In *RM* and *RB* this long passage of Saint Paul is replaced by short quotations from Psalms 21 and 87, which are prophecies of the Passion.

The suggested attitude of the faithful soul is thus none other than Christ's own attitude. The implicit reference to the example of the Lord helps us to understand both the proximity and the distance of similar experiences among the mystics of other religions. Let us consider two characteristic examples.

Among the Hindus, one of the precepts for the devotees of Shiva, called Virashaïvites, is:

Consider all the faithful as superior to yourself.[45]

In this school, respect for others is thought to be given to the divine presence that dwells in them.

In a manual of the Tibetan monks, we find:

Each time I meet someone, I should consider myself as inferior to all, while thinking that the other person is my superior.[46]

One can find numerous texts, in the Hindu *Bhakti* devotion, in Zen, and even among the Sufis,[47] which advocate the total gift of self, including self-annihilation, as the condition of entry for the final stage of contemplation.

Many of these mystics seem to have had a fundamental spiritual experience that is very close to that of the Christians. Nevertheless, its expression in diverse cultures and theologies introduces notable divergences. It is not just that there is no reference to Christ among them, but also that humility is conceived as an effort to remove from a man the things that stop him from reaching a union that would otherwise be well within his natural grasp. This is the case even with those Hindus and Sufis who strongly emphasise dependence on grace, and even more with the Buddhists. These all insist on the need for human effort, without recognising the gift of sharing in God's own life, the essential point of Christian humility.[48]

---

[45] SUDASIVAIAH, *A comparative study of two Virasaïva monasteries,* ch. 1, p. 56.
[46] *The eight verses for training the mind,* p. 1.
[47] For the Sufis, see, for example, J. SPENCER TRIMINGHAM, *The Sufi,* p. 155 ff.
[48] Nevertheless, all these religions can show us examples of people who are truly holy and humble. This fact makes me inclined to believe that the fundamental experience of a person of good will in his encounter with the All of God is very similar in the different religions. None the less, Christian revelation brings a new and distinctive light to the experience.

The last phrase of the text of *RB* brings us back precisely to such dependence on God, and the need to correspond with his will. We are given a quotation from Psalm 118, combining verses 71 and 73. This reference suggests a biblical theme frequently developed by Saints Basil and Cassian. For them, as in many texts of Scripture, *obedience to the commandments* means the acceptance of God's plan of love for humanity:

> *'I have been brought down, and reduced to confusion.' ... 'It is good for me that you have humiliated me, so that I may learn your commandments.'*

It was good that you humbled me: God takes the initiative. By means of our defeats, he detaches us from the mistaken projects in which we were engaged and, in his love, invites us to discover and do what is necessary to follow him.

The eighth step of humility: the common way (*RB* 7: 55)

> *The eighth step of humility is that a monk should do nothing except what is recommended by the common rule of the monastery and the example of those above him.*

The sixth sign in Cassian's system required a monk to avoid 'singularity' as he followed the example of the elders. That refers to the usage of the Fathers, both of former times and the present. *RM* restricted such imitation to the customs of the monastery and the example of the Abbot. By suppressing an explicit reference to the Abbot, Saint Benedict gives the expression a more general sense, in line with monastic tradition

Effort to avoid singularity is certainly a mark of humility, well demonstrated in the lives of the recently canonised male and female saints of contemplative orders.[49]

Some psychologists, who think that this step represents one of the summits of human development, also confirm avoidance of singularity as a road to sanctity. Such behaviour shows that a person has arrived at perfect maturity, acting, not with a frivolous or selfish motivation, but according to the essential values of the ideal that he has embraced, as exemplified in the conduct of the monks of old.

This degree also shows us the profound calm of one that has encountered the pacifying presence of God in the depth of himself,

---

[49] E.g. Saint Thérèse of the Child Jesus, and the recently beatified sons and daughters of Saint Benedict.

and knows how to centre all his activities on it. Such a person is rooted no longer in the narrow 'self', but in the transcendent God: *Christ lives in me*, and through him, I am in profound and peaceful relations with all others.[50]

If the regular observance is a strength, it can also become an excuse for passivity: the community has to endure our actions, without our having to bear the consequences. The educative value of such consequences is thus diminished, leading to both human and spiritual mediocrity. Keeping to the rules is not sufficient in itself, and each monk needs to take charge of his personal life, within the general dispositions of the community life. The overall tone of the community depends on the zeal of each of the brethren for doing what is pleasing to God.[51]

At the same time, there is always an equilibrium to be sought between tradition and *aggiornamento*, especially in our own days of rapid cultural changes. The customs of the elders are important for us as an example, but not as an absolute rule. The experience of our predecessors helps us to discover the necessary conditions to live our own experience in the present context.[52] As Saint Benedict himself put it,[53] it is the duty of the monastic authorities, aided by the considered opinion of the community, to decide how each generation may follow the tradition in a way that remains faithful to the Gospel.

The problem of adapting customs, codified in sacred texts, to modern ways of behaviour is one that is also shared by monks of other religions, and sometimes experienced more acutely by them than by us. This is one of the areas in which common reflection would be valuable, and dialogue fruitful.

The ninth, tenth and eleventh steps of humility: mastery of the tongue (*RB* 7: 56–61)

Having looked at the deep roots of humility in the heart of man, the Rule now turns to its outward expression. In fact, this change had already been felt in the eighth step. The three following deal with mastery over the tongue, and control of laughter. We have already

---

[50] English spiritual writers allude here to 'Still Point,' 'Centring Prayer', and 'Community Consciousness', technical terms which I have tried to paraphrase in the text. Cf. D. M. LAW, 'Journey to the inner Centre', in TJURUNGA, Oct. 1980; M. B. LUETKEMEYER, 'Resurrection in RB', in SPIRIT AND LIFE, March–April 1986.

[51] Cf. B. ROLLIN, *Vivre aujourd'hui la Règle de St Benoît*, p. 54.

[52] Ibid. p. 79.

[53] In *RB* 3, and in many passages of the Rule, Saint Benedict leaves the details of observance to the discretion of the Abbot.

touched on this, in dealing with silence. The aim of all these regulations is that each person, and the entire community, should cultivate an atmosphere of *seriousness-with-a-smile*, which is an expression of the truest heartfelt humility.

The ninth step deals with control of the tongue: to speak only when you are asked, and to exercise care about what you say.

The tenth step is directed against dissipation and noisy laughter – the opposite of the vigilance and concentration that were required by the first step of humility.

In the eleventh step, Saint Benedict replaces *holy words* (in *RM*) with *reasonable words*, or words adapted to the situation, a reaction coming from good sense, and not lacking in humour. It is perhaps here, in this step, that the comportment of the humble monk is best described:

> *When a monk speaks, he does so quietly, without laughter, with humility, with restraint, making use of few words and reasonable ones, as it is written, 'The wise man becomes known for his few words' (RB 7: 60).*

The twelfth step of humility: the publican *(RB 7: 62–66)*

Speaking of control of the senses, we pass naturally to control of the eyes and, in a more general way, to exterior conduct. Humility manifests itself in the posture of the body and, in its turn, the body helps to foster humility in the heart.

Saint Augustine[54] and, later, Saint Caesarius of Arles,[55] put the monk on guard against impudent looks. The twelfth step takes a more general perspective. We must control our eyes so that we can preserve concentration. Here the exterior posture and interior attitude reinforce one another, since the monk is invited to repeat to himself the humble words of the publican in the Gospel. The quotation of the Gospel leads the Master and Saint Benedict to generalise the attitude:

> *Whether sitting, walking or standing, he should always have his head bowed, his eyes fixed on the ground (RB 7: 63).*

However, the emphasis is placed not on the position of the body, but rather on the interior attitude that is symbolised in the parable of the publican:

> *[He] should at every moment be considering his guilt for his sins and thinking that he is even now being presented for the dread judgement.*

---

[54] AUGUSTINE, *Reg.* IV, 4–11.
[55] CAESARIUS OF ARLES, *Reg. Virg.* 23.

He should always be saying in his heart what the publican in the Gospel said with downcast eyes, 'Lord, sinner as I am, I am not worthy to raise my eyes to heaven.' (RB 7: 64–65).

It is interesting, however, that the Buddhist rules for monks prescribe a similar attitude. They are to go the villages to find food but, while on the way, must practise custody of the senses:

Let not your eye roam around like a bee in the forest, like a frightened deer, or a timid child. Let your eyes be cast down, not look forward more than one yoke's length. Let the monk not be enslaved to the power of his thoughts, like a fevered bee.[56]

Conclusion of the chapter *(RB 7: 67–70)*

By way of a conclusion, Saint Benedict selects just a few sentences from *RM*. He suppresses the long description of heaven, which he had resumed in a few words at the end of chapter 4:

We shall in return receive from the Lord that reward which he himself has promised. 'The things that no eye has seen, and no ear has heard, which God has prepared for those who love him' (RB 4: 76–77).

Without delaying over the details of the ladder, he takes up again the idea of a general progression towards love:

Thus when all these steps of humility have been climbed, the monk will soon reach that love of God which, being perfect, drives out all fear (RB 7: 67).

The next sentence is one of the rare passages in the Rule where Saint Benedict speaks of mysticism. It is worth stopping here to consider it, since it opens a new dimension in the text:

Through this love [of God] all the practices which before he kept somewhat fearfully, he now begins to keep effortlessly and naturally and habitually, influenced now not by any fear of hell but through the love of Christ, by good habit and delight in virtue (RB 7: 68–69).

The words *of Christ* were added to the text of the Master by Saint Benedict. Using a similar addition to the one in the third step, he insists on the duty of the Christian monk to take the Lord as his model, and follow him out of love.

But the path laid out by Saint Benedict also invites us to ponder the

[56] *Digha Nikaya*, 2: 293.

steps of humility as a description of the stages of union with God. First comes an effort to concentrate on him, then come the trials and the darkness, which purify the soul and unite it, in a obscure way, with him. This is the night of the senses, the night of the spirit.

> *I am like a pack animal before you, and yet I am always with you* (**sixth step**).

Yet, in spite of all this, the action of the Lord gives both joy and peace:

> *Yet unmoved, through their hope of divine reward they joyfully persevere, saying, 'These are the trials through which we triumph on account of him who has loved us'* (**fourth step**).

After this comes a kind of serenity that is also visible in outward behaviour. This is the peace and harmony with God, which spring from *good habit and delight in virtue*. As the Prologue puts it, *our hearts are opened wide, and the way of God's commandments is run in a sweetness of love that is beyond words.*[57]

The last phrase of the chapter implies (as Saint Augustine also tells us) that these moments of *sweetness beyond words* are transitory:

> *These things the Lord, working through his Holy Spirit, will deign to show in his workman, when he has been purified from vice and sin.*

The faithful person, even if pardoned, remains a sinner, and must constantly try to correspond with the action of the Holy Spirit, the Spirit of Christ, which ceaselessly invites him to make progress in his love.

So let us try, then, to make a rapid comparison between chapter 7 of *RB* and the non-Christian spiritual programmes.

There is unanimous agreement on the need for concentration on the divine, of a kind that allows a person to distinguish correctly things that are passing from things which endure. To fix the attention on the latter, there must be an effort to master the senses and the passions. Then, passing through the midst of painful trials, the disciple moves beyond the realm of the senses and mental concepts. Lastly, coming face to face with the Supreme Reality, he is led to realise that his being derives entirely from it, and that he is nothing in himself. Moments of illumination transform his view of things, and give an interior calm, which allows him to continue his path in peace, judging every matter in the light of its eternal value.

---

[57] *RB*, *Prol.* 49.

At this point, Christian revelation shows that the Supreme Reality is a loving Father, who invites us freely to participate in the intimacy of his life, uniting us with his only Son, Jesus Christ. The invitation of the Father is made constantly effective in us by means of the Holy Spirit, who transforms our inner being, little by little, into the image of Christ, if we allow him to do so, and makes us into sons with the Son of God.

In this chapter, Saint Benedict makes frequent mention of the soul's relationship with Christ, and recalls it also in connection with the work of the Holy Spirit. Following several of the Western Fathers, he describes this process as a way of humility, which makes us aware that everything in us comes from God, and that we have nothing in ourselves to make us superior to other people. The means of arriving at such humility are obedience (considered as an effort to conform our will to the will of God), and mastery of words and thoughts, so that we can listen to God and remain in his presence. Despite the trials (which he does not hide from us) Saint Benedict shows us the peace and joy which spring up in the heart of a person who has found harmony with God, by accepting the love which he offers.

PART II

LIFE WITHIN THE MONASTERY

CHAPTER IX

FROM PSALMODY TO CONTEMPLATION

The first chapters of *RB* laid down its doctrinal and spiritual basis. Chapter 8, however, begins a second section, dealing with the organisation of monastic life, and starting with prayer. Chapters 8 to 20 describe the Divine Office in the choir and private prayer. What is said here is complemented by other passages of the Rule, as we shall see further on.

As a whole, these texts indicate a way of prayer that is found in many religions. Reading of sacred texts and psalm singing lead to meditation and contemplation, which in turn lead to direct contact with the Absolute.

Seen from outside, psalmody and meditation form perhaps one of the main points of resemblance between the various world monastic systems. Attending an 'Office' or a silent prayer, in a Hindu ashram or Buddhist temple, a Christian monk feels a deep kind of spiritual kinship, and the desire to share such experiences.

Here we shall try to compare the ways that lead to contemplation in the diverse religions, beginning with the organisation of psalmody and reading of the sacred Scriptures.

1. THE READING AND CHANTING OF SACRED TEXTS IN HINDUISM

Many of the Hindu sacred texts are meant to be chanted or recited. This recitation follows very precise rules, which help to explain why the texts have been preserved for centuries, almost without adulteration. When it forms part of a sacrificial ritual, sacred chanting is often preceded by several days of fasting.[1] But, whatever its aim, the recitation is always accompanied with gestures of respect, well described in the *Laws of Manu*:

> *At the hour of study, the young novice, having made an ablution accord-*
> *ing to the law, should give the Holy Book a respectful greeting, and*
> *receive his lesson, clothed in a clean garment, while controlling his*
> *senses. He should read with hands folded – for this is the respect due to*
> *the Sacred Writings.*[2]

Some of the sacred books, such as the *Veda*, are held in higher veneration, because they contain the result of a particular contact with the Divine. In reciting from them, it is possible to share in the experience of their authors, the *Rishi*, *'those who have seen'*. Some passages however are considered especially useful for meditation. The *Laws of Manu* and other still more specific texts on monastic life, such as the *Aruni Upanishad*, limit the novice's reading to the *Vedanta* and, more particularly, to the *Gayatri* and the *Aranyaka*.[3] The more the ascetic progresses in concentration, the more will his recitation be simplified. It is reduced to a *mantra*, then to the sound *Aum*, a synthesis of all words, and finally,

> *The ascetic should get rid of all things, both the thread of sacrifice and*
> *the Vedas.*[4]

According to the *Laws of Manu*, recitation is performed standing in the morning, and sitting in the evening. In the latter posture, it is combined with the yogic meditation, well described in the *Bhagavad Gita*:

> *Having withdrawn to a solitary place, with his mind under control . . .*
> *having arranged a stable seat in a pure place, neither too high, nor too*
> *low, covered with an antelope skin or sacred grass, keeping the body*
> *firm, head and neck straight, and immobile, let him direct himself firmly*
> *towards me.*[5]

---

[1] R. PANNIKAR, *The Vedic Experience*, p. 34. The *Brahmana* of the *Sama Veda*, for example, gives a detailed description of the various fasts and austerities performed during the recitation of the *Sama Veda*, which is the ritual part of the *Rig Veda*.

[2] MANU, 2: 70–71.

[3] MANU, 6: 83. *Aruni Up.*, 2, DEGRACES-F, p. 106; 192. The *Gayatri* or *Savitri* is an invocation of the divinity, compared to the rising sun, which gives life to all things. The *Aranyaka* are texts to be meditated by forest-dwelling hermits.

[4] *Kathasruti Up.*, UR., p. 204. The 'thread' of sacrifice is a piece of cotton which is worn as a sign of the brahmin caste. The wearer is thus allowed to perform sacrifices.

[5] *B. Gita*, 6, 10–14.

Hindu monasticism is not limited to the solitary *samnyasi*, or holy man. Since the third century AD the *Bhakti*, or devotional movement, gave it a new and enriching quality by establishing the veneration of a personal God, who loves humanity and saves it by his grace. Theologians and poets composed hymns of praise, adoration and repentance, and other writings celebrating the mythological ventures of the divine *avatars* or saints of the group. These texts were gradually recognised as sacred, and were sung by the ascetics, repeated during pilgrimages, and used by families. Even today, they provide not only models of the social virtues that animate the Indian culture, but also ways of prayer that are followed by multitudes of men and women of all conditions.

Since the ninth century, some ascetics made these chants their speciality. They formed groups that encouraged the piety of the faithful, and fostered spiritual friendship and mutual encouragement between them. Their songs, even when not acted out in dance, involve the whole body. Indeed, according to the tradition, none of them can be beautiful if the performer does not feel the *raga* or emotion that wells up from the text.[6]

Sung or recited by groups, these poems help to bring about unity of heart in a shared love for God. In private, they lead to a kind of meditation that moves towards a union of love with him. Some songs were even specially composed for this effect: the *bhajans* (songs of praise) and the *japas* (litanies of divine names).

In this rich variety of expression, some chant demonstrates typical Hindu characteristics. The most striking is the intense participation of the body. In the gestures of respect for the sacred book, as much as in the immobility of the *yogi*, or in the refined dance of the *bhakta*, the body is fully involved in recitation and singing. Psalmody is a form of teaching that finds its summit in meditation. But as concentration intensifies, the importance of the text decreases progressively, or even disappears completely. Though such concentration on the inner Self is meant to be continuous, the beginning and end of the night are the most privileged times for psalmody and meditation.

Several Hindu theologians have studied the process that leads from the recitation of the text to contemplation. One of the first was Shankara. In his Commentaries on the *Brihadaraniyaka Upanishad*, and on the *Bhagavad Gita*, he shows how to proceed from exegesis (*shravana*) to theological reflection (*manana*), which helps the disciple to make the doctrine into a concrete part of his life. Such reflection, animated by tranquil faith, and freed from objections,

[6]　PANIKKAR, *Vedic*, p. 34.

leads to total concentration (*nididhyasana*) on the Self, present '*inside the city of the heart*'. Then

> the wisdom obtained from such science[7] is converted into one's own experience.

This is an experience beyond words and concepts – for the Absolute is, for Shankara, the *Nirguna Brahman*, who is infinitely beyond the field of reasoning.

Ramanuja adds the viewpoint of the devotional movement (*Bhakti*) to this vision. His Absolute is the infinite and transcendent Brahman, but with an infinite number of perfect qualities. He is the Lord who

> creates, sustains, and holds within himself the whole universe, so that he may save the souls that seek his love.[8]

In writings like the *Bhagavad Gita* or the *Puranas*, the disciple finds images of the Lord, which can be used as themes for meditation, and will help him fix his mind on God.[9] To arrive at this point, Ramanuja uses the yoga techniques, as did Shankara. Concentration on a *mantra*, or on an image or idea of the Lord, is first transformed by a kind of vision, and then by the direct presence of the Divine in the intelligence and imagination of the devotee.[10] Going beyond this level, which is conceptual, the Absolute is met as the source of the human existence:

> He crosses over, in the boat of the sound, 'Aum', to the other shore of the space within the heart, and enters it slowly, even as a miner in search of minerals. Thus, the inner space is revealed. Thus, he enters the hall of Brahman.[11]

The *Chandogya Upanishad* says, similarly:

> In this city of Brahman, there is a dwelling in the form of a lotus flower, and within it, there is an inner space. One should search for that which

---

[7] SHANKARA, *Brihadaraniyaka Up.* II, 4, 5; *Gita Bashya*, 6, 8, quoted by R. DE SMET, *Contemplation in Shankara and Ramanuja*, p. 209.

[8] RAMANUJA, *Shribashya*, 1: 1, 1; R. DE SMET. ibid. p. 216.

[9] Thirty-two types of meditation (*Brahma-Vidya*) are described in the *Upanishads*. The Lord can be considered as the One without equal, Truth, Knowledge, the Interior Master, etc. Cf. R. DE SMET, ibid. p. 218.

[10] R. DE SMET, *Contemplation*, pp. 213–214.

[11] *Maitri Up.* 6: 28.

is within that inner space. It is this we must seek. It is this that we should desire to know.[12]

Here is the meeting point between God and the human being, the *ground of being*, the inside of the *cave of the heart*, the inner *lotus flower*, and seat of the divinity. Ramanuja, and, in a way, Shankara himself, say that such contemplation is not the fruit of a technique of concentration, but is unforeseeable, since it is *caused by divine grace, because Scripture teaches it.*[13] This help from the divine is much underlined in the *Bhagavad Gita*, but it is already found in the very ancient *Katha Upanishad*, which says:

> *This* atman *is not attained by instruction or intelligence, or learning. Only the one whom He chooses attains* atman *... To him, the* atman *reveals his own being.*[14]

It should be noted, however, that for many Hindus, the contact with the Absolute source of being is not the encounter with 'another', but rather the awareness that a spark of the divine is part and parcel of the human essence. The goal is thus the *realisation*, or experience, of the identity of the *atman*, that is, the individual soul is united with the *Brahman*, the Absolute. This spiritual experience is beyond any concept, and the self disappears in the common source of all beings.[15] It is a foretaste, a pledge of the infinite beatitude which, when repeated, helps to free a person from the cycle of rebirth.

2. PSALMODY AND MEDITATION IN BUDDHISM

In contrast with the solitary recitation of sacred writings often used by Hindus, the Buddhist psalmody is mostly done in community. This derives in all probability from its origin, which was the recitation of the Buddha's teachings by his itinerant disciples during the rainy season, a time when they remained stable in certain places. The monks maintained this liturgical custom as their lives gradually became sedentary.

[12] *Chandogya Up.* 8: 1.
[13] *Vedanta-sutra Bhasya*, 2: 3, 41, quoted by R. DE SMET, *Contemplation*, p. 213.
[14] *Katha Up.* 2: 23.
[15] SHANKARA, says, for example, in his commentary of the *Gita*: '*The knowledge of Atma-consciousness is not an effect to be obtained ... Brahman is self-evident: we have only to eliminate what is falsely ascribed to Brahman by a-Vidya [ignorance].*' Gita Bhasya, 18: 50, quoted by R. DE SMET, *Contemplation*, p. 215.

As in the other religions, some common recitation of sacred texts is linked with ritual. On other occasions, recitation is a means of religious instruction. It can also be used for praising in common the heavenly benefactors, or to bring about a meditative concentration. According to the Indian custom, meditation is usually done morning and evening. It is sometimes shortened in the morning, when monks have to go out for begging their food, but it can also be carried out during the day.

The recited text, leading to meditation, varies according to the different schools. But, in general, it is a summary of the essential points of Buddhism: repeated praise of the Buddha, the *Dharma* and the *Sangha*, followed by the *Taking refuge* in these three, a kind of profession of faith.[16] Here, for example, is the conclusion of the Buddhist morning office, in Laos:

> *He raised up in the world the Perfect One, the Saint, the highest Lord, Buddha, and the Law* [Dhamma] *proclaimed by the Perfect One, so that all beings may be free, and find peace and quiet, Nirvana, and illumination. We have listened to the* Dhamma *and we know it. Birth is suffering, old age is suffering, death is suffering ... We turn to the Blessed One* [Buddha], *in whom we take refuge, to the* Dhamma *and the* Sangha. *We strive heartily to keep these teachings with all the strength of our minds. May our devotion put an end to multiform suffering.*[17]

This recitation is explicitly designed to prepare for meditation. After describing them, Father Zago concludes:

> *The diverse forms of monastic prayer lead to meditation and are, in any case, one of its expressions. The morning and evening rituals carried out by a Buddhist religious community aim at fixing mind and heart on the triple gem (Buddha, Dhamma, and Sangha). Thus the repetition of the same ideas in these formulas can be understood. Meditation should accompany gestures, words, corporal attitudes, and offerings.*
>
> *In these exercises, some ritual gestures are suggested: such as kneeling before a representation of the Buddha, fixing the eyes on his sacred image, kindling candles, making offerings, prostrations, etc. All this, however, is only an introduction to meditation, a means of fixing the mind, and has a value similar to that of bodily posture or the control of breathing.*[18]

[16] Let us remember that the *Dharma* (*Dhamma*, in Pali) is the universal law, discovered and proclaimed by the Buddha, whereas the *Sangha* is the community of his disciples, and above all, the monks.
[17] M. Zago, *Rites et cérémonies en milieu bouddhiste Lao*, p. 73 (our translation).
[18] Ibid. pp. 76–77.

These characteristics are found in most schools of Buddhism. The relationship with meditation is sometimes even stronger. Among the Tibetans, for example, the psalmody often consists of the practice in common of some of the meditation processes. In Zen, with its strong opposition to conceptual reasoning, psalmody is again centred on meditation and songs are only used as an introduction. Psalmody can also be prolonged in some way, by the recitation of mantras, *koans* or syllables as aids to concentration.

Among Buddhists, the participation of the body is very strong. It is manifested, from the moment the monks enter the prayer room, by the dignity of their folded hands, and their silence. Only some discreet whispering is allowed, then each one sits calmly in his place. The recitation is often accompanied with gestures of the hands which, at least among Tibetans, are used as an aide-memoire. They have a symbolic meaning, and help to put the whole being in harmony with the universe.[19]

In the *Mahayana*, and sometimes in Zen, songs of praise to the *Bodhisattvas*, or protecting beings, foster interior harmony by bringing the affective part of the personality into play.

Such participation of the diverse levels of the human being is expressly meant to influence the subconscious, so that it may not obstruct the search for the one on whom the mind meditates. It is interesting to note that Tibetan children have to memorise words, gestures, and dances that accompany the songs, before receiving the explanation of their meaning.

Studying the process that moves from reading the sacred text to meditation, the Tibetans recognise the same stages as Shankara: listening to the teaching, analysis of its contents, and intuitive contemplation.[20] Each school insists on the knowledge of its own traditional writings. Nevertheless, in the singing that leads up to the meditation, the body's rhythm and the breathing are more important than the meaning of the text.

For Buddhists, meditation itself is the most efficient exercise in following the path of the *Dharma*. A great number of methods have been elaborated to answer the various needs. That of *Samatha* aims to develop serenity and mastery of the passions, since these two

[19] The universe includes not only the material world, but also the world of the spirits. A person needs to be reconciled with them, attracting the favourable ones, and driving away the bad.

[20] This process has been described, in the Tibetan tradition, in the twelfth century. It is possible that Shankara (ninth century) or other Indian sources may have influenced it.

promote a desire for something beyond the senses. Then the spirit becomes 'empty', and remains at its 'centre', in contact with *Nirvana*. The methods known as *Vipassana* insist on the impermanence of all things, and lead to the dissolution of the sense of self in the presence of the Infinite. In the devotional movements, the methods used are close to the Hindu *Bhakti*, while Zen aims for *Satori*, in which the self disappears, since it shares a common existence with all beings.

As a whole, these methods show that reflection on a text is not the only possible base for meditation. Concentration can begin from a word, an object, an image, an idea, a posture, a bodily movement, attention to the present moment, and other similar things. But, despite the variety of starting points, the process seems always the same: attention is given to the chosen subject, helped by the repetition of a word and by posture, thus unifying the person and concentrating his powers on a single point, while withdrawing them from the external world. The result is a state of calm, peace and receptivity, which allows concentration to become ever deeper. The starting point diminishes in importance, until eventually it disappears into the Infinite, leaving the mind in the presence of *Nirvana*.

The experience of the loss of consciousness of the self, by fusion with all that exists, is highly sought by Buddhists, because it is considered as a means of salvation. According to Buddhism, the human being is a part, or an energy, which comes from the Absolute, to which it must return if it is to find its plenitude. The experience of union is one of the best ways to be freed from impermanence, to escape from the cycle of rebirths, and be united with the fullness of the Infinite.

Since Buddhism has no teaching about a personal God, the role of grace is rarely mentioned in the process of meditation. However, the followers of the *Mahayana* attribute some kind of help to the *Bodhisattvas*, and their assistance is invoked. Regular practice of meditation with a view to union with the Absolute implies a serious attitude to the religious search, and a style of life that is in harmony with it.

[21] *Lk.* 18: 1; 21: 36; *Eph.* 5: 19–20; 6: 18; 1 *Thess.* 5: 17; cf. *Rom.* 12: 12; *Phil.* 4: 6; *Col.* 4: 2; CLEMENT OF ALEXANDRIA, *Stromata*, 7; ORIGEN, *De Oratione*, 12: 2; *Contra Celsum* 7: 17–18. Cf. JEROME, *Let.*, 47, to Marcella, where he speaks of Origen.

3. PSALMODY AND CONTEMPLATION IN CHRISTIAN MONASTICISM

HOW TO PRAY CONTINUOUSLY

Christian prayer has its source in its Jewish counterpart, which is based on the singing of the psalms, and the reading of Holy Scripture, texts which are, in part, contemporary with the Hindu *Veda*. Christ, the Apostles, and the first Christians followed this usage. Saint Paul (*Eph.* 5: 19) recommends his communities to sing the psalms. However, like Jesus, he wants the faithful to *pray continuously*. These directions were passed down to the first Christian ascetics by Clement of Alexandria and Origen.[21]

From the moment he left the world, Saint Antony made it his practice to meditate continually on Scripture, as an answer to the call he had heard in the Gospel, *pray continually*. Later he recommended his disciples

> *to pray continuously, and to sing psalms before and after sleep.*[22]

Following his example, the Desert Fathers united psalmody with silent prayer and work. Thus Theodore

> *used to sit in his cell, plaiting ropes, and reciting passages of the Holy Scripture he had learnt by heart. When his heart felt so inclined, he stood and prayed.*[23]

The psalmody was carried out in common, mostly when the solitaries gathered at the end of the week for the Eucharist.[24]

During the lifetime of Saint Antony, the cenobitic tradition, inaugurated by Saint Pachomius, organised fixed times for psalmody, Scripture study, silent prayer, conferences, and work. All these Fathers recited passages of Scripture, interspersed with silent prayers. The psalms, considered as 'a summary of Scripture', had a privileged place in this recitation right from the outset.[25] However, Pachomius shows us that the rest of the Scripture was used in doctrinal catechesis, which nourished and sustained the life and prayer of the monks. Psalmody at fixed times, a Jewish inheritance, gave a framework to

---

[22] ATHANASIUS, *VA* 3; 39.
[23] PACHOMIUS, *Bo.*, 34; cf. *Apophthegmata*, Epiphanius, 3; 9; 10; Isidore, 4; Macarius, 33; Poemen, 202; etc.
[24] *Apophthegmata*, Poemen, 32; 79.
[25] EVAGRIUS, *Or.*, 85; ATHANASIUS, *Ep. Marcellus*, *PG* 25.

personal prayer. Recommended by the Fathers, it was organised by the first monastic legislators, Pachomius, Basil, Augustine, Cassian, followed by the small Rules of the West, the Master, and Benedict.[26]

The Fathers and Christian ascetics gave a special significance to the prayer inherited from the Jews, connecting it with events in Christ's life. Such fixed times of prayer became an approximate expression of the continuous prayer sought by Jesus, and were united to his own prayer. Indeed, most of the Rules ask that the common prayer of the Divine Office overflow into private prayer. For the same motive, silence during manual work, and when going from one place to another, is meant to foster the interior 'rumination' on the Scriptural words.[27] The hours of night in particular were always considered as a particularly favourable time for meditation.[28]

THE COMPOSITION OF THE DIVINE OFFICE

Within this framework, the number and composition of the offices varied considerably. At first, psalms were recited by heart, according to their order. Later, some of them were selected according to the hour of the day. In the longer offices, Scripture readings would complement the psalmody.[29]

However, the number of the psalms ascribed to the different offices were not the same everywhere. The Egyptian monks lent authority to a system they had themselves invented, by saying that it was 'revealed by an angel'.[30] Some large communities in Gaul, finding themselves

[26] *Acts* 3: 1; DIDACHE, 8: 3; TERTULLIAN, *De Oratione*, 24: 36; 25: 6; CYPRIAN, *De Dom. Or.*, 34: 3; CLEMENT OF ALEXANDRIA, *Strom.* 7: 7; 40: 3-4; ORIGEN, *De Or.*, 12: 2; *In Reg. Hom.*, 1: 9; *In 1 Pe.*, 1: 2; *In Mat.*, 16: 22; HIPPOLYTUS, *Trad. Ap.*, 41; PACHOMIUS, *Praec. et Inst., Intro.*, 14-15; *Praec. et Leg.* 10-12; BASIL, *LR* 37; AUGUSTINE, *Ordo mon.*, 2; CASSIAN, *Inst.* 3: 2-4; CAESARIUS OF ARLES, *Reg. Virg.*, 22; 66-69; *RM*, chs. 38-49 (quotations taken from AV *RB* 4 and 5).

[27] Cf. the quotations of the previous note. For union with Jesus, see: JEROME, *In Dan.*, 6; *Ep.* 22: 37; CASSIAN, *Inst.*, 2: 10-11; 3: 4; *Conf.* 9: 36; AUGUSTINE, *Ep.* 130: 18. Private prayer as a prolongation of the Divine Office: PACHOMIUS, *Praec.* 28; 59; 68; 94; 116; BASIL *LR* 5-6; *SR* 21-22; 202; GREG. NAZ., *Or.* 33; CASSIAN, *Conf.* 10: uses the verse *O God come to my help for this purpose; Apophthegmata*, Ammonas, 4; DOROTHEUS OF GAZA, 10, p. 39; CAESARIUS OF ARLES, *Reg. Virg.* 22.

[28] The Egyptian monks usually dedicated the full day, and half of the night to continuous prayer, accompanied by manual work (cf. CASSIAN, *Inst.* 3: 2). Nevertheless, several examples also show monks spending the whole night in prayer: *Apophthegmata*, Arsenius, 30; Isidore, 4; in the same way, *Philokalia*, Isaac the Syrian, 235.

[29] *Verb. Sen., Vitae Patr.*, 3: 116, quoted by Saint Benedict. Cf. A. DAVRIL, *La psalmodie chez les Pères du Désert*, COLLECTANEA, 49, 1987, 2.

[30] CASSIAN, *Inst.*, 2: 5; PALLADIUS, *Hist. Laus.* 32, 6.

with little work to do, increased the Office, so that there were twelve psalms for each of the so-called 'Little Hours' (Terce, Sext and None), and twenty-four, for each 'Nocturn' or part of the night prayer. By contrast, other communities, with a greater inclination towards the hermit life, gradually arranged long hours for private reading, and met only morning and evening to recite some psalms together, according to their order in the Psalter.

The same variety is seen in the number of the offices. The office of Prime, for example, appeared only a few years before Saint Benedict. However, the fundamental idea remained the same: *to pray continuously*. This is fulfilled through the traditional number of seven hours a day, a number that, in the Bible, acts as a symbol of plenitude, and indicates that the prayer of the office embraces the whole day.[31]

What was the attitude of the monks during their recitation or meditation of Scripture? The texts we have quoted offer us only occasional and short indications. The brethren usually sat for the reading and recitation, but stood, knelt, or prostrated for personal prayer. These are simple and natural gestures. More precise indications are given only much later, to ensure some kind of uniformity in the gestures of the community. The Rule of the Master is the first to offer a detailed ceremonial, which lends some importance to gestures and corporal attitudes that unify the person as he prays.[32]

The singing of the psalms could be joyful enough to captivate the audience. Saint Augustine, for example, was enthusiastic when he first read the psalms, and found himself subsequently moved to tears when he heard them sung in Milan. Cassian says that the monks of Gaul liked to sing long series of psalms, and other witnesses tend to confirm this.[33]

But if the singing of the psalms was sometimes exuberant, it always gave rise to silent prayer, the response, as it were, of the human being

---

[31] Before the introduction of the hour of Prime, the number, seven, included the Night Office. It is found in Cassian, Cassiodorus, and Augustine, cf. AV *RB* V, pp. 514–515.

[32] Theodore recited psalms while sitting, then stood for prayer, as we have seen. Arsenius prayed kneeling the whole night (*Apophthegmata*, Arsenius, 30), Orsisius takes care of the good behaviour of the monks during the office (CSCO, 160, pp. 83–85). Cassian, *Inst.* 2: 18, says that the monks were seated during the office, and in *Inst.* 3: 11, they stand up together. In *RM*, the brethren rise, then bow down to the ground during the prayer between the psalms. Other details are given to ensure respectful behaviour in the presence of God and of his angels.

[33] Augustine, *Conf.* 9: 4, 7–8; 10: 23 where the charm of singing the psalms fights against the old pleasures; Cassian, *Inst.* 2; *Cons. Zacchei*, *PG* 20, 1157–1158; S. Nicetius Trev., *PL* 68, 371–374.

to the Word received from God. Beside silence after the completion of the office, there was usually a time of prayer between the psalms.[34]

With his desire to pray continuously, the Christian monk organised his life so as to be in some way enveloped by the Word of God, which was sung, in the office, and meditated, in *lectio divina* and silent work. This external framework leant support to a whole spiritual journey, whose various stages have been studied since the first centuries. Origen and Clement of Alexandria based themselves on Scripture, as they attempted to describe the stages of union with God. Saint Augustine and Saint Gregory of Nyssa complemented that work. The description of the stages of this union was later developed by several mystics, particularly those of the Carmelite school, Saint Teresa of Avila and Saint John of the Cross. On their part, the monastic authors show a preference for studying the process that leads from reading of Scripture to contemplation.

LECTIO DIVINA

Evagrius and Cassian report the experience of the Desert Fathers on this subject. In the Middle Ages, Guigo the Carthusian schematised its various stages, giving us a list which, curiously, reproduces what Shankara had discovered three centuries earlier, and would also be used by Guigo's Tibetan contemporaries. Guigo distinguishes four stages, which he compares with the way a cow chews the cud:

> *Reading is like bringing solid food to the mouth; meditation is the chewing of it; while prayer is the tasting of it; and, in contemplation, we take delight in the sweetness we have found.*[35]

He explains also that the soul looks into the text for a word which can nourish it, then repeats it to itself, 'chewing' it over, and God allows it to find delight in this experience. Hence the beginning is rational reflection on the words with which the grace of God has touched the soul. Meditation and 'chewing' the word helps the meaning 'to go down in the depth of the heart', from which a delightful contemplation may arise. In the centre of this schema Guido puts prayer, which in reality envelops the whole process, because

> *The soul does not, itself, have the necessary resources to reach it (the sweetness of contemplation) ... but must receive it from above.*[36]

---

[34] Cf. AV, *Psalmodier n'est pas prier*, ECCLESIA ORANS, 1989, 1.
[35] GUIGO THE CARTHUSIAN, *L'échelle des moines*, No. 2, SC 163.
[36] Ibid., No. 4.

Insisting on the ascetic preparation necessary for union with God, Cassian set out to describe what would be, in fact, the latter stages of Guigo's schema. In monastic life there should be three renunciations: the first is 'corporal', that is, the ascesis necessary for a life of prayer; the second is renunciation of the heart and desires, without which the corporal observances are useless; the third controls wandering thoughts, and concentrates the mind on God.[37] Cassian gives us an example of words that God's grace had rendered 'tasty' to his soul in the phrase, *O God come to my aid – O Lord, make haste to help me* (*Ps.* 69). Here, we see an *intelligent* recitation of Scripture, which not only understands the words, but actually *experiences* them in some way, leading from an intellectual knowledge to a loving encounter with the Lord. Little by little, thinking is simplified. Prayer becomes *the prayer of fire*, having the enthusiasm of thanksgiving, or repentance, looking on God alone, and speaking to him as to a Father. Then the words themselves disappear:

> *Thus the soul reaches purity of prayer ... It does not cling to any image, nor express itself in words. But prayer springs up in a burst of fire, an unspeakable rapture, an insatiable impetuosity of spirit. Led beyond its senses, the soul offers itself to God, in unspeakable sighs and groans ... a prayer expressed by the Holy Spirit himself.*[38]

We shall have to consider Cassian's thought again, since Saint Benedict refers to it in his Rule. Here we could mention a saying of Saint Teresa of Avila, on how to move from a reflection on a word of Scripture to contact with God: the reflection is transformed into acts of praise and adoration:

> *Souls who occupy themselves with mental discourses ... would do well to try, from time to time, to make acts of praise to God, rejoicing in his goodness and in his infinite perfections.*[39]

4. FROM PSALMODY TO PRAYER IN *RB*

We have seen how, from the very beginning of the Rule, Saint Benedict wishes to guide the monk according to Scripture, asking

---

[37] The three renunciations: CASSIAN, *Inst.* 2: 3; *Conf.* 3: 7–8; 18: 7; 24: 2; 10–12.

[38] CASSIAN: *Intelligent* recitation of Scripture, *Inst.* 2: 11, quoting 1 *Cor.* 14: 5; *Conf.* 10: 11; pure prayer, purity of heart (recollected, free from passions) *Inst.* 5: 32–33; *Conf.* 9: 2–3; 15. Repetition of the verse, *O God come to my aid, Conf.* 10: 10; Our Father, *Conf.* 9: 18–25; prayer of fire, *Conf.* 9: 15; 10: 11.

[39] TERESA OF AVILA, *The Interior Castle*, fourth mansion, ch. 1.

him, as he did in the first step of humility, to stay in God's presence.
RB, following the tradition of the Fathers, considers psalmody as the
essential structure for *continuous prayer*, which will blossom into
contemplation. Beginning with the external aspects of prayer, Saint
Benedict leads his disciple towards a most profound union with God.

GESTURES AND CORPORAL ATTITUDES

In contrast with the overly detailed prescriptions of *RM* on the
gestures and ceremonies of the Divine Office, *RB* is very sparing,
and leaves such matters to the Abbot's discretion. Despite his
conciseness, Saint Benedict gives a precise significance to each attitude he indicates.

We spoke earlier of *gravitas* (*RB* 22: 6), an attitude of seriousness
and charity which the Rule asks the brethren to observe when going
to church. On arrival in the choir, the brethren are to go to their stalls

duly and in order ... with humility, gravity, and reverence,

a prescription which holds good for all changes of place during the
liturgy.[40] Such organisation is intended to create an atmosphere of
silence, respect, and humility, which will, in turn, lead to God.

THE PSALMODY

To show how the times of recitation of the Divine Office will bathe
the whole life of the monk in prayer, Saint Benedict discusses the
symbolism of the number seven:

*As the prophet puts it, 'Seven times daily I have praised you.' This sacred
number of seven will be performed by us if we carry out the duties of our
service ... and at night let us get up to praise him (RB 16: 1–2, 5).*

In fixing the number of hours and the disposition of the psalms, Saint
Benedict shows himself to be part of an evolving tradition. For

[40] *RB* 11; 2; 47: 3–4; 63: 4. Also: *As soon as the reader has begun the 'Gloria', let
all rise from their seats in honour and reverence to the Holy Trinity* (*RB* 9: 7).
During the reading of the Gospel *all stand with fear and reverence* (*RB* 11: 9).
When a brother makes a mistake, he is to prostrate himself on the floor, with
humility (*RB* 67: 3–4; 71: 8). *When the Work of God has been completed all are
to go out noiselessly, and let reverence for God reign there. So that if a brother
should have a mind to pray by himself, he will not be disturbed by the ill-conduct
of anyone else.* (*RB* 52: 2–3). Even when the Divine Office is said during work
in the fields, the brethren kneel *in reverence before God* (*RB* 50: 3).

instance, he adopts the hour of Prime, which had been only recently introduced, and improves the distribution of the psalms, selecting those which fit the time of day, while for the night Vigils he makes use of those which remain, taking them in order as they come. Nevertheless, he does not seem completely satisfied with this system, and makes allowance for alternative dispositions:[41]

> *Nevertheless, we emphasise that if anyone is dissatisfied with this arrangement of the Psalms, he is to organise them otherwise as he finds better (RB 18: 22).*

Speaking of the number of psalms for the various offices, Saint Benedict asks that twelve be said at Vigils, and the entire Psalter during the week (*RB* 18: 20–25). He is concerned that his monks may become lazy, and less fervent than the Desert Fathers. But it is evident that he is more concerned with measure and balance (*RB* 14: 2), that is, the length of the prayer, than its content, which he considers as variable. His main aim was thus to allow his brethren enough time to soak in God's word, and live in his presence.

The composition of the Divine Office as a whole indicates a care for the needs and tastes of the community in helping it to pray. The solemnity of an office depends on the number of the participants (*RB* 17: 6). Contemporary elements are introduced: usages of the Roman Church; hymns from Milan or elsewhere (*RB* 13: 11); the use of the *Te Deum*, a recent Western chant, and the Eastern *Te Decet Laus*.

The timetable of the monastery, in a similar way, takes into account the climate and the exigencies of work, attempting to envelop all the monks' activities in prayer. The liturgical offices are placed at the points where activities change, in order to offer to God what has just been done and entrust him with the next duty. This distribution is not to be thought of as a rigid framework, but rather as a living structure that supports the prayer of the community, as it is.

---

[41] A close examination of the text shows a lack of coherence in the times and composition of the Divine Office, which in turn suggests certain hesitations on the part of the manuscript redactors. For example, in the timetable given in *RB* 48, Prime is not mentioned in winter, nor is the office of Sext mentioned between the first of October and Lent. The chapter on those who come late to choir (43: 10) does not mention the hymn at the beginning of the day prayers. Several titles of the chapters on the Divine Office seem to be either fictitious or later additions (chs. 10; 13; 14). These details led some commentators to think that there have been perhaps several redactions of these chapters, either by Saint Benedict himself, or by his first disciples, at the time of their leaving Montecassino for Rome.

Another aspect of the Divine Office can be seen in the special meaning that is given to the word *service*.[42] Saint Benedict considers the life and prayer of the monk as a service to the Church, *a service of devotion* which should be carried out without laziness, but with courage and love. The notion that the monks' prayer protects and strengthens the Church had already been expressed by the Greek Fathers, especially Saint John Chrysostom:

> *They assist those in charge of the Church, strengthening them by their prayers, by their union with them, by their charity ... They are the ramparts that protect the cities.*[43]

Saint Benedict sees monastic intercession as a prayer of praise and thanksgiving to God. The night office is called the night *Praise*, in the title of chapter 10, and chapter 16 says that the brethren give praise to God by their prayer during the day and night. The same chapter mentions twice that during the night office the monks are to *give praise to our Creator*. All these expressions are in fact quotations from psalms, which shows how Saint Benedict was imbued with their spirit.

The insistence of *RB*, and of the Hebrew tradition, on the aspect of praise in the Divine Office is an original contribution that we have not yet come across. The psalmody is not merely a prelude to meditation or a framework for unceasing prayer, but has its own particular value as a prayer of praise, repentance and supplication. It is an acknowledgement of all that God's love unceasingly gives to humankind, from its existence in a universe full of order and beauty, supported by God's constant attention to all creatures, to the particular love he showers upon each human person, despite weaknesses and revolts.

Shot through with continuous prayer, gratitude and praise, the Divine Office constitutes so essential a part of the monk's life that he must strive to preserve it in all circumstances. Saint Benedict requires that the brethren working outside the monastery or travelling:

> *should not allow the hours prescribed for prayer to go unobserved, but they should do their best to carry out their duties in God's service and not neglect them (RB 50: 4).*

This sense of duty and flexibility characterises the organisation of the whole office. In his service of gratitude, the monk is also united with

[42] The monastery is *a school of the Lord's service* (*RB Prol.* 45); the monastic life is the *profession of holy service* (*RB.* 5: 3); the choir prayer is *the duty of our service ... a sacred service* (*RB* 16: 2; 18; 24).

[43] JOHN CHRYSOSTOM, *Contra Anom.* VI, *PG* 48, 496 D; *In 1 Tim.* 14: 3, *PG* 62, 574. Antony and Pachomius also prayed for all the needs of the Church.

the angels and wants to stand with them, before God, contemplating his mystery.

5. FROM PSALMODY TO CONTEMPLATION IN *RB*

A Rule is not a treatise on mysticism. Thus, as far as prayer and contemplation are concerned, Saint Benedict refers explicitly to Cassian, and the use he makes of his vocabulary gives us a fairly accurate account of his own thought on the subject.

We have seen how the way of entering the church, and all the gestures made during the Divine Office, foster within each monk an attitude of respect for God's presence. The same is required when beginning the hours of the office:

> *We believe that God is present everywhere, and that the eyes of the Lord are in every place, keeping watch on the good and the bad; but most of all should we believe this without any shadow of doubt, when we are engaged in the work of God [the Divine Office] (RB 19: 1-2).*

The chapter continues with a series of quotations from the psalms, on respect for God's presence. Saint Benedict adds the angels who for him are the sign of the divine Majesty and of its unceasing attention to us:[44]

> *We should therefore always be mindful of the prophet's words, 'Serve the Lord with fear.' And again, 'Sing praises [psalms] wisely.' And yet again, 'In the sight of the angels I will sing praises [psalms] to you (RB 19: 3-6).*

Such attention, like that of the angels, is not merely passive. The Rule invites the brethren to deepen their experience of God's word. Indeed, the second quotation, *sing [psalms] wisely*, refers to Cassian, who develops this theme first in his *Institutes* (2: 11) (quoting 1 *Cor.* 14: 15, where Saint Paul asks everyone to try to understand the words of the psalms) and then in *Conference* 10. In this last work, the monk is invited to recite the Scripture *wisely*, that is, not only to understand the meaning of the words, but in some way to *experience* them:

---

[44] *RB* mentions the angels three times: in chapter 7: first, on Jacob's ladder (7: 6), then, as the sign that *God is always looking down from heaven* (7: 13-26); and twice in ch. 19, concerning God's presence (19: 5-6).

Filled with the same sentiments with which the psalm was sung or composed, we become, in some way, like its author ... Taught by what we feel within ourselves, these words will not be like things learned by hearsay, but we shall, so to speak, touch the reality, because we have perceived it thoroughly ... It is not through reading that we understand the meaning of the words, but through acquired experience.[45]

Chapter 19 of *RB* concludes with a summary of this text:

As we sing our Psalms let us see to it that our mind is in harmony with our voice (RB 19: 7).

To penetrate the meaning of God's word, we need a thorough attention to his presence. *RB* Prologue had expressed the eager search of God through use of the images of hurrying and running: the monk arises, runs, hastens towards the heavenly dwelling.[46] His prayer, his desire of God is earnest, with tears, joyful zeal and repentance inspired by the Holy Spirit.[47]

Through the narrow way of faith, the psalmody leads to a personal contact with God. Thus, it was quite natural for Saint Benedict to continue his chapter on the manner of saying the Divine Office by one on *Reverence at prayer* (*oratio*).

Note the word *reverence*, followed immediately in the text by humility, (*RB* 20: 1) both referring to the context of the psalmody.

We should present our supplications to the Lord God of all things with complete humility and devout purity of mind. Indeed we must grasp that it is not by using many words that we shall get our prayers answered, but by purity of heart and repentance with tears (RB 20: 2-3).

Each time Saint Benedict speaks of prayer, he asks the monk to remember his rightful place before God, that is, the attitude of humble trust of the publican in the Gospel, as it is described in the *Prologue* and in chapter 7 (first and twelfth steps of humility).[48]

In describing the silent prayer that the monk continues in his heart, either after the choir office or when he goes to his work, Saint

---

[45] CASSIAN, *Conf.* 9: 11. The theme of the harmony between voice and mind is often treated in monastic literature (cf. AUGUSTINE, *Let.*, 48, 3; 211, 17). *RM* develops it at length. Saint Benedict limits himself to a well-cast sentence (*RB* 19: 7).

[46] *RB Prol.* 8: 22; cf. 7: 5; 73: 2; 4: 8.

[47] Earnest prayer, *Prol.* 4; purification by the Holy Spirit, 7: 70; supplication with humility, purity of heart, tears, 20: 2-3; 49: 4; with tears and fervour of heart 52: 4.

[48] *RB Prol.* 1-4; 7: 10-18, 65-69.

Benedict makes further use of Cassian. He chooses the phrases, *purity of heart*, which means the stripping of all egoistic ties, and *pure prayer*, which for Cassian means, precisely, the contemplation that results from the psalmody. We have seen it described above. It is a prayer inspired by the Holy Spirit, beyond images and words, in which the soul pours itself out in God, like a blazing fire.[49]

Saint Benedict summarises all this in a few words:

With tears and the attention of [one's] heart . . . our hearts are opened wide, with a sweetness of love that is beyond words.[50]

This reminds us of Guigo's ladder, which starts from an understanding of the text, and ends in prayer, in *contemplation that takes delight in the sweetness it has found.* Nevertheless, Saint Benedict, and all the Christian tradition, attribute spiritual progress solely to divine grace. He says this several times in the Prologue, and one of the Tools of Good Works (ch. 4) is:

Whenever one perceives any good in oneself to attribute it to God, not to one's self (RB 4: 42).

Similarly, it is the Lord who allows the ladder of humility to rise up to heaven. The monk obeys in difficult circumstances, trusting in the assistance of God. He fulfils the Rule *with the help of Christ*, and reaches the summit of perfection, *under God's protection.*[51]

The place given to Christ is the most characteristic point of Saint Benedict's thought. We have already noticed this aspect at the beginning of the Rule, and it is manifested again in the arrangement of the prayer and life of the monk. All organisation in the monastery is centred on the paschal mystery. In the course of the year, the timetable varies with the liturgical seasons, headed by the feast of Easter. In relation to its date, the times of the offices, of fasting, meals, work and *Lectio divina* are all fixed. In the weekly rhythm, Sunday, the Lord's Day, is celebrated in a particular way, with longer times of prayer and reading, while work is reduced to a minimum.[52]

Sunday is also pre-eminently the day of the Eucharistic celebration. In ancient times, an echo of the Eucharist was introduced into the

---

[49] CASSIAN, *Conf.* 10: 11, cf. n. 38. *On Purity of heart*; cf. *Inst.* 15: 32–36; *Conf.* 1: 6–7.

[50] *RB* 52: 4; *RB Prol.* 49.

[51] *RB Prol.* 20, 29–32, 41; 4: 42; 7: 8; 68: 5; 73: 8–9.

[52] *RB* 41; 48: 22–23.

rhythm of each weekday by the distribution of the Holy Communion at the end of the office preceding the meal.[53] Our present daily Mass can be seen in the same light, bringing the whole community life into contact with the mystery of Christ, as suggested in the Prologue:

> *To you, who, by the renunciation of your own will, are taking up the strong and glorious weapons of obedience in order to do battle in the service of the Lord Christ ... First of all, whenever you begin any good work, you must ask of God with the most urgent prayer that it may be brought to completion by him.*

Again, it is:

> *Christ [who will] bring us all together to life everlasting.*[54]

These two sentences which in a way encapsulate the whole Rule, give us a good indication of the centrality of Christ in the prayer of Saint Benedict's disciple. We now need to view all this within the context of all those ascetics who have strived to reach union with the Absolute for many thousands of years.

6. SACRED TEXTS AND CONTEMPLATION, CONCORDANCES AND DIVERGENCES

The fundamental point that defines the monk in all religions, is that he dedicates his whole life and all his activities to the search for union with the Absolute. This approach is made with the help of sacred texts, studied, read and sung, which support meditation, in which he may meet the Absolute, beyond words and concepts.

THE USE OF SACRED TEXTS

Everywhere the sacred texts are used in a complementary way for doctrinal formation, psalmody and meditation. The diverse traditions

---

[53] The usage of giving Holy Communion outside Mass during the week is attested by *RM*, and comes from the time of the Desert Fathers, as BASIL testifies in his *Let.*, 23 to the patrician, Caesaria. He recommended frequent communion, and said that this custom came from Egypt where, because of the persecutions, Christians kept the Eucharist at home. This custom was maintained by the monks, and Saint AUGUSTINE recommends even daily communion (*Tract. in Jn.*, 26: 13, *PL* 35, 1313). This communion was considered by the Fathers as a *participation in the holy mysteries*, that is, a prolongation of the Sunday Eucharist.

[54] *RB Prol.* 3–4; 72: 11–12.

also place the psalmody at fixed times, generally before meditation, especially at the beginning and the end of the day, in order to orientate the whole life towards a constant search of the Absolute.

Whatever the religious tradition, its holy texts are diverse and deal with many subjects. All of them are studied in a more or less specialised way. Some, however, are selected for public or private recitation, either as an accompaniment to a ritual, or as introduction to meditation. But ritual can itself become a kind of meditation.

Usually, texts selected for common recitation synthesise the essentials of doctrine. In the theist currents, they mostly express praise, love and repentance. Even the book containing the sacred texts is an object of veneration, since it contains an exceptional spiritual experience which all desire to share.

Bodily gestures, as a support for chanting and prayer, are found in all religions. They are not much emphasised in Christianity. However, simple actions are used to foster the unity of the person and create an atmosphere of respect and recollection before God. By contrast, among Hindus and Buddhists, and thanks to very elaborate techniques like Yoga and Zen, the body has its place in the chanting of texts, as well as in meditation. Such bodily gestures are a means of putting the human being in harmony with the universe. They also act on the subconscious, helping to produce definite psychological states. All acknowledge, too, the importance of breathing techniques and methods, which can have a great influence on prayer.

FROM READING TO CONTEMPLATION

Independently of the respect due to the sacred books, most religions ask the monks to have an attitude of silence and respect when they enter the place where chanting or ritual will be performed. This is part of the ascesis leading to the mastery of senses and passions, always considered a necessary precondition for contemplation.

It is evident that Hindus, Buddhists and Christians have separately discovered a similar process, used for passing from exegesis, necessary to understand the text, to theological reflection. Such reflection is slowly changed, so that contact may be made with the Absolute.

A similar process can be found in all forms of meditation. Starting with a text, an object or an idea, the disciple enters into an ever more intense concentration that unites the senses, the imagination and the mind. Thus all external things are eliminated from the mind's consideration, so that it has merely 'a single point' to meditate on. Hindus and Buddhists make systematic use of bodily gesture to help this concentration.[55]

The result is a feeling of calm and peace, which has some similarity with the *apatheia* described by the Fathers of Christian monasticism. But all this implies a relaxed mind and body, something which is threatened by the stress of the modern world. These Asian methods may none the less help the disciple to achieve it. Thus he will enter into *the cave of the heart*, the place of encounter with the Infinite.

THE WAYS TOWARDS THE ABSOLUTE

Despite all these convergences, there comes a point where methods differ, because the philosophy and doctrine of each religion inevitably condition the ways of union with the Absolute that it proposes.[56]

Hindus and Buddhists look for an experience of concentration which, by eliminating the impermanent, allows them to discover in themselves the Reality from which the human being springs, so as to be immersed in this Reality, and be freed from the circle of rebirth. The *atman* realises its identity, and the *Brahman, or Buddha nature*, present in each and every person, becomes again one with the Absolute Nature. This leads to an experience of loss of consciousness of the Self, together with a sense of fusion with the source of the universe.

The Christian aim is different. The disciple tries to follow the example of Jesus, who in return introduces his disciple into the infinite love of the Holy Trinity.

Thus, we see a divergence in methods of approach. On the one hand, there is the search for a superior experience, considered as salvific, on the other, conformity through love with a person who saves. The stages of concentration, based on human nature, may be similar, but they are lived in a different way according to the desired goal. One group seeks fusion with the source of all beings, involving

---

[55] This conclusion may seem too simple. Nevertheless, I came to it after having studied, over a period of several years, the many Hindu and Buddhist methods of meditation that were readily available to me.

[56] Cf. Y RAGUIN, 'L'expérience personnelle de Dieu dans le christianisme', in *Moines Chrétiens*.

the loss of the self; the other seeks union, through Christ, to a God who is Love.[57]

Another difference is found in the way of understanding the means that are used. Yoga, and the Buddhist method, puts the stress on personal effort to reach liberation from the circle of rebirths. Christians, however, acknowledge the action of the Holy Spirit in the transformation that occurs in them by grace. The Christian's effort will therefore consist in opening himself to the Holy Spirit.

The use made of the sacred texts is also indicative of the diversity of approaches. Hindus and Buddhists, as we have seen, feel that the text becomes less and less important as progress is made. Some Tibetan monks even said to me on one occasion that the meaning of the text had little importance. The essential was the chanting, which gives the body and the breathing a rhythm conducive to meditation. For the Christian, however, the Word of God remains always alive and creative. In the Scripture text the disciple finds, and keeps in mind, words that touch the heart, words chosen by God, loaded with the grace of his Presence. Received in faith and love, they create something new within him. The Word is no longer merely a concept, but a living presence which nourishes, purifies and transforms the soul. This Word communicates the Spirit of Christ, and makes a humble person, who trusts in him, to be like him. We have seen this process described by the Fathers and by Cassian, and later summarised by Saint Benedict.

The particular originality of *RB*, in regard to the Divine Office, is found in its stress on the spirit of praise during the psalmody, and in the zeal required in praying the psalms, where the disciple must *yearn for eternal life with all possible spiritual desire*.[58] An atmosphere of humility and deep respect before God gives *RB* a relationship with Saint John Chrysostom, who had given the Eastern liturgy this same sense of God's greatness.[59]

---

[57] The experience of loss of consciousness of the Self, through communion with the whole universe, is not in itself contrary to Christian faith, which believes in God as the unique source of all that exists. Nevertheless, from the Christian point of view, this experience has no special salvific value. It is rather a psychological phenomenon in which, as it were, we 'cannot see the wood for the trees': one aspect of God fills the field of consciousness, and prevents other aspects from being seen. Whoever is searching for the God of Jesus Christ, will always have a relationship with him, based on knowledge and love, a share in the relationship which unites the Son with the Father. This is the experience reached by Abhishiktananda (Fr Le Saux), after a long and painful search.

[58] *RB* 19: 7; 4: 46.

[59] The fight against the Anomean heresy (which refused to see any mystery in God) led Saint John Chrysostom to meditate on the attitude of the Prophets and of the Apostles before their experiences of *theophany*, or revelation of God. He drew from that his great sense of the divine majesty.

But the most remarkable aspect of Benedictine prayer is its essential relationship with liturgy. In *RB* the life of the monastery, from the timetable and the kind of food to the texts of the Divine Office and Mass, is settled according to the liturgical season. So when the monk goes out of the church for silent prayer or work, his meditation revolves around the mysteries of the Lord he has been celebrating by singing or reciting the liturgical texts. The 'Work of God', the choir office, framing the daily activities of the community, is thus one of the most characteristic features of the Benedictine way of life. It nourishes the monks' spiritual life and is a *duty of service* (*RB* 50, 4) entrusted to them by the Church. Through it they pray and praise God in the name of the whole of mankind.

This liturgical aspect of prayer, characteristic of Saint Benedict in the Latin Church, is also found in the Oriental Churches. But the referral of all life to an Infinite Principle that governs it, beyond all the impermanence of this world, is also a trait that Christians hold in common with Hindus and Buddhists. Thus despite many differences, chanting and meditation, the search for union with the Absolute, respect, humility, singing, and silence before the divine Infinity, are all points held in common, which invite us to a dialogue in depth, between the different religions.

CHAPTER X

THE OFFICIALS OF THE MONASTERY:
Deans, Cellarer, Prior

Saint Benedict speaks in his Rule of *Deans*, elders in charge of a group of the brethren and used as counsellors. He also speaks of a bursar or *Cellarer*, and of a *Prior* who assists the superior. Hindu and Buddhist monasticism have similar offices. If we compared them with the Christian tradition, we shall find some common ground, and the particular aspects that each religion gives to these various duties. It may help also to see how they differ from similar positions in the secular world.

1. OFFICIALS IN HINDU MONASTICISM

Ancient Hindu monasticism did not have much structure, and its modern Orders, like the Ramakrishna Mission, copied the organisation of the Christian missionary Congregations. Nevertheless the ashrams, though generally small, give us some interesting clues.

The *Laws of Manu*[1] show that from the beginning there were different duties in the ashram. The guru, who is principally a spiritual master, is also sometimes called teacher, *acharya*. Besides him there is sometimes a paid teacher, specialising in some parts of the Veda, and called *upadhyaya*. Another helper, the *ritwidj*, is in charge of the sacred fire and family sacrifices.[2] There is also a certain hierarchy among the teachers, according to their learning.[3]

The qualities required for teaching, beside competence, are kindness,

---

[1] MANU, 2: 140–143.
[2] MANU, 2: 142.
[3] MANU, 2: 155.

self-mastery, and humility, which allows the master's words to penetrate the heart of his disciple:

> *A Brahmin who does not study the sacred books is like an elephant made
> of wood, or a stuffed deer. The three of them bear a name that is empty
> of meaning ... Any instruction, which has good as its object, should be
> communicated without ill-treating the disciples, and the master who
> wants to be just, should use kind and pleasing words.*
>
> *The one whose speech and mind are pure and well regulated in all
> circumstances, reaps all the advantages attached to the knowledge of the
> Vedanta. One should never give way to a bad mood, even when afflicted,
> nor try to do harm to others, nor even think about it, nor say a word
> which could offend somebody.*
>
> *A Brahmin should always fear worldly honour, as if it were poison.*[4]

From the point of view of economics, the Hindu monk lives essentially from alms. The origin of an ashram is a guru who gathers
disciples, and takes charge of them. He is thus responsible for the
whole group, and has full authority in material and spiritual fields
alike.

When the size of the ashram grows, the master asks a trustworthy
disciple to take charge of donations received, and to give board and
lodging to the members of the group. He is thus more free to dedicate himself to meditation and spiritual direction.

The monk in charge of the management has full responsibility for
it, and refers to the guru only for important decisions. He may have
helpers, for example, for cooking and for receiving guests, but as the
ashrams are generally rather small, these junior officials are few.
What is expected from all of them is honest management for the peace
of the group.

2. OFFICIALS IN BUDDHIST MONASTICISM

The Buddha had decided that, after his death, the monasteries would
be governed by the assembly of professed monks. But, when the
monks grew in numbers, the necessity of looking after the discipline
of the group, of taking care of the goods given to the communities,
and pressure from the civil authorities led to the election of a superior, who was thus principally an administrator.

In the monasteries of Sri Lanka, for example, there were at the
outset spiritual guides (*upajhaya*) and some teachers (*acharya*), nomi-

---

[4] MANU, 2:157; 159–162.

nated by the assembly of the professed monks for each novice.[5] After the twelfth century, the needs of the administration required some centralisation and at the request of the king a hierarchy was organised. The *Mahanahayake*, or Supreme Pontiff, appointed two assistants and a council of twenty members. In due course, one of these two assistants was chosen by the council to succeed to the Pontificate. The Council of the Twenty chose the regional superiors, who supervised the monasteries of their territory in economic matters, and the moral and spiritual education of the monks. They could eventually punish the heads of the monasteries if they were found to be neglecting their duties. In the same way, each monastery was headed by a monk, assisted by a council and by the assembly of the professed. The monks in charge of all these functions were elected democratically by the members of the community, and sometimes also by distinguished laymen. Each election had to be approved by the religious and lay authority of the next higher level.

Soon afterwards, the monasteries of several countries grouped themselves according to their spiritual families, and a complex hierarchy was created, often under the protection and supervision of the State. The officials varied, according to the country, and corresponded, as we have seen, to the organisation of the surrounding society.[6] In Sri Lanka, there are at present four Orders, each with its own main superiors and council. These Orders are sometimes divided into several branches, each one having its own hierarchy.

The role of the superiors and of their councils at each level was to see to the correct administration of the sometimes abundant goods of the monasteries,[7] and to settle the problems and conflicts between houses, between monks, or between monks and lay people. They had also, as we have seen, to take care of the monastic discipline and observance. But teaching and spiritual direction were done individually, each monk receiving his training from his master.

Nevertheless, the development of intellectual research slowly created other hierarchies among the monks. First came the spiritual masters, a group which developed into several branches, above all in the Mahayana Buddhism. Then there were the teachers, ranked

---

[5] In India, and Sri Lanka, the words *upajhaya* and *acharya* sometimes mean the spiritual master, sometimes his assistant. A personal enquiry, made in several monasteries of Sri Lanka, yielded the information which follows here in the text. This was later confirmed by reading *The History of Buddhism in Ceylon* of WALPOLA RAHULA.

[6] cf. M. ZAGO, *Rites et cérémonies religieuses en milieu bouddhiste Lao.*

[7] ZAGO, *Rites.* pp. 140–151 indicates the great wealth of Buddhist monasteries in some periods; hospitals were attached to some of them.

according to the degrees they had attained. This hierarchy is particularly developed among the Tibetans, who have other officials in charge of singing and ceremonies.

Furthermore, seniority never lost its rights, and created a form of precedence, which was combined with the other grades. In Laos, there were three degrees of precedence, first from 1 to 4 years, then from 5 to 9 years, and finally, over 10 years. They also had another hierarchy based on the honorary titles given by the king.

It is also customary for a monk to belong to several hierarchies, either by rota or simultaneously, since any elder can be the spiritual father of a younger one. In the Zen monasteries, for example, there is a section for meditation, and another for administration, each one with its own hierarchy of persons in charge. A monk belonging to one section cannot enter into the other without the permission of its head monk. But every six months the monks change section; those of the administration go to meditation, and vice versa. Buddhist authors give information about the conditions to be fulfilled for being appointed to each charge. So, at Sri Lanka in ancient times:

> *To be elevated to the rank of* Mahathera *or Regional Head, a monk had to fulfil five conditions: he had to have high moral standards, a deep knowledge of the* Dharma *and of the* Vinaya *[rules for community and monastic life] and of their commentaries, to be a competent spiritual guide, renowned by his good behaviour, to have at least twenty years' experience since ordination, be accepted by the Supreme Pontiff, elected unanimously by all the monks of the island, and formally installed by the king . . .*
>
> *The monasteries were well endowed with lands and other riches. Persons well-known for their non-attachment to gain were appointed to head them, so that it could be reasonably hoped that the income would be used honestly. Such a nomination [by the supreme Pontiff] had also to be approved by the king.*[8]

From these Hindu and Buddhist institutions taken as a whole certain features stand out. First of all, we find here again the two currents we noticed regarding the Abbot: in one of them the guru, or spiritual master, groups his disciples together and organises them; in the other, the organisation grows out of a pre-existing group which, at its origin, had been rather informal.

Along with the superior, other hierarchies sprang up: the spiritual masters, the teachers, the various fields of administration, and the cult.

[8]   Cf. G. PANABOKKE, 'The early Buddhist Sangha and its organisation', unpublished Doctoral Thesis, University of Colombo.

A superior is not always the spiritual master of the whole community, but, among the followers of the two currents, he always holds the final responsibility for the temporal administration. Thus the hierarchy of officials complements and assists the superior in the spiritual and material fields, but in different degrees according to traditions and circumstances. In the first group, an appointment is usually made by the guru, whereas, in the second, the community plays an important role.

Note the flexibility of the institution. It underwent a continuous evolution, adapting itself to the needs of the monasteries, as well as to changing times and forms of government, in the different countries. We shall speak later of the qualities needed for the spiritual master. But for the ordinary teachers, it is remarkable that the texts, even the oldest ones, place much emphasis on the correct way of speaking to young people. They have to be educated without being harmed.

Honest and competent people are needed to take responsibility for material assets and teaching. They have also to see to the welfare of the whole community. One of their roles is to ensure peace, both inside the monastery and in its external relations. For the same reason, the officials must have a good reputation among the people they have to work with.

3. OFFICIALS IN CHRISTIAN MONASTICISM BEFORE SAINT BENEDICT

During the life-time of Saint Antony, Saint Pachomius founded several communities, and brought Christian monasticism to its full development. His monasteries formed a kind of Congregation, with its Superior General and Bursar General. Each community was headed by a superior and his assistant. Inside the monastery, the monks were divided into houses of 30 to 40 monks. One of them was at the head of the house, and he was always helped by an assistant.[9] Each week he had to give the brethren a conference, as a complement to the one the superior regularly gave. They also brought him any problems arising in the house. The *Lives* of Pachomius mention brothers in charge of the main trades done in the monastery, like cooking, guesthouse, infirmary, weaving, etc. Other monks were spiritual fathers, whom the brethren were allowed to consult.[10]

---

[9] PACHOMIUS, VC *Bo.* 26; AV *Communauté*, p. 97, n. 1, citing JEROME, *Reg. Pac. Praef.* 2. A similar organisation exists in the big Tibetan monasteries that have taken refuge in India.

[10] PACHOMIUS, VC *Bo.* 26.

The qualities required by these offices are compared to those required by Scripture for the deacons. Pachomius and his successors insist on humility, charity towards the brethren, and zeal to take care of them.[11] The direction of particular duties required a special competence, such as the knowledge and meditation of the sacred writings for those who teach, a gift for guiding souls for the spiritual fathers, and, for all those in charge, the ability to give to each one a word suitable for his situation.[12]

Several scenes of Pachomius's life show that the appointment of the main officials belonged to the Superior General,[13] whereas the junior officials were appointed by his assistant and by the house superiors.[14]

Other writings, like those of Cassian and Palladius, inform us about the monastic centres of Lower Egypt contemporary with Pachomius. According to Palladius, the members of such centres sometimes reached several hundred in number, some of the monks living as hermits, the others in monasteries. Those of Nitria and of the Cells, for example, were headed by a body of eight priests, the eldest acting as superior. Other monks were responsible for the main trades, the guests and the infirmary.[15] Often the brethren were divided into groups of ten and a hundred, under the authority of an elder, following the example of the Hebrews in the desert.[16]

The role of these elders was to watch over the brethren, and give them what they needed, especially the newcomers. They had to train them in obedience, humility, and instruct them how to fight against their own will.[17] In return, the brethren would be open with them about their difficulties. Those in charge of the different offices had to inspect the tools during the weekly changeover of service, for all the objects of the monastery were sacred, since they belonged to God.

The officials were carefully selected by the elders who governed the monasteries. They selected only

> those who, in addition to the prerogative of seniority, gave witness of faith and virtue.[18]

---

[11] Ibid. 208.

[12] Ibid. 32. The necessity of a particular gift for spiritual direction was acknowledged by the Desert Fathers: *VP* 3: 170, PL 73, 297; *Sayings of the Fathers*, 4, Nos 28–30 (H. WADDELL, p. 102), also AUGUSTINE, *Enar. in Ps.* 103, 1: 19.

[13] PACHOMIUS, VC *Bo.* 26; 70–71; 121; 130.

[14] Ibid. 42; 74.

[15] CASSIAN, *Inst.* 4: 22.

[16] Ibid. 7.

[17] Ibid. 7–10.

[18] CASSIAN, *Inst.* 4: 19–20; *Conf.* 21; BASIL, *Reg.* 103–104; LR 11; SR 143

We need to mention the *Rule of the Master* (*RM*) written at a time very close to that of *RB*. The Master considers the prior merely as the coadjutor of a sick Abbot, at the end of his time of government. Speaking of the deans, and the cellarer, he lays down detailed regulations that made them only supervisors, without personal responsibility. All their activity is nevertheless designed to foster the spiritual progress of the brethren.

Cassian's perspective, followed by the *RM*, is essentially vertical. The superiors guide each monk towards God, but the mutual relationship between one brother and another is not much taken into account. Saint Basil and Saint Augustine, on the other hand, agree with Saint Pachomius in putting the stress on community life, and on the good influence the brethren ought to have on one another.[19] Saint Benedict would unite these two currents, in his own Rule.

4. OFFICIALS IN THE RULE OF SAINT BENEDICT

RB speaks separately of the deans, the cellarer and the prior. Each has its own chapter, but some of their functions are also mentioned elsewhere.

THE DEANS (*RB* 21; 22; 27; 46; 58; 62; 65)

The word *decani* (deans), as used by Saint Benedict, was new in the Christian monastic tradition. But, like Cassian, he also uses the word *elders* for them. The beginning of chapter 21 briefly summarises the authority and function of the deans:

> *They are to exercise care over their deaneries in all respects according to the commandments of God and the instructions of their Abbot. They should be chosen as deans who are such that the Abbot may be able to share his burdens with them with confidence (RB 21: 2).*

RB draws a parallel between the commandments of God and the instructions of the abbot. Hence, in both cases, the question is about general directives, and a spirit to be kept; it is not about detailed checking-up by the Abbot. On the contrary, the superior is to give a true responsibility to these officials: he trusts them to the point of sharing his burden with them. It will be the same for all the various

[19] Cf. AV *Structure et gouvernement*, p. 563 ff.; *Communauté*, pp. 319–320; AUGUSTINE, *Reg.* 13, 162–165.

officials of the monastery: cellarer, infirmarian, guestmaster, novice-master, doorkeeper. All are asked to have the qualities necessary for these functions, so that they can be trusted and allowed to take the initiatives useful for their work. In modern language, this is what we call subsidiarity.[20]

The elders also enjoy a spiritual role. The brethren reveal their secret faults to a spiritual father (*RB* 46: 4); an elder is in charge of the novices (*RB* 54); others are to help the brethren in trouble, as *senpectae* (*RB* 27: 2); and the elders form the Abbot's private council.

In some circumstances, the elders must keep an eye on what the brethren are doing, for example during *lectio divina*, or in the dormitory (48: 17–18; 22: 3). According to Saint Pachomius, their presence helps the brethren to be faithful to God. Cassian adds that they also take care that every monk may have what he needs in the matter of food and clothing.[21]

Saint Benedict's unique contribution is, first, his insistence on the qualities by which the deans are to be selected: they must be *brethren of good reputation and holy way of life* (*RB* 21: 1). The first words are an allusion to the text of *Acts* 6: 3, speaking of the choice of the deacons, and to *Deut.* 1: 13–15, where Moses chooses elders to assist him.[22] *Virtuous life and wise teaching* are similarly sought in the appointment of the Abbot (*RB* 64: 2) and refer to the same Scriptural texts.

These indications show that, for Saint Benedict, the deans form a monastic hierarchy of responsible persons. They should be united to the Abbot, allowing him to guide his monks, as Moses was helped by Joshua when he led the Jewish people towards the Promised Land. That comparison had already been used by Pachomius.[23]

THE CELLARER (*RB* 31)

The text of this section can be divided into several parts.

1) The choice and function of the cellarer

Like the deans, the cellarer is to be selected with care, and *RB* lists ten qualities he should have: *let him be sound in judgement, mature in character, sober etc.* (*RB* 31: 1). This attention to the qualities of the person contrasts with the detailed rules of *RM*. Saint Benedict is

---

[20] *RB* 2–3; 31: 1–2; 36: 7; 53: 21; 58: 6; 66: 1.
[21] PACHOMIUS, VC *Bo.* 84; CASSIAN, *Inst.* 4: 10; 17.
[22] Cf. also *Ex.* 18: 21–22 and *Nb.* 11: 13–17.
[23] PACHOMIUS, VC *Bo.* 78.

interested in the virtues which have to be put into practice in relation to people and to material things; the practical details are left to the care of the persons in charge.

The list ends with love for God and humanity, something which has a special meaning in the cellarer's duties:

> *He will be a father to the whole community. He is to have charge of all affairs, but he is not to act without the Abbot's approval, and he must carry out his orders (**RB** 31: 2-5).*

In material matters he shares the Abbot's role as father and, like him, has both to take care of things, and to contribute to the education of the brethren in the areas entrusted to him. The precise definition of the cellarer's duties is an instrument of peace, which he shares with the Abbot. The following sentences underline the spirit of charity needed by the cellarer in fulfilling his function:

2) The care of the brethren (*RB* 31: 6-9)

> *He must not sadden the brethren. If any brother happens to make an unreasonable demand of him, he should not upset him by showing contempt, but refuse the ill-advised petitioner with reasons modestly presented.*

As in the case of the deans, we see here obedience to the Abbot, linked with peace in the community. Saint Benedict insists more on the *way* of doing things than on what is to be done: the cellarer is to answer *reasonably* to an *unreasonable* request. He thus takes part in the formation of the brother, helping him to reflect on his conduct, and humbly explaining the reasons for his refusal. Here, once more, are the qualities that were requested at the beginning: *not self-important, not turbulent, not harshly spoken.* On the contrary, he should diffuse peace, and, precisely for that reason, *keep guard over his own soul*, meditating the recommendations of Saint Paul to Timothy about the deacons (1 *Tim.* 3: 8-13).

Saint Benedict entrusts to the cellarer, as he had done to the Abbot, the care of the weaker members of the house: *the sick, the children, the guests and the poor.* He has to watch over them, *knowing for certain that in the day of judgement he will have to render account for his treatment of them all.* This care for the weak is one of the characteristics of *RB*.

3) **Respect for the goods of the monastery** (*RB* 31: 10-12)

As we saw earlier, the Fathers, especially Saint Basil and Cassian,[24] considered the monastery and all its belongings as consecrated to God. In *RM*, the bursar was like the steward of Providence.[25] Saint Benedict takes these ideas up again, and asks the cellarer to take care of the goods of the monastery, just as the deacons attend to the sacred vessels. Hence the necessity of careful management:

> *He must neither succumb to avarice nor be a wasteful squanderer of the monastery's goods; but he should conduct all his affairs with prudence and in accordance with the Abbot's instructions.*

This concern for discretion and peace is shared by the Abbot and cellarer.

4) **The 'good word'** (*RB* 31: 13-16)

After dealing with material things, Saint Benedict comes back to the relationship of the cellarer with the brethren, giving it an even more positive emphasis. It is not enough to avoid grieving them; they expect the *good word [which] surpasses the best gift*. Speaking is also one of the functions of deacons. A word spoken with charity and humility, in line with directions given by the Abbot, becomes a word of God bringing peace, touching and transforming the heart. To make this attitude clearer still, Saint Benedict contrasts it with behaviour that is unruly, contrary to the Abbot's intentions, arrogant towards the brethren, and gives them cause for scandal. But he is answerable before God for such behaviour.

5) **Conclusion: peace and joy in the house of God** (*RB* 31: 17-18)

At the end of the chapter, Saint Benedict broadens the perspective, extending it to all the officials. He is the first in the tradition to show concern that the officials be not overloaded, but have helpers and a normal timetable, so that their work may be done in peace and in harmony with the whole community. But for this the collaboration of all is needed: things are to be asked for and given at the proper times.

The chapter is summarised with a well-chosen sentence, and one that is very characteristic of Saint Benedict:

[24] BASIL, *Reg.* 103-104; LR 11; SR 143; CASSIAN, *Inst.* 4: 19-20.
[25] *RM* 16; cf. *Mt.* 6, 25-33.

***That no one may be upset or saddened in the household of God* (*RB* 31: 19).**

THE PRIOR (*RB* 65)

In *RB*, the word *Prior* designates the Abbot's assistant. In order to understand what is said about him, this chapter should be placed in the context of history.

A. THE MONASTIC TRADITION

1) The meaning of the word in monastic history

Before 450, in the works of Jerome, Cassian and Augustine, the word *praepositus* indicates a superior. In the fifth century, some texts use it to indicate the head of a group within the monastery.[26] However, from the sixth century onwards, *praepositus* was used for the prior (or second-in-command), the superior being called Abbot. Thus, *RM* belongs to the second period, and *RB* to the third.[27]

2) Nomination

Among the Pachomians, the nomination of a prior was made by the Superior General, who also appointed the head of each monastery. According to Saint Gregory the Great, this custom was sometimes still in use in Saint Benedict's time, but the general practice was the nomination of the prior by the superior of the monastery.[28]

3) His function

To help the Abbot
For Pachomius, the assistant replaces the superior when he is absent. But, more often, he collaborates with him in various duties. In Saint Basil's Rules, in *RM*, and in the small Western Rules, his function is only to replace the Abbot.[29]

His own role
Until the sixth century, the prior was in charge of organising the

---

[26] AUGUSTINE, *Ordo monasterii; Rule of the 4 Fathers, Regula Orientalis.*
[27] AV *Communauté.*, pp. 390–400.
[28] AV ibid. p. 142; cf. BASIL, LR 45; *Reg. Orient.* 3, etc.
[29] AV ibid. p. 416.

work, and sometimes, the discipline of the brethren.[30] In the seventh century, the office of prior gradually took on a growing importance, due to the increase in size of the monasteries, and the fact that the Abbot was more engaged in external relationships, and study. His assistant thus had to take care of the community's observance, and its practical organisation. He was helped by a *formarius*, or subprior,[31] and by the cellarer, in material affairs.

Saint Benedict (480–547) lived at the end of the fifth and beginning of the sixth centuries. His Rule is thus a little in advance of its time, heralding the evolution that would follow.

B. CHAPTER 65 OF *RB*

The place of this chapter in the Rule, and the absence of any allusion to the prior among the officials of the monastery in the first part of the Rule, seem to indicate that his function was a late addition to the monastic regulations of Saint Benedict. The text also alludes to dissension between prior and Abbot. This seems to indicate a painful memory of past events in Saint Benedict's life, and would explain his reluctance to nominate a prior, as well as some of his recommendations to the other officials of the monastery.[32]

These special points make this chapter significant, in showing us how Saint Benedict dealt in practice with a delicate problem, using the advice of the council of the elders and of the community. It also gives the key to the relationship between the Abbot and the officials.

A delicate problem: the appointment of a prior

The beginning of the chapter showed that Saint Benedict would have preferred not to have a prior, but was led to change his mind. Before taking the decision, he reflects on what the purpose of the prior would be: *the preservation of peace and charity* in the community, something that had already been mentioned in regard to the cellarer (*RB*

---

[30] AV ibid. p. 417, *Reg. Orient.* 3: *disciplina fratrum et diligentia monasterii*; CAESARIUS, *RV*; *Reg. Tarn.* 10–19; *Reg. Isid.* 19; *Reg. Fruct.* work and direction of the main offices.

[31] CAESARIUS, *RV* 42.

[32] Saint GREGORY THE GREAT does not say anything about Saint Benedict in his *Dialogues*, but the only episode which might suggest such a situation of grave tension in a community is that of the saint's departure from a *monastery in the vicinity of Subiaco* (*Dial.* 2: 3), usually called Vicovaro. It is possible that a part of the community had been set against him by a jealous prior, appointed by the local bishop.

31: 19). Then he listens to the community, examines its motivations, and the circumstances in which officials might need help.[33]

If ... local conditions require it, or the community makes a reason-able and humble request (RB 65: 14).

The question of *utilitas monasterii*, that is, the needs of the internal organisation of the monastery (*RB* 65: 12), belongs to the competence of the council of deans, so, after consulting them, the Abbot makes the appointment:

If the Abbot judges it to be expedient, then the Abbot himself should appoint as his prior whomsoever he chooses after taking the advice of God-fearing brethren.

We have here the practical application of the indications given in chapter 3, about the calling the brethren to council: consideration of the problem, listening to the brethren in council, and decision. But the chapter as a whole shows a strong, almost violent, reaction of Saint Benedict to a situation of division, which represents a danger for his community. He suffered from it, and wants to protect his brethren against it.

The unity of the community

The unity of views between Abbot and prior is thus essential to the smooth running of the monastery. So the more he is set above the rest, the more should the prior be an example for the community. More than all the other officials, he should thus act *according to the Abbot's orders*, that is to say, according to his directions, to ensure that order and peace prevail in the life of the community.

For his part the prior is to perform respectfully whatever functions the Abbot lays upon him, and do nothing contrary to his will or arrange-ments. For inasmuch as he has been placed over others, he should the more carefully keep the precepts of the Rule (RB 65: 16).

To do what the Abbot requests, do nothing against his regulations, to observe the Rule – these words refer obviously to the situation force-fully described at the beginning of the chapter, which seems always to be present in Saint Benedict's mind throughout the Rule. These circumstances explain the frequent recommendations to the various

---

[33] Cf. *RB* 35: 4 in connection with the cooks.

officials to act *according to the Abbot's orders*. The aim is clearly to avoid the trouble caused to the brethren by initiatives contrary to the directions given by the superiors. These frequently repeated recommendations do not diminish the responsibility of the officials, nor the trust placed in them. They aim only at ensuring peace and concord in the community.

The final part of the chapter shows the realism of Saint Benedict. As with the deans, he envisages the possibility of faults in other officials, as well as in the Abbot, and gives the means to correct them. There is a series of warnings, given, however, with respect for the persons concerned. The higher the official, the more the warning should be given: three times for the deans, four times for the prior. The possible sanction of dismissal shows the seriousness of the situation, and the importance given by Saint Benedict to unity in the community. Here, as in all important cases, he reminds the Abbot of God's judgement (*RB* 65: 18–22).

5. AN OVERVIEW

Common aspects

We have found, among Christian monks, features quite similar to those we met in Asian monasticism. In most traditions, the officials in charge of temporal matters have a superior, whose function is either that of a spiritual father (guru), or to look after good order and peace inside the monastery, as well as in its relations with the exterior. Such an arrangement means that the management is not carried out in view of making a profit, but for a spiritual motive. This orientation is also stressed by the fact that many Hindu and Buddhist monks live off alms; the first Christian monasteries always gave particular attention to the poor.[34]

The different monastic hierarchies in the communities of all religions can be seen to have shared a single aim: to foster the spiritual progress of the monks, either in guiding and encouraging them directly, or in helping them by the necessary peace, harmony and security in the community.

The habit of keeping this essential aim in view contributes to the flexibility of the institutions, which everywhere adapt themselves to the religious traditions and to the circumstances. An interesting detail is, for example, that the turns of service among the Buddhists follow

[34] CASSIAN, *Inst.* 4: 14; *RB* 4: 14; 31: 9; 53: 15; 53: 24.

the monthly cycle of their cultic exercises, whereas among Christians, there is a weekly cycle centred, like the Liturgy, on Sunday.

The aspects proper to Christianity

Other elements are specifically Christian, such as the constant reference to Scripture. The models of organisations are, if not borrowed from, at least justified by it. The influence of the organisation in Roman military camps seems rather clear in the organisation of Pachomian monasteries. Nevertheless, Pachomius, like Cassian, refers only to the example of Moses in the Desert, and to the qualities required for deacons.[35]

Christ is the example constantly proposed as a model for monks, as well as superiors. He is the supreme example of obedience, humility, and total self-surrender for the good of others.[36]

The total dispossession required of all Christian monks makes them entirely dependent on the monastery and the community, in all the details of their lives. The various officials should, therefore, be most attentive to the needs of their brethren.[37]

The Abbot and his collaborators in Saint Benedict's mind

Saint Benedict comes into the Christian tradition with his own special characteristics. One of his main concerns seems to be the choice of officials. The qualities they need are similar to those required for the Abbot, for they share his burden. A more detailed list is given with regard to the cellarer, and summarised in the case of the other officials, where each one's particular qualities are described.

So, for Saint Benedict, the officials are true collaborators. They have to fulfil their task with care and competence, *being capable of performing this duty (RB* 53: 17), and *neglect[ing] nothing (RB* 31: 11), so that *God's house [may] be wisely cared for by wise men (RB* 53: 22). They are responsible not only for their own work, but also for that of the brethren. Above all, they should look to the quality of their relationship with them, so that everything may be done with order and charity.

Unity of mind between the Abbot and his officials is thus of the highest importance. Its base is in the meetings of the council, whose competence is defined in *RB* with the same words as that of the deans:

---

[35] PACHOMIUS, VC *Bo.* 78; CASSIAN, *Inst.* 4.
[36] CASSIAN, *Inst.* 4.
[37] CASSIAN, *Inst.* 4: 10; 17; PACHOMIUS, VC *Bo.* 26; 70; 104–105; 191.

'utilitas monasterii' 'the ordinary business of the monastery'.[38] In these meetings, as in the community meetings, all together should seek God's will, and the practical means of carrying it out. Unity is forged in that context, and the Abbot's duty is to see that it is maintained in the daily life of the community.[39]

This duty gives meaning to the recommendations made to the officials, to act *according to the instructions of their Abbot* and, to the brethren, *that the commands of the Abbot or of the superiors appointed by him must come first.*[40] This does not mean an over-zealous control, opposed to the mind of the Rule, but a harmonious co-ordination of the activities of the monastery, in view of the peace of the community. To go against these directions is a cause of trouble, and ruins the calm needed for the spiritual quest. Saint Benedict had had the painful experience of such troubles, and wanted to prevent them recurring for the sake of his brethren.

The main duty of all officials is that, in fulfilling their duty conscientiously, they strive, by giving a *good word* and by the way they work, to create in and around the monastery an atmosphere of peace and charity that will lead souls to God. In the same way, those who have a spiritual responsibility should not only guide the brethren towards God, but help them to have a trusting relationship with the Abbot and the community.

The proper role of the Abbot is to make appropriate decisions, with the advice of his council, to determine the field of activity for each official, to see that the directions they give do not give rise to disputes but foster the harmony of the community, and finally, to take care that the weaker members of the community may be given due consideration in a fraternal way.

What is said about the relationship between persons applies also to material things. They have to be treated with care and respect, because the monastery is:

> **the household of God [and] its whole property should be looked upon as if it were the sacred vessels of the altar (RB 31:10).**

In short, it can be said that in monasteries of all traditions, especially if their members are numerous, the superiors are helped by officials in the domains of material organisation, teaching, and often in spiritual direction.

The main role of these officers is to ensure, by means of good

[38] *RB* 3: 12; 65: 12.
[39] *RB* 3.
[40] *RB* 21: 2; 31: 12; 65: 16; 71: 3.

management, the order, harmony, and spiritual progress of the brethren. If they are to carry out their duties well, they need competence and concern for peace in the community, and with people outside. Christians find examples in the Bible, especially in what it says about deacons; but the model is always Christ, who is attentive to each person, devoting himself even unto death.

The role of the assistant superior varied according to the needs and the times. Saint Benedict was placed in surroundings where the prior was sometimes in competition with the Abbot, thus creating trouble in the community. He reacts strongly against this dreadful defect, insisting on the necessity of mutual harmony in their decision-making, which will create a climate of peace in the community. This situation explains the numerous recommendations in the Rule *not to do anything against the Abbot's orders*. Far from being authoritarian, they express the concern for *the preservation of peace and charity (RB 65: 11)* so that *no one may be upset or saddened in the household of God. (RB 31: 19).*

Saint Benedict asks the Abbot to be both the spiritual father and the administrator of the monastery. He will be able to fulfil this twofold role only if he is helped by officials with whom he *may, with confidence, share his burdens (RB 21: 3)* and who become, with him, *like fathers to the community (RB 31: 2)*. For them, more than for any other in the monastery, it is important that they look for the common good, that *they love their abbot with sincere and humble charity*, so that *Christ ... may bring [them] all together to eternal life (RB 72: 10–12)*.

CHAPTER XI

WORK

In current language, work means all gainful activity, manual as well as intellectual, which provides a living for the monastery and is the opposite of leisure with its connotations of rest and pleasurable pursuits. The monks of all religions have always engaged in manual and intellectual work, according to the mentality of their time and place. Thus intellectual work was sometimes called leisure, and manual work sometimes used as a method of prayer. In this chapter, we shall use the word 'work' in its usual sense of gainful activity, whether intellectual or manual. The opposite tendency is mendicancy, or begging.

Why are some activities forbidden to monks, whatever their religion? Why do some of them work for their living, while others go begging? The responses of the various religions to these questions will help us to understand the special contribution of Christian monasticism, and the qualities that contact with other religions invites it to develop.

1. WORK IN HINDU AND BUDDHIST MONASTICISM

IN HINDUISM

To understand the attitude of Hindu monasticism towards work, we have to remember that traditional Indian society was divided into several periods, as we have seen at the beginning of this book. The

Laws of Manu[1] give a more precise division, separating childhood, in which one is under the care of one's mother, from the time of studies under a Master. Then comes marriage and adult life, that is the time in which men have to fulfil their duties as householders by working for society. And finally, *'when a man's hair turns grey, and he sees the sons of his sons, let him retire to the forest'*,[2] and devote himself exclusively to the search for the essential, that is, for union with the Absolute.

Monastic life thus assimilates the two age groups in which men are usually dependent on society, namely, as students, and as retired people. It is only by way of exception that some persons choose to remain celibate students, *brahmachari* for life, without assuming the life duties of the householder.[3]

Nevertheless, work is never totally excluded from Hindu monastic life. The *bramachari* (student novice) has to collect firewood for the sacred fire. He helps keep the house clean and provides offerings of food. He must also care for the needs of his guru.[4] In the same way, the mature man who has retired to the forest (*vanaprashta*) has to procure food and clothing from the local plants and trees. He should be hospitable to visitors, and give alms to the needy.[5]

Begging is thus compulsory only in the first stage of monastic life, when the novice is too busy with his studies to care for himself, and during the final *ashrama* of *samnyasi*, when the old man, having left everything behind, concentrates all his energies on the inner search for the Absolute.[6] In the Hindu context, this form of religious mendicancy, above all for young monks, is not opposed to work;[7] it is an ascetic practice, aimed at controlling pride and bodily desires. For this reason, it is compared to fasting.[8]

For the ascetics belonging to the devotional tradition called *bhakti*, to adopt mendicancy is a form of loving trust in their venerated Deity. For others, like those who are itinerant *samnyasi*, or for the Jains,[9] it

---

[1] MANU, 6: 1, 36–39. The chronological division given by the *Laws of Manu* fits here better than the classical division into states of life (*ashramas*) given in ch. 1: student (*Brahmacharya*); householder (*grihasta*); retirement in the forest (*vanaprasta*); life of renunciation (*samnyasa*).

[2] MANU, 6: 2.

[3] MANU, 2: 243–249. *Apastamba Dharma Sutras*, Prasna II, Patala IX, ch. 22, Sûtra 6.

[4] MANU, 2: 182; 186; 243.

[5] MANU, 6: 2–21. *Apastamba D.S.*, Sûtra 1–2; 13–14.

[6] MANU, 6: 20–28. The *samnyasi* lives a solitary and usually itinerant form of monastic life. Cf. *Laghu-samnyâsa Up*.

[7] MANU, 6: 55–59.

[8] MANU, 2: 88–108; 188.

is an expression of the effort to liberate oneself from all worldly attachments, in order to gain union with the Absolute. This position is often strengthened by a philosophy that considers detachment from the world as a necessary condition for transcending the impermanent, in order to attain the Absolute.

Finally, we note that the Hindu sect of the *Lingayat* extols respect for all human beings (because of God's presence dwelling in them), the sacredness of the body and the dignity of work. Work is compulsory for these monks and begging forbidden, unless help to be given to the poor make it necessary. The monasteries organise collections on the occasions of the main annual feasts, during which food is distributed to the needy.[10]

In all branches of Hinduism, study is an integral part of monastic life. We have seen how the young man must apply himself to read and meditate the sacred books. Similarly, each of the main schools owes its origins to monks who, like Shankara, Ramanuja and others, were both philosophers and theologians.

Nevertheless, the *Laws of Manu*, like the *Upanishad of Renunciation*, show that though manual as well as intellectual work is useful in the first stages of monastic life, it is incompatible with the life of the wandering *samnyasi*, whose quest is beyond the world of senses and concepts. Having symbolically swallowed up the ritual fire, having left the thread (sign of his caste) and even the signs of monastic life (*kavi* dress, pilgrim stick and begging bowl) he concentrates all his energy on the presence of the Self in the cave of the heart:

> *Having his hands and his stomach as his bowl, 'Ohm' is the whole Upanishad ... All desire left behind, well established in the Supreme One ... in the Self; he has come to know the awakening to the One who is plenitude and felicity.*[11]

IN BUDDHISM

In later Upanishadic times, the early Buddhist Masters had begun to found those *viharas* (monasteries) that were to become famous centres

---

9 In the *Bhakti current*, or devotion, the devotees dedicate themselves to the divinity by love. The Jains also have itinerant monks.

10 D. M. SADASIVAIAH, *A Comparative Study of Two Virasaiva Monasteries*, ch. 2, pp. 91–113.

11 U.R. *Aruni Up*. V; *Paramahansa Up*. III, IV. Similar texts are found in most of the *Upanishads of Renunciation*. Nowadays, some of such ascetics are frequently found along the sacred rivers, like the Ganges, which, for them, are symbols and almost sacraments of the Divine presence.

of study and meditation. From these the Buddhist schools developed, spreading the *Dharma* throughout South and East Asia.

Buddhist monks begged for their living for the same motives as the Hindu ascetics, stressing detachment from all recreative activities, in order to dedicate themselves fully to the spiritual quest. Later the development of community life, and close relationships with lay people in the surrounding areas, led them to discover other values in both mendicancy and work.

Begging came to be seen both as a way of detachment for monks, and as a virtuous act for the faithful followers, who would fill the monks' begging bowls daily with offerings of food, and who might offer alms to sustain institutional monastic life.

Some kinds of work, such as digging and tilling the soil, involved the risk of harming living creatures, and thus they were forbidden to monks by their vow of non-violence. However, other works were encouraged as fit for monks, such as personal hygiene, or household cleaning and maintenance. In the course of time, care of buildings developed into architectural skills, and monks themselves made or inspired great masterpieces, which can be still admired all over Asia.

In some country regions, important Buddhist monasteries were established. The monks thus had to work for their living, because they were then situated far from a population from which they might have been able to beg. Having taken up work because of their need, they soon discovered that it had psychological consequences, which could foster their spiritual quest. Manual work prevents wandering thoughts, encouraging concentration of mind. It is thus particularly useful for beginners.[12]

Eventually, Zen Buddhism actually made use of some kinds of work as a way of meditation, using the activity of the body to focus the mind. This came to include such arts as archery, gardening, pottery, painting, and the tea ceremony.

Thus, anything that can be done with care can become a work of art, developing an aesthetic sense which leads to silent communion with nature, consciousness of realities beyond words, and finally to illumination.

On the level of community life, the monks noticed that manual work strengthens humility. The feeling that one shares the lot of the poor is always an appropriate one for monks. In various regions, social and pastoral activities have been entrusted to monks, while others have dedicated themselves to study or meditation.[13] Whatever

[12] WALPOLA RAHULA, *History of Buddhism in Ceylon*, pp. 186–187.
[13] Ibid., p. 193.

may be the importance given to manual work, it is a natural part of the daily activities of any monastic community. Perhaps not all would accept the saying of a Zen master:

> *A day without work is a day without eating.*[14]

Nevertheless, nearly all will agree that, beyond its practical usefulness, work has a genuine monastic purpose, and is one of the main ways of moving ahead in the spiritual journey.

Begging often provides for the monks' material needs, but it is also an ascetic practice leading to humility. The lay people who make offerings see it as a way of gaining in virtue for themselves, by making gifts to the monasteries. Monks are forbidden to do work that would imply a violation of their vows, especially that of non-violence and detachment from worldly goods.

2. WORK IN THE CHRISTIAN MONASTIC TRADITION

As we saw at the beginning, the categories of thought about work used by the first Christian monks were markedly different from our own. All was centred on the quest for union with God, and manual work was for them an exercise of the *praktikē*, that is, a struggle against vices and a support for prayer. Intellectual activity was considered as contemplative leisure, and study included in the time of *lectio*. Training for monastic life implied learning by heart parts of Scripture, at least the Psalms. The books of the Fathers show us what the fruit of such practices might be. Basil, for instance, and Gregory Nazianzen, during their stay in the monastery of Anessi, wrote the *Philokalia* (an anthology of Origen's works). Jerome, Augustine, Cassian, and other monks, of whom many became bishops, both in the East and in the West, were famous for their writings. All this shows that the reputation of knowledge later attached to monasteries already had its roots in the first centuries. Monastic work is thus a complex activity, and we shall study it under several aspects: its history, its Christian meaning, and its place in monastic life.

---

[14] Pai-chang, quoted in H. DUMOULIN, *A History of Zen Buddhism*, p. 103.

A. HISTORY[15]

1. Its evolution in the first centuries

In both East and West, Christian monasticism, after a period of hesitation, opted in favour of work. During the initial period of monasticism, many monks seem to have been so immersed in an ideal of intense prayer that they did not work. In Syria, in the fourth century, to live on alms was a sign of perfection and trust in divine Providence.[16] The extreme representatives of this movement were the followers of the Messalian heresy.[17] They claimed that the Evil One can neither be expelled from a man by Baptism, nor by asceticism; only prayer induces the presence of the Holy Spirit and makes the soul immune to evil. So monks should above all pray without ceasing.

At the same time, in the West, the only work that Saint Martin allowed his disciples to perform was to copy manuscripts, and even this was meant exclusively as a help to beginners. Senior monks dedicated their whole day to prayer.[18]

About the year 400, Messalian trends were found among the monks of Carthage, who wanted to pray without ceasing and to be fed and clothed, like the birds and the lilies of the field, by the heavenly Father, without doing any work. Their bishop asked Saint Augustine to refute their beliefs, which he did in his *De Opere Monachorum*.

Cassian took up the same themes as Saint Augustine, to persuade the monks of Gaul to work. He did it so well that some monks of Lérins who became bishops, such as Saint Hilary of Arles, continued their daily manual work in the midst of their spiritual endeavours. Manual work even became compulsory for clerics in the *Statuta Ecclesiae Antiqua*, and during the same period the African bishop, Fulgentius of Ruspe, enjoined it upon his clergy.[19]

In the East, the reaction was the same. The Desert Fathers did not hesitate to follow the letter of Saint Paul, saying '... *to deprive of food those who claim to be able to live without working*'.[20] Antony, Pachomius and Basil urge their disciples not only to live from their work, but also to earn enough to be able to give alms.

[15] On the history of work in Christian monasticism, see *Dizionario degli Istituti di perfezione*, art. 'Lavoro': 'East', by J. GRIBOMONT; 'West', by A DE VOGÜÉ.
[16] We find in these practices one of the many points of contact between the Syriac and Hindu monasticisms.
[17] The Messalian heresy appeared in the fourth century, in Syria. Its followers wanted to pray without ceasing, despised other activities, and lived on alms.
[18] SULPICIUS SEVERUS, *Vita Martini*, 10: 6. St Martin died in November 397.
[19] *Vita Hilar.*, 11, 15, 19: *Vita Fulg.*, 59. Cf. *AV, Dizionario*.
[20] *Apophthegmata*, John the Dwarf, 2; Sylvanus, 5; *PL* 73, 768; 807–812.

Following the great legislators of monastic life, the Rules of the later centuries presented work as an element for individual perfection and fraternal service. But, although the principle was no longer questioned, the very insistence of the regulations on this point shows that its observance often met with greater or lesser obstacles. Saint Basil, in the East, the Rules of the Master and of Saint Benedict in Italy, Ferreolus in Gaul, and Isidore in Spain, all mention these difficulties, and encourage monks to overcome them with a generous spirit.

This brief overview of monastic history shows that work, for Christian monks, has always been both an observance and a problem. The hesitations among the first monks, and the reaction that followed, need to be studied so that we can distinguish the common human problems met in each generation from the obstacles which arose from the historical context.

2. Obstacles to monastic work in the first centuries

At first, we are not surprised by the hesitations of the first Christians, confronted by the contradictions among Scripture texts with regard to work. Indeed, the Scripture summons men to a sense of responsibility towards the created world. But some miracles, and even some parables in the Gospel,[21] seem to intimate that God's Providence provides all that is necessary to those who strive to reach the end of the spiritual journey, concerned only with being absolutely faithful to God.

Jesus did not work during his three years of preaching, and his disciplines left their trades to follow him. The *Acts of the Apostles* do not speak of work in the first community of Jerusalem, but of selling land to support it. Saint Paul, like Jesus, invited Christians to pray without ceasing.[22] Thus in some places eschatological expectation seems to have wiped out all earthly involvement.[23] Many believed that the Lord's return was close at hand, and that working was useless.

Saint Paul reacted strongly against these feelings, both in his example and in his letters:

> *If anyone will not work, let him not eat ... These hands of mine have provided for my own needs and those of others, and I have shown you, in every way, that by working in this way we must help the weak.*[24]

---

[21] Cf. *Gen.* 2: 51. The manna in the desert, *Exod.* 16, Elijah miraculously fed, 1 *Kings* 17: 2–5. In contrast, work is a slavery imposed by Pharaoh; *Mt.* 6: 25–34.
[22] 1 *Thess.* 5: 17.
[23] *Jn.* 6: 27; *Lk.* 10: 42.
[24] 2 *Thess.* 3: 10; 1 *Cor.* 4: 12; *Acts* 20: 33–35.

Let us note that the condemnation of Saint Paul is really directed against the selfish idleness of those who want to live off other people and have no care for the poor. The scriptural texts leave the door open to other charisms, which the mendicant orders will later develop. The vocation of the monk to earn his living was probably the most urgent, in a time where sociological conditions were unfavourable to manual work.

It is true that Jewish tradition required the knowledge of a trade, even for the most literary persons, and that Stoic philosophers were appreciative of work and some kinds of social service. Nevertheless, it can be said that, as a whole, Greek philosophy and the Greco-Roman world were not in favour of manual labour. For them, even paid work was considered dishonourable. Free men lived from the income of their estates, run by slaves, to whom all manual labour was entrusted. According to Aristotle:

> *Citizens must not live the life of artisans ... for such a life is ignoble, and inimical to virtue ... we call those arts vulgar which tend to deform the body, also all paid employment, for they absorb and degrade the mind.*[25]

These attitudes were old and widespread in the Middle East.[26] But, at the same time, the philosophers saw that idleness could have a corrupting effect. Again, Aristotle says:

> *It is a mistake to place inactivity above action, for happiness is activity, and the actions of the just and wise are the realisation of much that is noble.*[27]

The pursuit of virtue was thus the most fitting activity to occupy the leisure of everyone.

So when free people became Christians they naturally followed this trend, while retaining the customs of their milieu. This fact can partly

[25] ARISTOTLE, *Polit.* 1328B and 1337B, 9–14. Quoted by C. PEIFER, *The Relevance of Monastic Tradition to the Problem of Work and Leisure, AMERICAN BENEDICTINE REVIEW*, Dec. 1977, p. 374.

[26] HERODOTUS, *Hist.* 2, 167, quoted by C. PEIFER, ibid.: *I could not say for certain whether the Greeks got their ideals about trade, like so much else, from Egypt, or not; the feeling is common enough, and I have observed that Thracians, Scythians, Persians, Lydians – indeed, almost all foreigners, reckon craftsmen and their descendants as lower in the social scale than people who have no connection with manual work; only the latter, and especially those who are trained for war, do they count among the 'nobility'. All the Greeks have adopted this attitude, especially the Parthians; the feeling against handicrafts is least strong in Corinth.*

[27] ARISTOTLE, *Polit.* 1325A.

explain the lack of interest in manual work in several Christian monastic communities of the East, as well as of the West. These feelings also provided a favourable climate for the Messalian tendency. But, on the other hand, and in other cases, quite different factors produced the same results.

It is remarkable, for example, that the communities in the East where monks did not work, are situated mostly in Syria, a country well known for its commercial and cultural relations with India. This fact is only one of the many similarities between Syrian Christian monks and Hindu ascetics. It was also in Syria, and probably for the same reasons, that Messalianism sprang up and developed. In Gaul, the absence of work among the disciples of Saint Martin can perhaps be attributed to some Messalian tendency. But Sulpicius Severus notes that a good many of the monks were of noble origin and often had little physical strength.[28] It may have seemed quite normal for these men to live without the manual labour they had never practised before joining the monastery. People of their time already found them praiseworthy enough for having left their grand houses to live, like the poor, in caves or wooden huts.[29] It is also significant that these monks were the companions and helpers of the Bishop, and as such were considered as clerics, men who depended on the Church for their support. In Martin's words:

> *It belongs to the Church to feed and clothe us. We should not hoard up things for our needs.*[30]

Work, on the contrary, did not raise problems for Saint Antony, Saint Pachomius, and the first Egyptian monks. Most of them came from families of farmers or craftsmen. They were used to manual work, and continued it on becoming monks. They merely selected the kind of work that was better suited to monastic life. Intellectuals, like Arsenius, former teacher of the Emperor's sons, or Evagrius, cleric of Constantinople, are seen as exceptions. Basil, and several members of his family, embraced monastic life, thus following his example, and had the courage to live from the work of their hands, putting themselves on the same footing as the former slaves. In this monastic world full of good sense and deep faith, work soon took on a great importance.

But all the difficulties were not so easily solved: social pressure, contempt for manual work, incapacity, all such factors can be found

[28] SULPICIUS SEVERUS, *Vita Martini*, 10; *Dialogi*, 3: 8.
[29] Id *Vit. Mart.* 10.
[30] Id. *Dial.* 3: 14.

through the centuries. Nevertheless, work remained one of the main features of Christian monasticism. It is all the more interesting to consider the reasons put forward by the first monks to work with their hands, and to persuade their successors to follow in their footsteps.

B. THE MEANING OF WORK IN CHRISTIAN MONASTIC LIFE

In the *Life of Saint Antony*, the first Christian monastic text, work is presented as an essential part of his life:

> *All his desire and diligence were directed towards ascetical labour. He worked with his hands, for he had heard 'He who does not work, should not eat' [2 Thess. 3: 10]. He used a part of his wages to buy his bread, and distributed the rest to the needy. He prayed continually, having learned that one should pray without ceasing. He was so attentive to the readings that he knew the Scriptures well, and his memory was, for him, like a book.*[31]

This text gives us a kind of synthesis of Christian monastic life and situates work in the context of prayer and meditation on Scripture, which gives it its full meaning. Work is an ascetic practice that develops charity, and makes prayer easier. It thus proclaims God's Kingdom and becomes a prophetic witness to the world.

1. An ascesis

In Saint Antony and Saint Pachomius's lives, work, with fasting and vigils, is one of the means that help the monk to gain mastery over his body and passions, an essential condition for any spiritual quest.[32] It is true that among the Desert Fathers we may find some examples of monks who wanted to tire their bodies by uselessly carrying sand, or going to fetch water at a great distance.[33] Nevertheless, Christian monastic literature as a whole considers work as a way of eliciting generosity in the practice of monastic virtues. Cassian, for example, says:

> *The solitaries of Egypt ... never remain idle. They measure the disposition of their hearts, and their progress in patience and humility, according to their earnestness in working.*[34]

---

[31] ATHANASIUS, *VA*, 3.
[32] ATHANASIUS, *VA*, 3: 53. PACHOMIUS, *VC Bo*. 10: 14.
[33] *Apophthegmata*. Coll. Syst. 7: 3.
[34] CASSIAN, *Inst*. 10: 22.

The various works required from the brothers are, of course, a good occasion to practise charity and patience, and to fight against laziness and idleness which are the enemy of the soul.[35]

But work has its own ascesis. For a diligent worker, the love of God and the effort to remain in his presence produced a quality of care and respect for things and persons, leading him on to greater perfection. Cassian remarks that:

> *Any object once brought to the monastery, should be treated with great respect, as something sacred.*

Theodore taught the young monks to strive to discover new methods to make the mats beautiful and fine.[36] Basil too prescribes that the tools should be kept like things dedicated and consecrated to God.[37]

Saint Benedict adopted these ascetic practices, highlighting certain aspects. Still more than his predecessors, he insists on performing work with particular care: the house should be well kept, nothing should be lost or spoiled.[38] These dispositions are inspired by a sense of respect, which *regards all utensils and goods of the monastery as the sacred vessels of the altar.*[39] Later, this same desire for perfection for God's sake will lead the *craftsmen of the monastery* to become the artists and technicians, whose contribution to the creation and development of European civilisation was immeasurable.[40]

He knows that the work is sometimes hard, but this is part of the difficulties that the Rule invites monks to overcome with generosity, in union with Christ's Passion, as a sign of obedience and humility. But in contrast with Cassian he never imposes artificial trials, either in the work or elsewhere.[41] His care is rather to relieve the weak in order to avoid murmuring; his desire is that *No one may be upset or saddened in the house of God.*[42]

A constant reference to God, together with a search for beauty,

---

35 CASSIAN, *Inst.* 4: 10; 19–30; 2: 12; 10: 14; *Conf.* 10: 14; BASIL LR 37; 42; SR 105; 115; 116; 142; 160; 167.

36 CASSIAN, *Inst.* 10: 24; PACHOMIUS, *VC Bo.* 72.

37 BASIL, SR 143–144; LR 41; cf. CASSIAN, *Inst.* 4: 19–20.

38 The kitchen of the guesthouse should be wisely cared for by wise men. *RB* 53: 22; 35: 1–3; 36: 7–10. Nothing should be neglected, spoiled or lost: *RB* 31: 10–12; 32: 1–5.

39 *RB* 31: 10; cf. 32; 35; 46; 55; 57.

40 Cf. J. DÈCARREAUX, *Les moines et la civilisation en Occident.* In the same manner, the Oriental monks developed the art of the icon and Byzantine architecture.

41 *RB*, housework: 31: 17; 48: 7; 53: 18. Circumstances which can make work heavier: 7: 35–43; 68: 1–5.

42 *RB Prol.* 46–48; 7: 35–43; 68: 1–5; 31: 19; CASSIAN, *Inst.* 4: 8–10; 24–30.

gives Christian monastic asceticism a note of love and joy. If we respect men and things because of God, we love them also as he does. Sufferings and trials cannot block this response. Indeed, Saint Benedict stresses it all the more in such circumstances, saying, for example, that

[obedience] should be offered by the disciples with good will, because 'God loves a cheerful giver.'

Further, he adds:

Yet unmoved, through their hope of divine reward they joyfully persevere, saying, 'These are the trials through which we triumph on account of him who has loved us.'[43]

This joyful zeal is indeed one of the features of monastic asceticism stressed by Vatican II.[44]

Comparison with other religions reveals another quality of monastic work; detachment, not only from material goods, but from financial worries that distract the mind and prevent concentration on the goal. Mentioned by Saint Benedict in connection with the Abbot's duties, it had been emphasised by the Cappadocian Fathers. They advised that it was best to live by cultivating the soil in remote places in order to avoid involvement in worldly affairs.[45] For similar reasons, in the *RM* the administration of the monastic estates was entrusted to farmers.[46]

The same desire for detachment which led Hindu and Buddhist ascetics to a life of itinerant begging, induced most of the Christian monks to refrain from leaving the monastery unnecessarily and, upon their return to the monastery, to avoid speaking of events which might disturb their recollection.[47]

In *RB*, these regulations are joined with the idea of concentration on God through the notion of stability.[48]

---

[43] *RB* 5: 16, quoting 2 *Cor.* 9: 7; *RB* 7: 39 (fourth step of humility), quoting *Rom.* 8: 3.

[44] *PC*, 7.

[45] BASIL, *Ep.* 132: 2; LR 6; 8; 9; GREGORY OF NYSSA, *Life of Saint Macrina*, 5: 40–50; 11: 1–20.

[46] *RM* 86.

[47] ATHANASIUS, *VA*, 84–85; *Apophthegmata*, Arsenius, 1; 2; 7; 11; 13; 38; SYNCLETICA, 6; Syst. Coll. 7: 24; 26; 30; 36; 8: 9; PACHOMIUS, VC *Bo.* 26; *Praecepta*, 1: 49–60; 84; 108; 118; AUGUSTINE, *Reg.* 4: 2–3; 5: 7; CASSIAN, *Inst.* 10: 3; *Conf.* 6: 15; 24: 5; CAESARIUS ARL. *RV* 1–2; 28; 50; *RM* 55–67; *RB* 66–67.

[48] *RB* 4: 78; 58: 9–29; 60: 9; 61: 5–10.

Nevertheless, seclusion in the monastery should not be viewed as a selfish flight from other people's worries and anxieties. Charity is the keynote of monastic work.

2. An act of charity

The excerpt from the *Life of Saint Antony*, quoted above, shows that the precept of the Apostle, on the duty to work in order to earn one's living, was understood as an act of charity, and of social responsibility. The monk should not be a burden on society; rather, he should care for the poor.[49]

Pachomius had the same conviction and, describing Theodore's monastic ascesis, he unites also prayer, work and charity.[50] Cassian adds that Egyptian monasteries had organised a kind of Catholic Relief Service, providing regular help to *prisons, hospices, hospitals, foreigners and needy persons* and making large donations to people in regions struck by natural disasters.[51]

Saint Basil, who had to take the Messalian tendency into account, emphasises trust in Providence. He does not stress the duty of earning one's living, but urges his disciples to avoid becoming a burden to others. He is nevertheless adamant on the monk's duty to work. His aim is that they should follow Saint Paul's example, and fulfil the Lord's commandment, when he said, *I was hungry, you gave me food, thirsty, and you gave me drink.*[52]

Saint Augustine had to fight the same Messalian tendencies. He desired that monks should work so that they would not become a burden on other Christians. Work would also allow them to give more to the poor, among whom he includes ministers of the Church who are ill or overburdened with responsibilities.[53] Saint Jerome is of the same opinion, and says that monks, like the Apostles, should work to support themselves, and be able to give alms.[54]

---

[49] Athanasius, *VA* 44. Antony's disciples *worked in order to give alms*, 50; Antony himself grew wheat, to spare others the trouble of bringing him food, 53; work is considered both as a penance and as a means of giving something in exchange for the food visitors brought him.

[50] Pachomius, *VC Bo.* 10: 17; 106; 133. Orsisius, *Testament*, 160.

[51] Cassian, *Inst.* 10: 8–18; 22 (works as a means of ascesis); *Conf.* 24: 10–12. Cf. Augustine, *De moribus ecclesiae*, 36 (organised help to the poor); *Hist. Mon. In Egyp.* 18.

[52] Basil LR 37, quoting *Eph.* 4: 28, and *Mt.* 25: 34–35. Cf. LR 41–42; SR, 207; 272; Gregory Nys. *Vit. Macr.* 8; 12; 20, shows the constant care for the poor of the Basilian monasteries.

[53] Augustine, *De opere monachorum*, 16–25; 17.

[54] Jerome, *Ep.* 125: 4; 52: 2–3.

Charity is practised within the monastery as well as with outsiders. Monks often work in teams, or for the service of the community. Thus they have many occasions for fraternal charity. Already the Desert Fathers, Pachomius, Orsisius, Basil and Cassian give many examples of it when describing the organisation of their houses, and the spirit which animates them.[55] They also mention that the work should be assigned according to one's strength. The brethren are invited to help each other, in order to avoid murmuring, and to provide all with enough freedom of heart to praise God in their work, and to fulfil their task with joy.[56]

This unanimous tradition is summarised by Saint Benedict when he reminds his brethren that

Truly are they monks, if they live by the work of their hands.[57]

But he also sees it above all from the point of view of charity, under its twofold aspect of mutual service and help to the needy. The care for the poor appears at the beginning of the Rule, in the Tools of Good Works. It is also one of the main duties of the Abbot, the cellarer, the guestmaster, and the doorkeeper. Finally, those who enter the monastery are invited to leave at least a part of their goods to the poor.[58] Saint Benedict's life still shows that he pushed charity as far as heroism, not hesitating, in time of famine, to give to the poor the little food which remained for the community.[59] The characteristic of Saint Benedict's charity is that it applies to the whole person. He takes care both to *console* and to *clothe*, to quiet the heart and to avoid overburdening work. So that when an official cannot give what he is asked for by one of the brothers he should find words which touch the heart and give hope.[60]

The attention Benedict gives to each person is expressed in his desire to organise the monastery so that

no-one should be upset or saddened in the household of God, [and requests that] *the brothers should serve one another ... because through this service the reward of an increase in charity is gained.*

[55] *Apophthegmata*, Syst. Coll., 16–17; PACHOMIUS, *Praec.* 5; 12; 58–66; 108–111; 116; 120; 124; 129, etc. BASIL, LR 34; 41; 42; SR 141–156; 207; CASSIAN, *Inst.* 4: 29–30; 5: 37–39.
[56] *Apophthegmata*, Syst. Coll., 17: 16; 20. ORSISIUS, *Test.* 7. BASIL, LR 29; SR 149; 151; 152; 156; 157; 160–162. CASSIAN, *Conf.* 2. PACHOMIUS, *Praec.* 5.
[57] *RB* 48: 8
[58] *RB* 4: 14–19; 31: 9; 53: 15; 55: 9; 58: 24; 59: 7; 66: 3.
[59] GREGORY THE GREAT, *Dialogues*, 2: 28.
[60] *RB* 4: 14–19; 31: 6–9, 13–14; 35: 3–4; 39: 6; 41: 3–16; GREGORY THE GREAT, *Dial.* 2: 27–29.

We could multiply these quotations for here we touch one of the main traits of *RB*, namely its care for each person, especially for the weaker members of the community, and for the poor.[62]

3. Work as prayer

The Fathers constantly link prayer to the duty of charity. The texts we have quoted often juxtapose the two precepts of the apostle, concerning incessant prayer, and work. They considered keeping the hands busy to be one of the means by which to focus the attention of God; thus work itself came to be perceived as a prayerful activity. Saint Antony, the Desert Fathers and the Pachomians led the way.[63] Saint Pachomius's *Life* describes his disciple, Theodore,

> *sitting in his cell, making ropes and reciting Scripture texts he had learned by heart. Whenever he felt the need in his heart, he stood up and prayed.*[64]

Basil, too, considered manual work as a privileged time for prayer, and he explained how one supports the other:

> *While our hands are occupied, we can praise God, aloud, if it is possible, or useful for the other's edification, or at least in the heart, with Psalms, and spiritual canticles, according to Scripture (Col. 3: 16). We thus fulfil our duty to pray while we work. In this way we thank God, who gave our hands skill for working, and our mind the ability to learn. Moreover, he has provided the materials, both the tools and the supplies we work with in the various trades. Finally, we ask that the work of our hands may be directed in the right way, and be pleasing to God. When busy, a good way to keep our soul recollected is indeed to ask God to bring our work to a good end, to thank him who gave us the means to carry it out, and, as we have just said, to keep in view the purpose of pleasing him. Otherwise, how could we reconcile the words of the apostle, 'pray without ceasing' (1 Thess. 5: 17) and 'working day and night' (2 Thess. 3: 8).*[65]

Cassian repeats the same lesson, illustrating it with examples,

> *Solitaries interrupt neither their work nor their meditation. They equally train the faculties, both of mind and body, to combine the efforts of the*

[61] *RB* 31: 19; 35: 1–2.
[62] *RB Prol.* 46–48; 2: 31–36; chs. 22; 27; 28; 42; 58; 64–65; 68; 70, etc.
[63] ATHANASIUS, *VA*, 3; 44. *Apophthegmata*. Lucius, 1.
[64] PACHOMIUS, *VC Bo.* 34; cf. *Bo.* 10 for Palamon.
[65] BASIL, LR 37.

exterior man, and the progress of the interior person. The weight of the work is like a firm and immovable anchor they oppose to the dangerous movements of their hearts and the tumultuous waves of their thoughts.[66]

Further, he explained why Abba Paul continued to plait baskets though he could not sell them:

Paul taught us that ... our work should be done, even if we are not obliged to do it because of need, in order to purify the heart, to make the intelligence steady, to stay in the cell, and to win the victory over laziness.[67]

In practice, the interdependence of work and prayer is expressed by the atmosphere of peace and silence in which the monk's activities are performed. Pachomius's *Rules* are strict in this respect. It was always an important yet troublesome area, since Pachomius's *Life*, as well as the writings of Orsisius, Basil, Cassian, Augustine and their successors, comes back to it again and again.[68]

Silence, as we have already remarked, is both protected by, and filled with, *meditatio*, that is, recitation, or rather, the repetition of Scriptural texts while meditating on their meaning. The Fathers explained it at length,[69] and Saint Benedict recommends both repeating a word of the Scriptures in the heart, and keeping an habitual silence.[70]

We note, moreover, that for him, the occasions for gossip are found in idleness rather than during work.[71] The community had to earn its living and work was taken seriously. Several scenes of Saint Benedict's life show that he had to moderate the brothers' zeal, to invite them to detachment, and to help them to remain in God's presence when they worked.[72]

---

[66] CASSIAN, *Inst.* 2: 14; cf. 2: 12.

[67] Ibid., 10: 24.

[68] PACHOMIUS, *Praec.* 58–60; *VC Bo.* 74–77; BASIL, LR 13; SR 208; CASSIAN, *Inst.* 2: 33; *Conf.* 14: 9; AUGUSTINE, *Ordo mon.* 9.

[69] PACHOMIUS, *VC Bo.* 10; *Praec.* 3; 28, 59–60; 36; BASIL, LR 37; CASSIAN, *Inst.* 2: 15; *Apophthegmata*, Achilles, 5. PACHOMIUS, *VC Bo.* 66–77, and AUGUSTINE, *De opere monachorum*, 20, recommended reciting or singing Psalms when the brothers were working together, while some of the later Rules, like that of CAESARIUS, *Regula Virginum*, 20, and *RM*, 50, prescribe reading aloud, when the work allows it.

[70] Saint Benedict does not use the word *meditatio* in its traditional meaning of repetition. For him it means rather to memorise Scripture (cf. AV *Les deux fonctions de la méditation dans les Règles monastiques anciennes*, *RAM*, 1975, 1–2), but he recommends the monk to *remember always* a good thought (*RB* 19: 3; 31: 8; 57: 5; 63: 3; 64: 7) or to *say constantly in his heart* a word of God fitting to the circumstance (*RB* 7: 18, 65; cf. 7: 50–52).

[71] *RB* 43: 8; 48: 18.

[72] GREGORY THE GREAT, *Dial.* 2: 9–10; 28.

Work, as an act of charity and prayer, will spread these values by itself. The concern of perfection for God has given to monastic labour a cultural influence which was not looked for. But at a deeper level it became a sign for the world which, like that of the Prophets, witnessed to the Gospel ideal.

4. A prophetic gesture

The economic and cultural services rendered to society by monasteries have often been celebrated. However, it has been less noticed that, in freely choosing poverty for the love of Christ, monks have also wanted to care for the poor and have, by that fact, challenged the societies which were oppressing them.

Monastic work, as a prophetic gesture,[73] is especially striking during the first centuries, when manual work was left to slaves. Monks then constituted a classless society, where work was held in honour. A typical example was given by Saint Basil and his family.[74] They were rich intellectuals, owning large estates and numerous slaves. In dedicating themselves to God, Macrina and her mother retired into the countryside and transformed their family house into a monastery:

> *Macrina persuaded our mother to renounce her usual mode of life, her manners as a noble lady, and the services she used to receive from her slaves. Thus she shared in the common way of life of the virgins she had with her. From the slaves and servants they had been, she made them her sisters, living at the same level, eating at the same table, using the same bedding, adopting the same means of living: all differences of rank were suppressed in their lives.*[75]

Macrina and her companions lived from the work of their hands and, *though they did not send the beggars away, neither did they search for benefactors.*[76]

When Saint Basil organised a monastery nearby, he too united manual labour with monastic poverty:

---

[73] The prophets of Israel were considered as the natural protectors of the weak and oppressed; 2 *Sam.* 12: 1–6; 2 *Kings* 4: 13; *Amos* 5, etc.

[74] The family life of Saint BASIL is described in his *Letters*, and in the *Life of Saint Macrina* by Saint GREGORY OF NYSSA. The holiness of their elder sister, Macrina, attracted Basil and several of his brothers, first Naucratios, then Peter (later bishop of Sebaste), and finally Gregory of Nyssa, to dedicate themselves to God.

[75] GREGORY OF NYSSA, *Life of Saint Macrina*, 7.

[76] Ibid., 20.

*Renouncing worldly glory, and despising the glory his eloquence had
acquired for him, he came, as a fugitive, to a hard life of manual
labour. His practice of poverty removed the obstacles which might have
impeded him from leading a virtuous life.*[77]

The example given by Basil and Macrina was not an isolated one; it
followed the general custom of the early Christian monasteries. In the
Egyptian desert, the senator Arsenius placed himself on the same level
as the peasants of the Nile valley, and as the black Ethiopian Moses,
who was a former robber. In the monasteries of men and women
established by Martin and Cassian in Gaul, by Jerome in Jerusalem,
and by Augustine in north Africa, slaves were incorporated as *brothers and sisters.*[78] It was this courageous attitude of the monks, so
contrary to the usages of the time, which taught Europe the Christian
values of the dignity of work and of discovering a brother in each
man.[79]

We understand easily that these transformations were not done
without difficulties. Monastic institutions had sometimes to take into
account the fact that persons coming from different social origins had
ways of life difficult to unify. So Saint Jerome says that sisters of the
monastery founded by Paula really were *sisters*, wearing the same
habit, practising the same poverty, and meeting for prayer. But, for
work and meals, they were divided into *three sections or monasteries*
according to whether their origin was *noble, middle class or low.*[80]

In Saint Augustine's communities, probably smaller, all brothers

---

[77] Ibid. 6. This work was not a joke. Saint Gregory Nazianzen, who shared Basil's
life for a while, says, in his letters: *How can I keep silence about the manure we
had to take out of the Augean stables, which we then spread on the gardens. We
had to pull the cart, made for carrying earth, with this very neck and these hands,
which still bear the traces of our efforts. (Ep.* 5: 5). He reminds us, elsewhere,
about his daily manual work: *The wood we had to carry! And the stones we had
to shape! The plants we took care of and watered! (Ep.* 6: 5).

[78] JEROME, *Ep.* 108: 2; cf. SULPICIUS SEVERUS, *Dialog.* 3: 8; AUGUSTINE, *De op.
mon.*, 22; *Apophthegmata*, Arsenius, 6; 68; CASSIAN, *Conf.* 24: 12; the most vivid
pages of the Fathers about the illegitimacy of slavery come from the monastic
milieu, for example, GREGORY OF NYSSA, *In Eccles. Hom.*, 4.

[79] In the Middle Ages, where important lands were given to monasteries, new relations were created with the workers to free them from serfdom. These conventions
are at the origin of the present farming contracts.

[80] JEROME, *Ep.* 108: 2; 20. This division was not foreseen at the beginning, but
imposed by the circumstances; nevertheless the differences did not confer any
privileges. It did not exist in the initial project of Jerome, who wrote to
Eustochium, '*Are they some servants who want to share your religious life? Don't
be distant towards them, don't keep the haughty appearances of a mistress. You
have the same spouse, you sing psalms together in honour of Christ, why would
you have a different table?*' (*Ep.* 22, 29).

and sisters led the same life, but the holy bishop mentions tensions between the former rich and those coming from labouring classes. The difficulties came sometimes from distribution of goods, but were above all about work, where the differences of physical force and competence are particularly emphasised.[81] The realism of these monks' struggle is shown by the reference to these difficulties, and underlines the idea of fraternity in Christian monasticism.

In a general way, we can say that monks have always been the natural defenders of the poor. Antony had given the example, and since then the interventions made by abbots in their favour are a well-known page of history.[82] Finally, the monastic way of life, which cares for the poor and avoids all superfluity, is a constant challenge to a society which seeks profit and egoistic comforts. The recent Monastic Congresses of Asia and Africa have invited us to maintain the dynamism of these principles in our own times, when poverty is so acute and so visible. To be a prosperous island, without relationship with the world of misery which surrounds it, is a counter-witness. The monastery's work should thus be just, not only for its own living and spiritual profit of its members, but should also be concerned with the good of the surrounding population.[83]

C. THE PLACE OF WORK IN MONASTIC LIFE

Work takes up a large place in the monastic timetable. How is it integrated in the search of God, what are the obstacles which prevent it, and what kind of work makes it easier?

1. The balance between prayer, work and *lectio divina*

We saw how the first Egyptian monks used to pray, meditating on Scripture while working in their cells. They also brought their work with them when they recited the Psalms in common.[84] At that time, they earned their living by plaiting mats, and making baskets or ropes, work which could be done seated, and which required few materials.

---

[81] AUGUSTINE, *De op. mon.*, 22–23.

[82] ATHANASIUS, *VA*, 87. The *Apophthegmata*, Poemen, 5, shows that the interventions of monks in favour of the poor were already so customary that Poemen provoked astonishment by refusing this service. The scandal that the monks provoked in all times, when they become rich and attached to money, shows that society expects from them the service of recalling the ideal of justice and charity.

[83] Cf. reports of the Monastic Congresses of Bangalore, 1973; Abidjan, 1979; Kandy, in Sri Lanka, 1980, Ed. AIM.

[84] *Apophthegmata*, Isidore, 4–5; Lucius, 7; Pambo, 8; PACHOMIUS, *Praec.* 5; 7; CASSIAN, *Inst.* 2: 12–14.

Later, more varied kinds of work became necessary. Monks were to work in the fields or in specialised workshops. Then they had to stop their work in order to recite the choir office. Basil and Pachomius already prescribed that *when travelling, or in the fields, monks should not omit the times of silent prayer and of the psalmody.*[85] Thus, little by little, work was separated from the recitation of the Psalms in the oratory of the monastery. Finally Saint Augustine, followed by the Western tradition, prohibited that anything be done in the oratory besides prayer.[86]

Though separated, work, reading and prayer remained in harmony, and the various Rules carefully arranged their respective times, so that the happy alternation could sustain the monks' attention to God.[87]

The usual custom prevailing in the West was that the community choir offices divided the day into four parts: three of them were dedicated to work and one to reading.[88] Sundays were a time of rest, for monks were among the first Christians to initiate the biblical Sabbath on the Lord's Day. It was under their influence that Sunday as a day of rest became a general Christian custom, from the sixth century onwards.

Such was the tradition received by Saint Benedict. However, the needs of the times, as well as his own character, led him to modify traditional usage in a significant way. Most of his predecessors earned a living, either by cottage industries, which are easy to interrupt for the times of prayer, or in part from gifts and revenues, which made the monks' work less important to the general income of the house.[89] Under these circumstances, the monastic timetable could be centred around the Offices of Terce, Sext and None, artificially dividing the day into equal parts.

Saint Benedict and his monks had to earn their living. They needed

---

[85] PACHOMIUS, *Praec.* 142; BASIL, LR 37.

[86] AUGUSTINE, *Reg.* 2: 20; CAESARIUS, *RV* 10, forbids work during the office, but prescribes it to fight against sleeping during the long readings of the Vigils: *RV* 15.

[87] PACHOMIUS, *Praec.* 15–22; *Praec. et Inst.* Introd. 1: 14–15; *Praec. et Leges*, 10–12; BASIL, LR 37; CASSIAN, *Inst.* 2: 2–5; 3: 2–4; JEROME, *Ep.* 22, 34–36, Ad Eustochium; AUGUSTINE, *Ordo Mon.* 3: 9; *Reg.* 2.

[88] CASSIAN, *Inst.* 3: 7; cf. AV, *Dizionario*. The division of the offices throughout the day comes from the Jewish tradition, which gave three times of prayer in the day. Cf. *Dan.* 6: 10–14; *Didache* 8: 3; the time of reading was either in the morning, or in the middle of the day.

[89] The Egyptian monks specialised in making baskets, mats and ropes: AUGUSTINE, *De op. mon.* 17, says that alms made up for the lack of income, due to the monks' insufficient work. The Master's monastery lived partially off the revenues of its estates.

sufficient time to do real work, while not neglecting prayer and reading. So he was careful to balance the alternation of the monks' duties, taking into account the economic, spiritual, and psychological needs of the brethren. The horarium, originally based on the prayers of the third, sixth and ninth hours, is thus made more flexible, to fit the work schedule conveniently, and to allow *lectio divina* to be done at the most suitable time.[90] He placed the community prayer at the central points which separate the various activities of the day. In this important position, they are meant to centre the whole life on God. Coming to the Divine Office when their duties are fulfilled, the brothers have their minds at rest; they can offer the Lord what they have achieved, and the common prayer helps them to remain in his presence, and to foster charity, which will permeate the next activity.[91]

Therefore, Saint Benedict abandoned his predecessor's artificial framework, and followed the natural rhythm of human life. He respected its alternation of stress and rest, of manual and intellectual labour, and placed the times of prayer in order to centre everything on God.[92] That *discretion* may be one of the reasons why his influence spread far beyond monastic circles, his Rule supporting the efforts of men *seeking God* in various states of life.

Saint Benedict summarises there the whole monastic tradition, which has always sought in the alternation of work, reading and prayer, a balance of life which leads to God, determining the output of the monastery in accordance with its needs and those of charity, leaving the monks the necessary contemplative leisure. So work done

[90] During the hot season, work was done at the coolest hours of the day: early morning, and in the evening. In winter, on the contrary, it was placed in the middle of the day, when it would be warmer. In the same way, *lectio divina* was done when people liked to stay indoors, that is, early morning in winter, and during the hottest hours of the day in summer. Saint Benedict gives *lectio* a little more time than the Master. He divides it into short periods, to make it easier, taking into account the low cultural level of his times. It is longer during Lent, and is considered as one of the penances of that season. Perseverance in this duty is assured by the rounds of the elders: *RB* 48: 14–18; cf. AV, *RB*, p. 597. At present, the Conventual Mass is placed at the time provided by the Rule for the *lectio divina*. If, for some reason, it is not possible to have this Mass, its time should be given back to *lectio*.

[91] In the winter, and during Lent, Sext falls during the work period (*RB* 48) and is not mentioned in the community horarium. This office was probably said in small groups, at the place of work (*RB* 50: 1–3) and in choir only by those who stayed at home. The two signals given for None show that the brothers were scattered at some distance for work. How could they have been promptly gathered for Sext? (AV, ibid, p. 593, n. 14).

[92] This natural rhythm seems to have been that of early monasticism, cf. GREGORY OF NYSSA, *Life of Saint Macrina*, 11.

in the presence of God, and for the service of Christ in one's neighbour, is full of prayer. Moreover, according to the Fathers, the true work of the monk is his continuous striving to orientate his whole being towards God. *What is a monk? asked Abba John the Dwarf. It is the labour of the fight.*[93]

These numerous factors show the riches, but also the fragility, of monastic work. And so it would be helpful to examine the dangers and the errors which in all times have threatened it.

2. The heresies of work

The care and preponderance of details given in all monastic Rules to ensure a good distribution of the times of work, prayer, and reading, shows the fragility of this balance. It is constantly threatened either by the natural human inclination towards indolence, or, on the contrary, by an activism which is equally disastrous for spiritual life.

Cassian, following Evagrius and the Desert Fathers, placed laziness (*acedia*) among the eight main vices, and explained at length how work can remedy it. Saint Augustine also detects this defect in the claims of some monks, who neglect work under the pretext of incessant prayer.[94] One of Saint Benedict's tools of good works is directed against laziness, and he exhorts his brethren to undertake hard work courageously, being careful to avoid overburdening them.[95]

An exaggerated or misguided zeal for work is a danger far worse than laziness. The Desert Fathers, and Cassian, noted that one might work for motives of pride or personal advantages. They knew that the Devil might sometimes impel the brothers to overwork, in order to exhaust and discourage them.[96] Many disciples of Pachomius were caught up in the allurement of profit. Theodore was very sad about it, and this defect was one of the causes of the decline of the congregation.[97] Moreover, monastic history shows us time and again that among Christians, as in other religions, to become rich and attached to wealth, precipitates the irremediable decline, if not the death, of a monastery. From a more individualistic point of view, Saint Basil fears that not only attachment to money, but above all murmuring

---

[93] *Apophthegmata*, John the Dwarf, 44.
[94] CASSIAN, *Inst.* 5: 1; 10; AUGUSTINE, *De op. mon.*, 25–27.
[95] *RB*, 4: 38; 7: 49–50 (sixth step); 48: 7–9.
[96] CASSIAN, *Conf.* 9: 6–7; *Inst.* 2: 7–12; 4: 14.
[97] PACHOMIUS, *VC Bo.* 145; 192; 197–198; AUGUSTINE, *De op. mon.*, 34, forewarned his monks against serving mammon, by being over-anxious about their needs.

and a proud independence, which can become a source of disobedience and a cause of scandal among the brethren, as well as for the laymen involved in the monastery's affairs.[98]

It was against these defects that the Fathers urged their disciples to develop a detachment which limits the work to the needs of the brethren. Abba Silvanus thus restrains the zeal of his disciples, and he did not allow them to extend the vegetable garden, which was sufficient for them.[99] In the same spirit, *for the edification of all, and the preservation of religious life*, Basil requested his monks to sell the produce of the monastery at a lower price, rather than trying to make profits by selling at the usual market price. He also points out the temptation to prefer personal success to the common good of the community and, if a monk is stubborn, says that he should be deprived of his office.[100]

Saint Benedict also worries about the craftsman who becomes proud of his work. He uses the opportunity to mention that transactions should be fair, and should demonstrate that the aim of the monks' life is not profit, but *so that God may be glorified in all things*.[101]

These temptations are always present; Basil, Augustine and Benedict desire that all monks be careful to integrate their work into the service of the community, take an interest in it, and make themselves available for helping others.[102]

A common project to be realised through the work of the community can be an important factor of unity. It should nevertheless be remembered that the true basis of unity is not work, but the monastic ideal of search for God and fraternity in Christ vowed by all.

All these requirements impose a need for selectivity concerning the works to be undertaken in the monastery. What kinds of works are suitable for monks? This question has been raised since the beginning of Christian monastic life.[103]

---

[98] BASIL, LR 29; 38–39; 41; SR 18; 37; 39; 105; 117; 125; 195; 207; SAINT AUGUSTINE had to fight more against laziness of some monks than against excesses of work. He nevertheless forewarned against needless hoarding and egoistic use of the charity shown to the monastery, *De op. monachorum*, 25–27.

[99] *Apophthegmata*, Silvanus, 8.

[100] BASIL, LR 39; cf. SR 141; 143; 285; PACHOMIUS, *Praec.*, 61–70; AUGUSTINE, *De op. mon.*, 16; *Reg.*, I; IV. Cassian, Pachomius and Augustine are of the same opinion. Cassian and Augustine stress more the mastery over desires and freedom of heart. The other two provide more concrete examples: CASSIAN, *Inst.* 7: 24–31; *Conf.* 1: 6; 4: 20; 18: 7; 20: 5.

[101] RB 57: 9.

[102] RB 53: 18–20; BASIL, LR 29; SR 123–125.

[103] BASIL, SR 157; 184; 207; AUGUSTINE, *Reg.*, IV; *RB* 53: 18–20.

3. The selection of monastic work

In the same way as the Hindu and Buddhist monks excluded work which could cause them to break their vows, we see among Christians an impressive unanimity among the Fathers about the selection of the trades fitting for monks. Saint Basil defined them in his *Long Rules*, 38:

> *We should prefer trades which keep our life recollected, and attentive to the Lord, and which do not prevent those who want to train themselves in piety from devoting themselves to prayer, psalmody, and other religious practices.*

Then he advises activities which not only are acceptable to Christians, but which also avoid unrest and agitation. Another source of disturbance could come from lay people. Basil says that they should not come to chat in the brothers' workshops. He also wants to avoid business discussions, travel, and all occasions in which the brethren are contextualised in a world where they are no more considered as religious but are led to react as lay people, defending their private interests, thus running the risk of losing their monastic identity. Along the same lines, a saying of the Fathers shows monks giving up the Oriental habit of bargaining.[104] In conclusion, Basil requests that monks choose trades which

> *keep our life peaceful and quiet, and do not cause too many problems in procuring raw materials, or selling products, which do not involve us in unbecoming or harmful encounters ... and do not require a lot of travel.*[105]

Saint Augustine required also that work should allow the monk to keep his mind attentive to God, and Cassian gives the same reason to explain why the Egyptian monks

> *established themselves in places where the soil was not so fertile as to tempt them to engage in extensive agricultural efforts.*[106]

Saint Benedict continues this tradition but, avoiding most of the detailed descriptions of his predecessors, he trusted his monks, and above all, recommended that the tensions inherent in such matters be resolved through prayer.[107]

[104] BASIL, LR 38–40; SR 141; *Apophthegmata*, Agathon, 16.
[105] BASIL, LR 38.
[106] CASSIAN, *Conf.* 14; *Conf.* 10: 14; 9: 6; AUGUSTINE, *De oper. mon.*, 14; 16; 20. He requests that work *should not occupy the whole mind.*
[107] *RB* 50–51; 66–67.

We should note here that the economic autonomy suggested by Saint Benedict and several of his predecessors was for them a means of limiting their travel.[108] It is worth notice also that these methods were usual in this time. When he says that the monastery should have *all necessities, such as water, mill, garden, and the various crafts*, he is simply following the treatise on agriculture of Cato the Elder.[109] This parallel helps us to discern the spiritual motivation and permanent values in the monastic regulations imposed by the necessities of the time. It is not that the monastery needs to possess much property; rather the preoccupation is that monastic work should not take place outside, but

within the monastery, so that the monks have no need to wander round outside it, for that does not profit their souls at all.[110]

Within the monastery, Saint Benedict neither forbids nor recommends any particular work. In the course of time his disciples, men and women, have undertaken any kind of works, manual and intellectual. But history shows that, though there is no specific monastic work, there is a monastic way of doing work. The Rule, following the whole tradition, indicates that work should not impede but foster religious life, and indicates its conditions.

Some of these characteristics are typically Christian; others are found in monasticism of diverse religions.

3. THE WORK OF MONKS

1. Common values

It is a general observation that, in all religions, dedication to union with the Absolute leads to detachment from the impermanent, that is, from the world, from business, and from possessing material goods. Conversely, as we have already noted, wealth and attachment to money are deadly sicknesses for monasticism, whatever the religion. In most non-Christian religions this is understood to demand a radical renunciation of any lucrative activity and, among Christians, a duty to take care of the poor.

But wherever cenobitic monasticism is organised, monks do some

---

[108] *RB* 66; *RM* 95; Basil, LR 38.
[109] Cf. P. Grimal, *La civilisation romaine*, pp. 211–212.
[110] *RB* 66: 7; cf. *RM* 95: 17–18.

work, at least for the domestic service of the house. In some traditions, especially in Zen, work is used as a means of concentration and meditation. Everywhere, also, big communities became important intellectual centres. Hindu and Buddhist monks exclude work which is incompatible with their vows, and which disturbs their spiritual quest.

The kind of work selected by Christian monks shows that they also consider work to be a means of liberation from the pressure of society and all its businesses, in order to centre their whole life on the search for God. Poverty also provides them with an occasion of trusting in God, like the Hindu *bhakti*.

In all religions, these attitudes are meant to bear witness, in society in general, to the primacy of the spiritual in man's life. The acknowledgement of these common values will help us to discern the aspects of monastic work proper to Christianity.

2. Christian values of monastic work

Biblical revelation has led Christian monks to take a particular stance towards work. God's creation is a *good thing*,[111] and Christ's incarnation sanctifies work as any other bodily activity. Therefore the Christian does not need to escape matter in order to be united to God. He considers work as a collaboration with God's activity, a praise of God, a service to mankind and an act of love for the Lord present in all.[112] A monk, even a hermit in the desert, cannot lose interest in the human family without ceasing to be Christian. Through his prayer, penance and love, he works for the salvation of all. In a community, the service of the brethren becomes a means of encounter with God. Finally, for the Christian, work is part of a balance of life which leads to God: balance in business, where the profits go to charity, but are also used for technical progress; balance between concern for efficiency and work for the glory of God in beauty and detachment, and finally; balance or rather unity of prayer and work.

These Christian values are not exclusive. Some of them have been adopted by monasticisms of other religions, thus developing God's Kingdom. Conversely, Christians can perceive that some of the values which had existed in their own tradition are now stressed by others. Dialogue may help to rediscover and develop them.

---

[111] *Gen.* 1: 10; 2: 15; 9: 1–10.
[112] *Mt.* 25: 10. Saint Benedict constantly refers to serving Christ in others.

248   *The Rule of Saint Benedict*

3. Challenge and dialogue

Some monastic traditions, particularly Zen Buddhism, use work as a means of concentration. This reminds us that Cassian, Basil, and the Desert Fathers, and later William of St Thierry, also understood the care and concern for beauty when working as a means of quieting the mind for prayer.

The detachment we see among Hindu and Buddhist monks may invite us to develop a sense of gratuitousness. This may be done by taking more *contemplative leisure*, spending time with God, and also by caring about our work, not only for profit, but for the sake of doing it well for God.

The *bhakta*'s trust in God challenges us to put into practice the word of Christ, quoted by Saint Benedict: *seek God's kingdom first*, with the trust that *all things will be given you besides.*[113]

At the deepest level, we see that sometimes the most profound spiritual experiences can be very similar, despite the differences among the religions. This is the case in the relationship between action and contemplation. Work and prayer are not separate activities. The real work of a monk is the constant fight to turn his whole being towards God.

4. Monastic work today

The conditions of life are very different in the monasteries of the diverse continents. Some still have the chance to do manual work close to nature, and can profit directly from the advice of the Fathers. Many others have to work on machines and computers. Nevertheless, the experience of our Christian predecessors, summarised in the Rule, may help to discern some criteria.

The Rule insists, first, on work done in the monastery, and in a community spirit. This corresponds to the definition of a cenobite, who lives in a monastery under a Rule and an Abbot, and to the persevering stability often demanded, conditions which imply a work done for God in prayer, obedience and humility.[114] So primacy of the search for God, perfection in beauty, balance between work, *lectio divina*, and prayer, care for the common life, attention to the weak and the poor, such are the traits which characterise the activity of the monk, according to Saint Benedict.

Finally, in all monasticisms, work is never considered as the supreme value: it is an element of the spiritual labour, so that, in the

[113] *RB* 2: 35, quoting *Mt.* 6: 33.
[114] *RB* 1: 2; chs. 4, 58, 66.

midst of the most intense activity, the heart of the monk is at rest. Many centuries before Christ, the author of the *Bhagavad Gita* had perceived that unselfish work is an introduction to contemplation:

> *He who sees inaction in action, and action in inaction, is wise among men.*[115]

Saint Bruno, in very similar terms, expressed how work and rest in God are combined in spiritual labour:

> *Here we celebrate a leisure full of business and we are inactive in an action full of rest.*[116]

[115] *BG* 4: 18.
[116] *Hic otium celebratur negotiosum et in quieta pausatur actione*. In the *letter to Ralph of Rheims*, SC 88, p. 70. GUIGO II notes at the beginning of his *Monks' Ladder* that he conceived it *during manual work*.

CHAPTER XII

THE FORMATION PROGRAMME

Formation is a complex and difficult topic, and its various aspects are often treated separately in spiritual writings. We shall first try to see what is meant by monastic formation, then its aims and its agents, comparing the *RB* with the texts and traditions of other religions as I encountered them in various places.

1. WHAT IS FORMATION?

In all trades, competence is gained at the cost of a period of apprenticeship or preparation, which can be long or short. One is said to have a good formation when one has received not only the necessary intellectual knowledge, but the means of putting it into practice. Each activity has its own specifics. The *art of living*, however, which constitutes monastic life, is shaped into concrete form by models which define it.

The description of the ascetic given by the Hindu *Laws of Manu* indicates the ideal sought by many monastics.

> *Sitting in delightful meditation on the Brahman, needing nothing, inaccessible to any desire of the senses, without any other company than his own soul, may he live here below awaiting the eternal beatitude.*[1]

Buddhism has two main models: the *arhat* and the *bodhisattva*. About the first, it is said:

---

[1] MANU 6: 49.

> *Having disciplined the desire for sensual objects,*
> *Alert, with mind released in full,*
> *This monk, as he studies to think aright,*
> *Alone in time, and uplifted –*
> *– O may the darkness rend.*[2]

The *bodhisattva* puts into practice the same detachment, but with the aim of helping others to reach *Nirvana*:

> *As many beings as the universe contains – all these I have to lead to Nirvana.*[3]

In Jewish literature, the *Rule of Qumran* thus sets out the aim of its followers:

> *To seek God with all their heart, all their soul; to do what is good and just before one's brother, according to what God has prescribed through the intermediary of Moses, and of all his servants, the prophets, ... not walking any more in the hardness of a guilty heart and depraved eyes, doing any kind of evil.*[4]

Saint Benedict, summarising the Christian tradition, is concerned that the monk:

> **sincerely seeks God, ... is earnest at the Work of God, in obedience and under severe words, and will bear all the things that are hard and repugnant to nature in the way to God.**[5]

These few quotations are enough to show that monastic formation is organised around two main axes: the primacy of the search for union with the Absolute, and control of the passions. After examining these two aims of formation, we shall discuss the formators, and their function.

2. TO CENTRE ONE'S LIFE ON THE ABSOLUTE

INITIATION

Initiation, at least in societies that have a strong religious culture, is about gaining the necessary knowledge to be able to make the definitive

---

[2] *Sutta Nipata*, 975, trans. E. CONZE, *Buddhist Scriptures*, p. 79.

[3] *Diamond Sutra*. Ibid. p. 164.

[4] *Rule of Qumran*, in: *Les textes de Qumran*, trans. J. CARMIGNAC ET P. GUIBERT, Paris 1961.

[5] *RB* 58: 7–8.

choices that will govern one's life. The process begins with a with-drawal from the family group, to undergo a transformative experience. By means of trials and teachings, initiation gives access to a new source of strength. After that, the initiate may re-enter his world, though he will see life in a different way ever afterwards.

In Africa, the trials faced in an initiation ritual teach a person to confront fear, and to overcome the difficulties of life by relying on its Source.

> *When the one to be initiated has conquered fear, a new dimension is added to his personality. He has lived through this period. He has experienced the terror, and the exultation. At the root of his being, he has experienced deep ecstasy. He is a human volcano.*[6]

Entrance into the monastic life follows a similar pattern. The Hindu or Buddhist novice leaves his family, and lives under the guidance of a Master before taking his vows. The Jewish *Rule of Qumran* foresees a similar progressive admission into the community, with two years of preparation before each grade.[7]

Christianity underlines the special dimension of free choice, because initiation is not made under the pressure of society, but as an answer to an interior call.

In Christian monasticism, the first trial to be met is the difficulty of admission. At the beginning, the hermit Palamon refused to receive the young Pachomius, the future founder of the Cenobitic Life, and afterwards imposed on him a time of trial. Later, in Pachomian monasteries, newcomers had to stay for some time under the careful watch of the doorkeeper, in his quarters, before being allowed to live in the monastery itself.

Cassian, and Saint Benedict also have the same process of an initial refusal given with unkind words, followed by a stay at the door of the monastery, and later in the guesthouse.[8] The aim is to maximise the disciple's desire to enter the monastery, and to discern his motivation.

> *This first refusal is, as it were, the shock needed to make his heart ring, to measure the resonance of his soul.*[9]

---

[6] Birago Diop, *Breaths*, quoted by Fr Anselm Adodo: *The Way of African Mysticism*, in *AIM Monastic Bulletin*, 1997, No. 63.

[7] *Rule of Qumran*.

[8] Pachomius, VC Bo. 10; *Praec.* 99; Cassian, *Inst.* 4: 3; Basil, in LR 8–15, requires a period of experimentation before joining the community; *RB* 58: 1–4.

[9] M. Geneviève-Marie, ocso, *Pedagogy in the school of charity*, in *AIM Monastic Bulletin*, 1997, No. 63.

The purifying experiences of humiliation and patience invite the postulant to strip himself of his own will, in order to follow God's call, and enter the narrow way that leads to him.

After the trial of refusal comes that of distance. Moving to another place is the symbol of a desire for interior transformation. The novice enters into a new world, where he learns to consider the eternal outcome of his actions. This discernment is represented in some schools of Hinduism by the symbolism of the opening of the *Third eye*, the eye of the wise, for the wise person is able to discover the Absolute at the root of all beings, and find a way to It:

> *The wise person, seeking immortality,*
> *Turned his gaze inward, and saw the Self within ...*
> *The wise, discerning immortality,*
> *Does not seek the permanent among the impermanent.*[10]

In Buddhism, this sign became one of the thirty-two characteristic marks of the Buddha, which indicate 'perfect monks':

> *Detached from all objects of desire,*
> *their beatitude lies in renunciation.*
> *After mastering all their desires,*
> *They are free from all fetters.*
> *Full of light, and illuminating those around,*
> *They have reached the Nibbana.*[11]

Islam gives evidence of a similar tendency:

> *The initiation of the novice into the first stage of the Sufi Path, means he has deliberately chosen to redirect his life from self to God, by following a proved path. A proved path implies a course which leads to the surrender of self-will, and the transformation of desire from being centred in self to being centred in God ... and thus enter into a timeless experience.*[12]

Among the Christian writers, Pachomius, Basil, Cassian and Benedict require a preparatory stay before admission into the community. This delay would be felt more acutely in a society that cultivates immediate satisfaction of desire, where distances can be shortened. Nevertheless, the novice has to enter into himself, to meet the One who is calling him, and experience his love. Christian initiation is *conversion*, a loving response to God's love.

---

[10] *Katha Upanishad*, 4: 1–2; PANIKKAR, *The Vedic exp.*, p. 839.
[11] *Dhammapada*, 89.
[12] J. SPENCER TRIMINGHAM, *Sufi*, p. 199.

Already present in the Prophets, this idea also appears in the New Testament, where it is connected with Baptism, the Sacrament of Initiation, which makes the disciple share in Christ's life, promising to live not according to the world, but by the Spirit.[13] The Fathers often link entrance into monastic life with Baptism. For Pachomius, Basil and Augustine, it was its logical consequence. Saint Jerome considers it as a kind of 'new Baptism', an act of perfect love for Christ. The Prologue of *RB* presents monastic life as an encounter with a *loving Father*, who gives the disciple the *strong and glorious weapons of obedience*, allowing him to *follow God to glory*. The *Tools of Good Works* summarise all this, in two lapidary sentences:

> *To avoid worldly behaviour.*
> *To set nothing before the love of Christ.*[14]

ENTERING INTO A TRADITION

Monastic life cannot be improvised, except in the case of the great charismatic Founders. In general, it derives from a long line of spiritual Masters. To enter monastic life means to enter into their tradition, to study their doctrine and their interpretation of the sacred texts.

In Hinduism the guru, often helped by a specialist teacher, comments on such texts at length, asking his disciples to memorise them, with the tune and exact pitch of each word in Sanskrit. We have noticed this practice in the *Laws of Manu*, and the tradition continues even now in many ashrams. Similarly, the first Buddhist monks dedicated their free time during the rainy season to repetition of the teachings of the Buddha. The custom continues, and when one goes round a Tibetan monastery, for example, one can hear the young monks repeating the texts out loud for several hours each day.

Saint Antony, the father of Christian monasticism, knew long passages of the Scriptures by heart. It was the same for the Desert Fathers, the monks of Saint Pachomius and of Saint Basil. Saint Benedict continues this tradition by recommending several times that the Bible and the *Catholic Fathers*[15] should be studied. This study, as we have seen, is not only an intellectual exercise, but leads to a 'taste' of God's word in *lectio divina*. The disciple then *repeats in his heart* the words which have touched it.

This insistence on study can be explained by the determining

---

[13] *Mt.* 3: 1–2 (John the Baptist); *Mt.* 4: 17 (Jesus); *Acts* 2: 37–40 (The Apostles).
[14] *RB* 4: 21–22.
[15] *RB* 8: 3; 73: 3–4.

influence of religious knowledge on mysticism. In all religions, the meeting with the Absolute is made according to the conception that each religion has of it. For some, it is a union of love with a personal God. For others, it is a 'fusion' of the self in an Infinite beyond words. Mysticism and theology are always closely linked.[16] Each monastic group, whatever its religion, cultivates a particular way of expressing the doctrine which is common to all. To enter into a tradition means to know, to make one's own, the spiritual and intellectual patrimony of the particular religious family.

Nevertheless, the tradition is not an object in a museum, where everything remains frozen in its own time zone. It is rather like a living plant, rooted in its past, yet adapting itself to the changing seasons. One of the roles of formation is to make known the values of the past in order to express and develop them, using the means given by the actual time and place of the monastery. This is also one of the aims of the ongoing formation.

THE TRANSMISSION OF AN EXPERIENCE

All this knowledge would remain cold and ineffective, if the young monk could not see it concretely lived out by persons he could take as models. In the Hindu sacred texts, the *Mahabaratha* presents many heroes who have this role. Similarly, the Buddha's sermons are nearly always based on the example of persons he had met. Each branch of these religions also has its great Masters, venerated by the monks who follow them. The Christian tradition has Christ, and the saints of each Order. Saint Benedict reminds us of this fact, in the eighth step of humility:

> **A monk should do nothing except what is recommended by the common rule of the monastery and the example of those above him.**[17]

As we have seen in chapter 7 of *RB*, this text is a quotation from Cassian, who, when he speaks of 'those above him', means all the Fathers of the monastic tradition.

Teaching, made alive by the example of venerated Masters, invites the disciple to share their experience, as it comes from a higher 'intuition'. Shankara said:

---

[16] The Hindu philosopher RADHAKRISHNA noticed the same closeness: cf. M. DHAVAMONY, *The Bhakti experience in contemporary India*, in RELIGIOUS EXPERIENCE, ITS UNITY AND ITS DIVERSITY, Bangalore, 1981, p. 202.

[17] *RB* 7: 55.

It is by interior illumination, by direct experience, and not by the intermediary of a sage, that an aspirant comes to know the true nature of things (the Brahman). If I want to know what the moon is, I must see it with my own eyes. All that the others could tell me about it would not make it known to me.

Elsewhere he praises his guru for having introduced him to this experience. But he considers him as a means of union with an internalised guru or Master:

This sovereign splendour, given by the one who illuminates the Self, I have received from the majesty of your grace. This is a substitute for you, O glorious teacher, O my guru. It is you who, moved by compassion, awakened me from my torpor.[18]

The role of the tradition is seen again here, where the Masters of each religious school hand over their experience, by example as much as by words. Such activity goes on equally while they are alive and after their death. Hence the veneration given to them by their spiritual descendants.

We have noticed the example of Shankara, and many other Masters in Hinduism. Each Buddhist school venerates its Masters in a similar fashion. The Tibetans give particular honour to their 'Root Lama', an elder who incarnates the whole line of the previous Masters, and hands down their spiritual gifts. The Zen Masters have a similar method. A disciple cannot teach validly until he has lived with one of them, and received from him the acknowledgement that he has shared his experience, and is able to transmit it. This is still more emphasised among the Sufis, where the Master, or *sheikh*, is the holder of a *baraka* (holiness and spiritual power), which he hands down to his successor, and which has an influence on all the members of the Order.

In Christianity, under the action of the Holy Spirit, the Founders of Orders have made use of some aspects of Christ's life in teaching their disciples, for example: *praying on the mount, preaching, or curing the sick.* The Second Vatican Council asked Religious to return to the spirit of their Founders, and to make the Church shine with the gifts they received from God.[19] The return to the spirit of their origins has been the source of most religious reforms in Christianity, as well as

---

[18] M. SANTOU and Y. LELOUP, *Rôle du gourou dans l'hindouisme*, citing SHANKARA (SHRI CHANKARASHARYA) in *DU MAÎTRE SPIRITUEL AU MAÎTRE INTÉRIEUR*, p. 42.

[19] VATICAN II, LG 46; AG 40; PC 2.

in the other religions.[20] Its transmission to newcomers is thus an important part of formation.[21]

A LASTING EXPERIENCE

The desire for union with the Absolute, or for a loving union with God, can be the occasion of very strong experiences which have an impact on one's whole life. Such an effect, however, can diminish or even vanish if the deep contact with the Absolute, or God, is not renewed and vivified through interior silence, and by a life in harmony with the spiritual quest. Hindu and Buddhist sages, using the methods of meditation of their various schools, show that persever-ance is a necessary prerequisite for success. Similarly, the Desert Fathers insisted on remaining in the cell, while Saint Benedict tells the monk in trouble: *do not run away!*

We have seen, in connection with the work of the monastery, how overactivity can be an evasion of the spiritual quest. At an earlier stage, we saw also how Saint Benedict, following the Fathers, empha-sised the centrality of the love of God. This relation of love is deepened and renewed by prayer. If the young monk is aware in himself how this contact with God builds up his personality, gives him freedom, and makes changes in his life, his love for Christ will be strengthened. When he is also able to see that every difficulty is an occasion of progress, he is encouraged to persevere in a generous faithfulness to what is required of him.

As we progress in monastic observance and in faith, our hearts are opened wide, and the way of God's commandments is run in a sweet-ness of love that is beyond words (RB Prol: 49).

3. CONTROL OF DESIRES

Who ... desires life, and is eager to see Good Days? (RB Prol: 15).

With these words, Saint Benedict introduces the idea of control of the senses into his Rule. Similarly, the beginning of the Hindu *Laws of Manu* had said:

---

[20] The periodical renewals in Buddhist monasticism, in past centuries or in our own days, originated with hermits who had rediscovered the asceticism and the taste for meditation of the first disciples of the Buddha.

[21] Cf. Pot. Inst. No. 35.

The man who follows the rules given [in the sacred texts] wins glory in this world, and perfect felicity in the next.[22]

The efforts necessary to gain self-control can be made willingly only if their aim is well understood. For this reason, the formation period should be seen as a positive way of acquiring a better state. For the Christian, it is a means of developing the personality received from the Creator. God really wants to collaborate with each person, making them like a piece of art, each with its own beauty.

In the texts we have quoted concerning the search for the Absolute, control of the thoughts and senses is a prerequisite for an objective judgement on the situation, and for making the right choices. The *Laws of Manu* say:

When the sensory organs are in contact with attractive objects, the experienced man should struggle to control them, just as a charioteer tries to control his horses.[23]

The Buddhist *Dhammapada* is filled with similar pieces of advice, such as this verse:

If a person averts his eyes from the vanity of things, is well behaved, prudent and full of ardour, Maya [the illusion] cannot tear him down, but will be like wind blowing on cragged rock.[24]

The remarkable thing, in these two religions, is that they consider meditation as the main means for attaining such control. The *Bhagavad Gita* says:

Renunciation is difficult to reach without yoga, the discipline of the disinterested action. The ascetic whose energies are focused, through this discipline, would not take long to reach Brahman.
   When one is focused by the unitive discipline, the soul is purified, the faculty of the senses controlled ... He can act rightly, he is without stain.[25]

Yoga, together with ascetic discipline, has the twofold aim of unifying the person, and detaching him from any selfishness. For Hindus,

[22] MANU, 2: 9.
[23] MANU, 2: 88. Chs. 5 and 6 of the *Bhagavad Gita* deal with the same topic: *When one is no more attached to the objects of the senses nor to one's acts, having renounced any project of self-interest, one is said to have climbed up all the steps of the yoga* (5: 3).
[24] DHAMMAPADA, 8.
[25] BG 5: 6–7.

the control of the senses is a prerequisite for contemplation. It is also a means of discerning (*viveka*) the permanent from the impermanent, for acting justly:

> *Holding all [the senses] in check, he should sit, intent on Me. For he whose senses are under control is sure to come to understanding ... to see the Self.*[26]

A similar process is found in Buddhism. The rules of the *Dhammapada* settle the details of monastic life, which show the disciple how to remain in continual control of the senses. The effects of such discipline are strengthened by a progressive set of meditations, adapted by the Master to the needs of the novice. A consideration of the repugnant aspects of the body are used, for example, as an antidote to sensual desires. But the mind should also apply itself to the analysis of sensory perceptions and distinguish their various components: the external stimulus, the perception by the sense organs, the reaction, and the desires that are aroused. This objective reflection checks a passionate reaction, stops an indiscriminate admission of thoughts to the mind, and controls its manner of receiving them:

> *As rain cannot go through a well-thatched roof,*
> *So desire cannot penetrate a well-trained mind.*[27]

In Christianity, the Desert Fathers advise a similar vigilance, for:

> *All sin begins with a thought.*[28]

They ask the brethren to reveal their thoughts to their elder, before carrying them out.[29] Evagrius, on the basis of these observations, gives as a first step towards contemplation the *Practical life*, which aims at *purifying the part of the soul from which arise the passions*.[30] Such a purification will lead to charity, and then to contemplation. The same author, still basing himself on the Desert Fathers' teaching, made a study of the passions. Cassian[31] and all in the Christian tradition have maintained the principal points.

---

[26] BG 2: 61. Cf. T. K. JOHN, *Contemplation and action, the Bhagavad Gita in the light of Ramanuja's Commentary*, in THE SIGN BEYOND ALL SIGNS, pp. 37; 50.

[27] DHAMMAPADA, *Twin Verses*, 14.

[28] *Philokalia, Saint Mark the Ascetic*, p. 71. Cf. *Apophthegmata*. Syst. Coll. XI, 47. The whole chapter is about vigilance over thoughts.

[29] ABBE ISAIE, *Recueil Ascetique*, SPIRITUALITÉ ORIENTALE, 7 bis.

[30] EVAGRIUS, *Praktikos*, 50.

[31] CASSIAN, *Inst.* 5–12; *Conf.* 5.

The specific Christian contribution in this field is to insert prayer, and especially recourse to Christ, between the thought and the reaction of the senses. The Desert Fathers instructed their disciples not to enter into discussion with temptation but:

To flee towards God, as a man climbs a tree to escape a wild beast.

or

To pour prayer on temptation, as water on fire.

Many Fathers also use the image of Psalm 136:

To dash the evil thoughts on Christ, as soon as they arise.[32]

Saint Benedict echoes them, when he says:

To dash the evil thoughts that invade one's heart immediately upon Christ, as upon a rock, and to reveal them to one's spiritual father.

The same reflex is valid for good thoughts:

Whenever you begin any good work, you must ask of Christ with the most urgent prayer that it may be brought to completion by him.[33]

All these pieces of advice mean that, if intellectual formation is necessary, it remains useless unless the novice gets into the habit of checking his thoughts as soon as they arise, so that they may not stir up the instinctive reactions of the passions.[34] Meditation helps to introduce a distance which will allow him to observe the thoughts and make a discernment about them, for such is the distinctive feature of the human being. For the Christian, this discernment is done with Christ's help and light. A wise choice of meditation methods allows him to become aware of the thought processes, before they have a chance to gain a hold on the senses. To summarise, he must dash the

---

[32] *Apophthegmata*, Macarius, 19; John the D., 12; Poemen, 154; Martin of Dumes, 3-4.

[33] *RB* 4: 50; *Prol.* 4; cf. 7, first and fifth steps of humility.

[34] Pot. Inst. No. 37: *The ascesis, which implies a refusal to follow our instincts and spontaneous reactions, is an anthropological need before being specifically Christian. The psychologists point out that young people (and others) need something to resist (educators, rules, etc) in order to build their personality ... The teaching methods used in religious formation, for men and women, should help them to undertake with enthusiasm a progression which requires effort. It is in this way that God himself leads the human person he has created.*

bad thoughts on the rock of Christ, and direct the affective powers of his heart towards him.

The work of self-mastery lasts for life, but it is not an aim in itself. It brings a certain peace, called *apatheia* by the Fathers. All agree, however, that it should be thought of merely as a prerequisite, the threshold, as it were, of loving union with God, which is the real goal to be sought.[35] The Desert Fathers used to conclude their pieces of advice with the words:

Do this, and you will live!

4. THE FORMATORS

THE SETTING

Location of the monastery

Initiation brings the disciple into a new mode of living. The choice of a new physical location is intended in all cultures to make the *inner* changes easier. In Africa, during the period of initiation, young people live in the forest, or in the enclosure of a temple. In old India, the young man left his home to dwell with his guru. The location of Buddhist monasteries is always carefully selected. Here, for example, are the reflections of King Bimbisara, before offering a piece of land to the Buddha:

Where may I find a place for the dwelling of the Blessed One to live in? not too far from the town and not too near, suitable for going and coming, easily accessible for all people who want to see him. By day not too crowded, at night not exposed to much noise and alarm, clean of the smell of people, hidden from men, well fitted for a retired life.[36]

Tibetan monasteries are generally situated in the mountains, with splendid scenery.

The first Christian hermits went into the desert, but the Pachomian monasteries and those of Lower Egypt were on the skirts of the cultivated lands. They found, as by instinct, the arrangements for

---

[35] We mentioned this process described by the Fathers in the chapter on humility. In CLEMENT OF ALEXANDRIA, *apatheia* allowed openings to a knowledge which ends in love (*Strom.* 7: 10). For ORIGEN, the soul, having purified its moral fibre and become used to discernment, is capable of being lifted to the contemplation of the divinity, by means of a spiritual love (*Com. in Cant.* 78).

[36] *Vinaya*, 1: 143. (Trans. G. Panabokke.)

262 The Rule of Saint Benedict

withdrawal from the world and for accessibility determined eight centuries earlier by the Buddhists. This situation symbolises the continuous initiation the monks live and want to share with their visitors.

The place of worship

Inside the monasteries of all religions, particular consideration is given to the place in which prayer is performed. The style, the ornamentation, statues, use of incense, music and ritual gestures, all is minutely organised, to unify the senses of the human being and lead them to the Absolute, as it is understood in each tradition. The Formation programme teaches respect and care for sacred objects, helping the disciple to understand their underlying symbolism, and the aspects proper to each religious school. In Hinduism and Buddhism, the disposition and shape of the statues express the teaching of the religious group to which they belong.

In the monastic tradition of Saint Benedict, a Cistercian church, constructed for the monks' use alone, is generally unadorned. By contrast, Benedictine monks have a tradition of welcoming visitors to their churches, which are often also places of pilgrimage. Hence their church environment shows a concern to educate the faithful, by means of paintings and sculptures. History also shows that the monks have often changed the interiors of their churches, in order to adapt them to the mentality of the time, and to make prayer easier. They instinctively held in their hearts Saint Benedict's recommendation:

The oratory should correspond to its name: [a place of prayer].[37]

The cloister

The cloister is a place of silence, which has a complex dual role of relationship and recollection. It unites the different parts of the monastery: church, refectory, chapter-room, cells. But it is also the place of the *statio* (or silent assembly-point of the monks, before entering the church) and the brethren like to walk or sit in it peacefully, meditating God's word.

Embedded in the heart of the monastery, the cloister reminds the monk that all his activity should be filled with God's presence. Its traditional architecture, with its row of arches based on the straight line of a wall, invites him to '*ruminate*' God's word, slowly repeating it in his

[37] *RB* 52: 1.

heart. Its bays may open out either on to a well-kept garden, centred on a well, symbol of the Living Water and of God's presence, or on to beautiful scenery, which raises the mind to God.

THE COMMUNITY

The role of the brethren

In the Monastic Congress of Bangkok in 1968, it was a Tibetan monk who first drew attention to the important role of the community itself in the formation of its young members. An atmosphere of kindness allows the newcomer to feel at home and welcomed. The example of the elders show, better than any word, what is to be done and what to be avoided. The community also provides a rule of life, spiritual Masters and teachers. All these benefits are common to all religions, but each one gives its own particular note.

For the Buddhists, the *Sangha* (community) is, with the *Buddha* and the *Dharma*, the *refuge*, that is the guidance, security, and 'compass-bearing' needed by monks and lay people.

The groups of Hindu *Bhakti* ascetics attract their disciples through their joy and their trust in the divinity they worship. The gurus hold the main position in the ashrams, but the community plays a more important role in the modern Orders.

The organisation of Christian monasteries shows the 'vertical' Godward dimension, through the Abbot and his assistants, interacting constantly with the 'horizontal' dimension of finding Christ in the brethren. In return the brethren are also bearers of Christ's love, which is both the cement and the dynamic force of the community. Saint Pachomius put it thus:

> *May all things bring profit to you, so that you, in turn, may bring profit to all.*[38]

Saint Basil was always concerned about the influence that the behaviour of each monk might have on the others,[39] while Saint Benedict, in the first chapter of his *Rule*, gives equal importance to the community, the Abbot and the Rule, and the same balance is found with regard to the Councils.[40] The last chapters speak in more detail of fraternal relationships. Mutual relations, imbued with simplicity and trust, bear witness to the love of Christ, and lead the disciple to

[38] THEODORE, *Catech. CSCO* 159, p. 38.
[39] BASIL, SR 38; 98; 119; LR 7; 24; 47.
[40] *RB* 1; 2; 3: 1, 7; chs. 71–73.

respond with a generous fidelity.[41] To see Christ in others makes the community a place where the personal attitude of its members is tested. Are you able to serve joyfully, to accept people's different ways, to find your place in a group, harmonising your personality with others', and accepting responsibilities? It is the relationship with the others, with respect and love, which helps a monk to show to others the particular aspect of the mystery of Christ to which his own vocation has called him.

Another aspect of the formation given by the community is found in the religious ceremonies. The members of the Hindu ashram meet for singing praises to the divinity, the *Bhajans*, and for reciting sacred texts, sometimes accompanied with dances, whose refined symbolic gestures carry a profound teaching, and put the whole human being in harmony with his spiritual quest.

Buddhist monasteries sometimes have very long community rituals, during feasts in honour of the divinities. The singing of sacred texts occupies most of the time, but these are themselves a form of teaching, and lead the monks into meditation. Simple daily rituals offer the humble things of life: fruit, flowers, water, and oil. These unite life and meditation. Some groups, especially the Tibetans, have sacred dances, with many participants. Taught from childhood, such dances teach control of the body, and their symbolism, as it is progressively revealed, contains a deep teaching leading to meditation.

Muslims also have their daily rites of prayer, while the Sufis use religious dances, like the *dhikr*,[42] which has a strict connection with meditation. All who are present perform some part of it, but the ceremonies are developed and taught only in the houses of the different Sufi Orders.

Right from the beginning Christian monks met for prayer, while the hermits sometimes walked long distances to participate in the Sunday liturgy. Later on, up to our own time, the monasteries have always treated and developed the liturgy with care. The common recitation of the Divine Office and the Eucharist are both a school of prayer and its support. The mystics found their inspiration here, and the Rites, along with the Word of God, are the main source of meditation for all concerned.

In Christianity, the religious community as a whole helps its members to find landmarks based on faith which direct their behaviour and give meaning to their commitments. It also gives each monk the spiritual and affective support which allows him to be faithful to

[41] Cf. Pot. Inst. No. 27.
[42] Cf. J. Spencer Trimingham, *Sufi*, pp. 194 ff.

his vows, and develop his own personality. Nevertheless, all religions require certain conditions for joining the community.

THE CONDITIONS FOR JOINING THE COMMUNITY

Before Christ

The question of discerning vocations is not directly taken up in the pre-Christian texts, but they do indicate the dispositions required for those who want to join monastic life. After describing the renunciation of the family, the signs of caste, and sacrificial acts, the *Brahma Upanishad* shows the goal of the disciple: knowledge of the Supreme One, the Brahman:

> *The Supreme Self is the Supreme Brahman, who shines in the pure space of the heart. This is pure knowledge. This cave is the space that should be known ...*
>
> *There is only one God, hidden in all creatures. He penetrates all, he is the inner self of all beings, the controller of all actions, residing in all beings. Witness, absolute Conscience, free from all attributes ... this hidden God is discovered through meditation ... May the self be united, by knowledge, to the Supreme Self.*[43]

Commenting on the *Katha Upanishad*, Shankara speaks of the necessary prerequisites for the disciple, stressing an attitude of goodwill, and receptivity to the words of the guru.

When considering chapter 4 of *RB*, we quoted the words of the Buddhist vows. Here, let us recall the Master's words, at the end of each one:

> *Are you capable of observing it?*

The positive answer of the novice makes it clear that the Master was already sure of his ability to do it, since he had found that out during the time of probation. The novice strengthens his fidelity by

> *taking refuge in the Buddha, the Dharma and the Sangha.*

Trust in the Buddha, his teaching, and his community, is another essential condition for persevering in his way.

The beginning of the Jewish *Rule of Qumran*, written some centuries later, expresses the goal pursued by this community, and what was expected from those who joined it:

---

[43] Translated from A. DEGRASSE FAHD, *Upanishad*, p. 216; *Brahma Up.* I, IV.

From the Master of Wisdom, to all his brothers:
here is the book of the community Rule.
The aim is: to seek God with all your heart and all your soul;
to do what is good and just before his face, according to what he
has prescribed by the intermediary of Moses and of all his
servants the prophets;
... not to walk any more in the hardness of a guilty heart, with
depraved eyes, doing any kind of evil ...
All those who are willing to receive his faithfulness will bring all
their knowledge, all their strength, and all their wealth into the
community of God.[44]

The Christian tradition

The primitive literature of Christian monasticism was, from the point
of view of literary genre, much the same: there was no systematic
reflection on discernment, but rather pieces of advice, or isolated
stories. Rules, *Apophthegmata*, and Lives of the Fathers, give examples to be followed or avoided: it is the love of God which drove Saint
Paul the Hermit into the desert, while it drove Amoun, at Nitria, and
the one whom Palladius calls 'the young Alexandrian' out of the
world.[45]

When Saint Pachomius came to the hermit Palamon, asking to
follow his way of life, the old man tried first to discourage him,
describing all the difficulties of being a monk. Finally, he said:

I have explained the rules of monasticism to you. Now, go and examine
yourself on all these points. If you are able to do what I have explained,
you will come back, and I shall rejoice with you.

As Pachomius was unwilling to go, he had to ask several times before
being accepted for a period of trial, and finally he received the monastic habit.[46] Later, he made his prospective disciples wait in a similar
way, and appointed a monk

to instruct those who were arriving to become monks, up to the day on
which they were clothed with the monastic habit.

[44] QUMRAN *Rule*, 1: 1–12.
[45] PALLADIUS, *Lausiac History*, 1: 8; cf. AV *Critères du discernement dans la tradi-*
tion monastique ancienne; J. DANIELOU, *La direction spirituelle dans la tradition*
ancienne de l'Eglise, CHRISTUS, No. 25; I. HAUSHERR, *La direction spirituelle en*
Orient autrefois.
[46] PACHOMIUS, VC *Bo.* 10.

After that, we see him educating the young Theodore, teaching him to repel temptations and *acquire great kindness*.[47]

Saint Basil recommends an enquiry into the past life of the new recruits, and:

> *To those who already live a good life, the perfection of the command-ments should be explained. For the rest, they must reform ... to seek perfection in the knowledge of God. Their character should be exam-ined, for fear they may be unstable and easily swayed, and to see if some form of shame be not preventing them from confessing their secret faults, and from accusing themselves.*
>
> *One form of test that would be good for all, is to see if a man accept, without blushing, having to do the humblest tasks which are judged to be fitting ... When someone is thus seen to be an easy instrument for the Master, ready to do any good action, he can be admitted to the number of those who are consecrated to the Lord.*[48]

For Basil the main points are, the right intention for *serving God*, the ability to open one's heart, and a generous acceptance of the work and ascesis of the monastery.

In Cassian's monastery, those who wanted to join the community had to wait ten days at the door and endure insults. In the novitiate, the newcomer is entrusted to an elder:

> *who has to educate the novice, teaching him, first of all, to control his own will ... asking him to do things that he dislikes, to see if he is living in illusion, or, on the contrary, sincere and humble. To train them well, they should be taught not to hide any bad thoughts, but manifest them at once to the elder.*[49]

We find here the same criteria as in Saint Basil: sincerity, humility, openness of heart, but with an insistence on obedience, which includes absurd orders.

Saint Benedict knew most of the Desert Fathers' teachings, and explicitly referred to them, though giving them his own stamp.

Saint Benedict's Rule

Saint Benedict dedicates the chapter 58 of his Rule to *The rules for receiving [new] Brethren*. He begins by adopting once again the prac-tice of a not very friendly welcome: the newcomer has to wait at the

[47] PACHOMIUS, VC *Bo.* 32–38.
[48] BASIL, LR 10.
[49] CASSIAN, *Inst.* 4: 3–8.

entrance, where there was probably a place for casual visitors, and then in the guest house.

> *Easy admission is not to be granted to anyone as soon as he applies to enter the monastic state, but as the Apostle says, 'Test the spirits to see whether they are of God' (1 John 4: 1). But if the newcomer continues to knock on the door, and it is seen that he puts up patiently with the unkind replies and the difficulty of getting in, and that after four or five days he is still persisting in his request, then let him be allowed to come in, and remain in the guest quarters for a few days (RB 58: 1–4).*

Up to that point, Saint Benedict follows the tradition. His innovation, however, comes in his appointment of an elder for the formation of the newcomers as a group.

THE NOVICE MASTER

His qualities

In Hindu and Buddhist texts
In Hindu monasticism, the role of novice master is held by the guru. The *Upanishads* speak at length of the qualities he should have to train his disciples: to be of easy access, kind in his words, knowledgeable, of virtuous life, and with the gift of teaching. But before all else he must have an unselfish love, the kind that will help him to ask and elicit effort from his disciples.[50]

The Buddhists have similar recommendations, expressed with their own humour. Once, attending a lecture on this subject in a Buddhist monastery, the Lama concluded his list of qualities by saying: '*It is obvious that such a Master cannot possibly exist!*', and he explained his view with an image. The Master is like a snow-covered peak and the disciple is like the sun. If there is sunshine on the East, water will flow on the eastern slope, if it shines on the South, there will be water on the South, etc. This is to say that the answer of the Master depends on the quality of the disciple's question.

In the Christian tradition, and in RB
In the Christian tradition, the Abbot is responsible for formation, though he is often helped in this task by some elders. According to

---

[50] GURUSHIP, B. B. CHAUBEY, *The nature of guruship according to Hindu scriptures*, pp. 17–20 gives 5 pages of qualities taken from the *Arthavaveda*, from *Apastamba Dharmasutra* and from *Kularnava Tantra*. It excludes physical defects, sickness, bad conduct, incapacity to express oneself correctly, pride and jealousy.

Cassian, the newcomers were mingled with the community, and probably entrusted individually to an elder, as was the custom among Hindus and Buddhists. Saint Benedict makes the novitiate a particular group in the community: this is part of his innovation. The postulant had, as we have seen, to wait a few days:

> *After that he should be in the quarters of the novices, where they work and eat and sleep. And to them should be assigned a senior monk who has the gift of winning souls, and he should pay them the closest attention (RB 58: 5-6).*

New as it is in the Christian tradition, the idea is nevertheless found elsewhere. The fact of grouping the candidates together corresponds to the African tradition of initiation, where the youngsters help each other to dedicate themselves fully to the work of interior transformation which is assigned to them. That same intention is found in *RB*.

Next, *RB* specifies the qualities required in the novice master: he must have *the gift of winning souls*. This is a natural gift, but will be enriched by grace and by experience, so that the candidates can be really understood, and led to God. This is a gift that the whole monastic tradition acknowledged as necessary. Saint Basil said that the adult newcomers are to be examined by *discerning minds*.[51] Among the Tibetans, the monks destined to direct long retreats are trained for several years for this work, through a collaboration with senior Masters. Gifted though he may be, a spiritual Master is not made by chance.

The *RB* describes the novice master's way of attending to the novices with suggestive words: *omnino curiose intendat*. It is difficult to express, in so few words, the entire richness of this phrase. We can suggest, perhaps, *he looks at everything with interest, and with the utmost care*. In the following sentences, we see the repeated change from singular to plural (*He should be in the quarters of the novices, where they* ... and further: *pay them the closest attention ... find out whether* he *sincerely seeks God*). This serves to underline the twofold attention the novice master must give: to the group, and to each person, to each with affection and care. This attention is to be given especially in two particular areas: the discernment of vocations, and the difficulties met in monastic life.

---

[51] BASIL, LR 10. The corresponding text of the *Regula* translated by Rufinus says: *by those that great shrewdness has made able to scrutinise the dispositions (of the newcomers) and test them (Reg. 7: 13).*

The discernment of vocations

In Saint Benedict's time there were no religious Congregations to offer various fields of activity according to personal inclinations. The only choice was between life in the world, and consecration to God. All the attention of the novice master was therefore centred on the capacity of the postulant to persevere in the religious life.

RB describes the criteria for discernment: the way the novice lives in the novitiate, the signs of God's calling, and the novice's capacity to persevere in his response to it. This discernment begins, on arrival, with a test of perseverance (*RB* 58: 1-4). The life in the novitiate is then traced, in a few words:

> **He should be in the quarters of the novices where they study and eat and sleep (RB 58: 5).**

The Latin word *meditent* (*study*) means, in *RB*, that they learn by heart, through repetition. It was certainly Scripture that was learnt, beginning with the Psalms. They were recited without books, in the choir, and a study of them is recommended once more during free time in Lent (*RB* 48: 13). Curiously, and contrary to Basil and Cassian, there is no question of work, nor of special dispositions for any particular work. One probable reason is that it was done outside the novitiate itself. But perhaps the most cogent explanation is that the Master studies the disciple's qualities, revealed in the *way* that he works, rather than in any particular activity.

> **[The senior's] care must be to find out whether the newcomer sincerely seeks God, whether he is earnest at the Work of God, in obedience and under severe words (RB 58: 7).**

Sincerely seeking God: this is a quality that Saint Basil also insisted on, in saying *be sure that he works for God*. The essential question is: does the novice devote himself fully to God's service out of love? Generally there are several motivations, which have to be purified, little by little, as the novice makes progress in monastic life. But at the beginning, it is important to know whether the novice surrenders himself to God or whether, without realising it, he wants God to be at the service of his personal project, whatever may be its religious appearance. One does not enter the monastery to do this or that job, but to belong to Christ, to have a lifelong friendship with him, and a preferential love for him, a love that will grow as we make progress.

Saint Benedict does not give monastic life any 'secondary aim', or specific apostolate. The *search for God* is the essential. The rest may vary enormously, as determined by place and circumstances, but will be always directed towards this search.

Earnest at ... Mere external fidelity leads to a legalistic observance, which easily becomes intolerant. Here Saint Benedict uses the word *sollicitus*, which means zeal, love, and responsibility.[52]

The first object of this zeal, and this love, is the *opus Dei*, or the work of God, a phrase which Saint Basil had already used with the broad sense of God's service, in prayer, ascesis and work. In *RB*, the stress is put on prayer, and particularly on the Divine Office recited in common, an aspect which would become profoundly characteristic of the future Benedictine Order.

Like his predecessors, Saint Benedict leads on to the subject of obedience and humility. As in the case of '*sincerely seeking God*', we are here dealing with a fundamental disposition of the person, a deep and lifelong attitude. *Listen, ... incline the ear of your heart,* – these are the first words of the Rule. The monk, like the Virgin Mary, should always be ready to say: *Behold the servant of the Lord, let it be unto me according to your word* (*Luke* 1: 38) and, like Jesus, *I did not come to do my own will, but the will of him who sent me* (*John* 5: 30). Such an attitude demonstrates trust, and openness to the legitimate superiors. They have the task of speaking God's word to the disciple, a word which will transform his soul and shape it in the likeness of Christ. We have already spoken of these virtues. The question here is how to know whether the novice really wants them, and practises them.[53]

Training for the spiritual combat

To help the well-disposed novice, Saint Benedict asks the novice master to inform the newcomer of the obstacles he is bound to meet. This is something like a military officer, who explains to his men the terrain where they will have to fight, and gives them the appropriate weapons:

> **All the hardships and trials through which we travel to God are to be expounded to [the novice] (RB 58: 8).**

[52] The word '*sollicitus*' is used in *RB* to qualify the attention that the Abbot and the various officials should have towards the brethren (*RB* 21: 2; 22: 3; 47: 1), especially the weak, the guilty, the sick, the seniors, the poor, etc. (*RB* 27: 1; 31: 19; 71: 4). By contrast, the Abbot should avoid too much solicitude for material problems (*RB* 2: 33).

[53] Cf. *PENTECOTE D'AFRIQUE*, No. 13, Sep. 1993: *Formation, problèmes et défis*. As my own findings agree on many points with the reflections made in this issue, I have referred to it in writing this chapter.

The mention of *all the things that are hard* shows a concern for truth and a desire that the young brother should not be surprised and dismayed by unexpected obstacles. All the possible difficulties are not listed there, for they have already been mentioned in the course of the Rule. The Prologue already informs us that there will be *some degree of restraint, for the correction of faults and the preservation of charity* (*RB Prol.* 47).

The steps of humility, especially the fourth, describe in a realistic way some of the more painful trials: *opposition and abuse, injustice, adversities and rebuffs* (*RB* 7: 35–43).

Nevertheless, it is remarkable that Saint Benedict adopts such a positive attitude to these difficulties, seeing them as steps leading to God. The role of the novice master is to encourage the novice to follow with enthusiasm *the Lord Christ, the true King, taking up the strong and glorious weapons of obedience* (*RB Prol.* 3) given to us by his example. In the same way, when he speaks of *restraint*, he immediately adds that this is *for adequate reason, for the correction of faults, or the preservation of charity* (*RB Prol.* 47). It is the same for the *school of the Lord's service*, where Saint Benedict hopes *to lay down nothing ... harsh or hard to bear* (*RB Prol.* 45–46). By these words, as by the *adequate reason* mentioned above, Saint Benedict refuses the artificial testing foreseen by Cassian. On the contrary, he wants to encourage and inspire confidence in facing the trials. So he says to the novice:

> *Do not then and there be overcome with terror, and run away from the way of salvation, for its entrance must needs be narrow. On the contrary, as we progress in monastic observance and in faith, our hearts are opened wide, and the way of God's commandments is run in a sweetness of love that is beyond words* (*RB Prol*: 48–49).

A similar concern appears in the fourth step of humility, where the description of the difficulties is followed by words of encouragement and hope:

> *A man should, with an uncomplaining spirit, keep a firm grip on patience, and as he endures he should neither grow faint nor run away; even as Scripture says, 'Let your heart take courage and hope in the Lord.' ... Yet unmoved, through their hope of divine reward they joyfully persevere, saying, 'These are the trials through which we triumph on account of him who has loved us'* (*RB* 7: 35–39).

In the Prologue, *the strong and glorious weapons* are mentioned at the same time. These are, first, *obedience*, understood in the broad sense given by Saint Benedict, then, attention of heart, to follow Christ and, with him, the will of the Father who loves us. Then comes listening to the word given by the Abbot, and finally, the fraternal help of the community. Given all these:

the weak are not afraid (*RB* 64: 19)

and

May [Christ] bring us all together to life everlasting. ... Whoever you are, then, who are hurrying forward to your heavenly father-land, you will come at the end, under God's protection, to those heights of learning and virtue which we have mentioned above (*RB* 72: 12; 73: 8-9).

In his guidance of the novice, the novice master should know him thoroughly, and for that reason, begin by listening to him.

Listening to know

Saint Basil asked that the past life of the postulant be known. It is useful to give him an opportunity to review his life and see God's desire for him. In a general way, it is important to know his previous surroundings, if the novice master is to get to know him, especially if he comes from a different culture. A meeting with the family often allows the novice master to distinguish attitudes and reactions belonging to the monk in question from those which come from his background.

To know how to listen, to receive confidences, without forcing the novice's conscience or becoming an accomplice, is a difficult art. It supposes that, as Saint Benedict puts it, the monk can speak without fear of having what he says repeated to a third party. When the elder feels that there is something else which may be difficult for the novice to say, he should not end the session himself, but ask the brother if he wishes to add anything further.

The novice master has to discover the gifts and capacities of each novice, so that he can invite him to acknowledge and develop them in service to the community and the Church. To enable gifts that have been received to be used will assist the personal equilibrium and dynamism of the brethren, and their gifts are an enrichment for the whole community.

Listening to heal

In Hindu ashrams, all confidences are generally made to the guru. But when the structures become more developed, there are also elders to whom the monks can open their hearts. Among the Buddhists, besides the public accusations of the *Uposatha*,[54] in some places a brother may confess his fault to another, provided that he did not himself commit the same fault. In Zen and Tibetan monasteries, during the retreats, the participants regularly tell the retreat Master how they feel.

Christians understand healing as a gift of God. The word of the elder should thus correspond to what the Inner Master says, in the depth of the heart. To the novices, who were surprised at the pertinence of her answers, Saint Thérèse of Lisieux remarked that, before speaking, she always asked the Lord to make her say what was needed.

Do this, and you shall live, said the Desert Fathers. Pachomius had great skill in helping the brethren reveal their difficulties.[55] The Head of the house also performed this role, though referring difficult cases to the Founder. Saint Benedict used the same teaching methods as the Desert Fathers, when he asked the elder to

> *give unofficial consolation to the wavering brother, and induce him to make humble satisfaction, and give him comfort, 'so that he is not overcome by too much sadness'.*[56]

So the comforted brother may follow Christ and *run, [with] heart opened wide, in the way of God's commandments* (*RB Prol.* 49).

Listening to guide

The image of the guide is found in several religions, especially among Tibetans, while in Islam among the Sufis everyone has experience of mountains and desert: the guide is one who, having already made the journey, can indicate the right track.[57]

---

[54] *Uposatha*, a monthly meeting, where the monks recite part of their rules, and accuse themselves of their faults.

[55] PACHOMIUS, VC *Bo*. 42.

[56] *RB*, 27: 3–4, quoting 2 *Cor*. 2: 7.

[57] Cf. in QUESTION DE No. 64, 1991, *Du Maître Spirituel au Guide Intérieur, en Orient et en Occident*, FAOUZT SKADI, *Le Maître spirituel en Islam*, p. 36. C. O. McMULLEN, GURUSHIP, S. A. ALI, *The place of the murshid (guide) in the Mathnawi of Runi*, pp. 51ff.; LAMA DENIS TENDROUP, *Maître intérieur et maître spirituel dans le bouddhisme tibétain*, pp. 43–44.

Similar qualities are required in Christianity.[58] Nevertheless, the greatest Christian mystics, like Saint Bernard, Saint John of the Cross and Saint Teresa of Avila, said they were unable to direct themselves. Each person needs an outside opinion to evaluate his own position, and see what is the step to be taken at the moment. But the human guide has his own limitations. Zen Buddhism speaks of the *Patriarchs' gate*, while all the other religions acknowledge, albeit in different words, a threshold beyond which one is guided by direct contact with the Infinite.[59]

For Christians, the only true Master is Christ, and the Spirit which he bestows. A disciple needs to discern what he is saying in the depth of the soul and, according to the Gospel, follow Jesus by love. The role of the Master as spiritual guide, is to help his disciple to become aware of *inspirations* from the Lord, and show him how to follow them in the present moment.[60]

The personal contact between the monk and elder or novice master, as described in the *RB*, shows the development of the spiritual experience. The Master's *solicitude* will purify the disciple's motivations, and see if his lived response is in line with his vocation, and whether it is done out of love for Christ, or because of other motivations. The Master listens, encourages and guides, thus showing the way to God.

The word of the disciple

Yet, for all that, the Master's listening has no meaning, unless the disciple speaks. That seemed to be natural and simple for the Desert Fathers. The disciple referred to the elder all that seemed obscure in his heart – sometimes a fault, sometimes only a problem about something which was not a sin, sometimes even a grace received. The intention was to receive light to see things as they truly were, without obsessive introspection or scrupulous analysis.

Very often, the *Apophthegmata* give more importance to the disciple's questions than to the Abba's answer.[61] Their stories show how the temptation of a false kind of silence can conceal an aspect of self-

---

[58] Cf. Y. RAGUIN, *Maître et disciple*, pp. 13; 33 (DDB, 1985).

[59] P. DE BÉTHUNE, *Le Maître dans la tradition Zen du Rinzai*, in *DU MAÎTRE SPIRITUEL AU MAÎTRE INTÉRIEUR*, p. 72; LAMA DENIS TENDROUP, art. cit. p. 58; J. DORÉ, *Aperçus sur la direction spirituelle dans le catholicisme*, in M. MESLIN, *Maîtres et disciples dans les traditions religieuses*, pp. 205–208.

[60] Cf. POT. INST. No. 30.

[61] *Apophthegmata*, Paphnutius, 3; CASSIAN, *Conf.* 2: 11: Abba Theonas said to Serapion: *the confession of your fault has freed you even if I have not yet said a word of pardon.* Cf. DOM C. STEWART, *Radical honesty about self. The practice of the Desert Fathers*, in *AIM, MONASTIC BULLETIN*, 1997, No. 63, pp. 20–32.

will, which feels strong enough to solve problems on its own. The elder's role is to witness and encourage, for quite often the answer to the question arises by itself once the situation is exposed. Openness of heart, though sometimes difficult, fosters humility, frees from illusion, and purifies the heart. For, as the saying goes:

> *A fault that is hidden will multiply.*[62]

Cassian repeats this advice of the Fathers, when he asks that the brethren be trained:

> *not to hide any of their bad thoughts because of shame, but to manifest them immediately to the elder. They should not follow their own judgement, but that of the elder.*[63]

Further on, he repeats the same thought, in the text that both *RM* and *RB* quote, in the chapter on humility:

> **The fifth step of humility is that a man should in humble confession reveal to his Abbot all the evil thoughts that come into his mind, and any wrongful actions that he had done in secret (RB 7: 44).**

It is not a question of assuaging a guilty conscience, but of lightening the burden. To make known our way of seeing the events allows us to see them more objectively, and receive salutary advice. Often, it is the experience itself of opening the heart that brings healing and interior light.

Saint Benedict asked the monk first to listen to the word of the elder, but here he unites the monk's words with the elder's listening. It is their solidarity, being both sinners and saved, that allows them to *hasten together to life everlasting.*[64]

THE ABBOT AND THE SPIRITUAL ELDER

We have spoken of the guru, and of the spiritual Master. In Christian monasteries, a question sometimes arises about the respective roles of the Abbot and the seniors delegated by him to take care of the brethren's spiritual progress.

In *RB*, the first person to work with the Abbot in the formation process is a *spiritual father*, whose role is to listen to the good or bad confidential thoughts of the brethren. In *RB* 4: 50, this function is

---

[62] *Apophthegmata*, Anonymous, 50.
[63] CASSIAN, *Inst.* 4: 9.
[64] *RB* 72: 12; 73: 8.

given to a *spiritual father*, in a short passage added by Saint Benedict to the text taken from *RM*. In *RB* 7: 44, however, the text of *RB* copies that of *RM*, whereas, in a passage proper to Saint Benedict, the Abbot and the spiritual fathers are mentioned together:

> *However, if the failing be an interior sin, he should declare it only to the Abbot or to spiritual fathers, for they, knowing how to heal their own wounds, know how to heal those of others, without revealing them or making them known (RB 46: 5).*

The text indicates clearly that the confidences made to an elder are as secret as matters mentioned during the Sacrament of Confession. If it were otherwise, there could be no possible trust. Nevertheless, the Abbot

> *Whatever the number of brethren under his care, must understand clearly that he will have to render an account on the Day of Judgement for all these souls (RB 2: 38).*

The Abbot should thus at least have a general knowledge of the spiritual state of each monk, in order to make the right decisions about him. The elder should help the brother concerned to discern the important matters to be made known to the Abbot, so that he may speak more easily, or perhaps suggest to him that he would be willing to speak to the Abbot on his behalf. *If he does not dare to speak, let him do it through another*, said Saint Basil.[65]

In fact, the Abbot is mentioned alone only in a passage coming from *RM*; in the rest of the text the elder prevails. This means that, while the Abbot may be perfectly capable of fulfilling this function, he entrusts it to others who are more readily accessible to the brethren. Speaking, in chapter 4, about *the elder*, and in chapter 46, of *elders*, Saint Benedict seems to indicate that there were several such elders in the monastery, but that each monk normally consulted only one of them. The organisation of a permanent help, by means of elders who were the Abbot's delegates and who would support the monk in the spiritual combat, is an inheritance from the Fathers much emphasised by Saint Benedict.

CHRIST

Spiritual Masters in all religions acknowledge that they wish to lead their disciples towards an Absolute which is beyond them. Once this

---

[65] BASIL, LR 47; cf. SR 227; 229.

Absolute has been found, their role comes to an end. A Buddhist tradition compares the Master to a raft, used to cross a river, and abandoned afterwards. In Zen, after crossing *the Patriarchs' gate*, that is, the threshold which opens on the Infinite, one can *come back home*. The presence of the Master, an image of the Buddha, is no longer necessary when the Buddha himself has been seen, or, more exactly, the *buddheity*, that is, the Infinite, which alone exists by itself, and is present in all beings.

Most of the Hindu Masters say that they lead their disciples up to a certain point, beyond which only the Inner Master can guide them. It is the same in Islam, and for the Jews.[66]

For the Christian, the *form* (or way) is Christ, and formation consists in *conform*ing one's inner self to him, while being docile to the Spirit he has given us. Saint Paul and Saint John developed this teaching of Christ, followed by the Fathers, starting from the early years of the Church. Clement of Alexandria said that the teacher has a special dignity for *he represents God and leads people to him*, while for Origen, the Master's chief role is to lead his disciples to the only true teacher, the Divine Master himself.[67]

So the formation programme ends when the monk knows how to enter into himself and discover the *spring whose water is Life*, the Spirit, who shows him how to rid himself of the *old man*, so that his place may be filled with Christ. Then he can say, with Saint Paul: *I live, or rather not I, but Christ lives in me.*[68] This is the kind of intimate contact with the Lord that allows the disciple to find him present in others.

The monk has only to *practise* the first words of the Rule:

Listen my son ... incline the ear of your heart, willingly accept and carry out effectively the advice of your loving father (RB Prol. 1).

In conclusion, for most religions, the monastic formation programme teaches awareness of an Absolute, conceived in various ways according to the religions, whose fullness and infinite bliss are desirable for human beings who want to share in these things. Monastic life is a way to this goal. The newcomer enters it by accepting the tradition which defines it, leads towards this aim, and teaches him to control the senses and passions which are opposed to it.

For this purpose, the monk is entrusted to an experienced Master (novice master), who guides him and sees whether or not he is able to persevere in this kind of life.

[66] Cf. *Du maître spirituel au Maître intérieur*, QUESTION DE. No. 84, 1991.
[67] CLEMENT OF AL. *Strom.* 7: 91; ORIGEN, *Com. in 1 Cor.*; *Scholia in Apocalyp.* 9.
[68] Cf. *Apoc.* 7: 17; *Gal.* 2: 20.

The distinctive note of Christianity is to see in Jesus the model and the way towards the God who is love. Saint Benedict himself entered into a tradition, enriching it by the creation of a novitiate, a particular group within the life of the community. He sees monastic life as a *search for God*, without giving it any secondary aim, while the organisation of each house is left to the Abbot and the community.

In the formation programme itself, he insists that trials be seen in a positive light and as an encouragement to do better. He ends his Rule with the words:

> *with Christ's help ... you will come at the end to those heights of learning and virtue.*

CHAPTER XIII

SUPPORT FOR THE CONSECRATED LIFE:
The Vows and Penal Code

1. THE VOWS

In all religions we find that monastic formation leads on towards a definite moment of consecration to this unusual way of life, by means of *vows*. The form and the spirit of these vows vary according to the religion, and each one highlights different aspects.

THE VOWS IN HINDU MONASTICISM

Its first texts, the *Vedas*, the oldest known texts about monastic life, describe ascetics who have rid themselves of all possessions as having already reached a high degree of mysticism:

> *Girded with the wind ... they are carried along by the gods.*[1]

But a little later, the *Laws of Manu* describe the normal route using the *Upanishads*, each one having its own obligations. Monastic life is presented as the summit of human experience, the way that is closest to liberation from the cycle of rebirth. It is thus reserved to the highest castes, and especially to the Brahmins. Their young men are trained in ashrams under the guidance of a spiritual master. Entrance into ashram life is carried out with a ceremony of initiation that marks the passage from the state of childhood to that of celibate student (*Brahmachari*). After a bath, symbol of purification and of communion with the divine,

---

[1] *Rig Veda*, 10: 136.

the young man receives the sign of his caste, the sacred thread, which entitles him to officiate in sacrifices. Henceforth he has also the right to recite the *gayatri*,[2] but

> *When he has received the initiation, he is required to submit himself to the established rules and to study the Sacred Texts methodically, having observed the usual ritual.*[3]

He has thus to respect and obey his guru, to remain strictly celibate, to fulfil the daily rites of prayer, meditation and study, to wear a distinctive dress and to master his senses by an austere style of living:

> *He should abstain from honey, meat, perfumes, tasty juices, women . . . from ointments for the body, from sensual desires, anger, cupidity; he must not dance, play, he must not quarrel, slander, deceive, nor look at or kiss a woman; and he must do no harm to others.*[4]

These promises are temporary; most of these youngsters, in fact, once they have finished their cycle of studies, will leave the ashram to get married. Nevertheless it is expected that some of them will decide to stay for life in this celibate state, dedicated to study and meditation.[5]

After the establishment of monastic Orders, consecration (*diksha*) to this state was marked by a ceremony that was a development from the initiation rite. It begins with a bath, expressing purification, renunciation of the world, and communion with the divine life. The aspirant abandons his clothes in the river, receives the ochre dress of the ascetics, and a new name. His vows are the same as the promises of the *brahmachari*, but they are for life, because the way of those who *tend to the Self* knows no going back:

> *To abstain from harming all living beings, to tell the truth, not to steal, to keep chastity, to abstain from anger and levity, to obey the guru; to maintain cleanliness, and purity in food according to the laws.*[6]

From the very earliest times, other stages in monastic life were also provided for. Those who had fulfilled all their family duties could retire to a place of solitude (formerly in the forest itself) hence their name of *Vanaprastha*, or forest dwellers:

---

[2] The *gayatri* has been explained in the chapter on psalmody.
[3] MANU, 2: 172–173.
[4] MANU, 2: 177–179.
[5] MANU, 2: 243–247.
[6] *Baudâyana Dharma Sâstra*, 2, 10, 18; cf. *Asrama Up.* UR. p. 247.

When the head of the family sees his skin wrinkle, and his hair become white, and he sees the son of his son – let him retire to the forest. Renouncing the food that is eaten in villages, together with all that he possesses, and entrusting his wife to his son, let him go away alone, or he may even bring his wife with him.

Taking with him his sacred fire and all the utensils needed for the oblations, leaving the village to retire into the forest, let him stay there, controlling his organs of sense ... Let him honour those who come to his hermitage by presenting them with water, roots and fruits. He should constantly apply himself to reading the Veda, bear everything with patience, be kind and recollected, always giving and never receiving, showing himself compassionate towards all beings.[7]

Then comes the ultimate stage, that of the total renunciation, extremely difficult and hence more rarely performed; it is nevertheless abundantly described in the *Upanishads* and thus gives the sense of all other forms of renunciation.[8]

Behold! a difficult and barely frequented path! But if a man do but follow it, he shall be pure for ever, and the sages shall see in him a man of the Veda, a man of greatness; for he keeps his mind always intent on me and I, in return, dwell within him.[9]

It is the ultimate stage of life, and is thus available to anyone of any background, especially when death draws near, either through sickness or war. It can even be a preliminary to 'religious suicide', brought about by *fasting, water or fire*, and also through the *great departure*.[10] If a man in good health wants to undertake it, he has to fulfil certain conditions: e.g. he must not use non-Hindu rituals; he must be physically and morally healthy and have previously fulfilled all the duties of his caste: i.e. studies in an ashram, the duties of a householder perhaps, and those of the hermit in the forest.[11] Before his departure the renunciant should obtain the approval of his family and relatives, for the separation should be done with joy. The son who

[7] MANU, 6: 2 ... 8. The rite of departure is described in the *Laghu-samnyâsa Upanishad*, I (UR, pp. 182–183, cf. the following note).
[8] A. DEGRACES-FAHD has published nineteen *Upanishads* concerning this ultimate stage in *Upanishads du Renoncement* (cited: UR).
[9] *Paramahamsa Up.* I. UR, p. 210. The ascetics using these different ways are divided in several categories according to the renunciation they use. The *Upanishad* enumerates them several times recording four or six categories in each group. Cf. *Jâbâla Up.* UR, p. 169; *Asrama Up.* UR, pp. 248–250; *Biksuka Up.* UR, pp. 253–254; *Nârada Up.* UR, pp. 295–298; *Sâtyâyani Up.* UR, p. 367; *Brihat-samn. Up.* UR, pp. 378–379.
[10] *Paramahamsa-parivrâjaka Up.* 2, UR, p. 241.
[11] *Nârada-parivrâjaka Up.* 2–3, UR, p. 273.

sees his father leaving *should not shed tears for, if he weeps, he would forfeit his heritage and his knowledge.* It would be a sign of ignorance, a breaking of the thread of the knowledge of the Self, transmitted by his father.[12]

But still more important is the interior preparation. There should be a strong conviction, based on the study of the *Veda*, that the liberation is to bring about a union with the Self, present in all things; *concern for the body, linked to the individual self, should be abandoned.*[13] Thus, he should have reached perfect mastery of his senses and desires:

> *He should be one who leaves behind desires, anger, cupidity, aberration, drunkenness, hostility, pride, arrogance, selfishness ... one who practises chastity, non-possession, non-violence and truth, controls carefully his senses ... this one can 'realise' the Brahman.*[14]

Thus, when somebody desires this state, without being able to undertake it, he should become an ascetic, and make greater efforts to acquire the necessary self-control. So

> *when the spirit of detachment arises in the mind, then the sage should make his renunciation. If not, he would fall.*[15]

Once the decision has been taken *of his own free will*, the ascetic gives away all his goods and proceeds to the ceremony of renunciation. Those presiding begin by performing a symbolic funeral rite for him. He then symbolically absorbs the sacrificial fire by inhaling it, or by swallowing a few ashes in water, and recites, one last time, the *gayatri*, in order to make it, like the fire, return to its source, the interior Self. Finally he interiorises the signs that had given him the right to officiate in the sacrificial rituals:

> *He should get rid of the sacrificial thread, and put on, instead, an inner thread, saying: 'O give me glory, strength, knowledge, detachment and intelligence'. Then he should cut off the external thread (saying) 'Om Svâhâ', abandoning it to the waters with his clothes and his loincloth, while repeating three times, 'I have made the renunciation'.*[16]

---

12 *Katasruti Up.* 3, UR, p. 202.
13 *Nârada-parivrâjaka Up.* 6: 4, UR, p. 307.
14 *Paramahamsa-parivrâjaka Up.* 3, UR, p. 343.
15 *Maitreya Up.* 20, UR, p. 399.
16 *Brihat-samnyâsa Up.* 8, UR, p. 377. More detailed rituals are found in *Aruni Up.* UR, pp. 192 ff., *Nârada Up.* UR, pp. 274 ff., *Paramahamsa Up.* UR, p. 340. Each gesture is accompanied by a verse which indicates its symbolical meaning and is often a prayer. '*Om svâhâ*' refers to the Divinity.

This word seems to be the essential rite, even if sometimes it is said only in the mind; what matters is the inner decision to abandon everything in order to unite oneself to the Self.

After the ceremony the renunciant goes away alone, silent, constantly changing place to avoid creating links with anyone. His obligations listed in the *Laws of Manu* and in several *Upanishads*, are summarised in the *Aruni Upanishad*:

> *He must observe complete abstinence, non-violence; he must accept no offerings, and speak the truth.*[17]

The commentary says that these words should be understood at both the inner and outer levels: abstinence is chastity at the external level and, at the inner, unity with the Brahman; non-violence is directed towards the others and towards oneself; the non-acceptance of offerings is done in view of receiving nothing but the Brahman; and truth is the realisation of the true nature of the Self. The ascetic moves on without leaving any traces, intent only on the Self, like *the wild goose that flies towards the North*. Absorbed in his meditation, he is free from all ritual observances:

> *Indifferent to all, his conscience established in the non-duality which is 'being, conscience, felicity'; awakened to the One, all plenitude and felicity, he repeats without cease 'Om', until at last he hears the reply 'In truth I am the Brahman'.*[18]

He is essentially one *who tends towards the Self*. The constant repetition of this word in the *Upanishad*, and the frequent descriptions of the Brahman – *eternal, pure, always benevolent, fullness of existence, conscience, felicity, Supreme Self*[19] – bear witness to experience of deep contact with the Infinite which has the capacity to steer a whole life towards the search for the inner Self. This movement towards the centre gives the vows the meaning of a return of mankind and of the whole universe to their only Source. The ascetic thus participates, according to the Hindu theology, in the divine act that gave rise to the Universe and that will in the end re-absorb it. This is indeed a very worthy thing that

---

[17] *Aruni Up.* 3, UR, p. 193.

[18] *Paramahamsa-parivrâjaka Up.* 5, UR, pp. 346 ff. One of the most austere forms of the wandering monk is that of *Paramahamsa* (the supreme goose). These monks live in silence, and rid themselves of everything, not having even a cloth to protect themselves from bad weather and insects. But sometimes they *keep a loin cloth for the others' convenience* (*Paramahamsa Up.* UR, p. 210).

[19] *Maitreya Up.* UR, p. 377.

brings exaltation to sixty past generations, and to yet sixty more to come.[20]

Thus Hindu ascetics, though often solitaries, form one body with their people. They go out with their consent and their support[21] and they work for their good. The vows make them the spiritual summit of society, reminding all the people that the final end and happiness of the human being is to be found in the union with the Absolute, present in the inner depth of each person.

The Buddhist monks have their origin in the same surroundings and play a similar role, but with other means.

THE VOWS IN BUDDHIST MONASTICISM

The Buddha was, at the beginning, a Hindu monk, but his family belonged to the warrior group and not to the priestly caste of the Brahmins. He reacted against the ritualism of the sacrifices and against the excessive rigour of the ascetics; he was also struck by the incapacity of the human mind to catch the Infinite and by the omnipresence of suffering. He thus invited people to another kind of awareness, that of the origin of suffering, which is found in the never-satisfied desire for perishable and *impermanent things*. Moreover, unlike the Hindu ascetics, the Buddha's disciples have always formed a community, the *Sangha*, which follows the master, and the law of wisdom, or *Dharma*, which he discovered and handed over.

Thus if the Bhuddist monk's life remains orientated towards immersion in the *Ocean of Peace*, the *Nirvana*, beyond all knowledge, his rules show him the way to reject selfishness by means of a life lived in community, leading to self-mastery and universal compassion.

Entrance into Buddhist monastic life is made in two steps: first, the clothing in the monastic habit, marking the beginning of the novitiate; then, after about five years of formation, aggregation as a member of the *Sangha*, or monastic community. The vows are taken at the clothing ceremony and must be observed from then onwards. In front of the whole community assembled for the ceremony, the novice begins by entrusting himself, literally *taking refuge*, in the Buddha, his doctrine, the *Dharma*, and the community of the monks, the *Sangha*:

---

[20] *Brihat-samnyâsa Up.* 10, UR, p. 377.
[21] The ascetics live on alms and stay near the temples and the ashrams. Pilgrims and monks of the modern Hindu Orders show their solidarity with them in giving them what they need.

I, [novice's name], I take refuge in the Buddha, the Dharma and the Sangha. In imitation of the Buddha, I leave my family. I acknowledge [name of the master] as my master; I acknowledge the one who came, the Truthful one, and all the awakened as objects of my veneration.[22]

Having repeated this basic formula six times, the novice promises to observe the ten fundamental precepts:

1. *To abstain from taking life, this is the first precept of the novices. Have you the strength to observe this? The postulant answers 'I shall observe it'.*
2. *To abstain from taking what is not given, this is the second precept ...*
3. *To abstain from sensuous misconduct ...*
4. *To abstain from false speech ...*
5. *To abstain from intoxicants as tending to cloud the mind ...*
6. *To abstain from adorning the head with flowers and from anointing the body with perfumes ...*
7. *To abstain from dancing in the way of actors and street girls ...*
8. *To abstain from sitting on a high chair or a large bed ...*
9. *To abstain from eating, except at the prescribed times (from dawn to noon) ...*
10. *To abstain from touching gold or silver ...*

Behold the ten precepts of the novices! Until the very end of your bodily life you should never violate them. Will you be able to do it? – I will.

As you are now under the precepts, your duty is henceforth to honour and make honoured the three Treasures, the Buddha, the Dharma and the Sangha. You will apply yourself diligently to control of your thoughts, your words and actions. You will meditate, study and take your share in the common work.[23]

The Buddhist handbooks give detailed commentaries on these prescriptions, insisting on one or other aspect, according to the school they belong to. Those of the *Hinayana* (Small Vehicle) stress personal morals, those of the *Mahayana* (Great Vehicle) on the duties of benevolence and compassion towards others, based above all on the precept against false speech. Here is an example:

Truth and sincerity should hold the first place for a novice. No cunning words! Do not pour forth insults, do not speak lightly, do not embroider your speeches. Do not flatter someone to his face, only to denigrate him later, behind his back. Be slow to accuse, and never do it without

[22] *Ritual of the Dharmagupta School*, LW, p. 151.
[23] Ibid. p. 153.

proofs. Do not report others' defects. When you preach, explain the doctrine faithfully, without lessening or exaggerating. When you see people quarrelling, try to be a meditator for reconciliation. Speaking is like a sharp weapon that hurts the one who handles it clumsily. A novice who does not keep watch on his words does not have what is needed for his state.[24]

After promising the observance of all these precepts, the young monk begins his education under the guidance of his master. He has to learn numerous rules or minor vows, which define his daily behaviour in detail. They are enumerated in the *Patimokka*, one of the oldest Buddhist books. Their number varies a little, according to the different school. In the *Hinayana*, there are 263, distributed as follows:

Rules of behaviour towards the other sex	18
Food, drink, medicines	23
Dress and personal belongings	40
House, encounters, baths	10
Errors, schisms, bad behaviour	23
Chapters and recitation of the Rules (*Vinaya*)	17
Trade, acceptance of money	8
Killing, stealing, etc.	11
Rules of behaviour[25]	118

When the master considers the novice to have received enough training to become a monk, he presents him for reception as a member of the community. The novice does not make any new vows, since the first ones remain valid. Instead, the community, to see if he fulfils the conditions requested for admission, examines him. The first interrogation is done in private, with the master, and is later repeated in front of the assembled community.

Are you affiliated to any heterodox sect? Have you ever seduced a nun? Did you undertake this kind of life with evil intentions? While a novice, did you transgress any essential rule, either internal or external? Are you twenty years of age? Have you the three pieces of clothing and the bowl? Do you have the consent of your parents? Do you have any debts? Are you a slave? Do you belong to the king? Are you married? Do you have any unsightly or contagious sickness of the skin? Are you afflicted by any mental sickness?[26]

---

[24] *Dhammapada, Chinese School.* LW, p. 157.
[25] Cf. G. PANABOKKE, p. 5. Another book, the *Cullavaga*, developing the *Patimokka*, dedicates many pages to other rules, specially devised for preserving unity and good understanding in the community. All these rules together form the *Vinaya*.
[26] *Ritual of the Dharmagupta School*, LW, p. 197.

Then the four principal vows are repeated in front of the novice, and he is reminded that any transgression against them would be an offence entailing dismissal: impure conduct, theft, murder, pretension to have supernatural powers. After each vow, the novice is questioned: *Are you able to observe this all your life?* He answers *I am able.* Then he is dismissed, with the words:

> *You have now been received as a monk, and you have been informed of causes for dismissal. If you maintain good behaviour, it will be for your benefit ... Take advice, meditate, find your good in the Buddha's teaching. Thus you will rise, step by step, to the state of* arhat [passage to Nirvana]. *It is with this aim that you left the world. Do not deprive yourself, through your own fault, of the fruits of your renunciation.*[27]

The procedure is the same for the nuns, except that on entering the community the novice is first examined by her sisters, and later by the monks on whom the nuns' monastery depends.

In the *Mahayana* system, the vow of universal compassion is added to these other vows that are common to all Buddhism. This further vow flows from the idea of the *Bodhisattva*, who gives over all his merits for the illumination of others, and remains on the threshold of *Nirvana* until all human beings have entered there. He thus promotes universal salvation in the course of innumerable mortal lives. In the course of his profession ceremony, the novice proclaims:

> *May I, in a world without refuge, without shelter, without island, be the assistance, the refuge, the shelter, the salvation, the island. May I help all beings, who have not yet done so, to cross the ocean of existences, may I introduce into Nirvana those who are not yet there, and console those who are distressed.*[28]

The formulas used above show that monastic life knows no limit except the end of life. But we should note that the vows are considered as merely a means of progress in the way of perfection; the monk can stop when he thinks he has done enough. In some countries, there is even a provision for a ceremony of unclothing and return to the world.

The thousands of years of cumulative experience among Hindu and Buddhist monks allows us to see how the vows are a means of support to the monk, as he consecrates himself to a life dedicated to the search for union with the Infinite. The vows make a decision freely taken by the monk into an official status in society. He publicly pledges to lead

[27] Ibid. p. 201.
[28] *Bodhisattva Pratimoksa Sutra.*

a life without violence or sensuality, detached from material goods, in order to dedicate himself to study and meditation, considered as ways towards the Absolute: hence the obligation of celibacy, and an austere lifestyle, reducing comfort, food and clothing to the barest essentials.

This kind of life is acknowledged by society as a guide towards a blissful eternity. It is accepted that the monk leaves his family, and society supports him by providing training under a master and financial support, together with approbation and esteem. Society may even collaborate in building projects for stable religious communities.

In return, society expects from the monk – an expectation that is also a moral support – faithfulness to his vows, thus reminding everyone of the ultimate aim of human life. It also hopes that the ascetics' life will gain merits, which may help others in their own chosen path.

The differences between Hindu and Buddhist vows are also instructive. The Hindu dedicates himself to the Divinity in order to be united with It; his vows are thus naturally for life. The Buddhist's vows aim above all at acquiring merits, and so are not necessarily for life. The austerity of the Hindu has a purifying value and his way is essentially individual. Through his vows the Buddhist enters a community, which supports and controls his observance, hence the development of the virtue of compassion which is directed towards universal salvation.

THE VOWS AMONG THE ESSENES

In Palestine, the two centuries before Christ and the first century of our era were troubled times, in which some fervent groups of Jews, called the Essenes, met to practise the Law of Moses and the cult of Yahweh to the full, under a perceived threat of contamination by foreign influences. From these groups emerged an elite of *volunteers* who wished to dedicate themselves wholly to God.

We are aware of two groups of Essenes: the first, known because of the *Qumran Texts*, lived near the Dead Sea, under the direction of a priest, the *Teacher of Wisdom*, and prepared itself to become the Messiah's army which would deliver Israel and bring the entire world under its sway. The other group, described by Philo of Alexandria, lived at the fringe of the desert near Alexandria, and was dedicated to the study of Scripture, meditation and praise of God. But their ideal of faithfulness to God, through the observance of the Law, seems to be the same.

The texts of Qumran

The introduction of the Rule clearly expresses its aim:

*From the Teacher of Wisdom to all his brethren, the books of the Rule
of the community.*

*Their aim is to seek God with all their heart and soul, to do what is
right and just before His face, as prescribed through the intermediary of
Moses and through all His servants, the prophets ... to have no longer
a hard and guilty heart, and eyes debauched by all kinds of evil; to give
entrance to all who desire to carry out the commands of God and His
Covenant of grace, uniting themselves to God and living a life of perfection in His presence ... to love all the sons of light ... All those who
are willing to trust in His faithfulness shall bring all their intellect, their
strength and their goods to the community of God.*[29]

The beginning of the Rule gives a summary of its prescriptions:

*Here is the Rule for the men of the community who volunteer to turn
away from any evil and to stand firm in all He has prescribed, according to His wish: to separate themselves from the company of evil men,
to hold the Law and material goods in common, to rely on the views of
the sons of Sadoc, the priests, keepers of the Covenant, and on the views
of men of the community who remain steadfast in the Covenant.*[30]

The following paragraphs give details on each of these aspects. First,
faithfulness to the Law, seen as a means of interior purification:

*Any business concerning the Law, goods and rights will be settled
according to the judgement of the priest and community, so that they
practise together faithfulness and humility, justice and right, benevolent
charity and modesty of behaviour in all their ways.*

*No one shall go in stubbornness of heart, going astray according to
his heart, his eyes, and his instinctive desires.*[31]

The Rule specifies that this faithfulness comes from the heart and is
addressed to God, by renewing the Covenant made with him by
Moses:

*Whoever enters into the ideal of the community, enters into the Covenant
of God, under the eyes of all the volunteers. He must pledge by oath the
obligation to convert himself to the Law of Moses, to live according to
what He has prescribed, and this with all his heart and soul.*[32]

The obligation to part company from evil men is then recalled, along
with the duty of not admitting them to the community unless they

[29] QUMRAN, R. Colu. I, 1–12.
[30] QUMRAN, R. 5: 1–3.
[31] QUMRAN, R. 5: 4–5.
[32] QUMRAN, R. 5: 7–9.

convert. Inside the community, in dependence on the priest, the members of the congregation support and control themselves mutually, in their faithfulness to the Law and to charity,

> *in order to convert oneself to His Covenant in the community ... each one shall exhort his neighbour to faithfulness, humility and tender charity. No one shall speak to his neighbour with anger, either in murmuring or with stiff-necked harshness, nor shall he speak with the malice that springs from an unholy spirit.*[33]

Outside the main community of Qumran, smaller communities were provided for, where similar rules were to be kept:

> *Here is how one brother shall conduct himself in his dealings with another, in their dwelling-place ... The inferior will obey the superior in what concerns work and money. They will eat together, pray together, and consult together.*[34]

Entrance into the community was done by stages: first, a year of novitiate, followed by another year of probation. The vows were taken during the novitiate and, at the end of each period of preparation, the candidate was to be examined by the community. If the votes were favourable at both scrutinies, he could enter the community.

> *He shall be enlisted in his proper rank among his brethren, for the Law, the constitutions, the purifications, and for placing his fortune at the disposal of the community ... The community shall take his opinion and judgement into account.*[35]

The Rule ends with a penal code.

The *De Vita Contemplativa* of Philo of Alexandria

Philo called the ascetics whose life he describes *Therapeutes*, because

> *they practise a therapy that cares for souls in the grip of painful and intractable illnesses, freeing them from the chains of pleasures, desires and afflictions.*[36]

Further on he specifies the aim of their life:

[33] QUMRAN, R. 5: 23 ... 26.
[34] QUMRAN, R. 6: 2-3.
[35] QUMRAN, R. 6: 21-23.
[36] PHILO, *De Vita C.* 1-2.

The race of the therapeutes, whose constant effort is to learn to see with discernment, applies itself to the contemplation of the Being ... and never abandons this rule of life that leads to perfect happiness. Those who adopt this therapy, and are not moved by habit, advice or encouragement, but by celestial love, are possessed by God ... until finally they shall see the object of their desires.[37]

This great desire of God leads them to leave everything for him:

Their passionate desire for immortal and blessed life makes them believe their mortal life to be already over. They leave their possessions to their sons or daughters, or other relatives ... Those who have already understood the riches of the spiritual vision should indeed abandon blind riches to those whose intelligence is still blind ...

Stripped of their possessions, no lure can detain them, and they flee without looking back, leaving for ever brothers, children, wives, fathers and mothers ... friends and the land of their birth ... they dwell in gardens, and isolated places, looking for solitude.[38]

Their time is shared between study, prayer and contemplation:

God is always present in their minds, and even in their dreams they imagine nothing but the beauty of the divine perfections and powers.

They pray twice a day, in the morning and in the evening. At daybreak they ask for a happy day, truly happy, that is, for the light of heaven to shine in their minds ... Between morning and evening, they study Scripture and the works of authors of their sect ... they compose hymns to the praise of God.[39]

To support their contemplation they undertake a very austere kind of life:

They construct the other virtues of the soul on the foundation of self-control. None of them would take food or drink before sunset ... some even forget to take food for three days ... some six days, used as they are to living on air ... In a general way, they strive to eliminate pride, knowing that pride is the beginning of illusion, and absence of pride the beginning of truth.[40]

At the end of the text, while speaking of virgins, Philo explains once more the essential motivation of this pledge: the love of God that makes the soul crave for union with him:

[37] PHILO, *De Vita C.* 11.
[38] PHILO, *De Vita C.* 13; 18.
[39] PHILO, *De Vita C.* 26–27
[40] PHILO, *De Vita C.* 34.

Most of them are elderly virgins, who undertook chastity not by compulsion, like some of the Greek priestesses, but by a free decision, and a passionate desire that wisdom might envelop their whole life . . . they have the desire of the immortal children, and only God can give birth to such a desire [allusion to spiritual marriage] . . .

Their virtue has brought them into the friendship of God, the most precious of gifts.[41]

We recognise easily in these Essene texts several of the themes we have already met. The vows give public status to a personal decision, and are thus a means of support for a life fully orientated to the search of the Absolute, for one who has discovered that true goods are spiritual, and that happiness does not proceed from the satisfaction of selfish desires. This kind of life promotes control over the senses, detachment from material goods, and concentration on the search for the Infinite by means of study and meditation.

Thus bound by their vows, the ascetics are held in honour by society and are given material support that makes separation from the family possible,[42] either individually or in communities. Among the second group, the vows confer the right to participate in all community activities, and each member is sure of support from the others.

New elements also come to light. Among the Essenes, for instance, the individual decision to take vows in monastic life is motivated by the love of a personal God; it is the response to a *Covenant* that *he* has proposed, and which culminates in a mystical marriage. Other ascetics have to work for their living; their detachment is expressed by sharing their goods in common. The *Rule of Qumran* underlines the mutual support of the community members; the virtue of compassion, so dear to the Buddhists, seems here to be restricted to the members of the group.

THE VOWS IN CHRISTIAN MONASTICISM

Just as the commitment of the Essenes was viewed as a response to God's Covenant, in the same way the origin of Christian monasticism with Saint Antony and Saint Pachomius, is due to a particular call of the Lord: Antony obeys a word of Christ heard in the Gospel reading,[43] while Pachomius responds to successive calls from God.[44]

---

[41] PHILO, *De Vita C.* 68; 90.

[42] We can even note some curious similarities between the *Therapeutes* of Philo and the Hindu *Vanaprastha*. Most of them are elderly people who retire in solitude, with the support of their family in order to dedicate themselves to reading and meditation.

[43] ATHANASIUS, VA, 2.

[44] PACHOMIUS, VC *Bo.* 7.

The first explicit mention of a pledge to follow a rule is made at the beginning of *The life of Saint Pachomius*, when he was received as a companion by the hermit Palamon, a Rule which he later handed on to Theodore:

> *The Rule of the Church is to do all that is commanded without flinching, that is: unceasing prayer, keeping awake, recitation of God's Law, and our manual work, about which there are orders for us in Scripture, and which should allow us to stretch out our hands to the destitute.*[45]

The Rules of Pachomius enumerate the obligations: obedience, silence, withdrawal into solitude so as to dedicate oneself to prayer and meditation on Scripture *in order to have a pure heart ... and to see God after death;*[46] working for the sake of the poor. Theodore insisted on renunciation of all property:

> *All that belongs to the Congregation is not ours, but belongs to our Lord Jesus Christ, who has gathered us together ... Look first for the Kingdom of heaven and the rest will be yours without the asking (Matt: 6: 33).*[47]

In the next generation, Saint **Basil**, father of Christian monasticism in the East, gave words of advice, which were later called Rules. He considers entering monastic life as a pledge made to God:

> *(The monk) pledges himself to Him through a pact ... a promise made with personal judgement and conviction ... our ecclesiastical superiors should be made witnesses of this fact, so that they may consecrate the body of the professed as an offering made to God ... He is thus dedicated to God ... having reflected at length.*[48]

The aim of this life is clearly indicated:

> *Though marriage is allowed and worthy to be blessed, the life of ascesis is for those who, like Saint Paul, want to do what is pleasing to the Lord ... those who want really to follow Christ, should thus free themselves from the bonds of the passions ... and keep their heart vigilant, in order never to lose sight of Christ ... The aim of our acts is to tend towards him with all our energies.*[49]

---

[45] PACHOMIUS, VC *Bo.* 10; 35.
[46] PACHOMIUS, VC *Bo.* 33. Palamon stressed also ascesis by limiting food and sleep.
[47] PACHOMIUS, VC *Bo.* 183.
[48] BASIL, LR 14; 15.
[49] BASIL, LR 5.

To foster this continual focus on God, Basil recommends a community life in a solitary place:

> *To help the soul to be recollected, it is good to live in solitude ... [in order to avoid] multiple distractions and temporal cares ... those who aim at the same goal find many advantages in living together ... [A community of brethren] keeps the special character recorded in the Acts of the Apostles: they lived together and possessed all in common ... they had one heart and one soul, none of them called any of his possessions his own, and everything was shared in common.*[50]

Saint Basil further describes the necessary renunciations:

> *Is it necessary to renounce everything before consecrating oneself to God in this way? ... Most certainly! We renounced the devil, and the passions of the flesh, in the presence of all ... we renounced human company and any activity that is not in accord with the perfect and salutary practice of the Gospel. Still more necessary, however, is the renunciation of one's self, and the stripping of the 'old man' and his behaviour.*[51]

Having mentioned the promise of chastity (LR 5), Basil insists on the virtue of temperance, which masters evil instincts and keeps the senses within bounds. Working *with zeal* is also a part of monastic life. It is required by Saint Paul:

> *Work is necessary, not only for mortifying the body, but also for charity towards our neighbour, so that, through us, God may give to our brethren in need the means to be self-sufficient.*[52]

Work, however, must not interrupt the prayer, for

> *when our hands are occupied we can – with the mouth, if possible, or at least in the heart – praise God.*[53]

Engagement in monastic life allows of no turning back. Basil considers departure from the monastery acceptable only in the case of instability of character or because of a grave defect in the life of the community:

> *No other motive for going away is admissible, because such behaviour*

---

[50] BASIL, LR 6–7.
[51] BASIL, LR 8.
[52] BASIL, LR 37.
[53] BASIL, LR 37. This theme has been developed in the chapter on psalmody.

295

*would be to despise the unifying name of our Lord Jesus Christ, and also
because the others will with difficulty keep their conscience pure towards
their brother, because of the suspicions which may have arisen.*[54]

We see here the constant concern for the consequences that one's
behaviour may have on others.

With **Cassian**, a disciple of the Egyptian monks who had settled in
Marseilles, we move to the West. In his *Institutes*, he describes
monastic initiation, giving what he saw in Egypt as a model to be
followed by his monks. At the beginning of the book, he presents the
monastic habit as the *military dress of Christ's soldier*, the different
parts of the dress signifying mortification of the vices, according to
the word of the Apostle Paul:

'You have undergone death, and your life is hidden away now in Christ',
and still *'It is no longer I who live, but Christ who lives in me'.*[55]

In Book 4, set in the Pachomian monastery of Tabennessi, he shows
the trials of patience the postulant has to undergo at the door of the
monastery, then how he has to rid himself of all the money he may
have brought. He thus renounces all human advantages and freely puts
himself at the same level as all the brethren,

*for if he does not imitate the humility of Christ, he will not be able to
persevere in the monastic way of life.*[56]

The novice is then entrusted to a senior, who teaches him all the duties
of monastic life and the disciplinary code. Having introduced some
examples of other Desert Fathers, Cassian comes back to Tabennessi,
and describes the ceremony of profession and clothing presided over
by Abba Pinufius.

The old man gives a speech to the novice, reminding him first that
the trials at entrance are meant to strengthen his perseverance. He
then explains the symbolism of the main ceremony, which is to rid
oneself of one's worldly attire, in order to receive the monastic habit:

*Know that today you are dead to the world and to its desires and,
according to the Apostle, you are crucified to this world and the world
to you (Gal. 6: 4) ... for it is no longer you who live, but the one who
has been crucified for you lives in you. So you must live in the likeness
of the one who has been nailed to the cross for you ...*

[54] BASIL, LR 36.
[55] CASSIAN, *Inst.* 1: 4; cf. *Col*: 3: 3; *Gal.* 2: 20.
[56] CASSIAN, *Inst.* 4: 4.

We are crucified to vices of the flesh, and to all that belongs to the world, and the eyes of the soul are fixed on the place where we hope to be able to go at any time. Do not allow yourself to be distracted again by what you have abandoned ... memories of the family, and preoccupations of the world, for, according to the word of the Lord: 'If a man has once put his hand to the plough and looks behind him, he is not fitted for the kingdom of God' (Luke 9: 62). On the contrary, strive to persevere until the end in the poverty you have professed before God and his angels ... keeping till your last breath the humility and the poverty of Christ that you have now professed before him ...

Since you have come to serve the Lord, then, according to Scripture, 'Keep yourself in the fear of God' and prepare yourself, not for rest and tranquillity, but for temptations and labour ... narrow is the way leading to life and few are those who undertake it. Consider yourself as one of the few who have been chosen and, like this, you will leave behind the example and torpor of the multitude, in order to live with this small number, and find yourself, with it, in the kingdom of God.[57]

Abba Pinufius concludes by speaking of the progressive stages leading from the fear of God up to perfect charity:[58] the same list that Saint Benedict used, as we have seen in his chapter on humility.

IN SAINT BENEDICT'S RULE

Saint Benedict follows the Christian tradition which preceded him, and its main elements are found in chapter 58 of his Rule: trials at the entrance into the monastery, instruction under a master who explains the Rule and the difficulties to be overcome, and finally, the ceremony of profession. In his text, chapter 58 of *RB* is dependent on *RM* (summarising its chapters 87 to 90); but it also introduces new elements which are worthy of notice.

Saint Benedict, as we have seen, was the first to create a novitiate separate from the community. The newcomer thus feels freer, being not yet involved in the body of the community; the meaning of his pledge also becomes clearer, since, at the moment of his profession, he will enter the community forever.

Pachomius, Basil and Cassian had already indicated the need for a free decision, made after a time of reflection, whose duration varies according to the authors, but which is always experienced at the psychological level as *long*. Benedict, however, makes an innovation, preparing for the permanent commitment by means of temporary

[57] CASSIAN, *Inst.* 4: 34, 38.
[58] CASSIAN, *Inst.* 4: 39–43.

stages. The novitiate is divided in periods of two, six, and four months, after each of which the novice has to decide for himself if he wants to continue:

he is to be told, 'This is the law under which you are asking to live. If you can keep it, come in; if, however, you cannot, freely depart'.[59]

This exercise of taking decisions is formative for the personality of the novice; perhaps it would be good to restore this practice in our own days.

For Saint Benedict's predecessors, the vows were not expressed in verbal formulae. Monastic life was explained, with all its exigencies of renunciation, chastity, obedience, mastery of senses and passions, all this in view of seeking God and being consecrated to him. The newcomer pledged to enter this life by consecrating himself to the Lord. Saint Benedict follows this tradition, calling the *kind of life* led in the monastery *conversatio morum.* The modern formulae used for the religious vows of poverty, chastity and obedience have to be understood in the context of this tradition.

Poverty is, above all, dispossession: *not to possess anything as [one's] own.*[60] That implies not bringing anything from outside that may give a false sense of security or privilege in the monastery, but, as Cassian put it, *humbling oneself to the level of Christ's poverty ... He who did not disdain to be united with the poor and to be called their brother;*[61] then Benedict continues, *He must regard the chattels of the monastery and its whole property as if they were the sacred vessels of the altar,*[62] that is, as belonging to God, and finally, let him be concerned to *relieve the poor.*[63]

Chastity is seen in the context of mastering the desires of the body: *Not to seek pleasures ... To reject carnal desires;*[64] but Saint Benedict considers its positive aspect, which directs all the affective powers, not towards selfish satisfactions, but towards God and the good of one's neighbour:

In the first place to love the Lord God with all one's heart, with all one's soul and with all one's strength. Then to love one's neighbour

[59] *RB* 58: 10.
[60] *RB* 33: 3. Cf. *RB* 2: 35 where Benedict quotes *Mt.* 6: 33, as did Theodore (PACHOMIUS, VC *Bo.* 183).
[61] CASSIAN, *Inst.* 4: 5.
[62] *RB* 31: 10.
[63] *RB* 4: 14.
[64] *RB* 4: 12, 59.

as oneself ... To love chastity ... [to] labour with chaste love at the charity of the brotherhood.[65]

Lastly, obedience has the very wide sense of constantly putting one's heart and will in harmony with God's desires, as we have seen while commenting on chapter 5 of the Rule. Saint Benedict mentions it anew here because of its importance as the touchstone of a true gift of self to God.

Saint Benedict insists, in particular, on stability. The word '*stabilitas*', often used in the Rule, has a rich meaning: the 'holding fast' of a soldier in battle, and thus perseverance in the monastery until death;[66] it also implies belonging to a community, in contrast to the wandering gyrovagues.[67] These external aspects are meant to allow the monks to enter into intimacy with God, listen to his teaching, and praise him with the community, united with the celestial choirs.

To give to the pledge by vows its full religious and social value, a solemn promise is made

in the oratory, in the presence of all ... before God and all his saints, so that if he subsequently behaves otherwise, he will know that he merits condemnation by him the one whom he mocks.[68]

The promise, made in writing, citing as witnesses the Abbot in charge, and the saints who are present by means of their relics, is signed by the novice in a very obvious manner, and then placed by him on the altar, thus uniting his self-offering to God with that of Christ in the eucharistic sacrifice of the Mass.

After that comes the humbly confident prayer of the brother, repeated by the whole community: *Accept me, Lord, according to your word, and I shall live.* Prostration before each of the brethren in turn, and their individual embrace in reply, are God's reply, given through the community which receives the newly professed.

Lastly, comes the taking of the religious habit, a rite stemming from the oldest monastic times, symbolising a change in state of life. In the past, a kind of funeral rite took place: the newcomer lay under a black pall, and was later summoned to arise, as if to new life. This was perhaps too sentimental, but the gesture expressed a deep reality of death to the world, felt through the ages by monks of other religions.

Having made this act of dispossession, the monk rids himself of all

[65] *RB* 4: 1; 64: 9; 72: 8.
[66] *RB* 4: 78; 58: 17; 60: 8.
[67] *RB* 1: 11; 61: 5.
[68] *RB* 58: 17–18.

his goods, giving them to the poor or to the monastery *keeping for himself nothing at all*. Saint Benedict stipulates the legal form of these acts, so as to make them definitive and unquestionable, for he wants to be sure of the monk's perseverance.

Contrasting Saint Benedict's regulations with those of his Christian predecessors, we can see that he unites all the elements of integration into the monastery in the ceremony of profession: the solemn pledge, entry into the community, dispossession of goods, clothing in the monastic habit. But he takes particular care to inform and test the novice, so that his final pledge may be taken only after mature reflection and acceptance by the community.[69]

DIALOGUE ON THE VOWS

Asian monasticism has many similar requirements: casting off material possessions, mastery of the senses, chastity, the fight against vices and selfishness, obedience to a spiritual master and to a superhuman order, often indicated by sacred texts. These similarities are reflected in the ceremony which integrates the novice into monastic life: the formal reminder of the requirements, the stripping off of secular clothes so as to put on a new monastic form of dress, as a symbol for the monk himself and for society of the way of life he has chosen.

Everywhere the vows aim to concentrate the ascetic's mind on the essential purpose of his life: that is, union with the Infinite. At the same time they support his perseverance, inserting him into surroundings, or a community, which has the same aim, and giving him the mutual help of the brethren. The public character of the vows makes him more conscious that society expects him, by his way of life, to give meaning to human life in general, and to earn merit for the benefit of others.

There are nevertheless important differences.

The first is that the belief of Christians and Jews in a personal God makes the vows a Covenant, coming from the free choice of God, a consecration which ends and is fulfilled in love. For Christians, such a union is made in Christ, following his example and with his help; it is a mutual covenant, whose initiative comes from God, and in which they receive more than they give.

The reference to Christ, and to the Church as his members, transforms the notion of a function in society into that of service. For the

---

[69] Cf. R. YEO, *The Structure and Content of Monastic Profession*, STUDIA ANSELMIANA 83, Rome, 1982. The author makes a detailed comparison of the different elements of the monastic profession in Saint Benedict, Cassian and the *Rule of the Master*.

Christian, the monk is not the most perfect person in society,[70] he is, without any merit on his part, chosen by God to fulfil in the Church and in the world a particular service.[71] Like his colleagues of other religions, the Christian monk has to show his contemporaries the true meaning of human life.[72] But, for the Fathers, the monk is also a *spiritual physician*[73] and an intercessor with God. To all this is added the need for constant care of the poor. Still, following the example of Christ, this service is addressed not only to Christians, but to all people without distinction.

At the end of this survey, we could say that our present vows of poverty, chastity and obedience, and the ascetic effort they imply, have been held in veneration for thousands of years by those who are *seeking God*, as indispensable conditions for their quest and their ability to function in society.

The Christian personalises this quest by the knowledge of a God who is love, and of Christ, who is the way towards him. But he may profit from the experience of his predecessors in other religions, noticing that the starting point of the quest is a light that helps to distinguish the permanent values from those that disappear with the changing face of the world. He acknowledges there the action of Christ's Spirit who *enlightens every soul born into the world* (*John* 1: 9).

Saint Benedict adds stability, which roots the monk in his monastery and invites him to a persevering effort to seek God in prayer, study and work.

2. THE PENAL CODE

One of the most constant features of all monasticisms is the expression of sadness and pain felt by the spiritual masters and communities when a monk abandons the hard road of seeking the Absolute. Many have observed that these departures are the result of a progressive abandonment of the duties of their state of life. That is why they have

---

[70] Many stories of the Desert Fathers show monks tempted to pride sent by the Spirit to visit lay people more advanced in perfection than themselves.

[71] '*If you are a monk go to the mountain!*' retorted to Abba Arsenius a young girl, an Ethiopian slave, whom he had snubbed. This reaction shows clearly that, for the people, the monk had a proper place and role in the society, *Apophthegm.* Arsenius 32.

[72] The Vatican Council II (LG 44) has taken up this idea, saying that the religious life is a sign which manifests the heavenly goods and frees from attachment to earthly things.

[73] Saint Antony was called the *Spiritual physician of Egypt* (ATHANASIUS, VA 28).

established penal codes which serve to draw attention to weaknesses, and are means of warning and of making reparation and satisfaction. This type of check is meant to stimulate the interior reaction of the monk, but it can come only from outside, that is from the spiritual master, the community or the society.

THE PENAL CODE IN HINDUISM

The texts ruling the ascetics' life are full of encouragement, and sanctions are very few. They concern the cleansing from legal impurities by simple rituals like refraining from breathing, for a while; in faults regarding self-mastery, they strive to heal their roots through meditation.

> *May he blot out his sins by holding back his breathing; may he atone for his faults in giving himself to the most absolute recollection; may he restrain his sensual desires by imposing a curb to his sensory organs; may he destroy, by deep meditation, the qualities opposed to divine nature.*[74]

More serious is prolonged negligence of essential duties. The lazy student who sleeps at sunrise or sunset (the prayer times), has to fast a full day reciting the *gayatri*.[75] Grave faults have grave consequences: rebirth as an impure animal, or even a stay in hell.[76] Misconduct causing a scandal in society is punished by a downgrading from the caste. Such is the case with a student who refuses to say the ritual prayers or with a renunciant who tries to abandon his state. Such a one *has fallen from on high* and cannot be born again before 10 millions of *kalpa*.[77] The punishment is so serious because the renunciation made by the Hindu monk renders him legally unable to possess: he thus ends at the very bottom of the society, among the outcasts. His son would be forbidden to make renunciation.

As a whole these texts are very positive; among the 346 articles of Books 2 and 6 of the *Laws of Manu* on monastic life, only ten speak of sanctions; and the proportion is still less in the *Upanishad of the Renouncement*.

---

[74] MANU, 6: 71–72.
[75] MANU, 2: 220; the *Gâyatri* is also called *Sâvitri*.
[76] MANU, 2: 201; 6: 32.
[77] MANU, 2: 103; *Sâtâyani Up.* 29–31, UR, p. 320; *Brihat-samnyâsa UP.* 3–5. UR, p. 376. The *Kalpa* is the cosmic cycle which itself comprises several thousands of years.

THE PENAL CODE IN BUDDHISM

Fortnightly meetings of the *Uposatha*, during which the *Pâtimokkha*, that is, the list of the more or less 250 rules or vows quoted above is recited, control the community life of the Buddhist monk. One who has failed to observe a part of them should accuse himself, formerly in public, but now more often before a small group of monks, or even one alone, before or after the recitation.[78] These vows, as we have seen, are divided into several categories; there is a particular penalty attached to the breach of each one of them. The gravest is expulsion from the monastery, reserved for the four main faults: impure actions, theft, taking life, or lying. After that come about ten offences, from which one can be purified by a kind of excommunication,[79] more or less long according to the gravity. Originally, this penance began and ended with an act of the *Sangha*. Minor offences incurred less severe satisfaction.[80]

To understand this ceremony, it should be noted that the acknowledgement of fault is considered as an act that purifies and frees: to hide one's fault is *to sit on thorns*. Once hidden, the fault becomes graver, making the *karma* heavier and preventing *Samadi* (entrance into the Nirvana). We should note, however, that all these penalties are medicinal: they aim to purify the monk, helping him to come back to the right path. It is typical, for example, that the origin of the ceremony of reconciliation is described in the *Vinaya* as having helped the incorrigible monk Seyyasaka to correct himself. He had undergone various penances in vain, and was even obliged to repeat his novitiate. But having been encouraged by this rehabilitation, he became an exemplary monk.[81]

THE PENAL CODE AMONG THE ESSENES

The *Rule of Qumran* ends with a penal code.[82] The scale of the sanctions foreseen highlights the inner nature of the spiritual quest and the

---

[78] ZAGO, *Rites*, pp. 82–84.

[79] *Vinaya*, 11: 4. The monk who had incurred this penalty could neither give ordination, nor spiritual advice, nor preach to the nuns, nor participate in an act of authority; he had not even the right to have a novice in his service.

[80] Cf. A. WAYMAN, *Ancient Buddhist Monasticism*, in STUDIA MISSIONALIA, No. 28, 1979.

[81] *Vinaya*, 11: 1, quoted by PANABOKKE. The same author says that this ceremony comes from tribal customs. This reminds us of the African custom of the ceremonies of reconciliation, where all acknowledge their faults, and peace is thus restored in the village. Some Christian monasteries make use of this custom.

[82] QUMRAN, R. 6: 24–7: 25. PHILO describes the life of the *Therapeutes* as an ideal for Greeks; he does not speak of possible faults.

care for mutual encouragement among the community members. External faults against the ritual or in administration are briefly mentioned, while those that imply evil dispositions of the soul are described at length.

The heaviest pain is dismissal for those who have sworn falsely in the name of God, have slandered, or grumbled against the community or one of its superiors, or one whose

> *spirit betrays the community and who leaves ... to walk in the stub-bornness of his heart. He shall not come back to share the ideal of the community.*[83]

Bad dispositions of the soul: these are fraud, anger, disobedience, a grudge, vengeance, laziness, indecency in behaviour, and are punished by two to six months of exclusion from the community life. Lack of respect towards the community, in gesture or behaviour is punished by a month of penance. Carelessness and frivolous gestures are rectified by a ten-day penance, which consists in being excluded from the ceremony of purification of the community and in being deprived of a quarter of one's bread.

Nevertheless the Rule shows a particular benevolence towards the feeble:

> *A man should not be hated because of the perversity of his heart, but rather, on the same day he committed the fault, should be exhorted. In this way, others will not become guilty of his misbehaviour.*[84]

The *Document of Damas*, sometimes more severe than the Rule (even the death penalty is provided for),[85] shows that those who were expelled from the community were not abandoned:

> *Men of knowledge will reprove him according to his faults, until the day when he may resume his place among men of perfect holiness.*

Nobody will associate with him regarding money, business or work,

> *But let each one speak to his companion so as to lead him towards justice, supporting his steps in the way of God. God will be attentive to their word and will listen to them.*[86]

---

[83] Qumran, R. 7: 24.
[84] Qumran, R. 4: 26.
[85] Qumran, DD, 9: 1–6. The death penalty is foreseen, as a literal application of *Leviticus*, for someone who treats a member of the community as a pagan.
[86] Qumran DD, pp. 178–180.

THE PENAL CODE IN CHRISTIAN MONASTICISM

Saint Antony and the Desert Fathers did not leave any Rule or penal code. Big monasteries, however, like Scete or Nitria, may have had one, as we can see from a curious story: at Nitria, in front of the church, were

> *three palm-trees with a whip hanging on each of them; one was for the solitaries who had committed faults, a second, for the thieves, and the third, for the passing guests. Whoever makes a mistake deserving punishment, clings to the palm-tree and receives the stipulated number of lashes. He is then released.*[87]

This amusing story is, however, not very typical of the Desert Fathers. Their attention is focused rather on control of the passions, and the remedies they prescribed were applied according to the needs of each case, without any attempt at classification, beyond the broad nature of the fault itself.

The Rules of Pachomius deal very little with this question,[88] but by all accounts, there were rather strict rules on silence and obedience; the penances were usually periods of fasting, and prolonged prayers.[89] Pachomius and Theodore threatened the dismissal of any unfaithful monks who had committed theft, or unchastity, and simply refused to amend.[90] They would also send some of the brethren to visit the guilty parties, so that, by showing them kindness and understanding they could bring them back to the right path.[91] But, generally speaking, the lives of these two saints show their kindness:

> '*When we do good to an evil person, we help him to return to a positive attitude*'

said Pachomius to a superior; and his biographer describes him as

> *a shepherd who was close to the great Good Shepherd, Christ. He would often go from monastery to monastery to visit the brethren, warming them with the word of God, and taking care of them, like a mother that warms her children by the affection of her heart.*[92]

---

[87] PALLADIUS, *Lausiac History*, 7. Nitria. The guests mentioned here were generally monks.

[88] PACHOMIUS, *Praec.* 9–10 speaks of being late to the offices; there is more severity as to the day offices than as to those of the night.

[89] PACHOMIUS, VC *Bo.* 77; *S*, 6. Sometimes there was also deprivation of function, as happened to Theodore.

[90] PACHOMIUS, VC *S*, 10; 19; *Bo.* 75: 106–108.

[91] PACHOMIUS, VC *Bo.* 62–64.

[92] PACHOMIUS, VC *Bo.* 42; 89; likewise Theodore, *Bo.* 191–192.

Saint Basil speaks of correcting faults in several of his Rules, but he strives above all to lead the brethren to behave according to what is said in the Scriptures. As a model of correction he often quotes *Matt.* 18: 15–17 which advises the use of a reprimand, given in private, then before two or three brethren, and finally before the community. If all these efforts are in vain, the culprit is treated like a pagan or a publican. This extreme case is envisaged for those who persist in their faults: above all pride, murmuring, disobedience, and for those, also, who encourage them in their stubbornness.[93] Some deprivation of food is mentioned, but only incidentally.[94]

Two major concerns seem prominent in the Rules: the good of the community and that of the guilty brother. The sense of community or 'community-mindedness' is seen by constant allusions to the repercussion of faults, and of the corresponding penances, on the other (non-offending) members. One of the longest of the *Short Rules* (*SR* 64) is concerned with the treatment of different forms of scandal. Several other rules say that the dismissal of a brother is done *in order to avoid the sickness of one member spreading and affecting the neighbouring parts of the body*.[95]

The superior should behave towards each monk *without anger, with kindness, showing that he wants only to bring his sin to an end*. He wants to find the root of the vice and, by way of making satisfaction, he imposes a penance which gives the erring brother the opportunity to practise the opposite virtue: *For vainglory, humble tasks; for gossipers, silence; for murmurers, isolation*.[96]

The work of a superior is often compared to that of a doctor: *To impose a punishment is nothing else than to cure a soul*. Thus the penance is to cease when it has been well accepted, *and it shows that the culprit had amended himself*.[97] Like the doctor, the superior should adapt the medicine to the sickness, *taking into account the age, the health, the dispositions of soul, and the kind of fault*, making reproaches with kindness and compassion, *as a mother feeds her children and takes care of them* (1 *Thess.* 2: 7–8).[98]

Cassian shares the same thinking as the Desert Fathers. The greater part of his *Institutes* and *Conferences* deals with the passions, and

[93] BASIL, LR 28; 29; 47; SR 3; 9; 41–42; 57; 61; 102; 293.
[94] BASIL, SR 136: If a monk arrives late to the meal through negligence, he will have to wait for the next meal for eating. SR 122 speaks of monks deprived of *eulogia* which seems to be a complementary dish.
[95] BASIL, LR 28 and the others mentioned above.
[96] BASIL, LR 51.
[97] BASIL, LR 50–53.
[98] BASIL, SR 106; 184.

prayer. Nevertheless some chapters of his *Institutes* form a short penal code.

Book 4, chapter 16 describes excommunication from the oratory *for some fault*. The culprit prays alone, until reconciliation has been made, by means of a prayer for him, as he lies prostrate in the oratory. Chapter 7 of book 3 deals with latecomers to the choir office: one who arrives after the first psalm of the day hours, or after the second psalm of Vigils, remains outside and asks pardon of the brethren as they leave the oratory.

Book 4, chapter 16 gives more detail, mentioning the faults of negligence and disobedience, for which the culprit asks pardon before the whole community; he may not take part in the common prayer during his time of penance. For more serious infractions, especially of silence and obedience, there is exclusion from the oratory, whereas for faults indicating an attachment to evil, corporal punishment and even dismissal are envisaged.

The Rule of the Master dedicates several long chapters to correcting faults. Chapter 11 asks the deans to watch over the brethren, rebuking them and striving to eradicate what is contrary to God's precepts in their behaviour. For a small negligence, the culprit is deprived of *pure wine at the next meal*. If, after the two or three warnings recommended in *Matt.* 18, the monk shows himself *proud, murmuring, or disobedient*, the deans are to bring the matter to the Abbot,[99] who is to judge the nature and seriousness of the fault, and can impose excommunication from the table or the oratory.

Chapters 13 and 14 show the strenuous efforts to be made by Abbot and community, designed to lead the brother to make amends. They prescribe in detail a sophisticated ceremonial of exclusions, and requests for pardons, carried out between each psalm of the divine office. Children under the age of fifteen are not subject to these penances, but receive corporal punishment instead. The excommunicated monk eats alone, and his meals are shortened and delayed. If, after three days, he does not make satisfaction, he is to be whipped and then dismissed. Chapter 64 says that those who go away can be accepted again up to three times.

These excommunications are the monastic equivalent of the canonical penances used in the early Church. The guilty Christian would be excluded from the assembly of the faithful, and could obtain readmission only by submitting to the penance given by the bishop. In

---

[99] *RM*, 74, deals with coming late to the divine office; warnings are given on the spot by the Abbot; if there is repetition the culprits should stay out.

the same way, after the Abbot's verdict has been given, the guilty monk is excluded until he makes *satisfaction*.[100]

SAINT BENEDICT'S RULE

Chapters 23-30 of *RB* give Saint Benedict's penal code, and there is an appendix in chapters 43-46. It must be said that Saint Benedict owes a lot to his predecessors, especially *RM*, but adds his own flavour. Like *RM*, the beginning of the code is linked with the chapter about the deans, called *seniors* by Benedict. They have to warn the brethren according to the indications given in *Matt.* 18.[101] But *RB* reduces their role (they do not refer anything to the Abbot) and introduces breaches of the Rule to the list of faults. Another novelty is the distinction between the brethren who are aware of what they are doing, and the others. As in the chapter on the Abbot, Saint Benedict also takes care of the less intelligent, and provides appropriate measures for them.

The following chapters leave the assessment of a fault in the Abbot's hands, but make a clearer distinction between minor faults (which deprive the monk only of the common table) and graver faults (which exclude also from the oratory). In this last case, the monk is completely isolated from the community: nobody speaks to him or greets him, nor *blesses* him when he passes by. A short chapter (26) applies the same sanction to those who try to support his cause.

Leaving for a later moment the way of making satisfaction, Saint Benedict deals immediately with the case of the excommunicated. One of the most beautiful chapters of the Rule describes how solicitous the Abbot should be for the excommunicated (*RB* 27). The image used is that of Christ the doctor (*Matt.* 9: 12 – already used by Basil) and he also prescribes the use of intermediaries (called *senpectae*), which derives from Pachomius. But the central image is that of Christ the Good Shepherd, who goes in search of the lost sheep, makes use of all his knowledge to cure it, *and had so great pity for its weakness that he deigned to lay it on his own sacred shoulders, and so carry it back to the flock.*

The next chapter (*RB* 28) pays particular attention to difficult cases, those who will not amend after repeated corrections. After three days, the Master would have sent them away. Benedict wants the Abbot, like the wise physician, to make use of all possible treatment: if, after

---

[100] Cf. AV *Benoît et autour de lui*, p. 24. What is said below on *RB*, refers to this book.

[101] *Mt.* 18: 15-17, already cited by Basil and the Master.

his own exhortations, after corporal punishment and the prayer of the Abbot and of the whole community, the brother remains obstinate in his fault, then expulsion is necessary *for fear that one diseased sheep may infect the whole flock.* Here we find again Saint Basil's care for the community.

Finally *RB*, like *RM*, envisages the possibility of the brother's returning up to three times, a number that experience shows to be idealistic: a first return is often very fruitful; a second is already quite rare. But it is important to note that Saint Benedict, in his pastoral care, asks for a progressive reintegration into the community. This may sometimes make the adjustment easier, but it also gives the monk in question the opportunity of re-education. He is asked first to mend the defect that caused his departure, then he is given an opportunity to rebuild his spirit of humility: thus, he is to be received in the lowest place, i.e., with the beginners.

Chapter 30, about children, is careful not to specify their age and, as above, ranks them together with the adults who cannot understand the seriousness of the penalty of excommunication. Since they have let their body take advantage of them, it is their body that is punished, by fasting or corporal punishment. But, as often in the Rule, the last word of the chapter highlights the main thrust: *that they may be cured.* Similar words were found in the previous chapters after nearly all the mentions of penance.

The question of latecomers is treated in chapter 43. It begins by indicating the remedies for such a defect: promptness in responding to the signal for the work of God, and awareness of its importance as the prayer of the whole community; none of the individual activities may be put before it. Like Cassian's *Institutes*, *RB* is more severe on late-comers during the day than in the night but, instead of keeping the latecomers outside, they have to enter the oratory and stand in the last place, so as to benefit from the prayer and *being shamed ... may mend their ways.*

Satisfaction for faults is the object of the chapters 44–46. Of the long ceremony of the Master for the end of the excommunication, *RB* keeps only the central part where, as in Cassian, the community prays for the brother lying prostrate in the oratory. Benedict's interest is in the monk's healing, so he prolongs the satisfaction, giving a period in which the monk is still deprived of any active role in the choir office, and has still to prostrate himself at the end *until the abbot orders him to stop making this satisfaction.*[102]

Satisfaction for mistakes in the recitation of the office is made by a

---

[102] *RB* 44: 10.

gesture of humility, and for faults at work, by self-accusation. But if the matter is a secret sin of the soul this accusation is made *to the Abbot or to spiritual fathers, for they, knowing how to heal their own wounds, know how to heal those of others, without revealing them or making them known.*[103] Saint Basil had a similar remark.[104] We have here the germ of private sacramental confession, a practice which would spread, much later, under the influence of the Irish monks.

CONCLUSION

In all religions, the penances imposed for breaches of vows or rules aim mainly to put the culprit back on the right track; very rarely are they mere punishment.

The absence of community life makes Hinduism to some degree a distinctive case. In the ashram, the young man is under his guru, who, like the Desert Fathers, gives to each spiritual son the proper advice. The texts deal only with extreme cases, like dismissal by the guru or downgrading from the caste imposed by society. But the precautions taken before the final vows show that the aim of the sanctions is to help the ascetic to reflect on their serious nature.

In other religions, we find a particular attention by the community towards its weakest members, to support and ensure their faithfulness. For individuals, self-accusation of a fault is both a psychological liberation and a source of merits. Among the faults always considered as grave (besides breaches of the main vows) is pride, which renders a man obstinate in his bad behaviour and ill-disposed towards others. But the penances given are those in use in the surrounding society.

What characterises Christians is the imitation of the Good Shepherd, and the belief that he is present in each of his members, the human race. The Christian believes in God's infinite mercy; so the Abbot takes care of the monk, in union with Christ, and it is Jesus himself who is present in the wounded brother. Saint Benedict insists on the image of the Good Shepherd who not only takes care of the strayed sheep, but *carries it back to the flock on his own sacred shoulders*.

As a whole, these texts highlight the main traits of monastic life: the search for union with the Absolute, the common point uniting all monasticism; the public vows, which specify the conditions acknowledged by all as indispensable to this quest, and give the monk the support of society; the penal code, seen as a means of protecting the

---

[103] *RB* 46: 6.
[104] BASIL, SR 229.

professed monk against his weaknesses and giving him a way of recovery. In Christianity the vows are a mutual pledge of love between God and the person following Christ. Saint Benedict underlines the importance of stability in the total gift of self to God.

CHAPTER XIV

HOSPITALITY AND ENCLOSURE

Hospitality and enclosure – two words that seem mutually exclusive which are, nevertheless, quite closely connected. What distinguishes a guest from a member of the family is that the latter can walk freely throughout the entire premises, while the guest cannot. Receiving a guest is the first step of civilisation, where the foreigner is no longer an enemy but a welcomed person.[1] Often this change of attitude occurred when the reception of a guest took on a religious character. The isolated man is considered as emanating from the divinity and protected by it. This phenomenon is found in most of the world religions.

1. HOSPITALITY IN HINDUISM

For the Hindu tradition, the first guest is the Lord himself:

> He is the One, the all-pervading, and the guest of men ...
> O Lord, the guest most dearly loved.[2]

Hospitality was then considered as one of the five *'great sacrifices'* which contributed to support the order of the world:

> Day by day a man offers sustenance to creatures; that is the sacrifice of beings.

[1] J. DANIELOU, *Pour une théologie de l'hospitalité*, in LA VIE SPIRITUELLE, Nov. 1951, No. 367.
[2] *Arthava Veda*, 7: 21, PANIKKAR, *The Vedic Experience*, p. 661; *Rig Veda*, 186, 3, ibid. p. 183.

> *Day by day a man gives hospitality to a guest, including a glass of water; that is the sacrifice to men.*

Then comes the sacrifice to the ancestors, to the gods, and to Brahman.[3] Conversely, a man who refuses hospitality refuses a sacrifice, and *he will suffer the loss of all seven worlds.*[4] The forest hermit, the *Vanaprastha*, though retired from the world, keeps this duty of hospitality. The *Laws of Manu* prescribe that he should

> *make offerings to living beings, offerings taken from his own food. He should honour those who come to his hermitage, offering them water, roots and fruits.*[5]

The hermit shares his food, but he has above all to share his wisdom with those who come to him. The *Upanishad* speaks of kings who went to visit sages in the forest, in order to receive a spiritual teaching. We have already quoted the *Jâbâla Upanishad*, which reports a dialogue between the king Janaka and the hermit Yânavalkya about monastic life.[6] Several similar examples are cited in the *Mahabhâratha*. The 'renunciant', in his ultimate stage, is not able to give alms any more; it is he who is the guest of society and a source of blessing for those who receive him. But this is true also for any person received:

> *Look at your guest as at God himself, who wants to receive your attention,*

says the *Taittiriya Upanishad*,[7] and Toukaram was singing:

> *While you are making prayers to your God*
> *a man knocks at your door.*
> *If you ignore him, your prayer is impiety.*
> *You shut your house to the unexpected guest*
> *and offer a ritual meal to your God.*
> *If you make a distinction between the guest and God,*
> *said Tuka,*
> *Your liturgy is spittle.*[8]

So the Hindu tradition of hospitality goes beyond the respect of the guest, it makes it into a religious experience, in which God himself is received. Whether spiritual food is shared by teaching, or sustenance

---

[3] *Satapatha Brâmana Up.* XI, 5, 6, 1–3, ibid. p. 394.
[4] *Mundaka Up.* 1, 3, ibid. p. 414.
[5] Manu, 6: 7.
[6] UR, p. 166.
[7] *Taittiriya Up.* I, 1, 2.
[8] Transl. from Toukaram, *Psaumes du Pélerin*, Trans. G. A. Deleury.

of the body is shared by a meal, hospitality is an experience of encounter with God for both host and guest.

Neither the hermit nor the pilgrim monks have enclosure, but this does not mean that they can go anywhere. Even a novice has rules about asking for alms: he should avoid approaching people of bad repute, and should not always ask the same person; he has to avoid in the same way any physical contact with women, and should not even take a walk in a solitary place with one of them, even if she is his mother.[9] The rules of the renunciants are still more severe: he is to dwell in solitude, and when he goes for alms, he should ask only unknown persons, and do so without making any kind gesture, for fear of receiving a reward.[10]

The present-day important ashrams give generous hospitality, welcoming the many people who are eager to receive spiritual teaching, but men and women are accommodated in separate quarters.

2. IN BUDDHISM

The Hindu monk looks for a solitary place of meditation, while the Buddha in similar fashion selected for his followers

> *a quiet place ... not too far from the town and not too near, suitable for going and coming, easily accessible for all people who want to see them; not too crowded by day ...*[11]

For the Buddhist, the monastery is a place where the doctrine is taught, and where the lay person can practise it in a more perfect way, i.e. a way closer to monastic life. One comes to the monastery for an individual retreat, or on the occasion of a feast, to listen to a teaching and to practise five or eight of the monastic vows, for half a day, a night, or a few days. Such a one begins with an act of repentance for his faults, then promises

1. to abstain from killing any living being.
2. to abstain from taking what is not given.
3. to practise chastity.
4. to abstain from telling lies.
5. to abstain from taking any intoxicating drink.

---

[9] MANU, 2: 49–50; 184–185; 188; 211–217.
[10] MANU, 6: 55–59; most of the *Yâjnâvalkya Up.* is a warning against the attraction of women.
[11] *Vinaya*, I; 143.

To that, may be added

> 6. *to abstain from using flowers and perfumes.*
> 7. *to abstain from singing or dancing in a worldly way.*
> 8. *to abstain from using large seats or high beds.*

finally he should fast (in the afternoons like the monks).[12]

Monastic hospitality is very simple: the guests bring their food, and often something for the monks. But, in return, the monks have to prepare carefully the texts to be read or sung, and the teaching to be given.[13]

The guest house of the monastery is generally close to the temple and separated from the monks' quarters. Women cannot spend the night in a monastery of men, but during the day can go into the temple. It is the same for men in the nuns' monasteries. There is often also a pharmacy near the guest house, where a competent person prescribes medicines for the sick.

There are strict rules of separation between men and women. The male novice cannot ask alms in a house where there are only women, and if he is invited to sit down he cannot do it unless there are on the seat *neither arms nor precious objects, nor women's dress.* Only elderly monks are allowed to give talks to the nuns; but if a novice is sent to them,

> *He should address them in common, not individually, and only after having greeted the stupa of the convent, according to the ritual. If he is offered a prepared seat, he may sit down; if not, he has to stand up, for he should not, whatever may be the reason, sit on the same bench or divan as the nuns. If he is earnestly asked to give a pious talk, he will say only what is convenient. He should not gossip with the nuns, if he is offered clothes, shoes or any other elegant object, he should refuse all. When he comes back to the monastery he should not tell the monks his impressions of the nuns.[14]*

The monasteries of men and women have an enclosure; nobody, and above all no novice, is allowed to go out without the permission of the superior. All these restrictions are not only a safeguard for chastity; they also express reverence for the *Dharma*, the Universal Law, which implies the respect for all beings, in the harmony of the Cosmos. Thus in Zen the 'art of hospitality' the *Cha do*, the 'Way of

---

[12] *Vinaya*, Ritual of the Sarvâstivâda School, LW, pp. 147–150.
[13] Ibid. p. 178, precepts of male novices, Chinese school; ZAGO, *Rites*, p. 291. I have seen the same rites practised in Sri Lanka.
[14] *Vinaya*, ibid. p. 179.

Tea', becomes a means of union with the Infinite. Respectful of the mystery and difference present in the guest, this art

> *does everything possible that the guest may discover himself more truly, thanks to this welcome. This does not mean that he has to feel at ease (or at home) but that by the discreet incantation of the ritual and the quality of his host's presence, he will get a deeper awakening in this communion.*[15]

In conclusion let us note that the external aspects of monastic hospitality in Hinduism and Buddhism both intend to offer the guest peaceful surroundings that are conducive to prayer, doctrinal teaching, and meditation, together with an atmosphere of kindness which purifies the person and fights against selfishness. Enclosure promotes a spirit of peace, respect and prayer, which in turn protect chastity.

At the spiritual level, hospitality is considered, in a way proper to each religion, as an occasion of encounter and communion with the Infinite, both in the guest and in the host.

3. THE JEWISH TRADITION

THE OLD TESTAMENT

In the Old Testament Abraham, who in welcoming unknown strangers received a visit from God and was given the promise of having descendants, gives the most famous example of hospitality. By way of contrast, the town of Sodom was punished for having tried to abuse strangers.[16] Later the Hebrews were themselves received in Egypt and, in the Law, the commandment of being hospitable is based on the memory of their condition in that country:

> *The stranger who sojourns with you shall be as the native among you, and you shall love him as yourself, for you were strangers in the land of Egypt.*[17]

But it is also to imitate God

> *who is not partial ... He executes justice for the fatherless and the widow, and loves the sojourner, giving him food and clothing. Love the sojourner therefore: for you were sojourners in the land of Egypt.*[18]

[15] P. F. DE BETHUNE, *Par la foi et l'hospitalité*, p. 38.
[16] *Gen.* 18–19.
[17] *Lev.* 19: 34.
[18] *Deut.* 10: 17–19.

This duty of protecting the weak, and among them the strangers, was set out in many laws: there were towns of refuge, and there was a right of gleaning what had been left behind by the reapers, and of not working on Sabbath days. Job, Boaz and Tobias, who were rewarded for their generosity for strangers, provide us with other examples of hospitality.[19] The prophets repeat this teaching and forbid molestation of the weak.[20]

But Israel is also the guest of God, who nourished his people in the desert, received them in the Promised Land and introduced them into his tent, to enjoy his presence and to have intimacy with him:

> *Lord who will dwell in your tent or who will rest on your holy mountain?*
> *Let me dwell in your tent forever, and hide me under the shelter of your wings.*[21]

THE ESSENES

With their faithful observance of the Law the Essenes, quoting the prophets, recommended taking care of the strangers:

> *May each one love his brother as himself, strengthen the hand of the poor, of the unfortunate, and of the stranger . . .*
> *We should not ask the stranger to work on the Sabbath day.*[22]

That is nearly all we know about the Qumran group; but the *Therapeutes* of Alexandria give more precise indications. Philo said that he knew them from having visited them, and he quotes their example to others who could do the same. We can draw the conclusion that the solitaries were in the habit of receiving people who came to pray with them for a period of time. But the most interesting details are about the enclosure, which separated the twin communities of men and women. During the week, all of them lived as hermits in their small houses, and on the Sabbath day they met for a common prayer:

> *They sit according to age, with a proper posture, keeping their hands under their clothes . . . Then the eldest and most learned in doctrine goes forward to speak . . . This common sanctuary, in which they assemble on*

---

[19] *Num.* 35: 15; *Deut.* 24: 11; *Ex.* 23: 12; *Job* 31: 3; *Ruth* 2: 10–11; *Tob.* 1: 8.
[20] *Jer.* 7: 6; *Zech.* 7: 10.
[21] *Ps.* 77: 19; *Lev.* 25: 23; *Ps.* 14: 1; 60: 4.
[22] QUMRAN, DD VI, quoting *Deut.* 25: 7; *Jer.* 29: 7; DD XI, quoting *Isa.* 58:13; *Ex.* 20: 10.

the seventh day, is an enclosed space divided into two parts, one for men, and the other for women. For the women usually come to listen: they share the same zeal and the same kind of life. A wall of half-height separates these two parts, so that the women may both keep the attitude of reserve befitting them and yet may understand what is said.[23]

After the president's homily, there is a common liturgical meal, very likely in the same conditions. Later a sacred vigil takes place:

They stand up and form two choirs, one of men, the other of women ... They sing hymns composed in honour of God ... at one moment in separate choirs, then responding to each other in harmony, accompanied by gestures and dancing. Then, filled with inspiration, they move in procession, or stay in their place, and execute the verses and responses of the choir.[24]

At dawn they say together the Morning Prayer and each one

retires to his sanctuary and starts practising his philosophy once more.[25]

Philo concludes:

Citizens of heaven and of the world, they are really united to the Father and Creator of the universe, by the virtue which has given them the friendship with God.[26]

The Christian monks will use the same Biblical context, but seen through the lens of the Gospel.

4. THE CHRISTIAN TRADITION

THE GOSPEL

Jesus' teaching makes use of part of the tradition of the prophets. But he insisted that the host should be unselfish:

When you give a feast, invite the poor, the maimed, the lame, the blind, and you will be blessed, because they cannot repay you. You will be repaid at the resurrection of the just.[27]

[23] PHILO, *De Vita C.* 29–33.
[24] PHILO, ibid. 83–84.
[25] PHILO, ibid. 89.
[26] PHILO, ibid. 90.
[27] *Lk.* 14: 13–14.

But he adds a new note, inviting the host to see Him in the person received, or indeed, in the person who is sometimes rejected:

> *What you did to the least of my brethren, you did it to me ... I was a stranger and you welcomed me ... I was a stranger and you did not welcome me.*[28]

To understand the real importance of these words, we should note that the assembled persons are '*all the nations*' and that even the elect did not recognise the Lord in the needy they have assisted. The invitation to hospitality is thus extended to all those in need, without distinction of nation or religion.

There is something quite new in Christ's teaching on this point. The guest is no longer only a person protected by the divinity, as he had been in the ancient cultures of the West, nor, as in the East, a manifestation of the divine present in everything, nor even, as in the Old Testament, a messenger of God. Jesus identified himself so clearly with the poor as to become one with them. This text of Saint Matthew thus has a prophetic character, proclaiming the actual reality of Christ in need of help. It also has eschatological importance because fullness of union with him will take place only at the end of time.

Other evangelical sayings suggest various levels of reward, according to how much Christ has been discerned in the guest received. Jesus said to the Apostles:

> *He who receives you receives me, and he who receives me receives him who sent me. He who receives a prophet because he is a prophet shall receive a prophet's reward, and he who receives a righteous man because he is a righteous man, shall receive a righteous man's reward.*[29]

Hospitality is particularly required for preachers of the Gospel message:

> *You received without payment, give without payment.*

But those who have been evangelised should, in their turn, take care of their pastors:

> *Take no gold, nor silver ... for the labourer deserves his food.*[30]

---

[28] *Mt.* 25: 35 ... 43.
[29] *Mt.* 10: 40–41.
[30] *Mt.* 10: 8–10.

Christ invites all his friends to the eternal marriage-feast,[31] and even here and now wants to be the inner guest:

> *If a man loves me, he will keep my word, and my Father will love him and we will come to him and make our home with him.*[32]

MONASTIC CHRISTIAN HOSPITALITY

The Desert Fathers

The first Christians followed the directions given by Christ. According to the *Acts*

> *They had everything in common ... There were no needy persons among them ... distribution was made to each according to need.*[33]

Later, hospitality was mentioned as a good work in *The Shepherd of Hermas*. Clement of Rome congratulates the Corinthians for their well-known hospitality, and the Emperor Julian the Apostate attributes the success of Christianity to its *'humanity'* towards strangers.[34] The Desert Fathers, following the model of the Primitive Church, shared the little they had with all those who knocked at their door, and did not hesitate to modify their times of fasting and prayer in order to receive them. The *Apophthegmata* have a full chapter on this subject, here are some examples:

> *A monk went to visit a hermit and when leaving he said 'Excuse me, Abba, I have made you break your rule'. But the other answered, 'My rule is to refresh you, and send you back in peace'.*

> *A hermit lived near a monastery and led a very austere life. It happened once that some visitors came to the monastery and forced him to eat outside the usual time. After that the brethren asked him 'Abba, were you not displeased at that?' He answered: 'My displeasure is my own will'.*

> *It was said about an elder who lived in Syria along the desert road: this is his work: Any time a monk comes from the desert, he willingly gives him refreshments.*[35]

---

[31] *Mt.* 8: 11; 22: 2.
[32] *Jn.* 14: 23.
[33] *Acts* 4: 32–35.
[34] *Shepherd of Hermas, Mand.* 8: 19; CLEMENT OF ROME, *Ep. ad Corinthios* 1: 2; EMP. JULIAN, *Let. to Arac. Ep.* 84. Let us note that the word *humanitas* is used by Julian, as by many Fathers of the Church, in the sense of help to the poor and the giving of hospitality.
[35] *Apophthegmata*, Syst. Coll. 13: 8–10.

Most of the Desert Fathers' visitors were monks, looking for edifying examples or words. As a rule, women were not allowed in the vicinity of the hermitages. A Roman lady, who went to Egypt because she wanted at all costs to meet Abba Arsenius, had a bitter experience. She met him by chance outside his cell and bowed down to the ground before him. But he answered with indignation:

'How did you dare to journey here? Don't you know you are a woman, and that you cannot go just anywhere? Or have you come here so that you can return to Rome and say to other women, "I have seen Arsenius?" – and then the sea will become one long road of women coming to my place!' She said: 'If it please the Lord, I will not allow anyone to come here. But please, pray for me and remember me always.' But Arsenius answered, 'I shall pray the Lord to blot out your memory from my heart.' At these words, she left him, deeply upset.

She was so upset by this snub that she became ill, and would have died, had not the archbishop, Theophilus of Alexandria, assured her that, despite his hard words, the old man was praying for her.[36]

The Fathers also knew how to use a sense of humour to deal with tactless visitors:

Some monks of a community went to visit a hermit in the desert. He received them with joy and, as usual among hermits, seeing their tiredness, prepared the meal early and brought them all he had to refresh them. In the evening they recited the twelve psalms, and similarly during the night. While the old man kept vigil alone, he heard them saying among themselves 'The hermits in the desert have an easier life than us in the communities'. In the morning, when they were going to leave to visit an elder monk in the neighbourhood, he said to them, 'Please greet him in my name and tell him, "Don't water the vegetables".' So they did. Listening to these words the other elder understood their meaning, and kept them at work without eating until the evening. When the evening came he did the great office and said, 'That will do because you are tired', and he added, 'We don't usually eat every day, but because of you let us eat a little'. And he brought them dry bread with salt, saying: 'Because of you we have to make a feast' and poured a bit of vinegar on the salt. Rising from the table, they prayed until early morning. And he said to them: 'Because of you, we cannot fulfil the whole rule. You have to take some rest, because you have journeyed from far away'. In the morning, they wanted to go, but he entreated them, saying, 'Stay with us at least two or three days, according to the commandment, to follow our custom in the desert'. But they, seeing that he would not let them go, got up and went away secretly.[37]

[36] *Apophthegmata*, Arsenius, 28.
[37] *Apophthegmata*, Syst. Coll. 10: 97.

The big monasteries, like those of Scete and Nitria, attracted more visitors than isolated hermitages, so special quarters were provided for them. These guests, being generally monks, were invited to share the life of prayer and work of the monastery. Palladius said about Nitria:

> *Close to the church is the guest house, where strangers are welcome, even if they stay two or three years. But having allowed them to stay a week in idleness, they are invited to work in the garden, the bakery or the kitchen for the rest of their stay. If, however, the guest merits some consideration, he is given a book, but is not allowed to speak to anyone before the appointed time.*[38]

The Pachomians

The Pachomian monasteries had the same surroundings as those of the Egyptian deserts but, as they were often closer to inhabited places, the separation from the external word was more stressed. When Pachomius was building a monastery, we see by his *Lives* that one of his first cares was to build an enclosure wall.[39] Outside the wall, there was a porter's lodge, with enough space to receive separately the different kinds of persons who turn up: visiting monks, postulants and lay people. To look after this diverse group with appropriate care for each,

> *Pachomius appointed two monks 'having a tongue seasoned with salt' (i.e. with Wisdom). They had to receive the visitors according to their rank, and to teach those who came to become monks about salvation.*[40]

Hospitality was the responsibility of the whole community rather than of one individual. Other details confirm it: if, for example, someone brought food (even food which was allowed) to a monk, he had to give it to the porter, who allowed him to take a little, taking the rest to the infirmary for the use of the sick.[41]

The guests were received in a way appropriate to the situation of each person. Visiting monks initially mingled with the brethren, but later it was decided that they should join the community only for prayer, spending the rest of the time in the guest house, and taking

---

[38] PALLADIUS, *Lausiac History*, 7: 4.
[39] PACHOMIUS, VC *S.* 3, 19; *Bo.* 49; 58.
[40] PACHOMIUS, VC *Bo.* 26. 'The tongue seasoned with salt' is a qualifier used in the VC to designate persons gifted with discernment and wisdom.
[41] PACHOMIUS, *Praec.* 53.

their meals in a separate place.[42] This separation had a twofold aim: to avoid the guest being scandalised by the infractions of the rule, unavoidable in big communities, and to preserve the brethren from the gossip of the gyrovagues, or wandering monks, who hoped to find a welcome by criticising the monks of other places.[43] The postulants, as we have seen, had a separate regime, while concerning the visitors we have the example of Theodore's mother and his young brother. When they arrived

> *our Father Pachomius asked to take care of them in an appropriate place, according to their rank. They stayed there three days.*[44]

The guest did not have direct contact with the monks. All the visitors had to knock at the door; the porter informed the superior, who would come in person, or send someone to take care of them. So 'Denis the Confessor' had to use a pious trick to get Pachomius to come out of the monastery and go to the porter's lodge, where a sick woman approached him from behind, and touched his clothing in order to be cured.[45]

Another motive of these precautions was to avoid the community becoming contaminated by heretics. Most of the brethren came from the countryside, and had little culture. They could easily be deceived and fall into error, above all at this time when Arianism was protected by the State, and Origenism was beginning to spread. Pachomius was fiercely faithful to Saint Athanasius, and even refused to pray with Arians; he would not tolerate any book of Origen in his monasteries.[46]

At this time, contacts with the family seem to have constituted a serious danger for the monks, so they were avoided as much as possible. Pachomius did not even receive his own sister, although she was coming to be a nun. Theodore also refused to see his mother, and snubbed his young brother, who had sneaked in behind the monks of the community.[47] Such harshness astonishes us today, but it was probably required by local circumstances at the time. In other respects, Pachomius, Theodore, Orsisius and other superiors show a *motherly* heart towards those who approached them.[48] This kindness is found

---

[42] PACHOMIUS, VC *Bo.* 40.
[43] PACHOMIUS, VC *Bo.* 40; 88. Pachomius sees the gyrovagues in hell!
[44] PACHOMIUS, VC *Bo.* 37.
[45] PACHOMIUS, VC *Bo.* 41.
[46] PACHOMIUS, VG 33; VC *Bo.* 185.
[47] PACHOMIUS, VC *Bo.* 27; 37. This danger explains also the precautions taken by Pachomius to make sure of the consent of the family before receiving young postulants from well-to-do families, like Theodore the Townsman *Bo.* 89.
[48] PACHOMIUS, VC *Bo.* 91; 151; 191 ...

also in the *Praecepta* of Pachomius, which allowed relatives to enter the monastery, accompanied by a monk *of proved faith*, to go and see a brother in the place where he lived if he were sick, and bring him something to relieve him. But all this was under the control of the superior and head of the house.[49]

Many sick people came to find nursing care, or to implore the prayer of the superior that they might be freed from their infirmities. Pachomius was attentive to their needs and left his cell at once to take care of them, an eagerness which contrasts with his aversion for meeting important persons.[50] But his main concern was for sickness of the soul rather than of the body, and he would often simply invite the sick to bear their infirmity with patience, because he saw that, for them, it was destined to become a means of sanctification.[51]

Enclosure also implied restrictions on leaving the monastery. At the death of a relative, the permission of the superior was needed to attend the burial, and whatever the reason for the absence from the monastery, nobody was allowed outside alone, but must always have a companion. If, on coming back to the monastery, they found somebody wanting to see a monk, they were not to deal with him themselves, but should inform the superior. Similarly, they should not speak in community about worldly business.[52]

Pachomius developed monastic hospitality in several important ways. First, he organised it in such a way that the monastery would be able to receive different types of visitors. He also established an enclosure, which provided limits for both the community and the guests, while the welcome was provided not by an individual monk alone, but by the community as a body.

The Cappadocian Fathers and Saint John Chrysostom

Saint Basil was attracted to the monastic life by his sister Macrina who, with her mother, some friends, and some former slaves, retired to a country house that had been transformed into a monastery. Basil, having left behind a brilliant career and distributed his goods, had founded a monastery of men in the vicinity. When he had to leave it in order to enter the service of the Church at Caesarea, his brother Peter, later Bishop of Sebaste, succeeded him as the head of the monastery. Another of their brothers, Gregory of Nyssa, writes in his

---

[49] PACHOMIUS, *Praec.* 53–54.
[50] PACHOMIUS, VC *Bo.* 109–110. Pachomius sent a monk in his place to meet the 'philosophers' (*Bo.* 55) and he hid himself to avoid Athanasius (*Bo.* 28).
[51] PACHOMIUS, VC *Bo.* 110.
[52] PACHOMIUS, *Praec.* 55–57; VC *Bo.* 104.

Life of Saint Macrina of the hospitality received in both houses. As everywhere, sick and needy people were often seen at the door; monks and nuns considered it a duty to work, so as to have something to give by way of help.[53] But Gregory's account shows a type of guest that we have scarcely seen up to now: entire families coming to the monastery in order to pray. The women would go to the house of Macrina and the men to Peter's.

In his *Long Rules*, Basil also speaks of these different groups of visitors. One of the motives he gives to incite the monks to work is the relief of the poor. On that subject, he quotes Christ in the Gospel:

> *I was hungry and you gave me food, I was thirsty and you gave me drink.*[54]

Elsewhere, he distinguished several categories of persons among those who come and knock: visiting monks, relatives of community members, and people of the world.[55] The relatives who live *according to God* should be honoured by all as fathers and mothers, since Jesus said that whoever does the will of God is his brother and sister and mother. Those who come to *beg (God's) word* are to be treated in similar fashion. In both cases, the superior should take care of them himself or delegate another to do it.[56]

Everyone should be given the frugal diet of the monastery:

> *Is a guest due to arrive? If he is a brother with the same aim as us, he will recognise his own table. What he has left at home is what he will find again with us. But if he be tired, let us give him what is necessary to refresh himself.*
>
> *Another one comes. Is he from the world? Let him learn by deeds what words were not able to teach: let him be shown the model and example of frugality in food. Let him be reminded what a Christian table is, and poverty borne without shame, for the love of Christ. If he does not understand, and finds it ridiculous, he will not disturb us a second time ...*
>
> *While we should always take care to have a sufficiently generous table, we should never go beyond the limits of what is necessary. When we receive guests, let us take care to satisfy them with what they need.*

---

[53] Peter, in a time of famine even took care of providing food for the whole region (GREGORY OF NYSSA, *Life of Saint Macrina*, 12). Macrina and her sisters worked so well that *though not sending away the beggars, they did not look for benefactors* (*Life of Saint Macrina*, 20).

[54] BASIL, LR 37, quoting *Mt.* 25: 34–35. Cf. chapter 10 above on work, note 45.

[55] BASIL, LR 20; 32.

[56] BASIL, LR 32; 45.

The Apostle says, 'using the things of the world without abusing them'. Now abuse is use which goes beyond necessity.[57]

We can still find, among the guests, those who *live an ordinary life*, that is, who are not bothered about God. But Basil says, *we have nothing to do with them, we who are striving to practise without respite the law of God*, and as for those who reject the law of God, *we cannot receive them.*[58]

Basil obviously intends to preserve monastic life, in contrast with those *who put the enjoyment of pleasures in first place*. He says it would be *hypocritical and despicable to modify our diet in favour of those who are fond of good fare.*[59]

But the restrictions in contact with visitors, and especially with family members, have yet another purpose. Contacts with worldly people are avoided because to speak with them reawakens in some of the brethren the allure of the world. It makes them *return to Egypt* and causes their falling away ... This misfortune *happens frequently*, complains Saint Basil:

That is why we don't allow the brethren to speak with strangers, unless we are sure that it will be for the spiritual progress of their soul.

So when it is necessary to speak with visitors, let the charge be given to those who have received the gift of speaking, because they can speak and listen with wisdom and for the edification of faith.[60]

These reasons explain also the fear that the Pachomians had of the visits of families. Like Pachomius, Basil requests that the monk in charge of transient guests knows *how to answer them appropriately, in order to edify properly*. If a stranger consults another monk, the latter, even if he is able to answer, is to tell him to ask the person in charge. If another sees that he has not said something that perhaps he should have said, this is to be told him in private:

To be in a rush to speak would be a cause of disorder, and a sign of lack of discipline.[61]

Saint Basil speaks less of enclosure than Saint Pachomius, but like him limits talking and contacts with the guests, in order to preserve the spiritual life of the brethren and the identity of the community as a contrast

---

[57] BASIL, LR 20.
[58] BASIL, LR 32.
[59] BASIL, LR 20.
[60] BASIL, LR 32.
[61] BASIL, LR 45.

to the world. He nevertheless adds another dimension to monastic hospitality, instituting a tradition of spiritual counselling for lay people, a thing that the Desert Fathers would have done very rarely.

This new apostolate answered a need felt in the Church, and the bishops, who were often former monks, encouraged the faithful to go to monasteries, in order to pray and to strengthen their Christian life by the example of the monks. Saint John Chrysostom explained to his faithful that those engaged in monastic life

> *are established in solitude in order to teach us to despise the sterile agitation of the towns.*[62]

Hence their mission of welcoming:

> *The monasteries are like lights, shining on high, to lighten those who come to them from far away. Established in a safe harbour, they invite the world to share their tranquillity; they help those who see them to avoid shipwreck, and prevent them from remaining in the darkness.*[63]

That is why John Chrysostom invites people of his diocese to go there frequently for retreats:

> *I have no doubt that some of you may be touched by what I am saying to you, and that you conceive some liking for this life ... To prevent this ardent desire from cooling down, go yourselves to see these angels of the earth, so that your desire may thus be kindled still more. For such a holy spectacle will impress your spirits more than all I may say about it ... Don't say: Before leaving I have to speak about it to my wife, and put some business in order ...*[64]

On another occasion, he insists still further:

> *You say 'I have nobody to take me there' – Then come to me: I shall take you myself.*[65]

These texts show that monastic hospitality increased alongside the needs of the Church, and gradually became more specific about the roles of its practitioners.[66]

---

[62] J. CHRYSOSTOM, *In Mt. Hom.* 72: 4.

[63] J. CHRYSOSTOM, *In 1 Tim. Hom.* 14: 3.

[64] J. CHRYSOSTOM, *In Mt. Hom.* 68: 3–5.

[65] J. CHRYSOSTOM, *In Mt. Hom.* 72: 3

[66] JOHN CHRYSOSTOM is also one of the first Fathers of the Church to specify the role of the contemplative life in the Church. He said that a good monk does not make necessarily a good parish priest, but his prayer strengthens and protects the whole Church (*De sacerd.* 3: 15; *In 1 Tim. Hom.* 14: 13).

As bishop, Basil built a big centre outside the city, which included the cathedral, guest houses, and hospitals for the poor, the sick and pilgrims, with workshops and shops for their use. This centre, later called *Basileiad* according to the name of its creator, has been imitated throughout the East.

But Basil himself was only improving an older usage. We have seen how the big monasteries of the desert, in Egypt, Syria and Palestine, maintained hostels and hospitals for the service of the poor, and of the pilgrims in places of pilgrimage.[67]

Cassian, Augustine, *The Rule of the Master*

Cassian relates in his *Institutes* some examples of the Desert Fathers receiving other monks who came to visit them. The ascetics did not hesitate to modify their rules of fasting, because they saw Christ in the guest:

> *Fasting, though useful and necessary, is nevertheless the offering of a voluntary gift, whereas a work of charity is an absolute requirement of the precept. So, in welcoming Christ in you, I must refresh him, and when you have left, I can make up for the 'humanity' I have manifested for the sake of Christ, by means of a stricter fast. Indeed 'the bridegroom's friends cannot fast as long as the spouse is with them', but when he has gone, then they can do it.*[68]

Cassian takes up the question of hospitality when a meal had to be offered to a guest. He uses the word *humanity* (*humanitas*) already met in this context, to describe such a procedure.[69]

The monasteries cared for by Saint **Augustine** were in towns. They certainly had visitors, but it seems that they were not given meals. His Rule mentions only letters or gifts.[70] The saint speaks of hospitality mainly in sermons addressed to his flock.[71] A little later, Saint

---

[67] In Syria the monasteries had *Rules of Hospitality* given by Saint Euthymius; Saint Sabas had a guest house in his Lavra, one at Jerusalem and another in Jericho; similarly the monk Theodore used to receive near Bethlehem, monks, pilgrims, sick people and poor. Cf. D. J. CHITTY, *The Desert a City*, pp. 193–219.

[68] CASSIAN, *Inst.* 5: 24.

[69] Cf. note 34. In *Conf.* 21: 4, Cassian again takes the same idea of Christ served in the guests and uses twice again the word *humanitas* or another derived from it.

[70] AUGUSTINE, *Praec.* 4: 11; 5: 3.

[71] Cf. *LA VIE SPIRITUELLE*, No. 367, Nov. 1951, J. DANIELOU, *Pour une théologie de l'hospitalité*; and *Cinq sermons de saint Augustin sur l'hospitalité*, especially *Sermon* 103 and *In Jh. Tract.* 58.

Caesarius of Arles, whose *Rule for Virgins* depends on Saint Augustine, forbids the nuns to prepare meals for people of the town.[72]

With the **Rule of the Master**, we are again in a monastery isolated in the countryside, where the coming of guests causes problems of board and lodging. *RM* deals with particular cases as they arise. The Rule makes a distinction between passing visitors (chs. 65 and 72) and those who stay for several days (chs. 78–79), but all of them seem to be monks or clerics. They are received with respect, then the monks pray with them before giving them the kiss of peace. The prayer is made first in order to avoid the illusions of the devil, who, according to the Desert Fathers, might present himself under a human form[73] but disappear when prayer is offered. Because of the guest, the community is permitted to take meals earlier, but if he has to leave early, they will eat alone:

> *They will not be allowed to leave with an empty stomach, because it is in breaking bread that Christ made himself recognised.*[74]

The guests live in separate quarters closely watched by two monks with every semblance of kindness, who yet take care to stop any form of stealing. After two days, the guests are requested to work, or else to leave. This is to avoid the excesses of the gyrovagues. But, *to be charitable to a truly poor person makes us worthy of a beautiful reward.*[75] If a visiting monk wants to fix his stability in the community, he will have to undergo the periods of trial foreseen for the postulants.

RM ends with the chapter on the doorkeepers, whose place is inside the walls, giving details of their horarium and occupations. They inform the Abbot of the visitors' arrival, and have to shut the door of the monastery whenever they need to leave their post, i.e. for the divine office, or during the night.

Enclosure in *RM* was thus rather strict. Nothing is said of the relationship between the guests and the brethren, but the fact that the guest was always accompanied in his movements by a monk-invigilator, who was himself bound to keep silence, makes us think that the communication was reduced to the minimum. The fact that the door-

---

[72] CAESARIUS OF ARL. *Reg. Virg.* 39–40. Only the Sisters' relatives coming from far away could be given a meal, by way of exception.

[73] *RM* makes explicit reference to the example of Paul and Antony, but the fact is mentioned several times in the Lives of the Fathers: RUFINUS, *Hist. Monac.* 1 and *Lausiac History*.

[74] *RM* 72.

[75] *RM* 78.

keeper had to inform the Abbot of the visitors' arrival suggests that the contacts with the outside world were the responsibility of the Abbot.

5. SAINT BENEDICT

Hospitality

The monasteries of Egypt or Palestine mainly received visiting monks, pilgrims, and the poor. The diversity of guests became greater in Saint Basil's time, when ordinary Christians would come to monasteries in order to pray, but these are not much seen in Cassian's and the Master's houses. Saint Benedict, on the other hand, finds himself in new circumstances. He keeps the external forms received from the tradition, but he gives them a new character of his own.

As in *RM*, we find in *RB* a doorkeeper, who discerns the kinds of persons who turn up at the monastery. He takes care of passing visitors, and when guests have to come inside, the Abbot is informed. There is a ritual of reception, with a prayer to dispel the devil's illusions.[76] After that, the Abbot or his delegate looks after the guest.

RB chapter 53 summarises the indications given on hospitality in the four chapters of the *RM* we have just seen, but speaks of guests and of enclosure in other chapters, and on several occasions.[77] What Saint Benedict adds to *RM*, or subtracts from it, indicates his own special emphasis.

A first novelty is the variety of persons coming to the monastery. In *RB* and in the *Dialogues*, we see relatives and friends of the community, members of the clergy, monks, poor and sick persons, and finally even some powerful and hostile heretics.[78] All these people come to the monastery as a place where men are living close to God, hoping in general to receive either spiritual or material help from them.

A second new aspect, and the most important, is that *RB*, as usual,

---

[76] *RM* 71: 9; JEROME, *Vita Pauli*, 9; *Hist. Monach.* 1.

[77] *RB Prol.* 49–50, monastery-school; 4: 78, enclosure where the monk is stable; 31: 9, the cellarer has to take care of the guests, the sick and the poor; 42: 10, it is allowed to speak after compline when receiving guests; 55: 13, monks who have to go out; 56: 1–2, the guests eat at the Abbot's table; 58: 4, postulants are first received in the guest house; 66, the function of the doorkeeper; 67, brethren who are travelling.

[78] GREGORY THE GREAT, *Dialogues*, II, relatives and friends: 3; 13; 18; 22–24; clergy and monks: 15; 16; 28; 35; poor and sick: 26–28; 32; heretics, 15; 31.

leaves out the detailed description of the doorkeeper's function, and limits itself to a definition of the attitude of heart which should inform him, adapting it to the circumstances, since *Christ is received in the guest*. As often in the parts of the Rule which are proper to him, Saint Benedict expresses his attitude in the first sentence of the chapter:

> *All who arrive as guests are to be welcomed like Christ, for he is going to say, 'I was a stranger and you welcomed me.' The respect due to their station is to be shown to all, particularly to those of one family with us in the faith and to pilgrims.*[79]

Pachomius and Cassian had already used *Matt.* 25: 35,[80] but for them it was a question of receiving other monks. Benedict broadens the application of this evangelical precept to all those who turn up. Whoever may be the one who knocks at the door, he should feel welcome in the *house of God*. It is in this spirit that the doorkeeper is available at any time:

> *This doorkeeper should have a cell near the gate, so that persons who arrive may always find someone at hand to give them a reply. As soon as anyone knocks, or a poor man calls out, he should answer 'Thanks be to God' or 'God bless you'. Then with all the gentleness that comes from the fear of God, he should speedily and with the warmth of charity attend to the enquirer.*[81]

This monk should be *a wise old man ... capable of receiving a message and giving a reply*.[82] When somebody knocks at the door, the doorkeeper answers him with words of blessing, expressing *the gentleness ... from the fear of God*, and he hurries to answer his needs *with the warmth of charity*.

Twice again in chapter 53[83] the Rule insists on the attitude which ought to inspire this welcome: politeness, humility, charity, repeating that *Christ is received in* the person of the guests. If charity is equal for all, its truth is shown by adapting it to each case and in giving due respect to every person.

[79] *RB* 53: 1-2, quoting *Mt.* 25: 35.
[80] PACHOMIUS, VC *Bo.* 40; CASSIAN, *Inst.* 5: 24.
[81] *RB* 66: 2-3.
[82] *RB* 66: 1. In the *Dialogues* we see Saint Benedict himself doing this work: Zalla found him alone sitting before the door and reading (GREGORY THE G. *Dial.* 2: 31). Taking into account the beginning of the story and the meal offered to Zalla, we can guess that the scene happened at midday, and that the Abbot was doing his *lectio divina*, replacing the doorkeeper, perhaps to allow him to take rest (*RB* 48: 5).
[83] *RB* 53: 7 and 15.

Another aspect of the reception underlined by Benedict is that of prayer, and care for the religious formation of the guest. Prayer is mentioned at the guest's arrival, then:

> **When the guests have been welcomed they should be led to prayer, and then either the superior or someone delegated by him should sit with them. The Divine Law should be read to them for their edification.**[84]

This prayer is more than a mere tradition; Saint Benedict knows by experience that any man could bring both Christ and the spirit of the world. Prayer is thus both a protection for the monk, and a gift of the monastery to the visitor, by making him enter into a religious atmosphere. *Let the Divine Law be read*; few people at that time knew how to read; reading aloud was necessary for teaching. This care for the guests' religious education is to be underlined. The *Dialogues* show the Abbot speaking with them of spiritual matters, and the Rule provides that he can delegate that to another monk.[85]

The spiritual food goes along with bodily food: the meal, which in *RB*, as we have seen in the previous Latin texts, is called '*humanitas*'. So Saint Benedict finds an original solution to reconciling community fasting with the duty of hospitality: the guest is invited to the Abbot's table, and there is a special kitchen for the guests, run by competent brethren. To the hospitality of the table is added the gesture of washing of the feet, a sign of humility and of fraternal charity in which the whole community takes part.

The Rule also speaks of the *guest house*, distinct from the monastery, with a *sufficient number of beds*, entrusted to a monk *whose soul is full of the fear of God*, that is, in Saint Benedict's language, full of respectful charity, so that *God's house may be wisely cared for by wise men*.[86]

Saint Benedict thus insists that all the guests, without exception, should *be received like Christ*, giving to each person, with respect and humility, the welcome adapted to his situation. Already in the *Tools of Good Works* he had asked his monks *to honour all men*,[87] and Benedict's life gives a striking example of this in the way he received the furious heretic, Zalla, who arrived shouting insults at him. Instead of answering back, Benedict quietly called the brethren, and asked them to offer food and drink to the unusual visitor. Only after that did he invite him to stop his cruel behaviour.[88]

[84] *RB* 53: 9.
[85] Gregory the G. *Dialogues*, 2: 13; 15; 33; 35; *RB* 53: 8.
[86] *RB* 53: 21–22.
[87] *RB* 4: 8.
[88] Gregory the G. *Dialogues*, 2: 31.

Even if all are to be given honour, Saint Benedict as usual gives a special attention to the weakest members of the group:

Special care is to be shown in the reception of the poor and of pilgrims, for in them especially is Christ received; for the awe felt for the wealthy imposes respect enough of itself.[89]

The welcome given to the poor is traditional. Pilgrim means stranger, as explained at the beginning of chapter 61, the one coming *from some far-off locality*. Since he comes from far away, he is in a strange place and needs special attention. Chapter 53 also mentions *one family with us in the faith*. These words are a quotation from *Gal.* 6: 10 and can mean all the members of the Church, who come to the monastery in order to be closer to God. Rich or poor, they are not ordinary guests; Saint Benedict gives them religious teaching and invites them to pray.

A special chapter of the Rule is dedicated to *'travelling monks'* (*RB* 61). God can send these travelling brethren to *criticise or point something out* to the community, *reasonably* and *with humble charity*. The Abbot should take their opinion into account and perhaps even invite such a brother to fix his stability in the monastery.[90] In contrast, the *rich* are given *due honour* and nothing more; the persons concerned are obviously those whose spirit is foreign to that of the monastery.

In all these measures, however, Saint Benedict does no more than apply to new circumstances the traditional principle of receiving the guest as Christ. What is peculiar to him is his allowing the guests to associate with the community. As they *are never looking in a monastery*,[91] they are its 'regular members', not as part of the stable community but passing through; they are a symbol of the risen Christ. The Rule asks the community to take part in their welcome and to harmonise its other duties with that of hospitality. Monks and guests are two faces of Christ: one opens and gives; the other knocks and makes himself a beggar. The monastery is the *house of God* because of this perfect presence of Christ as all in all, in the one who welcomes and in the one who is received.

The enclosure

The integration of the guests into the family of the monastery is nevertheless made possible only by a refinement of enclosure. We have seen in the monasteries belonging to various religions that men and

[89] *RB* 53: 15.
[90] *RB* 61: 4–5.
[91] *RB* 53: 16.

women have no access to the quarters where persons of the other sex live. The Buddhists have even, in the old texts, a surprising abundance of precautions, probably made necessary by the environment. Rather similar dispositions are found in Christian monasteries, more strict in the communities living in towns, which seemed to be more exposed to abuses, than those in the countryside. The example of the Desert Fathers show that monks keep this distance to protect themselves more from thoughts than from persons. Hence the precautions taken to avoid those coming from outside using words which may be harmful for others.[92]

Saint Benedict enters into this tradition; the community has to keep its identity of silence, prayer and peace; the doorkeeper does not allow everybody to come in; the community keeps its timetable and its ascetic practices; the brethren who are taking care of the guests, in the kitchen or in the guest house, receive the necessary help. Use of speech is controlled: the guest receives the word of God in the divine office, and the *wise* word given with the *warmth of charity* by the doorkeeper and by the monk who *sits with him*.[93] Gossip and occasional encounters are replaced by a kind word. Peace is the fruit of a struggle; the monk has to keep purity of life – all the more demanding in that he aims to stay in Christ's presence and help others to share in it.

If the monk has to *set a guard to his mouth*,[94] a material enclosure is also necessary to preserve his identity, and for the benefit of those who come to visit him. As we have seen when speaking of the vows, Saint Benedict associates the idea of enclosure with that of stability. Permanence in a place is the sign of perseverance in the effort of seeking God. For him the monastery is *a school of the Lord's service*, thus the monk must not *flee* from the difficulty but,

> *persevering in his teachings in the monastery till death, let us share the sufferings of Christ through patience, and so deserve also to share in his kingdom ...*
> *Now the workshop in which we make diligent use of all these tools is the enclosure of the monastery combined with stability in the community.*[95]

These quotations of the beginning of the Rule show well how in *RB*, the idea of enclosure is linked with that of stability in the monastery, with the purpose of searching for God, the one conditioning the other. Nevertheless, if the enclosure prevents lay people from interfering in

[92] *RB* 67: 5.
[93] *RB* 66: 1; 4; 53: 8.
[94] *RB* 6: 1.
[95] *RB Prol.* 45 ... 50; 4: 78.

the life of the community, with its rhythm, its ascesis and its silence, this protection is not a selfish withdrawal. All the brethren who are directly engaged in the service of visitors should show, by their attitude full of *gentleness, fear of God and warm charity*, that they are being received into *the house of God*. The community itself, as a body, participates in this welcome, and accepts the guest as regular participant in the divine office and meals. The enclosure, giving thus both distance and participation, is the best means of allowing the guest to enter into the atmosphere of silence, prayer, and listening to the Word, which in turn, will lead him to God.

Saint Benedict does not speak of giving work to transient people. Participation in the brethren's activity was natural when the visitors were monks; it was less appropriate when the guests were mostly lay persons coming to pray.

By its hospitality and its enclosure, the monastery is, so to say, on the margins of the world, separated but not cut off from it. Solitude and communion in the monastery witness to the fact that human life is communion with God and with men. The community listens to, and brings to God, the unceasing call of the world, a world in which, at last, all religions are starting to meet.

BENEDICTINE HOSPITALITY AND INTERRELIGIOUS DIALOGUE

We have seen how Christian monastic hospitality, guided always by the evangelical principle of receiving the guest as Christ himself, has evolved in the course of time, according to the needs of the different kinds of visitors turning up at the monastery door.

For the last few years, Christian monks, and those of other religions, have started to come closer to each other, encouraged by the Church, for monasticism is *like a bridge between religions*[96] for mutual comprehension.

A first condition for dialogue is that all parties involved know their own doctrine. On this point, Christian monasteries can perhaps receive something from the Buddhists' zeal for well-organised teaching for guests within their monasteries. But this teaching needs to answer the questions of visitors who have only a vague idea of the teachings of various religions. Mutual information is thus necessary to understand and guide those who come. It supposes study and personal contacts.

---

[96] Cardinal Pignedoli's letter to the Abbot Primate Rembert Weakland (1973) *Bulletin, Secretariatus pro non Christianis*, 67, 1988, XXXIII/1.

These mutual relations brought about encounters and *Spiritual Exchanges* between Christian monks and others belonging to various religions, and also led some of their followers to visit monasteries. Pope John Paul II has explicitly requested Saint Benedict's disciples to apply the chapters of *RB* on hospitality to interreligious dialogue. Receiving some of them who had organised an encounter with Zen monks, he said:

> *Your specific contribution to this initiative does not consist merely in maintaining an explicit dialogue, but also in promoting a deep spiritual encounter, because your life is above all dedicated to silence, prayer and the witness of community life. You can do much through hospitality. Opening your houses and your hearts, as you have done, these last few days, you follow well the tradition of your spiritual father, Saint Benedict. With your brother monks, coming from all over the world and from various religious traditions, you apply the chapter of the Rule concerning the reception of the guests. In doing so, you offer a setting in which an encounter of spirits and hearts may take place. This encounter is characterised by the sharing of a sense of brotherhood in the unique human family, opening the way to an ever-deeper dialogue.*[97]

The Rule describes the laws of hospitality in a way that fits exactly the situation of an interreligious encounter.[98] First of all, the guest is received for his own sake: *As soon as anyone knocks ... [the door-keeper] should speedily and with the warmth of charity attend to the enquirer.*[99] This attitude of attention and care expresses well the driving force of the hospitality that the passing guest receives: the host listens to him and anticipates his desires. The welcome is always personal; it respects the guest with his religious and cultural background, receiving him without preconceived ideas or hidden motivations of selfish profit. The discreet incantation of a ritual – like that of the Japanese *Way of Tea* – allied with the quality of presence, in an atmosphere of silence and peace, gives the guest the favourable conditions for a more profound self-discovery.

Saint Benedict invites his guest to share the food of his house, a symbolic gesture that leads beyond superficial words, and invites the parties to ask of each other the reasons for living their faith. Sincerity and mutual respect in exchange allow each one to explain his convictions frankly, without arrogance or proselytising, respecting in others

---

[97] *Osservatore Romano*, 10/09/87. *Il dialogo interreligioso nel magisterio pontificio* No. 592.

[98] Cf. P. F. DE BETHUNE, *Par la foi et l'hospitalité, Essai sur la rencontre des religions*, pp. 28–39. The following paragraphs summarise this text.

[99] *RB* 66: 3.

the zone of mystery which gives them their own identity. So despite differences true friendship can grow, based on sharing the same spiritual quest, each one opening a space in his heart for the other person: this is the *Emptiness* of Buddhism, and the *Kenosis* of the selfish ego for the Christian.

This self-forgetfulness gives the meeting the dimension of an encounter with God. All the religions feel that hospitality is not only a dialogue between guest and host; the Latin *humanitas* can only be fully understood in the context of the Divine, uniting men among themselves and making them *brothers in the human family*, as the Pope put it.

In the ceremonial of *RB*, the guest is led to prayer. Respectful attention to the mystery of each religion avoids all syncretism, and beyond words and rites, which most of the time remain mysterious for the non-initiated, a true communion of thoughts takes place in the silence of prayer. God becomes the one who receives both parties, inviting them to come ever closer to him in the depth of their hearts.

Hospitality and enclosure together integrate the guest into the community and enable him to share its search for God. This results in a mutual increase in fervour, by way of shared study, meditation, friendship and peace.

CHAPTER XV

KOINONIA: FRATERNAL LIFE IN COMMUNITY

Saint Benedict writes at the end of his Rule of relations among members of the community. These chapters provide a preview of the summit of the mountain, so to speak, prior to the moment when the community will be reunited forever at the heavenly banquet. This Christian viewpoint will allow us to approach those of other religions with more clarity.

1. FRATERNAL RELATIONS IN HINDUISM

Community life did not develop to any great extent in Hindu monasticism, but the texts describing it indicate some form of mutual relationships among the members of its various groups.

The *Laws of Manu*

Monastic training, as described in its primitive form by the *Laws of Manu*, is no different from the formation given to all the boys of the same age and caste. Its natural milieu was the guru's family. The precepts on common life given in that situation concern both normal family life and monastic life. The guru and his family were held in great respect, since

> He teaches the divine science [union with Brahman] contained in the sacred books ... [Knowledge which is] the true birth, not subject to old age and death ... The guru, the father, the mother, the elder brother – these persons should never be treated with contempt by a novice, even when he feels he has been maltreated ... On every occasion, he should do what is pleasing to the guru, the father, the mother ... A respectful

devotion to the will of these three persons is recognised as the most
eminent devotion ... Indeed, they represent the three worlds, the three
orders, the three Sacred Books, the three fires ... one who respects these
three persons respects all his duties [and shall obtain the final reward].[1]

The guru, in the spiritual order, and the father and mother, in the
natural order, represent the whole universe, which, according to the
Hindu thinking, is full of the divine, and maintained in order by
means of sacrifices (the fires). The respect due to them goes through
them to the Divinity, the Absolute being that is their origin. This
respect is expressed by signs of deference, such as avoiding sitting
down at the same time as the guru, standing up when greeting him,
speaking with respect, not only to the guru but to any person, with
the special nuance required by caste and kinship. A special discretion
is recommended towards women.[2]

The novice has to carry out ordinary domestic chores: drawing
water, bringing flowers and all that is necessary for cult and meditation, collecting firewood, keeping up the fire, and begging for food.
In return for the teaching given by the guru, the novice is obliged to
be zealous in study:

> *Even if he has not received an order from the guru, the novice should*
> *apply himself with zeal and study, and strive to satisfy his venerable*
> *master.*[3]

When the ascetic has taken up the life of a hermit, he is freed from
his social duties, but he has to enter into communion with the whole
universe, and practise non-violence in everything. He walks carefully,
and filters his water in order to avoid killing even the smallest insect.
But he must also avoid hurting others by his words, and *purify them*
by truth. He should also

> *bear with patience insulting words, despise nobody and not nurse a*
> *grudge ... He should not lose his temper with an angry man; if he is*
> *insulted he should answer calmly ... meditating with delight on the*
> *Supreme Self (Paramatman) ... may he live here below in waiting for*
> *the eternal bliss.*[4]

The main concern of these laws is to put the novice, and later the
monk, in harmony with his surroundings and with the universe,

[1] MANU, 2: 114–118; 140; 148; 157; 193–202; 225–233.
[2] MANU, 2: 122–139; 210–222.
[3] MANU, 2: 182–191.
[4] MANU, 6: 46–49; 65–66.

creating the interior peace necessary for union with the Absolute. The community as such is considered only to the extent to which it may help an advance towards the Infinite or, on the contrary, prevent it. This tendency is still more pronounced in the *Samnyâsa Upanishad* which speaks of the wandering solitary, the last stage of Hindu monastic life.

The *Samnyâsa Upanishad*

The *Brihat Samnyâsa Upanishad* declares that to receive disciples for one's own sake is one of the six ways of perdition for the ascetic.[5] Similarly, one of the hermit's qualities is not to sit down with another, and not to take on disciples:

> *Like a dumb man, let him show the Self to men by his vision of the Self (only).*[6]

He masters his passions in himself and in his relations with others precisely so that he can find union with the Self:

> *Let him leave behind desire, cupidity, disorders, drunkenness, hostility, pride, arrogance, selfishness, envy, pretensions, self-will, hatred, joy, impatience, and the sense of self ... Let him turn away from riches and women, observe chastity, non-possession, non-violence, and truth, carefully controlling his senses, and living without attachment ... established in the contemplation of* Brahma-pranava [That is the sound 'Om', as an expression of Brahman].[7]

Neither solitude in the forest nor community life has any value in itself; only union with the Absolute is regarded as important:

> *Union with the Self, when truly achieved, is what makes the monastery.*[8]

Nevertheless, beside the traditional asceticism whose final stage is the wandering beggar who has left everything, organised communities were developed, especially from the eighth century with Shankara. But even before him and until our own time, the *Bhakti* (devotion) movement had groups of ascetics devoted to Vishnu or Shiva.

---

[5]   *Samnyâsa Up.* 101–102, UR, p. 388.
[6]   *Nâradaparivrâjaka Up.* V. 49–50, UR, p. 303.
[7]   *Paramahamsa Up.* 3, UR, p. 343.
[8]   *Nirvâna Up.* 33; *Maitreya Up.* 16, UR, pp. 237 and 398.

The *Bhakti* tradition

The followers of the *Bhakti* (way of devotion) found generally their inspiration in the *Bhagavad Gita* (written in the first or second century BC). This book emphasises the *Bhakti* as a privileged way to the Absolute. But poets, who saw union with the Absolute as love and self-gift, animated the groups of devotees. The presence of this Absolute, acknowledged in others, meant that more consideration was given to relations between the people in community life.

The first devotees of Shiva showed the love of God in love for humanity. The *Tirukkural* of Tiruvalluvar (seventh century) presents the love for Shiva as the essential source of family life and of human relationships. The ascetic should also have a compassionate love for all human beings. At the same period, Campantar said that the love of God frees a person from the six enemies – sensuality, hatred, envy, desire, pride, enmity – which prevent union with God.[9]

We should note the *Lingayat* or *Virashivite* among the first devotees of Shiva. These professed a belief in the equality of all human beings, based on the divine presence residing in each of them.

In the tenth century the *Sandilya Bhakti Sutra* taught that the signs of the true *Bhakti* are the acknowledgement of God's presence in all things, abstinence from anger, covetousness and impure thoughts.[10] A little later, the *Narada Bhakti Sutra* allude to a kind of community life among certain groups, whose members encourage each other in speaking of the Lord among themselves, and in singing his praises. Narada himself says that he was converted to the *Bhakti* when he was young by contact with some of these ascetics, who were going from pilgrimage to pilgrimage in order to sing the praises of Shiva:

To listen to and repeat the glories of the Lord, even in daily life ... to speak about him with emotion and tears ... this is what purifies the world.[11]

In *Bhakti* literature in general, the love of God destroys the passions and implies non-violence, so that the disciple may become pure and reach union with God.[12] All these authors, following the *Bhagavad*

---

9   M. DHAVAMONY, *Love of God according to Shaiva Siddanta*, Oxford 1971, Tirukkural, p. 25; Campantar, p. 143.
10 M. DHAVAMONY, ibid. p. 85; *Sandilya*, 57–59.
11 *Nârada Bhakti Sûtra*, 37; 68.
12 The idea of the love of God as purifying the disciple is found in the medieval poets: Manikkavacakar in the ninth century, Tirukkalirrupatiyar, twelfth century, Tiravarutpayam of Umapati, fourteenth century. They speak a little of the relationship with others, but always in the sense of a personal purification. Cf. M. DHAVAMONY, op. cit. p. 158 ff.

Gita, consider external actions (and thus relations with others) as the lowest but also the most fundamental degree of the *Bhakti*, while the superior degrees are those concerned with inner devotion. The same classification is found among the movements that gave birth to the present ashrams. Radhakrishna sees the *company of the holy men* as the lowest degree of *Bhakti*.[13] Shri Aurobindo, in similar fashion, puts the *spirit of equality* at the basis of love for the Supreme Self, present in everything:

> *The crown of this equality is love, founded on knowledge, fulfilled in action, extended to all things and beings; a vast, absorbing, and all-containing love for the divine Self, which is Creator and Master of the universe.*[14]

Hinduism thus acknowledges the love of God, but mostly as directed towards the individual; what is done to one person is not necessarily considered as done to God. The community is principally the place to find a spiritual master or guru. Relationships between its members are understood as mutual support and as a means of encouraging one another in fervour. Nevertheless, the Hindu tradition as a whole underlines very strongly the necessity of a respectful and delicate love for the neighbour, as a condition of union with the Absolute, because It is present in all things.

2. THE BUDDHISTS

We have already seen that the Buddhists promoted an atmosphere of peace and compassion for all in their communities, to help the spiritual journey. The organisation of regular Chapters (*uposatha*) in each house aimed mainly to strengthen the concord between the monks, as well as with the neighbours. But the formula of the monastic vows shows that the community *as such* has as much importance as the Buddha himself in the Buddhist system. Indeed, according to the monastic Rule known as the *Vinaya*, the monk, entering monastic life in the novitiate and at his profession *takes refuge*, that is, puts all his trust *in the Buddha, the Dharma and the Sangha*. The Buddha is the teacher of the doctrine, the *Dharma* is the law or the way he has taught, and the *Sangha* is the community of his disciples.

---

[13] M. DHAVAMONY, *The Bhakti Experience in Contemporary India* in RELIGIOUS EXPE-RIENCE, ITS UNITY AND DIVERSITY, Bangalore 1981, pp. 185–204.

[14] AUROBINDO, *Essays on the Gita*, Pondicherry, 1970, p. 321, quoted by M. DHAVAMONY, *The Bhakti exper.* p. 193.

What is the *Sangha*?

Etymologically the word *Sangha* means 'to come together', or 'the assembly'. In the ancient texts it designates first of all the assembly of the saints, the *Arhats*, those who are perfectly purified, ready to enter *Nirvana*. Then, by extension, the monks are made part of it, for they walk in the same way; and finally, all the Buddhists who practise, at least from time to time, some of the monastic vows are considered as part of it.

Commenting on this *taking refuge*, the *Abhidharma*, a work of philosophy, another volume of the Buddhists' sacred books, thus describes the *Sangha*:

> *The Community (Sangha) of the Lord's [Buddha] disciples is well behaved, upright, and correct. The four pairs of men, the eight persons[15] – these form the Community of the Lord's disciples. Worthy are they of offerings, worthy of hospitality, worthy of gifts, worthy of respectful salutation, they, without equal in all the world of the meritorious.[16]*

The first quality underlined in the description of the *Sangha* is what we would call holiness. It is also one of the marks of the Church (One, holy ... etc.). But, in Christianity, the Church is holy because it is redeemed and purified by Christ's blood. The Buddhist monk sanctifies himself *by his own efforts* and thus accumulates merits, burning away the weight of the bad *Karma* that prevents him from entering *Nirvana*.

The *Sangha* is holy because it is the assembly of the saints, those who are now struggling, together with all the masters of the past who continue to guide them by their examples and their writings. This conception is also close to the Christian idea of religious family. The Buddhist doctrines, and some powers, are transmitted from master to disciple, from the Buddha down to our own time. Since it is the assembly of the saints, the *Sangha* participates in some way in their holiness. It becomes a guide and a universal law, like the Buddha and the *Dharma*, and so it also joins the Absolute, *Nirvana*.

The *Sangha* defines the monk and the disciples

The *Sangha* is also concretely the monastic community that receives the novice, that is, as we have seen, the assembly of monks who

---

[15] These *pairs of men* are the perfect ones and those who, at various degrees, are close to perfection.
[16] *Abhidharmakosha* of Vasubadu, 9: 241–242, E. CONZE, *Buddhist Scriptures*, p. 183.

educate him and help him to understand the way of the Buddha and make progress in it. This community gives the monk his identity; through it he belongs to an established school of Buddhism after his monastic profession. The monasteries thus create a precise spiritual lineage. Masters who in some branches of Buddhism are like spiritual fathers, whose disciples will depend on them all their life, transmit their traditions. Relations in the community are governed by its superior.

With regard to the lay people, the monastery defines the religious group to which they belong. Its community is worthy of offerings and of respect: being composed of virtuous men, the gifts made to it are like a seed planted in a fertile field; they produce more merits than if they were offered to any individual person.

The monk in the *Sangha*

The text of the *Abhidarma* describes the well-trained monk in his community:

> *For a disciple who has been delivered, whose thought is calm, there is nothing to be added to what has been done, and naught more remains for him to do. Just as a rock of one solid mass remains unshaken by the wind, even so, neither forms nor sounds nor smells, nor tastes, nor contacts of any kind, neither desired nor undesired dharma, can agitate such a one. Steadfast is his thought; his deliverance is gained.*[17]

We see here the qualities of the *Arhat*, ready to enter *Nirvana*. The *Dhammapada* specifies that this perfect mastery over thoughts and passions is acquired by life in community:

> *Patience and endurance are the highest asceticism.*
> *Liberation [Nirvana] is supreme, say the Buddhas.*
> *Who hurts another is not religious.*
> *Who molests another is not religious.*
> *To avoid insulting the others, hurting the others,*
> *To restrict oneself according to the fundamental code of discipline,*
> *To moderate oneself in food, to live in a solitary place,*
> *To practise the high states of consciousness –*
> *That is the teaching of the Buddha.*[18]

The High States of conscience (*Brahma Vihara*) that seem to represent the summit of the monastic discipline in community life are four:

[17] Ibid.
[18] *Dhammapada*, 184–185.

benevolence (*Metta*), compassion (*Karuna*), joy and sympathy (*Mudita*), and equanimity (*Upekka*). Countless texts and methods of meditation speak of these virtues and invite monks to *radiate them in the whole world*. Let us quote only a passage of the *Metta Sutta*, or Sûtra of Benevolence:

> *May all beings be happy! May no one deceive another nor despise any being, no matter how small it may be! May no one, by anger or hatred, wish evil on another! As a mother risks her life to watch over and protect her only child so, with unlimited thought, should he cherish every living being, love the whole world, above, below and all around, without limitation, with infinite benevolent goodness.*[19]

These principles apply obviously to the monk's daily life. The *Vinaya* relates the words of the Buddha visiting some disciples living in small groups during the rainy season:

> *I hope that you, O disciples, live on friendly terms with everybody, living harmoniously like milk and water, looking at each other with eyes full of affection ... full of mutual respect and consideration, having different bodies but living in union of thought.*[20]

Elsewhere the Buddha insists that speaking to one another is an important means of keeping harmony in the community.[21] The monks assembled also to recite sacred texts, and for meditation, but their presence at these exercises does not have the importance given to it by Christians. When formation is over, this participation is left optional, under the control of the spiritual master. So the *Sangha* mainly fulfils a role of education; it fosters a common identity and develops the dispositions of benevolence and compassion that are essential for breaking the cycle of rebirths.

Benevolence and compassion

For the Buddhist, benevolence is an interior disposition by which the mind becomes used to forming non-violent thoughts, and is rid of selfish desires which bring about the need for rebirth. The practical application of this follows as it may, with patient but non-violent effort, because non-violence is applied also to oneself. Benevolence leads one also to avoid judging the neighbour's intention when he is seen doing something wrong, and in this way the disciple also discovers how to practise compassion.

---

[19] *Trans. from* MOHAN WIJAYARATNA, *Sermons du Bouddha*, p. 34, n. 5.
[20] *Vinaya*, 1: 158; 351; ibid. p. 174.

Compassion is an essential virtue for achieving Nirvana. It implies avoiding the killing or hurting of even the smallest living being. It is said in the *Swurnarprabhasa* that, in one of his previous lives, the Buddha, as a young prince strolling about in the jungle, came upon a tigress dying of hunger surrounded by her five seven-day-old cubs. He cut his throat so that she might drink his blood and then eat him. He explains his motivations:

> *Now the time has come for me to sacrifice myself! For a long time I have served this putrid body ... Today I will use it for a sublime deed. Then it will act for me as a boat that helps me to cross the ocean of birth and death.*[22]

Compassion leads also, as we have seen, to the ideal of the *Bodhisattva*, who offers his merits to allow the others to reach the Nirvana. But no communication between human beings is foreseen after death; the self disappears in the Ocean of Peace.

Buddhists and Hindus alike thus consider the dispositions of non-violence and universal compassion necessary for the union with the Absolute. But the Buddhists acknowledge a particular value in the community itself. The *Sangha* is the assembly of those who, in the past and the present, follow or have followed the way of the *Dharma*. The *Sangha* thus becomes the depository of the law and its teacher. Along with the Buddha and the *Dharma*, it becomes for monks a trustworthy way to the Infinite.

3. FRATERNAL LIFE IN THE CHRISTIAN TRADITION

Though some Hindus recognise the presence of the Absolute in all human beings, it is only with Christ, because of his unique position as God-Man, that the love for the neighbour is referred directly to God.

> *As you did to one of the least of these my brethren, you did it to me;* and also *This is my commandment: that you love one another, as I have loved you.*[23]

This *commandment of the Lord* (1 *Jn.* 4: 21) strongly influenced the

---

[21] *Kakacûpama-sutta*, ibid. p. 175 ff.
[22] *Swarnarprabhasa*, 206 ff., E. CONZE, *Buddhist Scr.* pp. 25–26.
[23] *Mt.* 25: 40; *Jn.* 15: 12.

first Christians of Jerusalem: *They had one soul and one heart* (*Acts* 4: 32) and their example has extended to Christian monasticism.

The Desert Fathers

In his youth, Saint Antony used to visit the ascetics of his region,

> striving to learn for his own advantage what was best in each one of them. He admired the kindness of one, the patience and charity of another ... In all, he observed the love of Christ, united with fraternal charity.[24]

Later he would teach his own disciples that

> From our neighbour comes life or death: If we win our brother, we win God, but if we scandalise our brother, we sin against Christ.[25]

The Desert Fathers had little common life, but their neighbour would remain present in their thoughts and they scrutinised the innermost recesses of the human heart so as to purify it by charity. The first step was to avoid judging the others. Abba Macarius said:

> Do not harm anybody and do not judge. Observe that, and you will be saved.[26]

Abba Isaiah said:

> To avoid judging one's neighbour, and to despise oneself, thus the conscience will find rest.

Many Fathers adopt a similar approach, and a full chapter of the Systematic Collection of the *Apophthegmata* is dedicated to it.[27] On a more positive note, the desert monk was asked to forgive others' weaknesses from his heart, and not to despise the guilty, but acknowledge himself to be a sinner:

> Abba Isaac said: I never allowed one thought against a brother who had grieved me to enter my cell, and I took pains to avoid a brother going back to his cell with a thought against me.[28]

[24] VA, 4.
[25] *Apophthegmata*, Antony, 9.
[26] *Apophthegmata*, Macarius, 28.
[27] *Apophthegmata*, Syst. Col. 9: 4; cf. Poemen, 173; Theodore of Pherme, 8; Macarius the Cit. 2, etc.
[28] *Apophthegmata*, Isaac, 9.

Abba Theodore of Pherme said similarly:

There is no virtue comparable with that of not despising.[29]

It is not enough, however, to watch one's thoughts; words also have to be controlled. Abba Poemen said:

If someone hears a word that upsets him, and if he, though able to answer a similar word, struggles not to say it; or if he is ill-treated and bears it without taking revenge; this one gives his life for his neighbour.[30]

To avoid speaking evil of others is necessary, but it is equally good to know how to thank, console and to praise them for the good that is in each one:

When an elder is heard praising his neighbour more than himself, he has reached a high degree of perfection, because it is perfection to praise the other more than oneself.[31]

Finally, to the words should be added acts of charity. Abba Pambo said:

Be merciful to all, because mercy gives us security in the presence of God.[32]

The whole of chapter 17 in the Systematic Collection of the *Apophthegmata* is on charity. Let us quote one of them in conclusion:

An elder said: Let us acquire the main virtue, charity. Fasting is nothing, late nights are nothing, and labour is nothing, if charity is not there. Indeed it is written: 'God is charity' (1 *John* 4: 16).[33]

Saint Pachomius

Saint Pachomius applied the principles of the Desert Fathers to a life lived in community. The governing principle of his organisation is mutual love that is devoted and peaceful; it sees God in the neighbour and makes *communion* in the community. This is the *holy Koinonia* (or fellowship), defined by the word of Pachomius:

[29] *Apophthegmata*, Theodore of Pherme, 13; cf. Pior, 3; Poemen, 92.
[30] *Apophthegmata*, Poemen, 116.
[31] *Apophthegmata*, Matoes, 7; cf. Poemen, 4; Hyperechius, 4.
[32] *Apophthegmata*, Pambo, 14.
[33] *Apophthegmata*, Syst. Col. 17: 31.

May all give profit to you, so that you give profit to all.

This *communion* implies encouraging one another in doing good, renouncing one's own ambitions, and giving up material possessions that create divisions. The model is *the life of the Apostles in the presence of the Lord of all.*[34] To be the cause of sadness to a brother is a fault:

> *The one who is in discord with his brother is at war with God; and he who lives in peace with his brother lives also in peace with God ... Be of one heart with your brother ... Let us love all human beings and we shall be friends of Jesus, the friend of mankind.*[35]

Pachomius adds in one of his letters:

> *Let us unite together in charity, carrying each other's burdens, like Christ, in order to be united in the future life.*[36]

His disciple Orsisius uses the same themes in his *Testament*: the strong ought to bear the weaknesses of the others; no one should seek what they like, but rather what is pleasing to the neighbour, seeing Christ in him; the brethren should become reconciled before sunset, remembering the request of the Our Father; they should imitate the kindness of the saints, and practise the Beatitudes, according to the word of the Lord: *This is my commandment: that you love one another as I have loved you (John* 15: 12). Orsisius concludes:

> *I say this to you because God has entrusted to me the direction of your life and that of the flock of the Holy Koinonia. Now I entrust you to God.*[37]

So the Pachomian *Koinonia* designates not only the monks as a whole but especially the link of fraternal communion which unites them. Thus, endowed with a very rich meaning, the word *koinonia*, fellowship, became a technical expression of the monastic vocabulary.

Saint Basil

We have already seen several times how Saint Basil was constantly concerned with the repercussions on the community of the actions of each of its members. His *Long Rules* begin with the two great divine

---

[34] THEODORE, *Catech.* CSCO. 159, p. 38.
[35] THEODORE, ibid. pp. 15, 2, 21.
[36] PACHOMIUS, *Let.* 2.
[37] ORSISIUS, *Testament*, 54–56.

commandments: to love God and one's neighbour.[38] He takes as a basis for monastic, as well as for Christian life the words of the Gospel:

> *A new commandment I give you: that you love one another.*[39]

It is this that convinces him that community life is superior to the eremitical or solitary way:

> *It is the will of God that we need each other, so that we may be united to one another, as the Scripture admonishes ... We are one body, having Christ as our head and are members of each other; and, with each doing his part, we begin the construction of a single body in the Holy Spirit, but this only by concord ... The brethren should thus treat each other as the members of the same body.*[40]

The *Short Rules* consider various problems, always basing the answers on the Gospel and on the example of the Lord. They quote *Mt.* 5: 23–24 several times, and comment on it:

> *If you remember that your brother has something against you, leave your gift there before the altar and go; first be reconciled to your brother ...*

to explain that we should grieve if we have been the cause of sadness for another brother. Similarly, Saint Basil exhorts us to mutual forgiveness, because to make another sad is also harmful for prayer.[41] Scandals, quarrels, and anger should be avoided;[42] and the brothers should not only

> *render good for evil but give consolation to one another, so as to lead the heart to full knowledge of the truth; they should help and support the feeble with the kind of solicitude which allows the strong to give strength to the weak.*[43]
>
> *Let them love, even as far as giving up their life ... let them be inwardly disposed to die for the sinners as well as for the just, without distinction, for God, says the Apostle, has showed his love for us in that, while we were yet sinners, Christ died for us (Rom. 5: 8–9) ...*
>
> *Above all let us practise the first and greatest of all the commandments: To love the Lord God with all your heart ... and the second: to*

[38] BASIL, LR 2–3.
[39] BASIL, LR 2, quoting *Jn.* 13: 34.
[40] BASIL, LR 7; LR 24.
[41] BASIL, SR 40; 42; 231; 265.
[42] BASIL, SR 64; 66; 68; 165; 243–244.
[43] BASIL, SR 177–178.

love your neighbour ... Moreover, try to resemble the Lord who said:
I leave you a new commandment, that is, to love one another as I love
you.[44]

You are told: 'Be kind and tenderhearted to one another' (Eph. 4:
32),[45] *so that your fraternal charity may be zealous and warm.*

Good example and zealous charity are expected from all, especially
from the elders:

When they are in good health, they show their zeal by giving a living
example of the whole observance; when they are infirm, by living in a
state of soul whereby their appearance and demeanour show that they
believe themselves to be in the sight of God ... and they thus manifest
the charity which the apostle requires: 'charity is patient, benevolent'
... All this can be realised in a body that is weak.[46]

Cassian

John Cassian lived for a long time in Egypt with the Desert Fathers,
and his writings show that he is concerned, like them, with the monk's
personal progress. In Book 4 of his *Institutes*, he speaks of the
novices' training and outlines the particular virtues that are to be cultivated:

Humility of heart; constant unity among the brethren; firm and lasting
concord, and long perseverance in the monastery.[47]

Further, he praises the spirit of faith that leads the brethren to serve
each other, in small ways,

like putting things in order, making repairs, cleaning an object, filling
the jug of drinking water ... for all these, they will receive a reward
from the Lord.[48]

He quotes as an example the story of some brethren working in the
kitchen, who went scouring the desert to collect branches and thorns,
a painstaking and laborious operation, in order to prepare the usual
cooked meal for the brethren.[49] Among the virtues to be practised, he
insists on the habit of not judging others, and concludes by saying:

[44] BASIL, SR 186; 163.
[45] BASIL, SR 242.
[46] BASIL, SR 200.
[47] CASSIAN, *Inst.* 4: 8.
[48] CASSIAN, *Inst.* 4: 20.
[49] CASSIAN, *Inst.* 4: 21.

I have understood that the monk is himself implicated in the faults of those he dares to judge and criticise.[50]

His remedy for anger is reconciliation, and forgetfulness of the offence, without which the Lord cannot accept our prayer.

Our avoidance of anger should not depend on whether or not the others are perfect, but should rather derive from our own virtue, acquired not through others' patience, but through our personal forbearance.

Searching together to find the truth, without relying on one's own judgement, develops good mutual understanding.[51]

Saint Augustine

The Rule of Saint Augustine is entirely based on the text of the *Acts of the Apostles* which it quotes in the opening lines:

The company of those who believed were of one heart and soul, and no one claimed that any of the things that he possessed was his own, but they held everything in common.[52]

This text also motivated Antony's decision to leave everything and dedicate himself to God. Augustine sees it as a prophetic call that assembles the monks, just as a trumpet calls the troops to battle:

Having heard this call, the brethren who wanted to live together rose up. This verse was their trumpet. It resounded in all the earth, and those who were divided assembled together; it was the cry of God, the clamour of the Holy Spirit, and a prophetic call.[53]

The Augustinian Rule can be divided into two parts, one outlining the principles of monastic life, the other drawing out the practical applications. The text from *Acts* we quoted above gives inspiration to the first part, and Saint Augustine comments on it at the beginning:

This is what we have laid down for you to observe in the monastery where you live: Before everything else – for it is the reason of your

---

[50] CASSIAN, *Inst.* 5: 30.
[51] CASSIAN, *Inst.* 7: 17. He comes back to the same topic in the *Conf.* 16: 8–11, where he quotes more explicitly *Mt.* 5: 23–24: '*If your brother has something against you, leave there your gift …*' because it is impossible to pray when maintaining grudges and sadness.
[52] *Acts* 4: 32.
[53] AUGUSTINE, *In Psalm.* 132, 2.

coming together – you must be unanimous, having but one heart and one soul turned towards God. There must be no talk among you of personal property; on the contrary, all shall be held in common, and from this common source each of you shall receive, according to his needs ... May you live thus in unity of heart and soul, and honour in each other the God whose temple you have become.[54]

The Holy Spirit, who is charity, makes possible this unity in peace, of which the Holy Trinity is the basis and the model. It is he who united the disciples at Pentecost, and who now attracts the hearts of the faithful to Christ, and unites them in him. Perfect union of hearts can be realised only in eternity, but Christ is already present in the Church. Monastic life is the expression of the Church's soul, rising towards the peace and unity of the celestial city. Saint Augustine illustrates this idea with an image taken from the stadium:

All the athletes join in the race at the stadium, but only one receives the prize; all the others go back defeated. But among us, this is not the case ... the one who arrives first waits for the last, so as to be crowned with him; for this contest is about charity, not about ambition. All those who run, love each other, and it is their love that makes the race.[55]

The Eucharist nourishes this union, as expressed by the *Amen* at the moment of receiving Holy Communion:

You reply 'Amen' to what you are [i.e. the Body of Christ] *thus indicating that you accept and approve it. Remember that the bread is not made of one grain, but of many ... and similarly the wine ...*[56]

In practice, unity is expressed by giving up the possession of material goods, thus making room for God in one's heart:

Let us indeed abstain, my brethren, from any form of private possession, or at least, from any attachment to them, if we cannot abstain from the possession itself. In doing this we shall make a space for God.[57]

Unity of hearts, care for the weak, and detachment: these are different aspects of the charity that should enfold everything. Saint Benedict borrowed from Saint Augustine all that has to do with the individual

[54] AUGUSTINE, *Rule*, I.
[55] AUGUSTINE, *In Ps.* 39.
[56] AUGUSTINE, *Serm.* 272: 1.
[57] AUGUSTINE, *Reg.* 6: 3.

brothers, their union in charity, sharing in common of goods, and the relationship between the Abbot and the monks.[58]

The *Rule of the Master*

This Rule follows the line of Cassian, and says very little about relationships between the brethren. Like him, the ladder of humility and perfection starts from fear and moves upward to charity. But we find charity recommended only in an exhortation given by the deans to their subordinates, inviting them to kindness, silence and charity, and asking them to avoid words of anger and to practise reconciliation.[59] Similarly the Abbot invites those who would like to succeed him to practise

> not hatred, but friendship; not falsehood, but charity; not anger, but peace; not quarrels, but patience.[60]

Fraternal charity will also lead a brother to visit the sick, and greet his brethren before going on a journey. But the Master feels that this virtue is so obviously required in the community that he does not see the need to speak about it. So his recommendations are mainly in regard to people outside the community, the guests, and persons met while travelling.[61]

Looking at the whole Christian tradition before Saint Benedict, the theme of fraternal charity occurs throughout, though it is considered from different viewpoints, which correspond to the two currents we have seen when speaking of the appointment of the superiors.

There is a vertical current which leads the community to God through the Abbot; it is present in the Desert Fathers, Cassian and the *Rule of the Master*, who consider the monk individually with his own dispositions towards others. To go towards the Lord is the common aim, which unites the brethren under the superior's direction. The Rule guides spiritual growth, and all help each other with fervour and charity, taking into account the diversity of the spiritual paths.

---

[58] The main passages where Saint Benedict is inspired by Saint Augustine are: in *RB* 3: 31, the attitude of the cellarer who has to comfort with a good word the brother to whom he cannot give what has been asked for; in *RB* 64, the recommendation to the Abbot to serve rather than to preside, to hate the vices, but love the brethren, to strive to be more loved than feared; with regard to material goods, an attitude of radical detachment, but of attention to the needs of each one (*RB* 33–34). Finally, in *RB* 52, Benedict requires, like Augustine, that the oratory be exclusively reserved for prayer, in order to foster the silent meditation of the monks.

[59] *RM* 11.

[60] *RM* 92.

[61] *RM* 27; 60; 71; 72.

The other current, called horizontal, is found with Saints Pachomius, Basil and Augustine. It considers the community as such, and recognises God's presence in each of its members; so what is done to one is done to Christ himself. The brethren thus strive to be kind and humble towards all, in imitation of him, and Christ is considered to be served in the other brethren. This presence of Christ in the monastery brings an atmosphere of love and peace, expressed and developed by tactfulness in relationships. The transformation of each person is brought about through his incorporation into the family of the community, and each can find harmony with God in listening to the brethren, and in loving and serving Christ in them.

4. THE COMMUNITY IN SAINT BENEDICT'S RULE

Saint Benedict's rule makes a synthesis of both these currents, in relation to the Abbot and the community. This is evident in many parts, but above all in the final chapters, which deal with fraternal relationships, and deserve our particular attention.

The monastery: meeting point between the love of the Lord and that of the brethren

The *Prologue* shows the Abbot as a spiritual father who indicates God's will, but who also preserves peace and order in the community, by protecting its weaker members. We have seen how the officers of the monastery help him in this role, so that

no one may be upset or saddened in the household of God.[62]

The community as such, and the horizontal relations between the brethren, are also discussed at the beginning of the Rule. In chapter 3, the Abbot and the community search together to find God's will, and it is acknowledged that *often* God speaks through the youngest members. Several of the *Tools of Good Works* (*RB* 4) describe these relations. At the beginning, they give positive directions that would be useful for all Christians:

To love one's neighbour as oneself;
To honour all men;

[62] *RB* 31: 18.

Not to do to another what one would not wish to have done to oneself;
To relieve the poor,
to visit the sick,
to give help in trouble,
to console the sorrowful
To speak with one's mouth the truth that lies in one's heart.[63]

After that come the defects to be avoided, by practising the opposite virtue:

Not to give way to anger ...
Not to abandon charity ...
Not to inflict any injury, but to suffer injuries patiently
To love one's enemies
Not to curse anyone who curses us, but instead to return a blessing ...
Not to cherish bitterness
Not to indulge in envy
Not to love quarelling
To flee vainglory.[64]

In conclusion, the tools that are more concerned with monastic life:

To revere the elders
To love the young
To pray for one's enemies in the love of Christ
After a quarrel to make peace with the other before sunset
And never to despair of God's mercy.[65]

The same attitude of humble patience is recommended in chapter 7 and, as in chapter 4, such generosity opens the monk up to a perspective of joy and love, things which are found already here below for those who follow the Lord with generosity:

The monk should not only say in words that he is inferior and less virtuous than all other men, but should really believe it in the depth of his heart ...
Thus when all these steps of humility have been climbed, the monk will soon reach that love of God which, being perfect, drives out all fear.[66]

When describing the monastery's organisation, Saint Benedict combines the hierarchical aspect of the community, headed by the

[63] *RB* 4: 1; 8–9; 14–16; 18–19; 28.
[64] *RB* 4: 22; 26; 30–32; 66–69.
[65] *RB* 4: 70–74.
[66] *RB* 7: 51; 67.

Abbot and his officers, with the concern of encountering Christ in each one of its members.

> *The cellarer is not to act without the Abbot's approval, and he must carry out his orders ... With all compassion he is to have care for the sick ... The care of the sick is to be given priority over everything else, so that they are indeed served as Christ would be served, since he said of himself, 'I was sick and you visited me,' and 'What you did to one of the least, you did to me'.*[67]

It is he also that is served in the guests, the poor and in all those who have some need or weakness:

> *The brethren should serve one another, and no one should be excused from kitchen duty except for sickness or because he is more usefully engaged elsewhere, because through this service the reward of an increase in charity is gained. For the weak, however, help should be provided so that this duty may not cause them dejection. Indeed all should have help according to the size of the community and the location ... [All] should serve one another in turn with charity.*[68]

The greatest sickness is that caused by sin. In this case, Saint Benedict asks even more insistently for collaboration between the Abbot and the whole community. Some elders are sent *to give unofficial consolation to their wavering brother ...* following *the loving example of the Good Shepherd ... who went after the one sheep that had gone astray.*[69] But the greatest remedy to be applied is *prayer [of the Abbot] combined with that of all the brethren that the Lord to whom nothing is impossible may work the salvation of the sick brother.*[70]

To be community-minded

One of the main novelties of Saint Benedict, as compared with the *Rule of the Master*, is his way of considering each monk as in some way responsible for the whole community. Even Saint Basil had been concerned about the repercussion of the actions of each brother on the others, but *RB* takes a still more general point of view, asking the Abbot not to act alone, but to bring the problems before the community, so that they may search together for the Lord's will, which *he often reveals to the younger.*[71]

[67] *RB* 31: 5, 9; 36: 1–3.
[68] *RB* 35: 1–6.
[69] *RB* 27: 3–8.
[70] *RB* 28: 4–5.
[71] *RB* 3: 3.

Saint Benedict feels that each monk should take an interest and an active part in the problems and decisions of the community. The officials are people with whom *the Abbot may be able to share his burdens with confidence*[72] and the care of the weak, so that *no one may be upset or saddened in the household of God.*[73] So all are to be community-minded, as members of one body, the Body of Christ, each one looking, not for his own advantage, but for the good of the house. All should feel responsible, not only for their own particular job, but for the whole community. Each activity is understood as a work done in the name of the community, and in common.

The result of this effort of mutual understanding and esteem is to give the community a creative dynamism. Each monk becomes sensitive to the action of the Holy Spirit on the others; his response is not a mere tolerance or a sterile refusal of his neighbours, but an effort to adapt himself to their needs. This striving is the source of progress for the whole community, and makes possible a collective creativity. This can be seen when personal initiatives aim at community progress, whether material or spiritual. They are not made at random, but by selecting what is good for all.

Thus in the whole Rule Saint Benedict weaves the community texture, twilling the warp of the love going to God through the Abbot, and the weft of fraternal links where each one finds Christ in the other. But this synthesis is still more evident in the last chapters of the Rule.

On the good zeal which monks ought to have (*RB* 71–73)

Fraternal relations, which unite the love of God with the love of the brethren, are one of Saint Benedict's constant concerns. The end of the Rule sees them being discussed once more, in a progression of thought that reminds us of the steps of humility. In chapter 63, the order of the community is settled according to a spiritual principle: seniority does not depend on age, but on *the time of their coming to the monastery.* The stress which this chapter puts on the respect of the *seniors*, can be partly explained by the fact that these could in fact be younger than others who joined after them. Nevertheless, respect for seniority is clearly underlined by the signs of respect and the modes of address to be used, as we will see further on with regard to the Abbot and the elders.

Then the Rule deals with the Abbot, prior and doorkeeper. Chapter

[72] *RB* 21: 3.
[73] *RB* 31: 19.

68, on difficulties in obedience, follows these, and throughout we see that the principle of authority still dominates. But Saint Benedict ends chapter 68 by asking his monks *lovingly to trust in God's aid, and so obey.* The following chapters show how relations among community members must blossom into fraternal love. Obedience is considered as a loving means of harmonising the entire human being with God's will; this explains why obedience is due not only to the Abbot, but to the whole community:

The goodness of obedience is not to be shown only through obedience to the Abbot, but the brethren should also obey each other, in the knowledge that by this path of obedience they will draw nearer God.[74]

Chapter 71 describes the relationship between seniors and juniors. More than merely giving due respect, charity goes beyond the rules of politeness, making use of a delicate concern in paying attention to the needs of each one. The seniors love the juniors and they, in turn, respect their elders, as chapter 4 had already indicated.[75]

Chapter 72 builds on these requirements by showing how *good zeal* makes the brother able to find God in all his relations with the community. Saint Benedict begins by explaining the nature of this zeal: it is opposed to the *evil zeal rooted in bitterness which separates from God and leads to hell.* On the contrary, the *good zeal* is full of love, it *separates from evil and leads to God and to life everlasting.*[76]

The Rule does not insist on the negative side of separation from evil; it is obvious that a true love of Christ implies rejection of its opposite, especially selfishness, which is directly contrary to the gift of self in charity. The *good zeal*, on the contrary, *is practised with the most ardent love.*[77]

In a series of sentences which remind us of Evagrius and of the Desert Fathers and, as with their sayings, could be followed by the words, *Do this, and you will be saved,* Saint Benedict shows the essential points of the way to God through the fraternal relations. It is good to look at them one by one:

They should forestall one another in paying honour.[78]

This sentence summarises what was said in chapter 4, on the relation-

[74] *RB* 71: 1–2.
[75] *RB* 4: 70–71.
[76] *RB* 72: 1–2.
[77] *RB* 72: 3.
[78] *RB* 72: 4.

ship between seniors and juniors.[79] Each one should recognise God's presence in others, and the particular gifts that define their vocation.

Love the young: this implies not being jealous of them, not despising them, not wanting to dominate them. *Revere the elders*: not to criticise them, but give them understanding and esteem. All this is nothing less than the Gospel message: *Do not judge*. The Christian attitude avoids judgement of the person. We may think that someone's action is not what it ought to be, but we must avoid imagining the motivations of the actions and condemning them. God alone can judge. Saint Benedict goes on:

> *They should with the greatest patience make allowance for one another's weaknesses, whether physical or moral. They should rival one another in practising obedience. No one should pursue what he thinks advantageous for himself, but rather what seems best for another.*[80]

To become aware that we can be a cause of suffering for others, and that on the other hand we share by patience in the suffering of Christ, may sometimes help us to bear each other's deficiencies. Similarly, to seek what is good for one of the brethren prevents us from taking pleasure in selfish satisfactions. To *make allowances for one another's weaknesses* means also to make up for others' misdeeds, helping them without despising or judging them. To be happy and proud of the qualities of our brethren is a sign of spiritual health; to acknowledge the good done by others is for them a source of hope and courage.

> *They should labour with chaste love at the charity of the brotherhood. They should fear God. They should love their Abbot with sincere and humble charity. They should prefer nothing whatever to Christ. And may he bring us all together to life everlasting.*[81]

These lines, which are the conclusion and the summit of the whole Rule, show Saint Benedict's insistence on fraternal love. The monk has a respectful love towards God, which also enfolds his Abbot and brethren; *all together* they go to God. The holiness of the monk is found not in the perfection of his observance, but in his love for God and neighbour. Saint Benedict repeats, in his own way, what Saint Paul had said:

> *Love is the fulfilling of the law.*[82]

[79] *RB* 4: 8; 70–71.
[80] *RB* 72: 5–7.
[81] *RB* 72: 8–12.
[82] *Rom.* 13: 8–10.

5. THE SPECIFIC CHRISTIAN CHARACTER OF *KOINONIA*

Koinonia based on the love of God

As we have just seen in *RB*, an essential characteristic of Christian community life is the response of love to a personal God who first loved us. The monk aims at union with God in love, and desires infinite beatitude in eternity. But already here below he lives in his presence, found both in the depth of his being and in the neighbour. The Christian love of God thus has its consequences in community life.

If we consider its vertical dimension, we find similarities between the various religions in the role of the spiritual master, which is to lead the disciple towards union with the Absolute. This union, however, is understood as fusion in Hinduism and Buddhism, whereas Christianity sees it as a relationship of love.

The horizontal dimension, however, reveals certain differences. Hinduism insists on mutual respect and the refusal of selfishness, and acknowledges the need for the practitioners to support and encourage one another. In Buddhism, an atmosphere of peace and mutual compassion is essential to the spiritual quest. For the Christian, harmony in the community fosters interior peace, but the presence of Christ in each person gives fraternal relationships eternal value: it makes them an act of love towards God himself. The neighbour becomes the sacrament and means of loving union with the Absolute. This personal relationship with Christ is, as we have seen, strongly underlined by Saint Benedict.[83]

Christian charity and Buddhist compassion

The virtue of charity, and the dispositions of *Brahma Vihara* – compassion, benevolence, etc. – still differ on several points.

First, in Christian charity, the emphasis is on the effort made to practise it. Without actions, faith and charity are *dead*.[84] Buddhism, on the contrary, insists on the inner dispositions. It strives to accustom the mind to think with compassion, in order to destroy the selfishness that brings the penalty of rebirth; hence the importance given to meditation. Salvation is in wisdom, and in the correct vision, which distinguishes the passing impermanent from the permanent or

[83] Cf. *RB Prologue*; chs. 4 and 7.
[84] *Jas.* 2: 17.

absolute value, which is present in all acts or things.

Nevertheless, these different points do also point to a common human basis. The Christian can learn from his Buddhist brother the importance of meditation as a means of unifying the human person and of fighting against a pharisaic behaviour, in which the external act does not correspond to an inner conviction. We see also how the methods of meditation on benevolence and compassion can also be useful to this end.

Another difference with Buddhism is that Christian charity, which unites man to God as his sovereign good and perfect beatitude, continues after death. *Charity will never come to an end,*[85] said Saint Paul. Human beings, members of Christ, enter into the eternal love that unites the divine persons. The Buddhist compassion, on the other hand, whose aim is to purify from selfishness, has no further purpose when this is achieved and Nirvana is attained.

The role of the community in the monk's life

When a person is received in a Buddhist monastery, his first impression is of its atmosphere of joyful kindness. Nevertheless, as we have said, he soon notices that attendance at community exercises does not have paramount importance. The *Sangha* is rather a milieu of education, which builds the monk's identity and fosters the interior dispositions necessary for getting out of the cycle of rebirth.

The Christian monks acknowledge these educative values, but they add a particular note, because for them the common exercises unite the brethren as members of the same body of Christ. *The community is built out of liturgical celebration, above all the eucharistic celebration and that of the sacraments.* The brethren, assembled together to listen to the word of God, and in fraternal charity, *become by that very action brothers and sisters.*[86] This assembly creates links that will blossom in eternity.

Another reason for the diversity of behaviour in Christian and Buddhist communities is the difference of their conception of human destiny. According to ancient Buddhism, human suffering here below impressed the Buddha. He indicated a way to relieve it and to reach eternal beatitude, but no relationship with others was envisaged in the world of eternal realities. The *wedding feast* of the Gospel,[87] symbol

---

[85]   1 *Cor.* 13: 8.

[86]   *Fraternal life in Community*, Nos. 11–14. Document of the CIVCSVA. As a whole this document shows community life as one of the most important means for the transformation of individuals into brothers and sisters, members of Christ.

[87]   Cf. *Mt.* 8: 11; 22: 1–4; 25: 1–13; *Lk.* 13: 29; 14: 15–20.

of the joy shared between *the members of God's family*,[88] does not exist in Buddhism. For Christians, community life is the preparation and anticipation of the eternal wedding where Christ, their head and spouse, *will lead them, all together*.

In conclusion, let us summarise the points common to the religions we have considered, noting the emphases of each faith.

For Hinduism, Buddhism and Christianity, non-violence, and the fight against selfishness and aggressive tendencies, are necessary preconditions, leading towards union with the Absolute. All these religions also admit a certain presence of the Absolute in human beings, though it is understood in various ways: *atman*, Buddha-nature, presence of God. Some Hindus acknowledge that this presence is a mutual love; the enthusiasm they show in singing about it can act as a stimulus for Christians. The Buddhists give pride of place to compassion, under the different forms of the *Brahma Vihara*, and insist on meditation to develop it. Christians may use these methods of meditation to unify the human person and reconcile exterior actions with inner convictions.

In each of these religions, the specific characteristics of their community life are seen above all in their differing perspectives on eternal life.

For Hinduism, all is centred on a personal union with the Divine, already present in the human being; the community is considered as a devotional incentive, or a school under a guru. The Buddhist *Sangha* is the educating environment, leading to the extinction of selfish desires and total liberation in Nirvana.

The Christian religious community strives to live ever more and more as brothers and sisters, as members of Christ, participating in his divine life by listening to his words, by prayer, by the sacraments and by universal charity.

Saint Benedict insists on mutual help as well as on the respect and attention due to each one, especially to the weakest, in whom Christ is especially present. He ends his Rule with an invitation to an attitude of humble and joyful trust in God:

> **Christ will bring us all together to life everlasting ... with [his] help fulfil this little Rule written for beginners; and then you will come at the end, under God's protection, to those heights of learning and virtue which we have mentioned above.[89]**

Let us note those words, *all together*, characteristic of Saint Benedict,

[88] *Eph.* 2: 19–22.
[89] *RB* 72: 12; 73: 8–9.

and the point of convergence in the Infinite that they indicate. The various religions say that the human being's fulfilment is to be found in an eternal union with the Absolute. Through community life, they help each other to progress in this union, by sharing their experiences and in cultivating harmonious relationships. For the Christian, all this is made possible only by his incorporation into Christ.

Saint Benedict's Rule: model of society

In writing his *little Rule for beginners*,[90] Saint Benedict, Abbot of Montecassino, had no idea of its being applied universally. His Rule, nevertheless, spread because of its intrinsic dynamism and value, first in Europe and then in all continents. Since the Middle Ages, it has defined the ideal of a society based on the Gospel, and called 'Christianity'.

Its basis is the respect of the human person – *'to honour all people'* – and above all the weak because in them, we worship and serve Christ.[91] All people thus have the right to be listened to and respected, because *often the Lord reveals to the younger what is best.*[92]

Authority is not an arbitrary use of power, but a service, which produces order while respecting the principle of subsidiarity, and protecting the weak.[93] A particular attention is given to the sick, to children, and to passing strangers.[94] The sanctions exist, but they aim to correct the guilty rather than punish them.[95] The economy of the monastery aims not at profit for the minority, but at a sharing of goods, *according to need* and so that *no one may be upset or saddened in the household of God.*[96]

This ideal has never been fully achieved. Nevertheless, for centuries, it has given monasteries their atmosphere of serenity, and it remains a safe guide towards peace and justice in any society.

[90] *RB* 73: 8.
[91] *RB* 4: 8; 31: 9; 36: 1; 53: 1, 7.
[92] *RB* 3: 3.
[93] *RB* 21; 31; 53.
[94] *RB* 31; 36; 37; 53.
[95] *RB* 23–29.
[96] *RB* 34: 1; 31: 19.

LIST OF SOURCES

Abishiktananda (P. H. Le Saux). *Prayer*, SPCK, 1925.
——, *Sagesse hindoue et mystique chrétienne*, Paris Centurion, 1991.
Acharya, F. *Le monachisme en Inde*, Coll. Cist. 1967, No. 3.
Adodo, A. 'The Way of African Mysticism', in *AIM Monastic Bulletin*, No. 63.
Apophthegmata Patrum, see Desert Fathers.
Aristotle, *Politics*, ed. & trans. J. Warmington, London, 1959.
Athanasius, *Life of Saint Antony*, *Letter to Marcellinus*, trans. R. C. Gregg, CWS, New York, 1980.
Augustine, *Confessions*, trans. R. S. Pine-Coffin, London, 1961.
——, *De Civitate Dei, PL* 41.
——, *De Opere Monachorum, PL* 40.
——, *De Moribus Ecclesiae, PL 32.*
——, *Enarrationes in Psalmos*, *PL* 36–37.
——, *Lettres, PL* 33.
——, *Rule of St Augustine*, Cf. Verheijen.
——, *Ordo Monasterii.*
——, *Sermones, PL* 38–39.
——, *Tract. in Jn. PL* 35.
Aurobindo, *Essays on the Gita*, Pondicherry, 1970.
Barzanuphe et Jean, *Correspondance*, Solesmes, 1993.
Basil the Great, *Moral Rules, PG* 31.
——, *Regula Basilii*, trans. Rufin, *PL* 103, pp. 483–554.
——, *Longer and Shorter Rules*, trans. W. K. Lowther Clarke.
——, *Ascetical Works of St Basil*, W. K. L. Clarke, London, 1925.
——, *St Basil Ascetical Works*, M. Monica Wagner, The Fathers of the Church, Washington, 1962.
——, *Letters* CC XLII 1993.
Basil (pseudo), *Admonitio and Filium spiritualem, PL* 103, pp. 683–700.
——, *Sermo Ascet., PL* 31.
Benedict of Aniane, *Codex Regularum; Concordia Regularum, PL* 103, pp. 425–1380.
Bhagavad Gita
Birago Diop, *Breaths in African Heritage*, London, 1964.
Borias, A. *Saint Benoît maître en patience*, in *Lettre de Ligugé*, 225, 1984, pp. 41–51.

St Bruno, *Lettres des premiers Chartreux*, SC 88.

Burchardt, T. Chaine d'Or, Maître et disciples dans l'Islam Maghrébin, *Hermès* IV, Le Maître Spirituel, Minard, Paris, 1967.

Butler, E. C. *Sancti Benedicti Regula Monasteriorum*, Stanbrook, 1930.

Caspar, R. *Cours de mystique musulmane*, Rome.

Cassian, J. *Conferences* N. F. and Cistercian Publications, and CWS, New York, 1985.

——, *Monastic Institutes*, trans. J. Bertram, Oxford, 1999.

Cato, M. *Porci Catonis De Agricultura Liber*, ed. G. Goetz, Lipsiae, in aedibus B.G. Tebverni, MCMXXII.

Chaubey, B. B. 'The nature of Guruship, according to Hindu Scriptures', in *The Nature of Guruship*, ed. C. O. McMullen, pp. 1–9, ISPCK Delhi, 1916.

Caesarius of Arles, *Reg. Virg. PL* 67, pp. 1103–1121.

——, *Sermons*, CC.

Chitty, D. J. *The Desert a City*, ed. Mowbrays, Oxford, 1977.

Clement of Alex, *Stromata*, SC 278.

Clement of Rome, *Ep. ad Corinthios*, SC 167.

Consultationes Zacchei Christiani et Apolloni Philosophi, *PL* XX, pp. 1071–1166.

Conze, E. *Buddhist Scriptures*, Penguin, 1971.

——, *Buddhism*, 1951.

Council, Vatican II, *Ad Gentes*.

——, *Lumen Gentium*.

——, *Perfectae Caritatis*.

Cyprian, *De Oratione Dominica, PL* 4, pp. 535–562.

Danielou, J. 'Pour une théologie de l'hospitalité', in *Vie Spirituelle*, 367, 1951, pp. 339–347.

——, 'La direction spirituelle dans la tradition ancienne de l'Eglise', in *Christus*, No. 25, Jan. 1960, pp. 6–26.

Davril, A. *La psalmodie chez les Pères du Désert, Coll. Cist.* 49, 1987, pp. 132–139.

de Béthune, P. 'Quand les chrétiens pratiquent le Zen', *Etudes*, Sept. 1987, pp. 235–247.

——, 'Le Maître selon la tradition Zen', in *Question de*, 84.

——, 'Par la foi et l'hospitalité', Cahiers de Clerlande, 4, 1977.

Décarreaux, J. *Les moines et la civilisation en Occident,* Paris, Arthaud 1962.

de Dreuille, M. 'Les voies de la prière chez Grégoire de Nysse', in *Colloque de Karma Ling*, 1983.

Degraces-Fahd, A. *Upanishad du Renoncement*, Paris, Fayard, 1989.

Delatte, P. *Commentaire sur la Règle de Saint Benoît*, Paris, 1913.

——, *The Rule of St Benedict: A Commentary*, trans. J. McCann, London, 1921.

de Monléon, Jean. *Les Instruments de perfection*, Paris ed. de La Source.

Desert Fathers (*Apophthegmata*)

——, Owen Chadwick, *Western Asceticism* (portion of Latin Syst. Col.) Philadelphia, 1958.

——, Benedicta Ward SLG, *The Sayings of the Desert Fathers* (Greek Alph. Col.) London 1983. *The Wisdom of the Desert* (Greek Systematic Col.) SLG Press, Oxford, 1986.

——, *History of the Monks of Egypt*, trans. Norman Russell, SLG, London, 1981.

——, *The Lives of the Desert Fathers*, intr. by Benedicta Ward, SLG, London, 1981.

Deseille, P. *L'esprit du monachisme pachômien*, Bellefontaine Spir. Orientale, 2, 1968.

——, *L'Evangile au Désert*, Martin de Dumio, Youssef Bournaya, Macaire, Cerf, 1965.

——, *Regards sur la tradition monastique*, Bellefontaine, 1974.

de Smet, R. V. 'The status of the Scriptures in the Holy History of India', in *Research Seminar on non-Biblical Scriptures*, Bangalore, 1973.

——, 'Contemplation in Shankara and Ramanuja', in *Prayer and Contemplation*, Bangalore, 1997.

Desprez, V. 'L'ascétisme chrétien entre le N.T. et le début du monachisme', in *Lettre de Ligugé*, 224, pp. 6–35.

Dhammapada, Trans. G. Serraf, Ass. Dhammaduta (Theravada), Paris 1985.

Dhavamony, M. *Love of God according to Shaiva Siddhanta*, Oxford, 1971.

——, 'The Bhakti experience in Contemporary India', in *The Religious Experience, its Unity and Diversity*, ed. T. Mampera, Bangalore, 1981.

Diadochus of Phot., (cap. 93) trad. A. G. Hamman, Migne, 1990.

Didache, SC 248.

Doré, J. 'Aperçus sur la vie spirituelle dans le catholicisme', in M. Meslin, *Maître et disciples dans les traditions religieuses*, Cerf, Paris, 1928.

Dorotheus of Gaza, *Discourses and Sayings*, Cistercian Studies 33, Kalamazoo, 1977.

Dumoulin, H. *A History of Zen Buddhism*, London, Faber & Faber, 1963.

Dupuis, J. *Toward a Christian Theology of Religious Pluralism*, Brescia, 1997.

Evagrius Ponticus, *Praktikos and Chapters on Prayer* trans. J. E. Bamberger, Cistercian Studies, Series 4, Spencer, 1972.

——, *Sent. Virg. PL* 20.

Faoutz Skadi, 'Le Maître Spirituel en Islam', in *Question de*, 64.

Ferrand, *Vita Fulgentii* (Fulgentius of Ruspe), *PL* 65, pp. 111–150.

Festugière, A. J. *Les moines d'Orient (IV/2, La première vie grecque de Saint Pachôme)*, Paris, Cerf, 1965.

Gardet L. et Anawati, G. C. *Mystique musulmane*, Paris, Vrin, 1961.

Geneviève-Marie, M. 'Pedagogy in the School of Charity', in *AIM Bulletin*, 63.

Geshe Ngawang Dhargyey (and others), *The Thirty-Seven Practices of all Buddha's sons and the Prayer of the Virtuous, Beginning, Middle and End*, Dharamsala, 1992.

Ghuruye, J. *Indian Sadhus*, Popular Prakashan, Bombay.

Gispert-Sauch, *The Narada Bhakti Sutra*, Kurseong.

Gougaud, L. *Ermites et reclus*, Rev. Mabillon, Ligugé, col. Moines & Mon. 5, 1928.

——, *Gaelic pioneers of Christianity*, trans. V. Collins, 1923.

——, *Epistolae*, SC 208.

Greg. of Nyssa, *Homel. in Cant. PG* 44–46.

——, *La Colombe et la Ténèbre*, trad. M. Canévet (Textes choisis).

——, *De Virginitate*, Introd. M. Aubineau, SC 119.

——, *Vie de sainte Macrine*, SC 178.

Greg. the Great, *Dialogues*, Collegeville, Liturgical Press.

Gribomont, J. *Saint Basile*, in *Théologie de la Vie monastique*, Aubies, 1961, pp. 99–113.

——, 'Lavoro', in *Dizionario degli Istituti di Perfezione* t.5 (1973), col. pp. 515–518.

Grimal, P. *La civilisation romaine*, Paris Arthaud, col. Gr Civilisations, 1, 1965.

——, *The Civilisation of Rome*, trans. W. S. Maguinness, 1963.

Guigues II le Chartreux, *L'échelle des moines*, SC 163.

Hausherr, I. *La direction spirituelle en Orient autrefois*, Lib. Orien. Chri. Analecta, 144, Pont. Int. Orient. Studies, 1955.

Heath, Sidney, *In the steps of the pilgrims*.

Herodote, *Histories*, Oxford Scriptorum Class. Bibl.

Hippolytus, *Trad. Ap.* ACW.

Humphreys, C. *The wisdom of Buddhism*, London, 1970.

Isaiah of Scetis, *Recueil ascétique*, trans. H. de Broc, *Spir. Orient. 7 bis*, Bellefontaine.

John Chrysostom, *Hom. 14 in Tim. PL* 62; *Hom. 22 in Mat. PG* 58.

John Climacus, *The Ladder of Divine Ascent*, trans. Colm Luibheid and Norman Russell, CWS, New York, 1982.

John of the Cross, *The Ascent of Carmel, The Dark Night*.

Jerome, *Epistolae, PL* 22, pp. 325–1224.

——, *In Daniel*, CC 1964.

John, T. K. 'Contemplation and action, the Bhagavad Gita in the light of Ramanuja's Commentary', in *The Sign beyond all Signs*, pp. 29–56.

Kabir, *Au Cabaret de l'Amour*, trans. C. Vaudeville, Paris.

Keating, T. *The two streams of Cenobitic Tradition*, Cist. Stud.

Lacombe, O. *L'Absolu selon le Védanta* An. Musée Guimet, 49, 1937.

——, *L'élan spirituel de l'hindousime*, OEIL, 1986.

Law, D. M. *Journey to the inner center in Tjurunga*, Oct. 1980.

Lefort, Th. Trans. *Les vies coptes de Saint Pachôme et de ses premiers successeurs*, Louvain Bib. Museon, 16, 1943. Trans. *Oeuvres de Saint Pachôme et de ses disciples*, Corp. Script Christ. Or. 159, Louvain, 1956.

Leroy, J. *La réforme studite*, Orient. Christ. Anal. 153, Paris.

Loiseleur-Deslongchamps, A. *Manava-Dharma-Sastra, Les Lois de Manou*, Garnier, Paris, 1903.

Lotus de la Bonne Loi, ed. Maisonneuve, 1973, Paris.

Luetkemeyer, M. B. 'Resurrection in the RB', in *Spirit and Life*, March–Apr., 1986.

Macarius the Egyp., *PG* 34, pp. 111–125; pp. 263–270; pp. 405–936.

Mohamed, *The Koran*, trans. N. J. Dawood, Penguin.

McMullen C. O. (ed.), *The Nature of Guruship*, ISPCK, Delhi, 1976.

Matus, T. *Yoga and the Jesus Prayer Tradition, An Experiment in Faith*, Paulist Press, 1984.

Meslin M. (ed.), *Maître et disciples dans les traditions religieuses*, Paris, Cerf, 1990.

Moschus, John, *Le Pré spirituel* SC 12.

Nicetus Trev., PL 68.

Origen, *Stromata, PG* 11–13.

——, *Com. in 1 Cor.*

——, *Schol. on Apocalypse*

——, *De oratione In Reg. Hom.*

——, *In 1 Pet.*

——, *In Mat.*

Orsisius (Horsiesios), *Testament trans.* A. Veilleux, *Pachomian Koinonia*, Vol. III, Th. Lefort, *Pachomiana Latina*, CC. 99–100.

Pachomius, *Vies Coptes*, cf. T. Lefort.

——, *Lives* etc. Trans. A. Veilleux, in *Pachomian Koinonia*, I–III, Cistercian Studies, Series 45–47, Kalamazoo 1980–82.

——, *Première vie grecque*, Festugière, Cerf, Paris, 1965.

——, *Praecepta*, in Pachomiana Latina, in *Bibliothèque de la Revue d'Histoire Ecclésiastique*, V. 3, fasc. 7.

——, *Praecepta et Inst*, ibid.

——, *Praecepta et Leges*, ibid.

——, *Catechesis* ibid., and CC. *Scriptores Coptici*, 23–24.

Palladius, *Lausiac History*, Trans. R. T. Meyer, ACW. 34. Washington, 1965.

Panabokke, G. *The Early Buddhist Sangha and its Organisation* (unpublished thesis), Colombo University, Sri Lanka, 1970.

Panikkar, R. *The Vedic Experience*, Univ. of California, Berkeley, Los Angeles, 1977.

Passio Iuliani et basilissae, (Salmon).

Pastor of Hermas, ACW, New York.

Peifer, C. 'The relevance of Monastic Tradition to the Problem of Work and Leisure', in ABR, Dec. 1937.

Pelagius, *Ep. ad Dem.*, *PL* Suppl., Pelagius, life and letters, trans. B. R. Rees, pp. 29–70.

Philo, *De vita Contemplativa*, Semitica X.

Qumran (Textes de), trad. C. Carmignac et P. Guilbert, Vol. I, *La Règle de la communauté*; vol. II, *Document de Damas*, Letougey et Ané, Paris, 1961.

Qumran (Texts of), *The Complete Dead Sea Scrolls in English*, G. Vernes, New York, 1997.

Raguin, Y. 'L'expérience personnelle de Dieu dans le christianisme', in *Les moines chrétiens face aux religions d'Asie*. Bangalore, 1973, pp. 36–48.

—, *Maître et disciple*, DDB, 1985.

Ramanuja, *Shri Bhasya*, quoted by R. de smet, *Contemplation*, pp. 216–220.

Rees, D. *Consider your call*, Cist. Stud. 20, *RB* 1980, Collegeville 1981.

[Rules], Aurelian *Ad Monachos*; *Ad Virgines*, *PL* 68; Ferreoli, *PL* 66; *Consensoria*, *PL* 66; *Cujusdam Patris*, *PL* 66; Fructuosus of bragia, *PL* 87; Isidore, *PL* 83; Macarii, *PL* 50; *IV Patrum*, *PL* 103; *Patrum II*, *PL* 103; *Patrum III*, *PL* 103; *Tarnatensis*, *PL* 66; *The Rule of the Master*, trans. Eberle, Cistercian Publications, 1977 (Cist. Studies ser. 6).

Ribb, *Les saints irlandais hors d'Irlande*, RHE, 1934.

Rinn, L. *Marabouts et khouans*.

Rollin, B. *Vivre aujourd'hui la Règle de St Benoît*, Bellefontaine, 1983.

Rufinus, *Historia Monachorum in Aegypto*, trans. Latin, *PL* 21.

——, *History of the monks of Egypt*, Trans. Benedicta Ward SLG, London, 1981.

Ryan J., *Irish monasticism*, Irish University Press, 1972.

——, *Irish monks in the Golden Age*, Dublin, Gill & Macmillan, 1971.

Sadasivaiah, *A comparative study of two Virasaiva monasteries*, Bangalore, 1970.

Shankara, *Selected works of Shankarâchârya*, Direct realistion.

Santou, M. and Leloup, Y. *Rôle du gourou dans l'hindouisme*, Question de, No. 84.

Shanta, N. *La voie Jaina, histoire, spiritualité, vie des ascètes*, Paris, OEIL, 1985.

Shorter, A. *Prayer in the religious tradition of Africa*, Oxford University Press, 1976.

Siauve, S. 'Expérience et amour de Dieu dans la bhakti Vishnouite', in *Les moines*.

Simon, M. *Plaire à Dieu selon les Règles monastiques de St. Basile*, Coll. Cist. 39, 1977, 4, pp. 239–249.

Spenser Trimingham, J. *The Sufi Orders in Islam*, Oxford, Clarendon, 1971.

Spidlik, T. *La spiritualité de l'Orient chrétien*, Rome, Pont. Inst; Orient. 1978.

Stewart, C. 'Radical Honesty about self. The practice of the Desert Fathers', in *AIM, Monastic Bulletin*, 63, 1997.

Subash Anand, *Bhagavata Purâna* (selected passages), Pune, 1975.

——, 'Discipleship in Bhagavata Purana', in *Christian Spirituality for India*, Bangalore, 1978.

Sukumar Dutt, *The Buddha and five after Centuries*, 1971.

Sulpicius Severus, *Vita Martini*, *PL* 20.

——, *Dialogues*, *PL* 20, pp. 183–222.

Sunyasampadaye, (texts of the Lingayat tradition), Bangalore.

[Sutras], *Apastamba Dharma Sutra*.

Tertullian, *De Oratione*.

Thartang Tulku, *Gesture of Balance*, Dharamsala, 1990.

Theodore, *Catéchèse*, CSCO, 160.

Theodoret, *Hist. Rel.*, SC 257.

Teresa of Avila, *The interior Castle*.

[Tibetans], *The Thirty-seven practices of all Buddha's sons*, Library of Tibetan Works and Archives, Dharamsala, 1975.
Tiso, F. V. (ed.), *The Sign Beyond All Signs*, Asirvanam, Bangalore, 1997.
Tukaram, *Psalms of the Pilgrim*.
[Upanishads] S. Radhakrishnan, *The principal Upanishads*.
van Troy, *Early ascetic movements*, All Asia Monastic meeting, Bangalore, 1973
[Vatican], *Codex Iuris Canonici (Droit Canon)*.
——, *Potissimum Institutioni*, civcsva.
Verheijen, L. *Nouvelle approche de la Règle de Saint Augustin*, T. I, Bellefontaine, TII, Louvain, Inst Hist., Augustin, 1988.
Vitae patrum, *PL* 73–74.
[Vita hilarii], *PL* 50, pp. 1219–1246.
Veilleux, A. *Pachomian Koinonia* 3 vol. Cistercian Sutides 45–47, 1980–1982.
Vogüé, A. de. *La Communauté et l'Abbé dans la Règle de Saint Benoît*, DDB.
——, *La Règle de Saint Benoît*, 4 vol., SC 181–186.
——, *La Règle du Maître*, SC 105–106.
——, *L'abbé vicaire du Christ*, Coll. Cist. 3. 1982.
——, Lavoro, in *Dizionario degli Istituti di Perfezione*, t. 5 (1973), col. pp. 518–522.
——, *Le monastère Eglise du Christ*, Studia Anselmiana 42, Roma, 1957.
——, *Les deux fonctions de la méditation dans les règles monastiques anciennes*, RAM, 1975, 1–2.
——, '*Sub Regula et Abbate*', Coll. Cist. 33/ 1971.
——, '*Perducatum Evangelii*', Coll. Cist. 35/ 1973.
——, *St Pachôme et son temps, d'après plusieurs études récentes*, RHE, 69, 1974.
——, *Structure et gouvernement de la communauté monastique chez Saint Benoît et autour de lui*, Act. Monastic International Congress 1980.
——, *Entre Basile et Benoît, l'Admonitio ad filium spiritualem*, Reg. Ben. Stud.
Wallis Budge, E. *The Paradise of the Fathers. The Wit and Wisdom of the Desert Fathers*, Syriac Systematic collection, London, 1934.
Walpola Rahula, *L'enseignement du Bouddha, History of Buddhism in Ceylon*, Colombo, 1956.
Wathen, A. *Silence*, Cist. Stud., 22, Kalamazoo, 1973.
Wayman, A. *Ancient Buddhist Monasticism*, in *Studia Anselmiana* 28, 1979.
Wieger, L. *Vinaya, Monachisme et discipline hinayana*, trans. from Chinese Cathasia 1931.
Wijayaratna, Mohan, *Les débuts du monachisme bouddhique, comparés à ceux du monachisme chrétien*, Coll. Cist. 1983, 2. T.44, pp. 69–76.
——, *Le moine bouddhiste selon les textes du Theravada*, Cerf, Paris, 1983.
——, *Sermons du Bouddha*, Cerf, Paris, 1988.
Yeo, R. 'The structure and content of monastic profession', in *Studia Anselmiana* 83, 1982.
Zaehner, R. C. *Hindu Scriptures*, (ed.) Dent & Sons, 1978.

Zago, M. *Rites et cérémonies religieuses en milieu Lao*, (ed.) Pont. Univ. Gregoriana, 1972.

Collections

Christian spirituality for India Bangalore, 1978.
Divine grace and human response, C. Vadakkekara (ed.), Bangalore.
Du Maître spirituel au Maître intérieur (Question de 84).
Maîtres et disciples dans les traditions religieuses (ed.) M. Meslin, Cerf, Paris, 1988.
Les moines chrétiens face aux religions d'Asie (ed.) AIM, Paris, 1973.
The nature of Guruship (ed.) Clarence O. McMullen, Delhi, 1976.
Prayer and Contemplation (ed.), Cletus Vadakkekara, Media House, Delhi, 1997.
Rapports des Congrès monastiques (ed.) AIM; *Bangalore*, 1973 (*Les moines chrétiens et les religions d'Asie*). *Abidjan*, 1979. *Kandy, Sri Lanka*, 1980.
Research Seminar on non-Biblical Scriptures, Bangalore, 1973.
Religious experience: its unity and its diversity, Bangalore, 1981.
The Sign beyond all Signs, F. V. Tiso (ed.), Bangalore, 1997.
Théologie de la vie monastique, Ligugé.

Periodicals

A.I.M. Monastic Bulletin.
American Benedictine Review.
Bharati Bulletin of Indology, Benares Hindu University.
Christus.
Cistercian Studies.
Collectanea Cisterciensis.
Dictionnaire de Spiritualité.
Etudes.
Lettre de Ligugé.
Hermés.
Monastic Studies.
Orientalia Christiana Analecta.
Pentecôte d'Afrique.
Question de.
Revue d'Ascétique et de Mystique.
Revue d'Histoire Ecclésiastique.
Spirit and Life.
Tjurunga.

INDEX